JOHN UPDIKE

Recent Titles in
Critical Responses in Arts and Letters

The Critical Response to Mark Twain's
Huckleberry Finn
Laurie Champion, editor

The Crticial Response to Nathaniel Hawthorne's
The Scarlet Letter
Gary Scharnhorst, editor

The Critical Response to Tom Wolfe
Doug Shomette, editor

The Critical Response to Ann Beattie
Jaye Berman Montresor, editor

The Critical Response to Eugene O'Neill
John H. Houchin, editor

The Critical Response to Bram Stoker
Carol A. Senf, editor

The Critical Response to John Cheever
Francis J. Bosha, editor

The Critical Response to Ann Radcliffe
Deborah D. Rogers, editor

The Critical Response to Joan Didion
Sharon Felton, editor

The Critical Response to Tillie Olsen
Kay Hoyle Neldon and Nancy Huse, editors

The Critical Response to George Eliot
Karen L. Pangallo, editor

The Critical Response to Eudora Welty's Fiction
Laurie Champion, editor

The Critical Response to Dashiell Hammett
Christopher Metress, editor

The Critical Response to H. G. Wells
William J. Scheick, editor

The Critical Response to Raymond Chandler
J. K. Van Dover, editor

The Critical Response to Herman Melville's
Moby Dick
Kevin J. Hayes, editor

The Critical Response to Kurt Vonnegut
Leonard Mustazza, editor

The Critical Response to Richard Wright
Robert J. Butler, editor

The Critical Response to Jack London
Susan N. Nuernberg, editor

The Critical Response to Saul Bellow
Gerhard Bach, editor

The Critical Response to William Styron
Daniel W. Ross, editor

The Critical Response to Katherine Mansfield
Jan Pilditch, editor

The Critical Response to Anais Nin
Philip K. Jason, editor

The Critical Response to Tennessee Williams
George W. Crandell, editor

The Critical Response to Andy Warhol
Alan R. Pratt, editor

The Critical Response to Thomas Carlyle's
Major Works
D. J. Trela and Rodger L. Tarr, editors

The Critical Response to John Milton's
Paradise Lost
Timothy C. Miller, editor

The Critical Response to Erskine Caldwell
Robert L. McDonald, editor

The Critical Response to Gloria Naylor
Sharon Felton and Michelle C. Loris, editors

The Critical Response to Samuel Beckett
Cathleen Culotta Andonian, editor

The Critical Response to Ishmael Reed
Bruce Allen Dick, editor
With the assistance of Pavel Zemliansky

The Critical Response to Truman Capote
Joseph J. Waldmeir and John C. Waldmeir, editors

The Critical Response to Robert Lowell
Steven Gould Axelrod, editor

The Critical Response to Chester Himes
Charles L.P. Silet, editor

The Critical Response to Gertrude Stein
Kirk Curnutt, editor

The Critical Response to Ralph Ellison
Robert J. Butler, editor

The Critical Response to John Steinbeck's *The
Grapes of Wrath*
Barbara A. Heavilin, editor

The Critical Response to D. H. Lawrence
Jan Pilditch, editor

The Critical Response to Marianne Moore
Elizabeth Gregory, editor

JOHN UPDIKE
The Critical Responses to the "Rabbit" Saga

Edited by Jack De Bellis

Critical Responses in Arts and Letters, Number 40

Westport, Connecticut
London

11·3·2005
WW
$97.95

This book is dedicated to my wife Patty with more gratitude than I can express.

Library of Congress Cataloging-in-Publication Data

John Updike : The critical responses to the "Rabbit" saga / [edited by] Jack De Bellis.
 p. cm. — (Critical responses in arts and letters, ISSN 1057–0993 ; no. 40)
 Includes bibliographical references and index.
 ISBN 0–313–30983–3 (alk. paper)
 1. Updike, John—Criticism and interpretation. 2. Updike, John—Characters—Harry Angstrom. 3. Angstrom, Harry (Fictitious character) 4. Updike, John. Rabbit run. 5. Updike, John. Rabbit redux. 6. Updike, John. Rabbit is rich. 7. Updike, John. Rabbit at rest. 8. Middle class men in literature. I. De Bellis, Jack. II. Series.
 PS3571.P4Z63   2005
 813'.54–dc22   2003058161

British Library Cataloguing in Publication Data is available.

Library of Congress Catalog Card Number: 2003058161
ISBN: 0–313–30983–3
ISSN: 1057–0993

First published in 2005

Praeger Publishers, 88 Post Road West, Westport, CT 06881
An imprint of Greenwood Publishing Group, Inc.
www.praeger.com

Printed in the United States of America

The paper used in this book complies with the Permanent Paper Standard issued by the National Information Standards Organization (Z39.48–1984).

10 9 8 7 6 5 4 3 2 1

Copyright Acknowledgments

The editor and publisher gratefully acknowledge permission for the use of the following material:

Richard Lyons, "A High E. Q." *Minnesota Review* Spring, 1961: 385-89. Reprinted with permission of *The Minnesota Review*.

Larry Taylor, *Pastoral and Anti-Pastoral in the Works of John Updike.* Carbondale, Illinois: Southern Illinois University Press, 1971. pp. 76-85. Reprinted by permission of Southern Illinois University Press.

Derek Wright, "Mapless Motion: Form and Space in Updike's *Rabbit, Run*." *Modern Fiction Studies* 37 (Spring 1991): 35-44. Reprinted by permission of The Johns Hopkins University Press.

Stacey Olster, "'Unadorned Woman, Beauty's Home Image': Woman in *Rabbit, Run*." *New Essays on Rabbit, Run*. Ed. Stanley Trachtenberg. New York: Cambridge University Press, 1993: 95-117. Reprinted by permission of Cambridge University Press.

Donald Greiner, "No Place to Run: Rabbit Angstrom as Adamic Hero." *Rabbit Tales: Poetry and Politics in John Updike's Rabbit Novels*. Ed. Lawrence R. Broer. Tuscaloosa, Alabama: The University of Alabama Press, 1998. Reprinted by permission of The University of Alabama Press.

Marshall Boswell, *John Updike's Rabbit Tetralogy: Mastered Irony in Motion.* Columbia, Missouri: The University of Missouri Press, 2001. 41-53. Reprinted by permission of University of Missouri Press. Copyright (c) by the Curators of the University of Missouri.

John Updike, "Henry Bech Redux" from *Picked-Up Pieces,* by John Updike. Reprinted by permission of Alfred A. Knopf, Inc.

Richard Locke, "Rabbit Returns: Updike Was Always There– It's Time We Noticed." *New York Times Book Review* 14 Nov. 1971: 1-2, 12-16, 20-21.

2. Reprinted by permission of the Reading *Eagle*.

Ralph C. Wood, "Rabbit Runs Down." *The Christian Century* 107 (21 Nov. 1990): 1099-1001. Reprinted by permission of *Christian Century* Copyright The Christian Century Foundation. From the Nov. 21, 1990 edition.

Thomas M. Disch, "Rabbit's Run." *Nation* 251 (3 Dec. 1990): 688, 690, 692, 694. Reprinted by permission from the 3 Dec. 1990 issue of *The Nation*.

Hermione Lee, "The Trouble with Harry." *New Republic* 203 (24 Dec. 1990): 34-37. Reprinted by permission of *The New Republic* (c) 1990. *The New Republic, Inc.*

Stacey Olster, "Rabbit Rerun: Updike's Replay of Popular Culture in *Rabbit at Rest.*" *Modern Fiction Studies* 37 (Spring 1991): 45-59. Reprinted by permission of The Johns Hopkins University Press.

Dilvo Ristoff, *John Updike's Rabbit at Rest: Appropriating History.* New York: Lang, 1998 pages 62-73. Reprinted by permission of Lang Publishers.

Judie Newman, "Rabbit at Rest: The Return of the Work Ethic." *Rabbit Tales: Poetry and Politics in John Updike's Rabbit Novels.* Ed. Lawrence R. Broer. Tuscaloosa, Alabama: University of Alabama Press, 1998. Reprinted by permission of Judie Newman and the University of Alabama Press.

James A. Schiff, "Rabbit at Rest: The Seed of Death Within." *John Updike Revisited.* New York: Twayne Publishers, 1998: 56-65. Reprinted by permissin of Gale Press.

D. Quentin Miller, *John Updike and the Cold War.* Columbia, Missouri: The University of Missouri Press, 2001: 63-71, Reprinted by permission of The University of Missouri Press. Copyright (c) 2001, by the Curators of the University of Missouri.

John Updike, "Why Rabbit Had to Go." *The New York Times Book Review* 8 Aug. 1990: 1, 24-25. Reprinted by permission of John Updike.

John Updike, "Introduction." *Rabbit Angstrom.* New York: Knopf/Everyman, 1999. ix-xxiv. Reprinted by permission of Alfred A. Knopf, a division of Random House, Inc.

David Heddendorf, "Rabbit Reread." *Southern Review* Summer 2000: 641-47. Reprinted by permission of David Heddendorf.

D[aniel] T. Max, "Noticers in Chief: John Updike and Rabbit." *Book* Nov.-

Dec. 2000: 32-36, 38-39. Reprinted by permission of Daniel T. Max.

A. O. Scott. "Still Wild About Harry." *The New York Times Book Review* 19 Nov. 2001: 11-12. Reprinted by permission of *The New York Times* copyright (c) 2001 by the New York Times Co.

Reasonable effort has been made to contact the owners of copyright materials used in this book, but in some cases this has proven impossible. The author and publisher will be glad to receive information leading to more complete acknowledgments in subsequent printings of this book and in the meantime extend their apologies for any errors.

Contents

"Rabbit Remembered"

Appendix:

Preface

The purpose of this collection of critical responses to John Updike's "Rabbit" saga is: first, to provide a sense of the reception of the four Rabbit novels and the novella "Rabbit Remembered"; and second, to show how these reviews and articles can illuminate for the reader the range of readings of the saga. The reader will discover how initial praise or objection lay the groundwork for critical arguments arguments using historical and biographical approaches as well as feminist, psychological and popular culture response. Also, Updike's own remarks have been included, amusing "interviews" by his own character Henry Bech and extended remarks on *Rabbit at Rest* and *Rabbit Angstrom* which reveal Updike's process of composition. In addition, a chronology will help the reader place the saga in the context of Updike's life and writing. To facilitate understanding of the critical responses, I have provided a timetable which will ease recall of the saga's episodes.

I have left British spellings and punctuation intact, and where the text is errant I have indicated with (sic) that the problem is in the author's text and not in my keyboarding. I have regularized spellings of characters' names to accord with those in Updike's *Rabbit Angstrom*, and I have placed in italics names ob books, etc. otherwise in quotes in newspapers and magazines.

I wish to express my gratitude to the many persons who have provided assistance in this project: To the contributors to this volume for helping to establish the significance of the "Rabbit" saga through their brilliance of their engagements with it; to Lehigh University for generous grants enabling me to purchase permissions to publish, and to Sandra Edmiston of Lehigh for offering extraordinary assistance in the intricacies of WordPerfect 9 and the HP Laserjet 4200n in creating "camera ready copy"; to numerous librarians who have answered queries cheerfully; to fellow Updikeans, particularly James Yerkes, who have energetically responded to this project; to John Updike for aid with his chronology and the "Rabbit" Timetable and for his warm encouragement every step of the way. Most of all I thank my wife, Patty, for providing her eagle eyes once again to the drudgery of collation, her eager spirit to the labor of proof reading, and her constant cheery devotion to my passion for Updike's work. Naturally, whatever errors remain are my responsibility.

A Chronology of John Updike*

1932 An eleventh-generation American, John Hoyer Updike was born March 18, in West Reading Hospital, Reading, Pennsylvania, to penurious parents, Wesley, (1900-1972) who taught mathematics at Shillington High School from 1934 to 1974, and Linda Grace Hoyer (1904-1989), an aspiring fiction writer. His mother's parents, John and Katherine Hoyer, lived with them at 117 Philadelphia Avenue, Shillington, a Reading suburb.

1944 James Thurber sends Updike a drawing of a dog which he still keeps.

1945 First publication, "A Handshake with the Congressman," February 16, Shillington High School *Chatterbox*. On Halloween his family moves eleven miles from Shillington to Plowville and to the sandstone farmhouse originally owned by Updike's mother's parents.

1946 Writes a murder mystery (published, 1994).

1948 Edits the Shillington High School newspaper, serves as class president. *The Yearbook*, which he edits, identifies him as "the sage of Plowville," who "hopes to write for a living." During the summer and the following two summers Updike works as a copy boy for the Reading *Eagle* where he writes some feature stories.

1949 First poem, "I Want a Lamp," published in the *American Courier* X (July 1): 11.

1950 Graduates as president and co-valedictorian of the senior class at Shillington High School. Updike had contributed 285 drawings, articles and poems to *The Chatterbox* which he also edited. In the fall he enters Harvard University on a tuition scholarship, majoring in English. That year he writes more than 40 poems and draws for the Harvard *Lampoon*.

1951 First published prose, "The Different One," appears in Harvard *Lampoon*.

1952 Named editor of the Harvard *Lampoon*.

1953 Meets Mary Pennington, a Radcliff ('52) fine arts student studying at the Fogg Museum, daughter of Rev. Leslie T. Pennington and Elizabeth Daniels. Marries June 26. While Updike publishes many parodies, sketches and cartoons in the Harvard *Lampoon, The New Yorker* buys a story and a poem.

1954 Graduates *summa cum laude*. Wins a Knox Fellowship to attend the Ruskin School of Drawing and Fine Art, Oxford, England. While at Oxford he meets E. B. White and his wife Katharine White, fiction editor of *The New Yorker* who hires him. The magazine publishes ten poems; his first story, "Friends from Philadelphia," appears there October 30.

1955 His daughter Elizabeth is born, April 1. Updike becomes a "Talk of the Town" writer for *The New Yorker*.

1957 His son David is born in January. In April leaves *The New Yorker* for Ipswich, Massachusetts.

1958 First book published, *The Carpentered Hen and Other Tame Creatures* (55 poems) with Harper and Brothers.

1959 His son Michael is born May 14. First novel, *The Poorhouse Fair* and first collection of stories, *The Same Door*, published with Alfred A. Knopf. Wins a Guggenheim Fellowship to support the writing of *Rabbit, Run*. "A Gift from the City" is selected for *The Best American Short Stories 1959*.

1960 Daughter Miranda is born December 15. *Rabbit, Run* published by Knopf. *The Poorhouse Fair* wins the Rosenthal Award of the National Institute of Arts and Letters. Publishes an often anthologized tribute to Ted Williams, "Hub Fans Bid Kid Adieu" in *The New Yorker*.

1961 "Wife-Wooing" included in *Prize Stories 1961*.

1962 *Pigeon Feathers* (stories) published, and *Rabbit, Run* is published in London by Deutsch with "emendations and restorations." This text was later used for the Modern Library printing and for Knopf reissues; he will make other revisions in the 1995 *Rabbit Angstrom* and in the 2003 Ballantine two-volume edition which re-issued the four "Rabbit" novels. Publishes a memoir, "John Updike (1940's)" (later collected as "The Dogwood Tree: A Boyhood") in *Five Boyhoods*. *The Magic Flute of Mozart*, with illustrations, adapted and arranged for young people. "The Doctor's Wife" included in *Prize Stories 1962* and "Pigeon Feathers" in *Best American Short Stories 1962*.

1963 *The Centaur* published and wins the National Book Award. *Telephone Poles and Other Poems* (60 poems).

1964 *Olinger Stories* published (taken from the two previous story collections). *The Ring of Wagner*, an adaptation of Wagner's "Ring" operas, is published for children. He is elected to the National Institute of Arts and Letters, the youngest member so honored. From Ursinus College Updike receives his first honorary doctor of letters degree. Travels to Russia and Eastern Europe for the State Department in the US-USSR Cultural Exchange Program.

1965 *Of the Farm* (novel) published. *Assorted Prose* published (parodies, articles and reviews). *Verse* published, combining his two previous poetry collections. *A Child's Calendar* (12 poems) published. Wins *Le prix du meilleur livre étranger* for *The Centaur*.

1966 *The Music School* (stories) published. "The Bulgarian Poetess," from this collection, wins the *First O. Henry Prize* award and is included in *Prize Stories 1966.*

1967 "Marching Through Boston" is selected for *Prize Stories 1967.*

1968 *Couples* published. Updike appears on the cover of *Time*, April 26, subject of the cover story "The Adulterous Society." "Your Lover Just Called" included in *Prize Stories 1968*. Receives an honorary degree, Litt. D., from Moravian College, Bethlehem, Pennsylvania.

1969 *Midpoint and Other Poems* published. *Bottom's Dream* (an adaptation for children of *A Midsummer Night's Dream*) published.

1970 *Beck: A Book* published (a story collection). Moves to Ipswich, Massachusetts. In May Gunther Schuller's opera *The Fisherman's Wife* is produced, using Updike's adaptation of the Grimms' story as the libretto.

1971 *Rabbit Redux* published. Receives the Signet Society Medal for Achievement in the Arts.

1972 *Seventy Poems* published. *Museums and Women and Other Stories* published. Appointed Honorary Consultant in American Letters to the Library of Congress (1972-75).

1973 Travels to Ghana, Nigeria, Tanzania, Kenya and Ethiopia on a Lincoln Lectureship from the Fulbright Board of Foreign Scholarships.

1974 *Buchanan Dying* (play) published.

1975 *A Month of Sundays* (novel) published. *Picked-Up Pieces* (articles and reviews) published. "Nakedness" is included in *Prize Stories 1975*. Wins the Lotus Club Award of Merit.

1976 *Marry Me: A Romance* published. *Buchanan Dying* premiers April 29 at Franklin and Marshall College, Lancaster, Pa. Updike is elected to the fifty-member National Institute and Academy of Arts and Letters. Given the "Special Award for Continuing Achievement" in *Prize Stories 1976*, which includes "Separating." "The Man Who Loved Extinct Mammals" selected for *Best American Short Stories 1976*. In March he and Mary Pennington divorce.

1977 *Tossing and Turning* (poems) published. *The Poorhouse Fair* published (revised edition with an introduction by Updike). On September 30 marries Martha Ruggles Bernhard.

1978 *The Coup* (novel) published.

1979 *Problems and Other Stories* published. *Too Far to Go* (stories) published. A film made from several of the stories appears on television.

1980 "Gesturing" included in *Best American Short Stories 1980*. Film *The Music School* televised over the Public Broadcasting Service as part of "The American short Story" series the week of April 28.

1981 *Rabbit Is Rich* (novel) published. It wins the following year the Pulitzer Prize and American Book Award, and the National Book Critics Circle Award three major American literary fiction prizes. Awarded the Edward MacDowell Medal for literature. "Still of Some Use" included in *Best American Short Stories 1981*. Updike is the subject of a BBC documentary, "What Makes Rabbit Run?"

1982 *Bech Is Back* (story collection) published. On his fiftieth birthday Knopf reissues, with revisions, *The Carpentered Hen*, the only trade book not previously published by Knopf. Receives an honorary degree from Albright College. For the second time he appears on the cover of *Time* (October 18) for the cover story "Going Great at 50."

1983 *Hugging the Shore* (essays and reviews) published; the following year it wins the National Book Critics Circle Award for Criticism. In May receives the Pennsylvania Distinguished Artist award from Governor Thornburgh. "Deaths of Distant Friends" included in *Best American Short Stories 1983*, and "The City" included in *Prize Stories 1983*. Wins the Lincoln Literary Award bestowed by the Union League Club.

1984 *The Witches of Eastwick* (novel) published. Edits and Introduces *The Best American Short Stories 1984*. Awarded the National Arts Club Medal of Honor. PBS film *The Roommate*, based on "The Christian Roommates" from *The Music School*, is shown January 27.

1985 *Facing Nature* (poems) published. "The Other" (*Trust Me*) included in *Prize*

Stories 1985. Receives Kutztown University Foundation's Director's Award, "in recognition of leadership, dedication and service to others in the community, especially in the area of education."

1986 *Roger's Version* (novel) published.

1987 *Trust Me* (stories) published. Receives the Elmer Holmes Bobst award for fiction. "The Afterlife" included in Best *American Short Stories.* Film of *The Witches of Eastwick* appears.

1988 *S.* (novel) published. "Leaf Season" selected for *Prize Stories 1988.* PBS film *Pigeon Feathers,* an adaptation of "Pigeon Feathers," is produced for American Playhouse. Brandeis University awards him its Life Achievement Award.

1989 *Self-Consciousness* (memoirs) published. *Just Looking* (essays on art) published. Mother Linda Grace Hoyer Updike dies October 10. President George H. W.Bush presents him the National Medal of Arts, November 17 at the White House.

1990 *Rabbit at Rest* published; next year it will win the Pulitzer prize and the National Book Critics Circle Award. *The South Bank Show* on London Weekend Television dramatizes scenes from the four novels, while Updike talks about his childhood and Rabbit books.

1991 *Odd Jobs* (essays and reviews) published. Wins Best Critical Work by the National Book Critics Circle Award. Awarded Italy's Scanno Prize for *Trust Me.* "A Sandstone Farmhouse" wins "First O. Henry Prize," first prize in *Prize Stories 1991* and is included in *Best American Short Stories 1991,* the first time a story garnered all three honors.

1992 *Memories of the Ford Administration* published. Received a Doctor of Letters from Harvard University.

1993 *Collected Poems 1953-1993* published. In July in Key West, Florida, awarded the "Conch Republic Prize for Literature" because his life's work reflects "the daring and creative spirit of the Keys."

1994 *Brazil* published. *The Afterlife and Other Stories* published.

1995 *Rabbit Angstrom: A Tetralogy* (a gathering of the four "Rabbit" novels) published by Everyman's Library. *A Helpful Alphabet of Friendly Objects* (26 poems with photographs taken by his son, David) published. Awarded the William Dean Howells Medal from the American Academy of Arts and Letters, an award given to the best fiction work of the previous five years. Receives the French rank "Commandeur de l'Ordre des Arts et des Lettres."

1996 *In the Beauty of the Lilies* published. Received the Ambassador Book Award for *In the Beauty of the Lilies* on June 3. *Golf Dreams* (essays, poetry and fiction) published.

1997 *Toward the End of Time* published. Updike begins and ends *Murder Makes the Magazine*, a story whose body is created from daily contributions from winning entrants on the website Amazon.com. Received the Campion Award September 11, given by the Jesuit magazine *America* to "a distinguished Christian person of letters."

1998 *Bech at Bay* (a "quasi-novel") published. Edited *A Century of Arts and Letters* contributing the "Foreword" and a chapter, "1938-47: Decade of The Row." Awarded the Harvard Arts Medal May 2. Received the Thomas Cooper Library Medal from the University of South Carolina, November 13-14.

1999 *More Matter* (essays and reviews) published.

2000 *Gertrude and Claudius* (novel) published. *Licks of Love: Stories and a Novella, "Rabbit Remembered."* (stories and a novella) published.

2001 *Americana* (poems) published. *The Complete Henry Bech* (stories from the Bech books, plus "Bech in Czech") published.

2002 *Seek My Face* (novel) published. Received on October 26 the F. Scott Fitzgerald Award.

2003 *Early Stories: 1953-1975* published.

2004 *Not Cancelled Yet* (poems) published. *Villages* (novel) published. Received the PEN/Faulkner award May 8.

*Prepared with the kind assistance of John Updike.

Introduction

Since1958, Updike has consistently been in the public eye by averaging two books a year for over forty years, appearing in magazines from *Forbes to Mother Jones,* providing dozens of interviews, and visiting conferences and colleges. His astonishing productivity, no less than his polished style, have earned him all major American prizes including two Pulitzer Prizes and two National Book Awards, the Howells Medal, the National Medal of Arts and, as an outstanding Christian novelist, the Campion award. He has been Honorary Consultant in American Letters to the Library of Congress and has been honored in several countries outside the United States. Novelists as dissimilar as Norman Mailer, John Barth, Joyce Carol Oates, Nicholson Baker, Margaret Atwood, Erica Jong, and Philip Roth warmly commend Updike as a writer's writer. He is regularly nominated for the Nobel Prize.

Updike's stories and novels have been received enthusiastically by critics and general readers; his poetry ranging from sophisticated light verse to a philosophical overview of his life has delighted both academics and casual readers; and his criticism, exploring not merely Kierkegaard, Borges and Melville, but, with equal aplomb, Ted Williams and Marilyn Monroe, has engaged specialists and the general public. Updike's *Buchanan Dying* illustrated his competency as a playwright, and his books for children convey a charming empathy. His prefaces, introductions forewords and afterwords for dozens of books have shown Updike to be a supportive colleague to fledgling and established writers. His work has enjoyed international readership, attested to by the translations of his books into more than two dozen languages. Appearances of his work in over two hundred anthologies have delighted generations of students. Films made from his fiction, and video reproductions of those films have been available for decades to academic and non-literary audiences, along with videos of his many readings and lectures.

It is difficult to say which impresses more, Updike's meticulous craftsmanship and wide-ranging style or his plentitude of ideas and characters. Updike suggested early in his career that the creation of an enduring character might be his life's ambition, remarking that a writer seeks, throughout his lifetime, to create an image that will outlive him, as Mark Twain with Huckleberry Finn. Whether or not he succeeded, Updike's exploration of Rabbit for forty years has left an indelible character on twentieth century literature. The Rabbit Angstrom Saga, with its depiction of middle class America during six decades has come to symbolize America itself to many readers. Perhaps this is why *Book* magazine in March, 2002, placed Rabbit Angstrom fifth on its list of the most memorable characters created since 1900.

American and foreign critics have been unanimous in praising the "Rabbit" Saga, though *Rabbit, Run* (1960) drew some objections about obscenity which dissolved by 1962 when censorship laws were overturned by the Supreme Court. Other critics mistakenly thought the book advocated irresponsibility, like a domestic *On the Road*, the book which Updike's novel in fact sought to answer. Other commentators felt Updike's lyrical style was squandered on inconsequential characters and self-indulgent description which disguised the fact that Updike had "nothing to say." But other critics found in Rabbit's flight from his family a rejection of post-war consumerism and the malaise of the Eisenhower years. Some reviewers went so far as to identify Rabbit as an "existential saint" rejecting his culture's alienation from meaningful work, expressive love and spiritual seriousness. To some, Rabbit's fade-out at the end of *Rabbit, Run* revealed Updike's indecision about his hero's fate. But for others, such a finish forced readers to consider that America might not deserve Rabbit, that all institutions from church to family have made life undesirable for him; thus, the novel tacitly criticizes the dark underbelly of American life. Rabbit may not be a tragic hero or saint, but his life invites a curious blend of abhorrence and commiseration.

What makes that ambiguous blend of emotions all the more troubling is the symbolic weight Updike attaches to familiar things. Small town America had never been so concrete yet simultaneously metaphorical: a pick-up basketball game, true in all details, reveals "change is time's sad secret," something Rabbit will not discover for decades. A perfect golf shot provides evidence of the thrill the body can provide when everything goes right, but it also indicates a transcendent reality. A congested livingroom contains all the accuracy of the "novel of accumulated details" since John Dos Passos, but it also reveals the poignant entrapment within ordinary American life. The details of Rabbit's job, like the TV kids' show Janice watches only reveal the ugly truth that "Fraud makes the world go round," and Rabbit unknowingly acts out the fact that the family is another case in point of such a "fraud."

Complicating our response to the meaning of *Rabbit, Run* also are the distinct similarities-with-differences of Updike's characters revealed through Joycean interior monologues of Janice and Rabbit. Such interior monologues reveal the essential separation of all people, as Janice worries about a mysterious "third person" in her house as she drinks to keep from feeling she has failed as a wife and is about to fail as a mother by drowning her baby. Rabbit's dream of sun and moon as like his two children provides him with a sense of grace that is impossible to articulate except in a brutish way. These representative elements from their interior monologues show how similar they are, but how tragically separated they remain just the same. Nevertheless, Rabbit discerns in his past first-ratedness, in his baby daughter or in sex with Ruth something that isn't fraudulent and something doesn't separate him, for it chimes with his religious sense.

A decade of such suppressed aspirations toward union-despite-differences causes explosions within the Angstrom family in *Rabbit Redux* (1971). Since Updike remarked in an interview that he conceived of his novels as debates with the reader, enquiring what makes the good man, it was logical that he would pursue the questions raised in *Rabbit, Run.* But instead of continuing where *Rabbit, Run* ended in June, 1960, Updike reintroduces Rabbit in "real time," July, 1969. *Rabbit Redux* undertakes the debate in earnest, through the confrontations of Rabbit and Skeeter, a black militant and Vietnam veteran, who hopes to overthrow America. Skeeter succeeds in making Rabbit perceive the similarities between his own life and the suffering of African-Americans. Rabbit also begins to question his pro-war position. Yet this re-education leads to the death of the rich runaway Jill, who also had pursued the same quest for something transcendent that Rabbit once felt was his mission in life. *Rabbit Redux* thus carries forward more dramatically the question raised and left unanswered in *Rabbit, Run*: does an intimation that one is chosen for a special mission in life justify the suffering of others? The novel asks the reader to join the debate.

Structural parallels ensure that the question is not only domestic and personal but nation and general. Let me cite two examples. First, the image of flight. At the beginning of *Rabbit Redux* Rabbit watches Apollo 11's flight to the moon, a feat which to him is personally meaningless since he is understandably obsessing about Janice's probable affair. The two are joined ambiguously as man steps on the moon and Rabbit tells his mother that "I know it's happened, but I don't feel anything yet," referring both to Janice's flight to Stavros's apartment and Armstrong's stepping on the moon. Again, Rabbit's mistress, Jill, breaks away from her family and brings the Sexual Revolution into Rabbit's home, just as Skeeter, a fugitive from justice, brings Black Power and Vietnam to racist, hawkish Rabbit. These aliens have arrived in Rabbit's home like astronauts on the moon. A second structural device is the war in Vietnam. Skeeter's consciousness-raising sessions lead Rabbit to accept violence as a personal solution for his own depression and frustration: beating Janice, Skeeter and Jill is his depression turned outward into rage. He can readily accept the war as a similar solution to frustration in Vietnam. Vietnam really "comes home" later when his home is burned; a Vietnam veteran is the ring-leader. Heroin, widely used in Vietnam, is used by Skeeter to hook Jill so that she can connect with God and confirm that he is the Black Messiah chosen to lead a holy race war in America.

Such parallels ask us to consider the relevance of science, technology, wealth and history to Rabbit's life. They ask us to consider the place of war and drugs in our culture, the causes of racism, the loss of love. Updike has led Rabbit back for education, and if he hasn't passed the final, he at least has been given a severe series of tests. When Janice returns he is sufficiently changed to recognize his share of responsibility for the alienation of his wife, the hostility of his son, the drugging and death of Jill and, perhaps, his part in the suppression of minorities. Only future novels of the "Rabbit" Saga could show if Rabbit had really learned anything.

Some commentators recognized formal connections Updike had created to tie together *Rabbit, Run* and *Rabbit Redux.* Some thematic connections raised in *Rabbit, Run* reappeared in *Rabbit Redux*, like, the need for significant work, spiritual longing and the failure of institutions to support that longing. Other connections were structural, like Rabbit's quasi-escape in *Rabbit, Run* paralleling Janice's breakout in *Rabbit Redux*, and Jill's death on Rabbit's "watch" resembling Becky's death at the hands of Janice. Minister Kruppenbach corresponds to evangelist Skeeter. Strands of images also lace the novels tightly together, like those derived from the "Peter Rabbit" story (which governs the entire saga), as well as images of the cosmos, food, and those drawn from popular culture– music, television and movies.

Now dedicated to writing about Rabbit every decade, Updike produced *Rabbit Is Rich,* ten years later, the most animated novel of the saga. In *Rabbit Is Rich,* Rabbit heads Springer Motors and has the leisure time and discretionary income to live the good suburban life. But lingering from *Rabbit Redux* is the old question about whether the good life can be bought at the expense of others. Rabbit's son Nelson had been infatuated with Jill in *Rabbit Redux* and has blamed Rabbit for her death throughout his adolescence and will not allow Rabbit to forget what he terms a "slip-up." The virtual Oedipal-conflict focuses on Nelson's effort to join Springer Motors, with Nelson supported by Janice who owns controlling interest. Rabbit thinks Nelson unready for such responsibility, and also incapable of taking care of a family. But because Jill looms between them Nelson rejects Rabbit advice that he not marry Pru Labelle, the woman he impregnated at Kent State, and have her have an abortion. Nelson thus, rejecting his father, follows his father's footsteps, since Rabbit had impregnated Janice before marriage. Also, where Rabbit followed unwillingly in his father's typesetter trade in *Rabbit Redux*, Nelson demands he follow in his father's. As in *Rabbit, Run* and *Rabbit Redux,* Rabbit discovers that a lover can come from an unexpected source, and in a wife-swapping, instead of Cindy, his "dream girl," he is chosen by Thelma Harrison, wife of his foe Ronnie Harrison. The joke on Rabbit is a variation on the way Tothero had chosen his lover Ruth in *Rabbit, Run* and African-Americans had procured Jill for him in *Rabbit Redux.* Commentators liked the book's comedy, satire and humanity, but others worried that Updike may have made an aesthetic error in allowing a "whiner" like Nelson to elbow Rabbit off center stage. General readers were bothered by sexually graphic scenes with Thelma, but critics recognized their thematic integrity and contribution to Rabbit's pilgrimage into "nothing" that began with Ruth in *Rabbit, Run* . Rabbit's pursuit of Ruth to discover if she did abort their child as she threatened at the end of *Rabbit, Run* as well as his continual disrespect of Janice caused a charge of misogyny to be leveled at Rabbit, and sometimes at his creator.

Rabbit at Rest (1990) treats Rabbit in retirement, yet still capable of being galvanized into action by the demands of his family and his quest for paradise. The action begins with Rabbit at a Florida airport. He imagines the plane bringing his son, daughter-in-law and grandchildren symbolizes his death, and in fact each will play a part in his death. His granddaughter prompts Rabbit's heart attack when she pretends she is drowning. When Nelson is discovered embezzling from the family business, Rabbit is forced from retirement and into a desperate effort to save Springer Motors. Finally, after Rabbit undergoes an angioplasty and returns from the hospital, he finds a kind of Edenic sexual comfort with his daughter-in-law Pru. When she confesses to Janice and Nelson, Rabbit runs as he had in *Rabbit, Run*, only this time he makes it to Florida. In his self-banishment, Rabbit plays a basketball game, is victorious but his athlete's heart, poisoned by a lifetime of bad eating, breaks. As he dies, Rabbit preserves the hope that his child by Ruth was not aborted, wanting to retain his vision of a daughter to the end, a dream of perfection. He still kept faith with his vision that he was a lead character in a cosmic drama.

The death of Rabbit dissatisfied many readers because it was unclear if his last words were spoken (Updike places them in quotes) or if they were only in his mind? Second, if, as Updike patiently explained in *The New York Times* that Rabbit "had to go," why did he make Rabbit's death ambiguous? Did he intend to revive him? Updike once explained that he always preferred a "quasi-death" of his characters and could not make the death unequivocal. Still, Updike's readers clearly did not want to let Rabbit go. But beyond Rabbit's passing, *Rabbit at Rest* completed the entropic disintegration of Rabbit's world as everything from movies to golf, and from the city to the country spiraled downward in the saga. Nonetheless, Rabbit's integrity counters such entropy by his mixture of beauties and faults. Fittingly, the four novels were issued in one volume by Everyman's Library as *Rabbit Angstrom,* allowing readers to evaluate the Rabbit novels as a single story, our story, the story of everyman. Critics agree that the tetralogy represents Updike's finest achievement. Some call it the finest work by an American in the past century.

As if amused by the Christ parallels some commentators had found in Rabbit of *Rabbit, Run*, Updike "resurrected" Rabbit in "Rabbit Remembered" in which Rabbit persists as an "absent presence." He not only "comes alive," in the conversations and recollections of his characters, but Rabbit is revitalized through his children Nelson and Annabelle. Nelson, having overcome his drug habit, now works as a counselor. Annabelle is a nurse. They work to heal bodies and minds, in contrast to Janice and her husband Ronnie Harrison, who treat Annabelle with suspicion and disrespect. The novel celebrates reunion and reunification as Nelson shelters Annabelle from their harm. Later he shelters her from a hurricane. Updike blends the domestic to the political, the private to the public, as discussions of President Clinton's sex scandal and the film *American Beauty* call for compassion and understanding in the face of the narrow-mindedness rooted in unremedied resentments. Such bigotry emerges when President Clinton's sexual misconduct and the homophobia in the film *American Beauty* are discussed. But for Annabelle and Nelson the president engaged in an act of affection and the film finds the homophobe shattered by the realization of his own misreading of the facts, while the innocent victim achieves transcendence. Affection (in Annabelle?) and transcendence seem to be what Rabbit himself represents in the lives of his children, and so the "Rabbit" Saga ends on a note of redemption. Annabelle will even apparently find her way from sexual trauma to marriage. Rabbit, operating through his son has led Nelson to rehabilitate his daughter. He is remembered indeed.

The critical reception of Updike's saga supplies the reader with four major insights: the criticism offers a diversity of opinion about Rabbit; second, it suggests that Updike may have achieved his goal of creating in Rabbit Angstrom a major character like Huckleberry Finn; third, it shows that Rabbit's story is emblematic of America in the last decades of the twentieth century; and fourth, it reveals a development of John Updike's artistry as a novelist capable of sustaining through nearly 2,000 pages inventive characters, exacting language, rich imagery and symbolic detail much that is meaningful to modern America and the world.

But what to do about Rabbit? Is he a misunderstood saint, an existential rebel without a cause? Is his mistreatment of women generally and his family acceptable because he seeks his own inner light? Updike has said that the title of *Rabbit, Run* is an imperative, thus endorsing the need for seeking one's own identity. But he has also said that the "social fabric unravels." The search for identity and the search for love may be, therefore, antithetical. Updike urges us to weigh and consider both options. Some critics seek a middle way and find that Updike's tactic, pursued for forty years, had been to show Rabbit as a complete man, one who rends the social fabric but is in fact a champion of marriage and the family, one who assumes a superiority to women but who also seeks and finds redemption through them, one whose omnivorous appetite for reality feeds upon the minute particulars of the everyday as mysteries, but who refuses to accept the commonplace facts of existence as the end of man. In fact, those minute particulars are the way, Rabbit believes, to find out how God may have "the last word." Updike reveals not only Rabbit's vulgar vernacular with which he converses with the world and himself, but his inward life in which metaphors and symbols are often the primary ingredients.

Meanwhile, it is worth recalling that Rabbit is only the protagonist at the center of a rich and complex community which Updike has brought together with remarkable variety and masterly command. The creation of this community is a daring goal for a modern writer, as Updike has acknowledged:

> What a wealth of material becomes accessible to a writer who can so simply proclaim a sense of community! We have writers willing to be mayor but not many excited to be citizens. We have writers as confessors, shackled to their personal lives, and writers as researchers, hanging their sheets of information from a bloodless story line. But of writers immersed in their material, and enabled to draw tales from a community of neighbors, Faulkner was our last great example. An instinctive, respectful identification with the people of one's locale comes hard now, in the menacing cities or disposable suburbs, yet without it a genuine belief in the significance of humanity, in humane significances, comes not at all. (Updike, *Picked-Up Pieces*, 489)

The following reviews and criticism, arranged chronologically, will give readers the opportunity to see if Rabbit can take his place along side Huck Finn and Jay Gatsby, and if the Rabbit saga expresses "a genuine belief in the significance of humanity."

Rabbit, Run

Richard Lyons

"A High E. Q."

Rabbit, Run is a poetic novel, but with certain exceptions it is not poetic prose. It is poetic in that like a good poem it cannot be paraphrased or summarized in any way that will fully enough suggest what it is. Its meaning is in its form. Nevertheless, I want to talk about the book. Sometimes one wants to talk about a thing that cannot be discussed more than he does about one that can. I am that way about this book.

Rabbit Angstrom, the hero of *Rabbit, Run* has been called a "disjointed simpleton" and a "hollow, spineless" character. He is not, although a summary of the events of the novel would lead one to think so. If one were to look for a literary cousin to Rabbit Angstrom, he would go to what appears on the surface to be the most unlikely of places– the fiction of J. D. Salinger. If Rabbit is like anyone else he is Seymour Glass in "Raise High the Roof Beam, Carpenters." There is, of course, a difference, but it is not in their nervous systems; it is in their respective intelligences and in their abilities at verbal analysis of their emotional responses to experience. Seymour's intelligence enables him to know what is happening inside himself. Rabbit experiences a personal life, a happiness, but he cannot identify it to himself or to others with words. Seymour can say, "I suspect people of plotting to make me happy." Rabbit, had he Seymour's capacity for introspection, could say the same thing. But he hasn't the vocabulary with which to externalize the emotional tinglings which vibrate through his nervous system. The nervous system is as illiterate as the brain is insensitive; words (art) are the medium of exchange between feeling and knowing, but only for the mind. If nervous systems, like brains, could be measured for their appropriate quotient, Rabbit would have a high E. Q. (emotion quotient). Since in Rabbit it is his nervous system and not his mind that is highly developed, he suffers because he cannot communicate what he feels, sometimes even to himself. While this situation is true of several of Salinger's characters, they all know who they are and what they are. With Rabbit, there is no one who knows him, not even, as an objectively conscious entity, himself. The one possible exception is the Reverend Mr. Eccles, the only one who feels that Rabbit is worth "saving." And yet it is not Rabbit but Eccles who is the lost character in this novel, a novel too, in which there is no one without pathos at one time or another, as, for example, Rabbit's wife, whose particularly tragic scene near the end is the artistic apex of the book.

Rabbit, with his inarticulateness (and he is inarticulate only because, unlike the rest of the characters, he has something to say), lives always in the present. This aspect governs the structural style. The book is written, except for one necessary transitional paragraph, in the present tense so that the whole experience of the book is always in the present. Rabbit is life, and life is always now. Tomorrow hasn't come yet; yesterday we remember, as Rabbit does. But we are actively conscious, alive only at this moment. When Rabbit speaks at such moments of greatest intensity, his voice says commonplace banalities. Others are unconscious of what he feels or that he feels. It is at such moments that people respond in the wrong way, break his sense of beatitude, a cleavage which produces further negative reactions in Rabbit by which others know him. Eccles, however, catches faint glimpses of Rabbit's essence, and it is he who calls him a mystic. The mystical experience is always in the present tense.

It is the curse of the mystic that his joy, which is not transferable, must be shared. To the creative artist there are escapes sometimes. For Rabbit there is no escape except through the act of love or through a delicately balanced sense of successful physical expression. From his past Rabbit remembers such an experience. It came during a non-conference basketball game during which everyone was relaxed and played the game for pure pleasure and Rabbit felt a complete control of his muscles. The game was played without reference to anything outside its own definition, a released, self-contained moment in time. During the period of the novel Rabbit communicates fully with another only once when he first makes love with Ruth and they share in touch what they can never share in words. In the world's mouth this desire for communion comes out as dirty lust. It is stained. It is such staining conversation among several people in a cheap tavern that goads Rabbit into his one lustful, loveless performance, also with Ruth.

That delicate emotional mechanism in Rabbit is much the same quality which Eccles searches for. Eccles, trained in the formalistic ritual of organized religious conscription, uses the term Grace. Grace is akin to mysticism (contrary to Rabbit, Eccles' background and training have prepared him, theoretically, to find it, but not to let himself be found by Grace, which cannot be pursued). What are in Rabbit selfish, physical indulgences become when translated into an acceptable traditional vocabulary respectable and transcendent expressions of saints who have touched God in the night. Rabbit, constructed of extrasensory but illiterate emotions and trying to maneuver through the world of cold intellect, continually crashes into negative responses from others. Yet people, life still excite him. He is delighted with Ruth when first they meet. That she is an itinerant prostitute is irrelevant to her humanity. She is not attractive. Like a Salinger character, Rabbit is receptive to some inner quality to which he responds without having to ask himself why. External circumstances are not important. He has been told that she is fat. He tries to suggest that she is not or that it doesn't matter. "He's talking just for happiness, but something he says makes her tense up." The tension turns out not to be bad at the time, but it is typical of the failure of emotional contact which must be translated into words to reach. He wakes up Sunday morning after sleeping with Ruth, sees people going to church. "The thought of these people having the bold idea of leaving their homes to come and pray pleases and reassures Rabbit, and moves him to close his own eyes and bow his head with a movement so tiny Ruth won't notice." His instinct is right, we see, from her response to his comment on the congregation. "'Sunday morning,' she says, 'I could throw up every Sunday.'" Nevertheless he tries to tell her that he believes. He cannot say quite that he believes in being alive, in living and in knowing it fully. Having no other word, he accepts Ruth's suggestion of "God."

This word he feels is not the right word, for it merely replaces one vagueness with another. To give some concrete dimension to this vagueness has been Mr. Updike's problem to solve. It is not an easy task, and he has chosen to make it more difficult. To be affirmative, to believe in life is at present, I gather, unpopular. To try to project this belief through an inarticulate athlete instead of through a highly articulate mystic, such as Seymour Glass, is to compound the difficulty. Modern savants have misunderstood Salinger. It is certain they will misunderstand Updike. Critics appear unable at times to recognize life in fiction, life without a program or a motto, without a tub-thumping manifesto for future proselytizing. Such readers flatten moments of emotional or spiritual doubt into morning sickness (as they did with Salinger's "Franny"). Positive thinking has become synonymous with not thinking at all because it has been usurped by non-thinking public-relations-type hacks and because it has become identified with some future material fulfillment. When affirmative art appears without the trappings of traditional beauties and unrealities, there is no critical apparatus currently available for analyzing it. The intellectual, by and large (myself as well), is so intent on his own cerebrations that he does not feel– that is, experience living as a moment of present time– and he does not admit that tragedy does not abrogate life and love any more than disease and ugly bodies and dusty streets and garrish (sic) neon signs do (and these ingredients are all accurately observed and included in *Rabbit, Run*) and that they make life and love more precious and more rewarding in the achievement. The tragedy in *Rabbit, Run* is that Ruth, Eccles and his wife, and Rabbit's wife fail to achieve it. Rabbit does. Even in his apparent defeat he is alive, and he even comes close to identifying himself to himself. "Good lies inside," he finally realizes. "There is nothing outside, those things he was trying to balance have no weight." To underline this theme Updike has used a quotation from Pascal as an epigraph. Its punctuation is important: "The motions of Grace, the hardness of the heart; external circumstances."

The greatest error to make in reading this book is to interpret Rabbit's running as escape, defeat. Such an interpretation fails to include the positive character of his running, especially at the end. It is a tremendously positive action. It is not so because of what it means in terms of something else or in relation to other actions. Its essence is not, as this book is not, in external circumstances. It is the only thing that Rabbit in his alienation from everyone he knows can do. Love, joy, happiness are intense accumulations of energy which demand release in some way. For the creative artist the release can take several (acceptable) forms. For the inarticulate athlete expression is more difficult. Physical response is all that is available to him. An early study of Rabbit appears in Mr. Updike's short story "Ace in the Hole." Here Fred (Ace) Anderson, once a basketball star, now fired from his job at a used-car lot (like Rabbit), runs with his daughter down the block from his mother's house to his own home. He just runs because he feels like it, he tells his wife, who doesn't understand. Ace and Rabbit are among those in Charles Hamilton Sorley's poem "Song of the Ungirt Runners." "We do not run for prize," they say in the poem. "And we run because we like it/ Through the broad bright land." It is with this response that Updike closes the novel: "he runs. Ah: runs. Runs."

*Richard Lyons, "A High E. Q." *The Minnesota Review.* Spring, 1961: 385-89.

from *Pastoral and Anti-Pastoral in the Works of John Updike*
Chapter 4: *Rabbit, Run*: An Anti-Pastoral Satire

Larry Taylor*

An *angstrom* is one ten-billionth of a meter. Harry ("Rabbit") Angstrom, the hero of *Rabbit, Run*, is blatantly christened by Updike, and turned loose in the novel to run and drive in circles, finger the "lettuce" in his wallet, sleep in the windowed "hutch" of his car, impregnate two women, become a gardener, and run off into the woods at the end. His wife Janet [*sic*] is a "Springer"; his old coach Tothero is a "Tot-hero"; his Lutheran minister Kruppenbach is a "horses's [*sic*] backside." [1] Is something satirical and allegorical going on behind this wild punning? One might not gather so from reading much of the major published criticism on *Rabbit, Run*— mainly criticism which somberly analyzes Rabbit Angstrom as a bleak Sartrian existentialist and post-Nietzschian seeker, a kind of ignorant but inspired folk-philosopher.[2] Are we to accept these name-puns and exaggerated details as

---

[1] "Kruppenbach," from German *Kruppe* (croup of a horse) and *Back* (backside). Kruppenbach, by the way, calls Rabbit a *Schussel*, p. 169, German (*coll.*) for a fidgety, hasty, or careless person. Compound German name-puns are a favorite trick of Updike's. For example, the neighboring farm in both *The Centaur* and *Of the Farm* is owned by "Schoelkopf,"an auditory pun on the German *Scholl* (clod or sod) and *Kopf* (head); thus, "Clodhead.."

[2] See especially Howard M.. Harper, Jr.'s "John Updike— the Intrinsic Problem of Human Existence," in *Desperate Faith* (Chapel Hill, 1967), p. 162 ff. Also see William Van O'Connor's "John Updike and William Styron: The Burdon [*sic*] of Talent," in *Contemporary American Novelists*, ed. Harry T. Moore (Carbondale, Ill., 1964), p. 205 ff. The last chapter of Ihab Hassan's *Radical Innocence* (Princeton, 1961), is a good general study of this type of hero.

whimsical linguistic indulgences within a highly serious realistic novel about the tragic paradoxes involved in the novel's epigraph: "The motions of Grace, the hardness of the heart; external circumstances?"[3] The name-tags are insignificant only if we accept names such as "Arden," "Touchstone," "Sir Oliver Martext," "Silvius," and "Phoebe" as mere whimsical indulgences in *As You Like It*; or "Chillingworth" and "Dimmesdale" and "Coverdale" in Hawthorne's novels. If they serve no other function, the names in *Rabbit, Run* warn the reader not to read the novel as a piece of simple realism; and they suggest from the beginning that the book is a type of fable with satiric overtones.

Like its baffling epigraph, *Rabbit, Run* is ambiguous, absurd, and moving. But, perhaps first of all the novel is satiric and ironic. Bent on exposing Rabbit Angstrom's failure to return to innocence and nature, the satire and irony spring from those "built-in" reflexes to the pastoral attitude– the reflexes which lead to mock-pastoral and anti-pastoral satire. Essentially the same satiric responses which make us smile at, love, and pity the "holy innocents" Don Quixote and Gulliver also make us smile at, love, and pity Sinclair Lewis' George Babbitt and John Updike's Rabbit Angstrom. They are all on quests for something which the reader knows cannot be found or attained. In addition to pity, we also feel a certain amount of contempt for Rabbit Angstrom. Questers, eremites, and saints should be celibate, like St. Paul, Don Quixote, and Thoreau. For example, Gulliver's sojourn in the pastorally ideal land of the Houyhnhnms separates him from humanity, and leads him to live in the stables with the horses at the end of *Gulliver's Travels*. Rabbit's flight to nature similarly separates him from humanity, and causes him to run off into the woods at the end of *Rabbit, Run*. But if our pity and sympathy is primarily for Gulliver and Rabbit, it is perhaps misplaced; in pursuit of their solipsistic pastoral ideals, they both abandon savable wives and children.

In our time, the paucity of genuine tragedy and heroism in both life and fiction has led us carelessly to call the merely pathetic "tragic"; and our readiness to identify our sorrows with our fictional heroes' sorrows may cause us to become so involved in their *pathos* that we forget to smile at their *folly*. This is a real danger in reading *Rabbit, Run*, despite the rather leading facts that an *angstrom* is one ten-billionth of a meter, and the "hero" is, ultimately, a "Hairy Rabbit Angstrom." He who feels compassion mainly for Rabbit rather than his wife and children is in danger of being a sentimental tragedy-monger who has missed the cutting anti-pastoral satire of the novel.

The novel has a sad ending, a pathetic ending; deaths of infants, imminent abortions, abandoned and neglected children can never, by any sophisticated intellectual appeal to irony or paradox, be funny or comic. But satire, by its very nature, is not a "pure genre," as comic parody and classical tragedy, for example, are "pure." If anything, satire is profoundly earthy, pragmatic, and moral, and deals with the important middle ground between comedy and tragedy. Both Updike's *Rabbit, Run* and Swift's "A Modest Proposal" talk about the deaths of infants, and

---

[3] The epigraph is from Pascal's *Pensee* [*sic*] 507.

the moral injunctions and pragmatic didacticism of both would seem indisputably clear. Yet critics and reviewers often like to talk quite seriously about twenty-six-year-old Rabbit Angstrom as an existentialist-sensitive-young-man-on-a-spiritual-quest, as if his decision to "Ah: run. Run." were little more than fifteen-year-old Huck Finn's decision to "light out for the territory." Treating Rabbit's quest as if it were philosophically valid, and interpreting the novel's epigraph as a cryptic *excuse* for Rabbit's behavior rather than as an *explanation of* such behavior, readers and critics often say much about Rabbit's theology, and little about his relationship to his two-year-old son. By giving us glimpses of the child throughout the novel, and by showing us how seldom Rabbit thinks of him, Updike shows that Rabbit's main sin is that he "has left undone those things he ought to have done." Tacitly de-emphasizing Rabbit's role as an antihero, readers and critics tend to talk about Rabbit's sorrow and tragedy rather than his son Nelson's. Like the characters of *Couples*, who would be "like nymphs and satyrs in a grove, except for the group of distressed and neglected children," Rabbit would be a sensitive pastoral swain, justified in his heroic flight from his alcoholic "dumb" wife, except for his distressed and neglected child (his "Knell-son"?). I submit that the satire of the novel should be emphasized as fully as the pathos; and this satire is perhaps most clear in the treatment of the "return to nature" motif in the novel. That the satirical elements exist by no means makes the pathos and poignancy less immediate or less painful– if anything, these elements increase the novel's value as a portrayal of what Updike calls "the mixed stuff of human existence."[4]

Updike, himself an accomplished and slashing parodist and comic satirist,[5] has written a telling essay on the function of laughter and satire in relation to pathos and seriousness: the essay is "Beerbohm and Others," collected in *Assorted Prose* (Knopf, 1965). In it he observes that the decline of parody and comedy as a distinctive genre, and the subsequent mingling of pathos and laughter may be a "symptom of recovery from nuclearphobia, cold war chilblains, hardening of the emotional arteries, and so forth."

> Laughter is but one of many potential human responses; to isolate humor as a separate literary strain is as unnatural as to extract a genre of pathos or of nobility from the mixed stuff of human existence. Insofar as "serious" literature is indeed exclusively serious, then humor, as in the Victoria age, was a duty, in the Parliament of Man, to act as the loyal opposition. But when, as in this century, the absurd, the comic, the low, the dry, and the witty are reinstated in the imaginative masterworks, then humor as such runs the risk of becoming merely trivial, merely recreational, merely distracting. A skull constantly grins, and in the constant humorist there is a detachment and dandyism of the spirit whose temporary abeyance in this country need not be cause for

---

[4] John Updike, "Beerbohm and Others," *Assorted Prose* (NY, 1965), p. 255.

[5] See Updike's *Verse: The Carpentered Hen and Telephone Poles* (New York, 1965), and his "Parodies" in *Assorted Prose* (New York, 1965), pp. 3-47.

unmitigated lamenting.[6]

Thus, the satirical elements of *Rabbit, Run* and *Couples* can be related to that "grinning skull," especially since infant deaths and abortions are involved in the ends of both novels. Indeed, Updike's work can be associated to some extent with the whole body of recent work currently referred to as "black humor." Unfortunately, the term is often used as if this were a twentieth-century phenomenon, a modern discovery that life is a mixture of horror and lyricism, pathos and laughter– as if the satiric and ironic treatment of pain, death, and damnation were not as old as Chaucer's "The Pardoner's Tale" and "The Sumonour's Tale," Shakespeare's *Hamlet*, Swift's "A Modest Proposal" and *Gulliver's Travels*, Voltaire's *Candide*, and Dickens' *Bleak House*. "Black humor" is merely a new name for an old technique, but the fact that recent fiction has prompted a renewed interest in the technique may, as Updike says, be a "symptom of recovery."

In the opening chapter of this essay, I suggested that a work is anti-pastoral when it challenges, refutes, and exposes the fallacies behind the dream of a return to nature. I also suggested that the concept of an elemental, simple life in a state of nature is a part of the American Dream and agrarian myth. Much of Rabbit Angstrom's failure can be attributed to his passionate pursuit of this ideal– an ideal which involves being in harmony with nature, rather than knowing one's relationship to nature. Those simple shepherds in the Theocritan *Idyls* were wonderfully adept at *being*, although their skill at *doing* and *knowing* was (to understate the case) limited. In terms of modern discussions about "essence" and "existence," they were wonderfully "existential."[7] No philosophical dialogues about the nature of God in Arcady; no soul-searching with priests between lyrical sexual encounters; no need to be concerned with the wages of sin in a place where sin does not exist.

First of all, Rabbit Angstrom is satirized through his very name, and through his inflated ideas of his past accomplishments. In assigning him the name "Rabbit," Updike associates him with a delicate, skittish, unintelligent and untrainable little animal noted for its prodigious breeding habits. In fright, which is often, it runs in circles. This process itself, i. e., equating a human with a certain animal, is an old satiric device as ancient as Aesop's *Fables*. The most common verbal associations with rabbits are "to be scared as a rabbit," and "to breed like rabbits"; secondary connotations are the soft, cute little anthropomorphic "Uncle Wigglys" and "Peter Rabbits" of children's fiction. Rabbit Angstrom's sensing he is in a "trap," his driving in a large circle, his fingering of his "lettuce," his following of his senses and animal intuitions, and so forth, are the linguistic tricks of fable, rather than, say, Howellsian Realism. The name and the rather farfetched symbolic details are part of an elaborate metaphor– rather in the way Aesop's *Fables* are metaphors, or Ben

---

[6] Updike, "Beerbohm and Others," p. 255.

[7] One of the best general studies of existential philosophy is William Barrett's *Irrational Man* (New York, 1958), available in Anchor Books Edition, 1962.

Jonson's *Volpone,* or Swift's "Houyhnhnms" in *Gulliver's Travels,* or D. H. Lawrence's "The Fox." In terms of the "return to nature" theme in *Rabbit, Run,* then, the metaphor suggests that Harry, as a Rabbit, is already an animalistic part of nature; never quite having become fully human, he has little humanity to lose. The reader sees a far greater need for him to nurture a superego than for him to indulge his already overactive id. Rabbit's illusions of grandeur about his single real accomplishment in life (that is, once setting a high school basketball scoring record– since broken) also suggests satire.

To finally reduce Rabbit's personality and his quest to the absurd and irrelevant, Updike gives Rabbit a proper name suggesting measurements in ten-billionths of a meter. Not only is he reduced to the level of a minor animal, but he is also reduced into an infinitessimally [sic] small rabbit– a kind of animal cipher. And, to complete the satiric pattern of making the tiny and insignificant seem grand and heroic, Updike causes Rabbit to see his flight from responsibility as a quest for ultimate meaning– for what Rabbit himself describes, with inspired vagueness, as "this thing."[8]

"This thing" Rabbit longs for and runs toward is the lyrical simplicity of his adolescence-- that is, his past glory as a high school basketball hero, and the exquisite titillation of exploratory sexuality. He has not realized that his youthful swainship is over– that Olinger (here Mount Judge) is a "state of mind." It is not enough to say that Rabbit is immature and an idealist; even Tothero tells him that. What is more important is that Rabbit still vaguely believes in the pastoral American Dream of eternal youth and transcendental harmony with nature. Escape. In terms of the American pastoral and anti-pastoral pattern, Rabbit is aligned with Thomas Morton's maypolers at Merry Mount– i.e., with sensuality and sexuality in Arcadia, rather than with Bradford's civilizing and disciplined Puritanism in Plymouth Plantation.

When Rabbit first runs at the beginning of the novel, he "wants to go south, down, down the map into orange groves and smoking rivers and barefoot women. It seems simple enough, drive all night through the dawn through the morning through the noon park on a beach take off your shoes and fall asleep by the Gulf of Mexico. Wake up with the stars above perfectly spaced in perfect health."[9] This is a version of the pastoral dream, and it is little wonder that he dreams it. For example, as he flees from his pregnant alcoholic wife and his small son, he is encouraged, consoled, and primed by the relentless idyllic lyricism of popular American culture. His car radio soothes him with songs about "Secret Love," "Autumn Leaves," and "fields of corn" where "it makes no mind no how. . .wihithout [sic] a song."[10] Agrarians singing in the fields; nymphs and swains secretly loving in the woods. Rabbit's "scalp contracts ecstatically" in response to these twentieth-century versions of the Theocritan idyl.

---

[8] John Updike, *Rabbit, Run* (New York, 1960), p. 132.

[9] Ibid., p. 25.

[10] Ibid., pp. 23-24.

We are reminded of George F. Babbitt's dream of the "Fairy Child" and of "really living," i.e., "plunging though the forest, making camp in the Rockies, a grim and wordless caveman!"– "like in a movie." Neither Rabbit nor Babbitt understands that idyls exist only in art (popular songs and movies, for example), rather than in real life.

As Rabbit rushes outdoors in flight from his apartment and his intolerable marriage, he sees a street sign as a "two-petaled flower," and a fire hydrant as "a golden bush: a grove."[11] Driving toward the "dawn cottonfields" on this heavily symbolic night of the vernal equinox, Rabbit mentally equates the land with a woman. His problem is to get west and free of Baltimore-Washington, which like a two-headed dog guards the costal [sic] route to the south. He doesn't want to go down along the water anyway, his image is of himself going right down the middle, right into the broad soft belly of the land, surprising the dawn cottonfields with his northern plates.[12] He envies an adolescent couple in West Virginia, and he gets lost in a park which turns out to be a lovers' lane. His tendency to see himself as a "lover" who wants sexual intercourse to be "natural," without "devices," is part of his image of himself as an amorous swain. The irony is that his attitude toward sex is more a rabbit's attitude than a sensitive human being's. Furthermore, Rabbit's pastoral vision engenders "pathetic fallacies" in more than a literary sense; it is pathetic in that it eventually leads to moral anarchy, terror, and death. Again, this is part of the American tradition in the pastoral pattern, dating back to Thomas Morton's eventual armament of the Indians. Seeing "two-petaled" street signs and "golden bush" fire hydrants is like seeing an untamed wilderness as a paradise. It is a lie; and John Updike seems to be asserting that it is a dangerous lie.

Further related to Rabbit's doggedly idealized vision of nature is his refusal to see rural life and nature as it really is; by this I mean that he has contempt for real farmers and the unattractive earthiness of real rural life. Without comprehending it himself, he wants "snowy flocks" and "naked girls on the seashore," rather than dirty sheep and manure piles. At first he idealizes the rural farmer who fills his gas tank-- he sees him as honest and law-abiding in a way that urban station attendants are not: "Laws aren't ghosts in this country, they walk around with the smell of earth on them." Then he discovers the farmer is drunk, and therefore corrupted; he doesn't fit Rabbit's pastoral ideal. Later, Rabbit, lost and circling back home, "blames everything on that farmer with glasses and two shirts."[13] Similarly, Rabbit at first idealizes an Amish couple in a horsedrawn buggy, and then mentally rejects them because their rural life is not ideal enough: First they are leading the "good life," "clear of all this phony business." Then they become "fanatics" who "worship

---

[11] Ibid., p. 15.

[12] Ibid., p. 31.

[13] Ibid., p. 36.

manure."[14]

Perhaps the most telling facts about Rabbit's return to nature are the types of nature he returns to– 1) in his all-night drive toward the "broad soft belly of the land," he never really leaves his car; 2) in his walk into the woods with the prostitute Ruth, after their first night together, he climbs up man-made steps and comes out in a parking lot; 3) in his conversations with the Episcopal priest Eccles, he returns to the "groves" of a man-made golf course; and 4) in his occupation as a gardener, he works on a luxurious estate raising exotic rhododendrons. Thus, he never gets close to real farms and agrarians. Significantly, the park, the green, the garden are about as far as Rabbit gets on his return to nature– not much further than the classic English "village green" with its maypole in the middle.

Rabbit has never really grown any older than the high school basketball hero he was as a teenager. His sexual fantasies about his first girl friends, his premarital sex with his wife, and even his relationship with Ruth are all idyllic norms against which he judges his happiness. His first night with the prostitute Ruth is a high point for him. Significantly, Updike ends the incident with a pastoral image– clearly satiric since it is purely from the narrator's point of view rather than Rabbit's. "He is asleep when *like a faun in moonlight* Ruth, washed, creeps back to his side, holding a glass of water."[15] This image is important because Rabbit and Ruth have temporarily played the roles of nymph and satyr this night. But in order to do so, they have become moral anarchists: Rabbit has abandoned all familial and social responsibilities, and Ruth has sold her body to him.

The next day, nymph and satyr that they are, they make an excursion into Arcadian groves– the city park on the side of Mount Judge. However, since Rabbit and Ruth are corrupted, pseudo-Arcadians, their groves are also corrupted, haunted with thugs by night, and strewn with litter by day. The city park is shabby and joyless; "the ornamental pool in front of the bandshell is drained and scum-stained."[16] The effect is similar to T. S. Eliot's use of pastoral and anti-pastoral ironies in *The Waste Land,* where Elizabethan lyricism is contrasted to twentieth-century aridity. Having shown Ruth as "a faun in moonlight" and having shown Rabbit as the young swain, Updike then presents the trip into the park as a parody of the folic in the pastoral grove. The description is satiric anti-pastoralism which establishes the discrepancy between the lyrical ideal and the tawdry reality. The couple take off their shoes and climb upward to the top of Mount Judge. At the top, in a parking lot, Rabbit looks over the city and is "bothered by God." He contemplates the inexorable power of death, and then, childlike, asks Ruth to put her arm around him. Then, in the satiric anticlimax, the ironic non sequitur, Updike curtly sums up the prevailing anti-pastoral tone of the entire incident: "They take

---

[14] Ibid., p. 28.

[15] Ibid., p. 86. My italics.

[16] Ibid., p. 110.

a bus down."[17]

The relationship between Eccles, the Episcopalian *ecclesi*ast, and Rabbit is similarly a part of the pastoral and anti-pastoral pattern of the book. Eccles is the heir of two traditions: 1) his grandfather's, a Unitarian transcendentalist who believed that "God is in the woods," and 2) his father's, a reactionary orthodox Anglo-Catholic. To the extent that he follows the forms of his church, Eccles is orthodox; to the extent that he liberally tries to see men as basically good and redeemable through individual transcendence, he is an Emersonian transcendentalist. As Jimmy, the "Big Mouseketeer" on television, translates "know thyself" into "be yourself," Eccles translates the King James pronouncement "love faileth not" into the New World Translation version "love never ends." Eccles is a romantic transcendentalist who finally admits, after his failure with Rabbit, that he has no faith.

And, of course, in terms of the American tradition, Eccles is the perfect sympathetic audience for Rabbit's pastoral vision. Ironically warning Rabbit that "all vagrants think they're on a quest, a least at first," Eccles doesn't seem to realize that he himself treats Rabbit as if Rabbit's quest were a valid one.[18] Eccles plays golf with him, gets him a job, discusses philosophy with him, but says little about sin, morality, and responsibility. Kindred souls, the two men clearly show the close relationship between Emersonian transcendentalism and the classic pastoral ideal. Both dream of Eden.

Rabbit's quest is satirized through an accident of gesture: when trying to explain to Eccles that he is seeking the mystery within and behind nature, Angstrom inarticulately gestures out of the car window toward what he means to be the unspoiled landscape. Eccles has just delivered Rabbit a mini-sermon about "outer darkness"and "inner darkness."

> Eccles' volunteering all this melts Rabbit's caution. He wants to bring something of himself into the space between them. The excitement of friendship, a competitive excitement that makes him lift his hands and jiggle them as if thoughts were basketballs, presses him to say, "Well I don't know all this about theology, but I'll tell you. I do feel, I guess, that somewhere behind all this"– he gestures outward at the scenery; they are passing the housing development this side of the golf course, half-wood half [sic] brick one-and-a- half -stories in little flat bulldozed yards with [sic] tricycles and spindly three- year-old trees, the un [sic] grandest landscape in the world– "there's something t hat wants me to find it." [19]

Ironically, "all this" is meant to be idyllic nature. Again, the effect is satiric anticlimax. It is later, in the groves of the golf course, that Rabbit explains to Eccles that he is searching for 'this thing."

---

[17] Ibid., p. 113.

[18] Ibid., p. 127.

[19] Ibid., p. 126-127.

The equation of transcendentalism with pastoralism, and Puritanism with anti-pastoralism also exists in the novel. Eccles, the Episcopalian, is pitted against Kruppenbach, the Lutheran minister. Kruppenbach, for all the narrowness of his vision, comes closer to being right about Rabbit than anybody else in the novel. Darkly Puritanical, he believes in sin and repentance; he takes the occasion of discussing Rabbit's "case" to attack Eccles for Eccles' own laxity and sentimentality. Howard M. Harper has rightly suggested that Kruppenbach's solution is "saner" than Eccles':

> Despite Kruppenbach's lack of interest in Rabbit's "case," his view, Updike seems to suggest, is saner than Eccles' ineffectual meddling .Kruppenbach talks of the force of belief, and it is the quality of force which Rabbit admires most in people. Kruppenbach and Eccles, then objectify two religious alternatives: one which Rabbit admires but cannot reach, the other which envelops him in its do-goodism but which he cannot respect.[20]

In terms of the American pastoral and anti-pastoral tradition, Kruppenbach would cut down the maypole and force reformation, whereas Eccles secretly tends to want to join the "frisking."

The rabbit takes a job gardening in old Mrs. Harry Smith's fancy rhododendron patch, the lavish garden on her wealthy estate. The garden is a version of Eden even to a direct comparison: an old woman had once told Mrs. Smith that "heaven must be like this." Mrs. Smith is a realist who prefers alfalfa to expensively unique flowers. Her dead husband, not she, had been the idealizing pastoralist. Rabbit becomes a type of surrogate for her lost husband, also named Harry. Rabbit feels the old woman is in love with him— *wants* her to be in love with him. And here we have curiously grotesque scenes in which the ex-basketball-hero and the ancient dowager stroll through the Edenic lanes arm-in-arm, at peace. Perhaps the strangest Adam and Eve in literature. The gardens in May are cloyingly lush, and Rabbit uses the perfume to prime fantasies of nymphs. Rabbit dreams of a type of girl "he had often wanted and never had, a little Catholic from a shabby house, dressed in cheap bargain clothes."[21] Rabbit really believes such lusciously innocent girls exist; unfortunately, he does not realize that they exist chiefly on Grecian urns and on the slopes of Arcadia. Finally, Rabbit is disillusioned with the ancient Mrs. Smith for the same reason he was disillusioned with the farmer station attendant and the Amish couple: they and Mrs. Smith represent the *real* agrarian world. Mrs. Smith, a farmer's daughter, prefers alfalfa and buckwheat crops to flower beds. She is too earthy for Rabbit's taste. The idyllic "little Catholic" is the dream; the wrinkled old woman is the reality.

Finally, with the depressing end to the novel, Updike seems to be saying that Rabbit's pastoral vision has devastating results. The Theocritan *Idyl* idealizes the

---

[20] Howard M. Harper, Jr., "John Updike– The Intrinsic Problem of Human Existence," *Desperate Faith* (Chapel Hill, 1967), p. 170.

[21] Updike, *Rabbit, Run*, p. 137

past in a dangerous way; that is, the attitude becomes dangerous when it is confused with reality, as it is in Rabbit Angstrom's mind. Rabbit's dream is the dream of eternal youth and immortality, the pastoral dream of "Heaven on Earth." His innocence is "radical" in the way Ihab Hassan defines it: "The anarchy in the American soul is nourished on an old dream: not freedom, not power, not even love, but the dream of immortality. America has never really acknowledged Time. Its vision of Eden or Utopia is essentially a timeless vision. Its innocence is neither geographical nor moral: it is mainly temporal, hence metaphysical. This is radical innocence."[22] Updike sympathetically celebrates that innocence, if anywhere, in his Olinger stories, not in *Rabbit, Run*. Simply that it is an American tradition is not enough to ameliorate its serious moral consequences. As Updike and other realists keep asserting, failure to acknowledge time results in failure to grow.

Thus, Rabbit is not a sympathetic hero on a quest, despite the allowances critics may make for him. Certainly, he makes an oversupply of allowances for himself. Perhaps the most charitable reading of the moral tensions in *Rabbit, Run* is William Van O'Connor's conclusion that Rabbit is no worse than the other characters in the novel.

> Presumably, Updike is not saying that Rabbit Angstrom is following the only honest course in rejecting the sententious platitudes offered him. The novel catches many little ironies– Rabbit's notion that he is praising his coach when he is praising himself, or the minister's wanting a glass of water while consoling Mrs. Springer, and many others. Human motives and actions show a welter of inconsistencies. But there are certain consistencies: Eccles is something of an ass, but he does help certain people; Ruth, the prostitute, is quite capable of loyalty and devotion, and, in her own way, maintains her self-respect. Janice is terribly weak, but she wants to make a go of her marriage. Tothero is a dirty old man, physically and mentally, but he'd prefer not to be, and his advice is on the side of the angels. The novel seems not to be saying that man's moral gestures are all fraudulent. It could even be saying, with Auden, Love your crooked neighbor with your crooked heart.[23]

In terms of the body of Updike's work, I believe this conclusion is perhaps too generous toward the characters, and especially toward Rabbit. Rabbit has an intelligence and sensibility which make him singularly responsible for his actions. It is not "external circumstances" which separate Rabbit from "the motions of [God's] Grace"; rather, it is "the hardness of the heart," which, I take it, is a result of willful moral acts, and not deterministic accidents. Rabbit is worse than the other characters.

The satirical anti-pastoral elements of the novel are related to the moral theme. Essentially, Rabbit is like the hero of Nathanael West's *Miss Lonelyhearts*, as

---

[22] Ihab Hassan, *Radical Innocence* (Princeton, 1961), p. 325.

[23] William Van O'Connor, "John Updike and William Styron: The Burden of Talent," *Contemporary American Novelists* (Carbondale, Ill., 1964), p. 211.

described in a critical essay by Roger D. Abrahams: "*Miss Lonelyhearts* is a novel of psychological development, one we might call the 'existential,' the 'chaotic experience,' or the antiromance novel." Abrahams continues,

> Here isolation is a permanent condition; the progress of the psyche, if there is any, is toward more intensive isolation, perhaps death. The tone of such works is ironic. Moments occur which might have become revelatory but which fail to transform the protagonist or resolve his problems. Consequently, the protagonist is never able to achieve the object of his search, the ability to act. He is immobilized. The search becomes a wait. This kind of progression characterizes Miss Lonelyhearts. The fixed moral and psychological dilemma of man is morbidly attractive; his search for answers is necessary but futile.[24]

The comments are pointedly applicable to Rabbit Angstrom's character. Rabbit's sin– the one which results in "the hardness of the heart"– is his solipsistic refusal to see himself as a sinner. Ready to condemn his fellows, he seems to be constantly thankful that he is not as they are. In fact, his self-righteous search for youth and innocence makes him more of a sinner than any of the others; it is an exorbitant and damning form of pride. In his search for Eden, he appears to himself as an innocent victim of a corrupt society.

> As in so many satires, a moral point of view is developed through the presentation of an innocent in the midst of the corrupt, corruption appearing that much more profound because it is presented by the naive observer. Further, the innocent is shown to be fully as deluded and vain as the corrupt; just as we discover that such satiric protagonists as Gulliver and Candide are the dupes of their own insular systems of thought, so Miss Lonelyhearts [and Rabbit Angstrom] is revealed to be deluded by his mystical sentimentalism.[25]

The ending of *Rabbit, Run* involves the melodramatic death of Rabbit's infant daughter, who slips out of his drunken wife's hands and drowns in the bathtub. It is an indefensible and exaggerated stroke of melodrama only if we forget the other exaggerations in the novel– the name puns and the parodic pastoral imagery, for example. Stylistically, the book is a mixture of moral fable and realism. The death is overdrawn in the way fables, allegories, and morality plays are overdrawn– as a symbol of the consequences of Rabbit's romantic view of the world. Driven by guilt to protest too much at the funeral, Rabbit is compelled to blurt out his innocence, and then run into the woods. He later seeks out Ruth, discovers that she is pregnant by him and considering an abortion, and then "he runs. Ah,[sic] runs: [sic] Runs."

In an excellent short article entitled "*Rabbit* [sic] *Run*: John Updike's

---

[24] Roger De. Abrahams, "Androgynes Bound: Nathanael West's *Miss Lonelyhearts,*" *Seven Contemporary Novelists*, ed. Thomas B. Whitbread (Austin, 1966), p. 55.

[25] Abrahams, p. 54.

Criticism of the `Return to Nature,'" Gerry Brenner arrives at the crux of the novel. Substantially, the only difference between my conclusions about the nature theme, and Gerry Brenner's conclusions is that I extend the subject to an historical tradition of pastoral and anti-pastoral patterns. Otherwise, we are in complete accordance. A portion of the Brenner essay merits lengthy quotation:

> Updike's focus upon the consequences of Rabbit's unconsidered blithe actions criticizes with calm insistence the omni-present desire to "return to nature" by showing the logical extension of that desire. More, he shows that instead of just a vague romantic ideal, it has become an integrated part of reality. Like all the values whose worth has depreciated in the twentieth century, the value of returning to nature, for example, has been immersed in the world of daily action, a colloquialization of the ideal. And made accessible, it is adulterated and abused until it is converted into a distorted way of life. The ideas of the past, which have value *precisely because* they spur effort for attainable goals, have become misinterpreted (like the "be yourself" interpretation of "Know Thyself"), debased (like the anarchy of authority), and pursued unconsciously without understanding. Now that the ideal has been lost, Updike suggests that a practiced return to nature, carried to its logical conclusion, ends in destruction. . . .The return to nature, like all impoverished ideas, is wrenched out of its original context and thrust into an alien situation. In the original context, the return was only to geographical nature. In the present-day context, the return has been to a psychological nature of physical impulse, lacking external, prescriptive refinements. The shadow of neanderthal man clearly hangs over modern man who, like Rabbit, possesses more id (in his impulse for nature) than ego, and possesses only wisps of a super-ego.
>
> Updike's philosophical conservatism conceives of the romantic dream of returning to nature, in its worst sense, as the ultimate extension of the loss of traditional values, ideals, laws. Set into a society that persists in adhering to some prescriptive mores, Rabbit, as a "noble" urban savage, images modern man's tradition-less character and portends his concomitant problems. And the effectiveness of the novel resides in Updike's projection of this statement through the use of the tacky social setting and a line-up of only moderately sympathetic characters.[26]

Those "external, prescriptive refinements" which Rabbit lacks are partly the sophistication and erudition required for seeing a return to nature in its historical context; that is, to see it in the tradition of Theocritus and Thoreau. The oldest myth in the Hebraic-Christian tradition is the myth of the loss of Eden; placed as it is, hard on the heels of the story of the creation of the race itself, this *should* be the first lesson Western man learns. It seems to be the last. The entire American tradition, from *The New English Canaan* to *Rabbit, Run*, contains characters who, like Theocritus two thousand years earlier, refuse to accept the loss of Eden as an inexorable fact, and consequently create Edens and Idyls in art and in their minds. Where is Rabbit Angstrom running to? To Olinger. And Updike has explained to us that Olinger is a "state of mind"– "like a town in a fable." Rabbit expects to find it

---

[26] Gerry Brenner, "*Rabbit, Run*: John Updike's Criticism of the 'Return to Nature,'" *Twentieth Century Literature*, 12, No. 1 (April 1966), p. 14.

physically, like finding a geographical location here on earth. Despite his ambiguity and subtlety, one point which John Updike makes painfully clear in the body of his fiction is that Rabbit Angstroms of the world will ultimately fail, no matter how long and how far they "Ah: run. (sic) Run."

*Larry Taylor, *Pastoral and Anti-Pastoral in the Works of John Updike.* Carbondale: Southern Illinois University Press, 1971. pp. 76-85. Reprinted by permission of Carbondale: Southern Illinois University Press.

From *Married Men and Magic Tricks: John Updike's Erotic Heroes*

Elizabeth Tallent*

"It has never occurred to me to face the terror but/ as to how to hide from it I'm a virtual booth of information," A. R. Ammons wrote in the long poem *Sphere: The Form of a Motion.* A parallel line of reasoning– if not a comparably introspective mockery, for Rabbit is Updike's creature, rather than a variant of his self– is pursued in the novel *Rabbit, Run.* The book is a record of the evasive maneuvers practiced by Harry Angstrom, nicknamed Rabbit, the hero of a life gone formidably wrong. The thing that he wishes to hide from is exactly the kind of terror– darkness, death, the decay of awareness and possibility– that the world relentlessly sends his way. Rabbit's chief certainty in *Rabbit, Run* is that *it* is right behind him, breathing down the back of his neck.

Even Rabbit's name acknowledges that he is, however unwittingly, an example, linking error and expiation as inevitably as any character in Beatrix Potter. According to the *Random House Dictionary*, an angstrom is "a unit of length, equal to one tenth of a millimicron; or one ten millionth of a millimeter, primarily used to express electromagnetic wavelengths." Crucial, in this definition, is not only the fact that a unit of measurement so astonishingly small exists, but that it exists to measure both the invisible– radio waves, x-rays, gamma rays– and the spectrum of light edging boldly toward the visible, for Rabbit's eyes "turn toward the light however it glances into his retina." (*Rabbit, Run*: 219) Rabbit is an instrument by which certain invisible forces– the willingness to seek the good; the desire to run, to err, to reconcile– can be judged, as well as some very visible things– the desertion of a wife; domestic ugliness and disorder; alcoholic sorrow following hard on the heels of adultery. Because he is always more than an instrument, however, Rabbit remains scaldingly aware of the electricity that runs through him, of the light that aches in the receptive cells of the eye. Long after the publication of *Rabbit, Run,* when he was discussing the Rabbit novels in an interview with John Callaway, Updike could speak of Rabbit's vulnerability to perception: ". . .his stream of consciousness, as it moves through these events which are squalid and disastrous– as real events often are– [is] nevertheless. . .a kind of praise-singing to the created world." (*John Callaway Interviews*: 13)

In the opening pages of the novel, Rabbit is wearing a sign of this vulnerability, the equivalent of his heart on his sleeve. "He wonders if he should remove the Demonstrator badge from his lapel but decides he will wear the same suit tomorrow. He has only two, not counting a dark blue that is too hot for this time of year." (*Rabbit, Run*: 13) This dark suit will figure in a grim way late in the novel, when rabbit wears it to the funeral of his infant daughter. "He opens the closet door as far as he can without bumping the television set and reaches far in and unzips a plastic zippered storage bag and takes out his blue suit, a winter suit made of wool, but the only dark one he owns." (*Rabbit, Run*: 261) It is still too hot for the suit– Rabbit's daughter was drowned on the summer solstice, and the funeral follows two days after– but the original mention of the suit, and the way it is retrieved, rather fearfully and ceremoniously, from a dark closet in the apartment where the death occurred, provides one of those pairings by which the novel is structured. It *is* a beautifully structured work, as full of machinations, premonitions, and pitfalls as a fairy tale, yet balanced by unexpected symmetries of sound and incident. Updike's accounting of Rabbit's life has been so exact that the reader not only immediately recognizes the contents of the closet, but knows something of the sour resentment Rabbit must feel at this, the sullen winter cloth worn to a summer burial.

Within a page of this first mention of the Demonstrator badge pinned to his lapel, Rabbit's wife Janice demands petulantly, "What are you doing, becoming a saint?" Though she could easily be the last to recognize it, sainthood is indeed one of the possibilities inherent in Rabbit's skittish progress through the world. His travails are those of the heart, and he suffers them with a heated purity. He runs from circumstances, never from his own emotions, which have acquired– when so much in his life is cheap and disordered– a value equivalent to that of the Krugerrands in *Rabbit Is Rich*. Emotions are the coin of Rabbit's realm, his only earthly good, his single clue: "He hates all the people in the street in dirty everyday clothes, advertising their belief that the world arches over a pit, that death is final, that the wandering thread of his feelings leads nowhere." (*Rabbit, Run*: 217) With whim as the *modus operandi* of sainthood, Rabbit charts his erratic course. He considers himself one of the elect, and tends to admire the nervous spontaneity of his own heart, no matter what chaos comes of his acts– that is the world's fault, not his. Late in the novel, during an argument with his lover, Rabbit finds that the "way she is fighting for control of herself repels him; he doesn't like people who manage things. He likes things to happen of themselves." (*Rabbit, Run*: 281) In an earlier quarrel with his wife, when he is about (sic) leave her for the second time, she voices a demand that seems, although irritable, just, and he replies according to his creed.

> "Why can't you try to imagine how I *feel*?
> I've just had a baby."
> "I can. I can but I don't want to, it's not the
> thing, the thing is how *I* feel. And I feel like
> getting out." (*Rabbit, Run*: 230)

In this– the italicized, anxiously forward-tilting *I*– Rabbit is most purely himself, and most purely a hero, however slender the thread that stretches ahead of him, however brutal the "things that happen of themselves."

In *Rabbit, Run* even language itself seems secretly anxious, as if confronting some fear it can neither precisely counter nor entirely evade. There is an almost placatory reliance on certain words– placatory in the sense that a prayer is placatory, and in the sense that any rhythm is, at some level, an attempt to stave off uncertainty, to fortify oneself against those things in the world that are frighteningly arbitrary. Still, these words recur with an insistence that is puzzlingly uncharacteristic of Updike's work, usually so wide-open to any fortuitous linguistic intrusion, so spirited and mobile, with a willingness to absorb the colloquial cadence, the exact names of streets and numbers of houses, the verbal *object trouvé*– in short, whatever is at once peculiar and apt. "You spend so much of your own energy avoiding repeating yourself," the psychiatrist in the short story "The Fairy Godfathers" tells the perplexed hero; the observation seems to apply to Updike, the craftsman, as well. He once admired Mark Twain's use of the word "scatteration" for its spur-of-the-moment exactness, and he himself has resorted to such curiosities as "jubilating" and "centaurine" with the ease born of immediacy. In *Rabbit, Run*, however, the language seems stubbornly closed, almost irritating in its impoverishment. It remains puzzling and irritating until you relinquish certain expectations of the language– that it is a formal system requiring forward movement, and implying a logical progression from *here* to *there* within each sentence. The language of *Rabbit, Run* is instead a vehicle of intuition, recognition, pattern, parable, and omen. The key words are smooth as mantras, narrow sounds snapped free of context, pure objects of contemplation, the stones that Rabbit touches again and again in his nervous circling. In the beginning of the novel these word-touchstones are "trap" and "net." "Run" remains a constant, as frequently invoked as in a primer, often rather hopefully, as if it were the verb particular to salvation. Near the middle of the novel, things are described as "tipped" or "tipping," until the entire physical universe seems precariously out-of-balance. In *Rabbit, Run* the world never rights itself. The novel ends, not with symmetry or release, exactly, but with a sigh that cold be either exhaustion or sly physical pleasure in motion itself: "Ah: runs. Runs."

Women, rooms, the twigs of a forest, the straps of a whore's shoes, all can be "nets" for Rabbit:

> The clutter behind him in the room– the Old-fashioned glass with its corrupt dregs, the choked ashtray balanced on the easy-chair arm, the rumpled rug, the floppy stacks of slippery newspapers, the kid's toys here and there broken and stuck and jammed, a leg off a doll and a piece of bent cardboard that went with some breakfast-box cut-out, the rolls of fuzz under the radiators, the continual crisscrossing mess– clings to his back like a tightening net. (*Rabbit, Run*: 18)

> At the upper edge of his headlight beams the naked tree-twigs make the same net. Indeed the net seems thicker now. (*Rabbit, Run*: 37)

> The names melt away and he sees the map whole, a net, all those red lines and blue lines and stars, a net he is somewhere caught in. (*Rabbit, Run*: 39)

> He feels the faded light he left behind in this place as a net of
> telephone calls and hasty trips, trails of tears and strings of words,
> white worried threads shuttled through the night and now faded
> but still existent, an invisible net overlaying the steep streets and
> in whose center he lies secure in his locked hollow hutch. (*Rabbit,
> Run*: 43)

In this last passage, "white worried threads shuttled through the night" is
an oblique reference to Rabbit's wife, whom he has earlier remembered as "just a
girl. Nerves like new thread. Skin smelled like fresh cotton." (*Rabbit, Run*: 18)
Thread can be woven into nets; even physiologically, she possesses the ability to
trap him. Entrapment is a fact of their life– she trapped by pregnancy, he trapped
into marriage– and an aspect of the world they share, where ashtrays are choked and
toys are "broken and stuck and jammed."

> Janice calls from the kitchen. "And honey pick up a pack of
> cigarettes, could you?" in a normal voice that says everything is
> forgiven, everything is the same.
> Rabbit freezes, standing looking at his faint yellow shadow on the
> white door that leads to the hall, and senses he is in a trap. It
> seems certain. He goes out. (*Rabbit, Run*: 20)
> He doesn't drive five miles before this road begins to feel like a
> part of the same trap. (*Rabbit, Run*: 29)

This incantatory play of language is essential to *Rabbit, Run*, for it reflects
and, in part, sustains the larger exigencies of the narrative– the passage of time, the
whittling-away of freedom, the constant underlying sense of dread that Rabbit feels.
The chronology of the novel is framed by a pair of events, the vernal equinox and
the summer solstice, that were crucial in the ceremonial lives of primitive peoples,
reverently observed by them as indications of consistency in the workings of the
universe, *knowns* in the flux of time; they were also ways of pinning down the
cycles of planting and harvest on which culture was dependent, of locating yourself
between the broad horizons of spring and winter. The universe mirrored the
trustworthiness of gods through the regular occurrence of solstices and equinoxes,
and their inviolate mystery through the chicanery of planets, which act according
to no readily decipherable law. Without a formal and rather scrupulous knowledge
of such events, only hunting and gathering was possible– you were forced to rely
on the whims of abundance and scarcity with which the earth alternately presented
you. The days for the planting of various crops, each according to the length of its
growing span, were calculated from the vernal equinox, while those until harvest
were counted from the summer solstice, making it a time of intense concentration,
and often of fasting, the ceremonial sequestering of priests or shamans, and
sacrifice. It is a procedure that Rabbit will echo with a curious precision in
mourning for his daughter. The narrative seems to stem from these events– equinox
and solstice– almost as much as it flows between them.

Now, just a few minutes after six a day before the vernal equinox, all the
houses and the gravel-roofed factories and the diagonal hillside streets are in the
shadow that washes deep into the valley of farmland east of the mountain. (*Rabbit,
Run*: 23)

> [Rabbit's] feeling that there is an unseen world is instinctive, and

> more of his actions than anyone suspects constitute transactions
> with it. He dresses in his new gray suit and steps out at a quarter
> of eleven into a broad blue Sunday morning a day before the
> summer solstice. (*Rabbit, Run*: 217)

The way in which each mention of the day and hour is fitted into the text hardly seems accidental: each is "a day before," although one deals in a preoccupied way with an enormous shadow, and the other with a "broad blue" morning light. The equinox is associated with a shadow that "washes deep into the valley of farm land," mimicking, at least to my ear, "Yea, though I walk through the valley of the shadow of death." In the second instance, the solstice is tied to a description of Rabbit's transactions with an unseen world. It seems to me somewhat oddly phrased, for who exactly is the "anyone" failing to suspect the belief behind Rabbit's actions? Does "anyone" mean the people near Rabbit, who are admittedly baffled by his behavior, or does it imply the reader of the novel, another, vaguer "anyone" existing on the periphery of Rabbit's world? Updike does have a way sometimes of turning unexpectedly from the fiction and poking his finger, whimsically or reprovingly, , at the reader– as he did in the aphorisms of *Couples*. "And I find," he has said, "I can not imagine being a writer without wanting somehow to play, to make these patterns, to insert these secrets into my books, to spin out this music that has its formal side." (*Picked-Up Pieces*: 481) It seems implied that *we*, at least, should suspect the basis for Rabbit's actions, his sense of a pact struck with an unseen world, or he appears far more intransigent and shallow that he really is, and would scarcely deserve a second glance.

Neither is it, I think, absurdly farfetched to see Rabbit in a priestly guise, yet another variation of the pilgrim-hero, this time with a rather more substantial aura of saintliness. Eccles, the minister, rebukes Rabbit by saying "saints shouldn't marry," and teases him that, "flexible time. That's what you want, isn't it? Flexibility? So you can be free to preach to the multitudes?" (*Rabbit, Run*: 121) "Oh all the *world* loves you," Ruth, the prostitute with whom he briefly lives, tells Rabbit. "What I wonder is why?" (*Rabbit, Run*: 135) The stress is exact, on *world*, confirming Rabbit's connection with the "unseen world," the encompassing cosmos whose signals are ignored by everyone but him. Why shouldn't the world love him? In a long list of the names of songs and sorts of commercials that Rabbit hears on his car's radio the first time he abandons his wife and really runs, it is mentioned that "the whereabouts of the Dalai Lama, spiritual leader of this remote and backward land, are unknown." (*Rabbit, Run*: 34) The paragraph concludes with a mocking lilt: "Where is the Dalai Lama?" (*Ibid.*) Clearly, it is Rabbit whose whereabouts are unknown; the "remote and backward land" of which he is the spiritual leader is that chaotic apartment he inhabits with his resentful wife, Janice, who is well into her second pregnancy. This identification between Rabbit and the missing Dalai Lama is subsequently strengthened:

> [Rabbit] feels freedom like oxygen everywhere around
> him;Tothero is an eddy of air, and the building he is in, the
> streets of the town, are mere stairways and alley-ways in
> space. So perfect, so consistent is the freedom into which the
> clutter of the world has been vaporized by the simple trigger

of his decision, that all ways seem equally good, all movements will put the same caressing pressure on his skin, and not an atom of his happiness would be altered if Tothero told him they were not going to meet two girls but two goats, and they were going not to Brewer but to Tibet. He adjusts his necktie with infinite attention, as if the little lines of this juncture of the Windsor knot, the collar of Tothero's shirt, and the base of his own throat were the arms of a star that will, when he is finished, extend outward to the rim of the universe. He is the Dalai Lama. (Rabbit, Run: 51-52)

Tothero (Tot/hero) was Rabbit's coach while he was a star basketball player, and serves as a sort of priestly mentor, whose shirt Rabbit literally wears. The paragraph is a little treatise on Tao, "that in virtue of which all things happen or exist," and under whose sway "all ways seem equally good," and the correct behavior is inspired by the moment, free of value judgements, unencumbered by social rigidities. For Rabbit, this perfect and unblinking recognition of Tao will be fairly frequent– in a sense, he is a man addicted to the seeking of *satori*, but ignorant of the codices and rituals that are meant to lend shape and dignity to such seeking. And, although frequent, these recogitions [*sic*] are fleeting. Rabbit customarily cares about the difference between girls and goats, and feels that both oxygen and freedom are rare commodities. But Brewer *is* his Tibet, his realm, circumscribed and impoverished; if he lacks the contemplativeness of a Dalai Lama, at least his presence seems, curiously often, to inspire love.

Rabbit will tend the world in more than the dainty adjustment of a necktie's knot. After his escape from Janice, while he is living with Ruth, he alters the way she lives, confines her for a time to housewifely things, cooking, the reading of paperback mysteries– in short, in almost Christ-like fashion, he renders a prostitute virtuous, and salvages from the disorder of her life something of affection and purpose. In the habit of Updike's heroes, he makes her, almost immediately, his wife.

She tries to twist away, but now he holds the arm he touched. She says, "Say, do you think we're married or something the way you boss me around?"
The transparent wave moves over him again and he calls to her in a voice that is almost inaudible, "Yes; let's be." So quickly her arms don't move from hanging at her sides, he kneels at her feet and kisses the place on her finger where a ring would have been. (*Rabbit, Run*: 75)

"I made you," he tells her. "I made you and the sun and the stars. . .I made you bloom." His passion cuts against her bareness. He insists, the first time they make love, that she be absolutely naked, naked as Eve, and– without her diaphragm– as defenseless. So Rabbit returns her to a woman's original functions, obedience and procreation, as chronicled in the admonitory tone of Genesis: "in pain you shall bring forth children, yet your desire shall be for your husband, and he shall rule over you." Her desire *is* for Rabbit. Makeshift husband that he is, and clumsily importunate Adam, he restores to her not only an aboriginal nakedness but also her own capcity [*sic*] for orgasm:

"I had forgotten," she says.

"Forgot what?"

"That I could have it too."

"What's it like?"

"Oh. It's like falling through."

"Where do you fall to?"

"Nowhere. I can't talk about it."*(Rabbit, Run: 83)*

Updike's Adams and Eves are often inarticulate with each other, but in this case the distance between them, the ability to talk, is profound.

While Rabbit is living with Ruth, the work that he finds is among other, literal blooms, for he goes to work in the garden of an old woman, Mrs. Smith, whose dead husband's consuming passion was for rhododendrons. The passages that deal with Rabbit's work in the garden carry a shy freight of happiness, and in their gorgeousness, they come to seem a kind of paen (sic) to richness, fecundity, and order.

Sun and moon, sun and moon, time goes. In Mrs. Smith's acres, crocuses break the crust. Daffodils and narcissi unpack their trumpets. The reviving grass harbors violets, and the lawn is suddenly coarse with dandelions and broad-leaved weeds. Invisible rivulets running brokenly make the low land of the estate sing. The flowerbeds, bordered with bricks buried diagonally, are pierced by dull red spikes that will be peonies, and the earth itself, scumbled, horny, raggedly patched with damp and dry, looks like the oldest and smells like the newest thing under Heaven. (*Rabbit, Run*: 127)

"Funny, for these two months he never has to cut his fingernails," the following paragraph begins. Rabbit is bringing these things forth by the sweat of his brow. When he plants the packets of seeds that the old woman gives him, he "loves folding the hoed ridge of soil over the seeds. Sealed, they cease to be his. The simplicity. Getting rid of something by giving it to itself." It is an equation even more ancient than Genesis, this metaphor in which the planting of seeds is linked to the insemination of a woman. Rabbit seems, for once, truly stable, dutiful, and at ease– all within the boundaries of the garden.

I would like to double back for a time to the peculiarities of the opening pages of the novel, because they contain further clues to Rabbit's character and fate; not only the language, but the dramatic stop-and-go movement of the narration, constructs a pattern for what will follow. These pages can be examined in grave detail, because they are very nearly as tightly coded and neatly interlocking as the sequences of rhyme in a sonnet. The dialogue bristles with omens. The very first word that Rabbit, hero of a trilogy that has spanned three decades so far, ever says is "Hey!" a shout of exaltation following a successful free throw (he has intruded into a boy's game in an alley, after the basketball thumps to his feet). *Rabbit, Run* opens with this hosannah, a cry of prideful greeting, and slips away from it, never to return to exactly this pitch of unthinking grace where luck and skill intersect.

None of this is casual, although Updike's use of the present tense (he has called it a "a mild adventure") renders the prose random-looking and quick. Free throws are granted to players who have been fouled, and Rabbit's life has been fouled, not in any technical sense, but in the meaning of having been obscurely dirtied at its source, diminished in purity. How this happens is not exactly clear, even to Rabbit; he only knows that it *has* happened, that his course has been a falling-off from a brief and original grace. He was once a basketball player, locally famous, so agile he could score twenty-three points in the first game he played. With his second word, the mater-of-factly inflected "Skill," Rabbit attempts to regain his old footing of nobility, for he was that most wonderful of heroes, a "natural," a "young deer," as Tothero calls him, who needed only the most rudimentary instruction to reach excellence. This initial metaphor, locked in place with the first exchange of dialogue between Rabbit and the boys, is one that will haunt Rabbit throughout his life. So neatly, so inevitably, did he once embody the metaphor– athletic prowess manifesting grace of spirit– that he rarely troubles to move beyond it. He believes that the graceful is the good; he only wishes to be good again.

Just after "Skill," Rabbit says, "Ok if I play?" The reader understands that this question– unpunctuated, off-handed plea that it is– will lie just below the surfaces of Rabbit's life, consuming his attention, for play is sexual as well as athletic, and the ingratiating "Ok" is Rabbit's ticket, a sort of open-sesame he will apply to women, to the world, as well as to young boys playing basketball in a Brewer alley.

It is odd, too, that in a series of novels whose hero will be so adamantly alert to sexual possibility– constantly speculating about other men's wives, rich women, poor women, women on the street, finally even, in *Rabbit Is Rich*, his own daughter-in-law– that the very first sexual imagery in *Rabbit, Run* is homosexual, occurring in the book's second paragraph: "The cigarette makes it more sinister still. Is this one going to offer them cigarettes or money to go out in back of the ice plant with him? They've heard of such things but are not too frightened; there are six of them and one of him." (*Rabbit, Run:* 9) Throughout the novel the ice plant will be an ominous symbol, a kind of fixed locale for iciness and evil:

> At the next corner, where the water from the ice plant used
> to come down, sob into a drain, and reappear on the other
> side of the street, Rabbit crosses over and walks beside the
> gutter where the water used to run, coating the shallow side
> of its course with ribbons of green slime waving and waiting
> to slip under your feet and dunk you if you dared walk on
> them. He can remember falling in but not why he was
> walking along this slippery edge in the first place. (*Rabbit,
> Run*: 20)

Rabbit is trapped at the level of a fairy tale, bogged down by an immense weight of detail, memories of "falling in." One of the things he has fallen into is marriage. He and Janice were caught in the classic way, by pregnancy, but their knowledge of why they were "walking along this slippery edge in the first place" is negligible. The first thing that she ever says, in the novel, is "It just locked itself." She is speaking of the door to their apartment, but the comment is so numbingly appropriate to Janice, the intensity with which she creates and then shuts herself into chaos, that Rabbit bewilderedly repeats: "Just locked itself." Within moments they are arguing:

"You're supposed to look tired. You're a modern housewife." "And meanwhile you're off in the alley playing like a twelve-year-old?"

It gripes him that she didn't see his crack about being a housewife, based on the "image" the MagiPeel people tried to have their salesmen sell to, as ironical and at bottom pitying and fond. There seems no escaping it; she is dumb. He says, "Well what's the difference if you're sitting here watching a program for kids under two?"

"Who was *shushing* a while ago?"

"Ah, Janice." He sighs. "Screw you. Just screw you." (*Rabbit, Run:* 17)

In this exchange they exhaust each other's limited resources— for gentleness, rue, companionability— with the abbreviated hostility of two people who consider each other so predictable that even a fight will yield nothing new. In fact, they know each other in ways that are almost unendurable. Rabbit is right to feel, as he does, somewhat frightened of Janice; in her haphazard depression she is a frightening woman. She is right to resent his vagrancy, for it threatens the little that they have. She detects his momentary freedom, and it throws her confinement into sharper relief. From her position, even aimlessness seems a gift. Saints shouldn't marry; if they do, their wives are in trouble.

Janice calls from the kitchen. "And honey pick up a pack of cigarettes, could you?" In a normal voice that says everything is forgiven, everything is the same.

Rabbit freezes, standing looking at his faint yellow shadow on the white door that leads into the hall, and senses he is in a trap. It seems certain. He goes out. (*Rabbit, Run*: 19-20)

This matching of "everything is forgiven" with "everything is the same" is the basis of Rabbit's terror, for in a world so shadowed with Christian nuance forgiveness ought to alter, to divest and purge the sameness from things; it ought to be a kind of lever by which things are forced to a newer, finer plane. Instead, this contradiction, hinged by something as slim as a comma, cause Rabbit to confront his shadow for the first time in the book. He knows that such sameness is a kind of dying, and that her forgiveness is simply a means by which he is nudged closer to his own death. Like the hero of the short story "Leaves" who basks in an epiphany in the form of light falling flat across the floor, "like a penitent," Rabbit is forced into awareness by the sight of this "faint yellow shadow." Shadows and light are often a mode of recognition in Updike's work. This instance is almost painterly in it its exactitude, because Rabbit sees not only a faint shadow, but a faint yellow shadow on a white door, and yellow— at least in the jargon of gradeschool playgrounds, a language not at all alien to Updike's imagination, nor, one assumes, to Rabbit's— is the color of cowardice, retreat from battle, and flight.

Even so, Rabbit's response fails immediately to crystallize. He thinks only that "it seems certain." In nearly everything, Rabbit shies from any too-definite architecture of response; that would be simply one more way of locking himself in.

It is almost difficult to imagine any circumstances in which Rabbit could be found thinking to himself, "It is absolutely certain." He is responsive, above all, to apprehension, the emotion you have when things *seem* dangerous or unpredictable. The physical environment of Brewer fosters this state of mind, for it is queerly numinous, in its kitchens, windows, alleys, and eaves, factories and flights of stairs, ice plants and cathedrals. How deftly Updike constructs a sacred wood:

> Outdoors it is growing dark and cool. The Norway maples exhale the smell of their sticky new buds and the broad living-room windows along Wilbur Street show beyond the silver patch of a television set the warm bulbs burning in kitchens, like fires at the backs of caves. He walks downhill. The day is gathering itself in. He now and then touches with his hand the rough bark of a tree or the dry twigs of a hedge, to give himself the small answer of a texture. At the corner, where Wilbur Street meets Potter Avenue, a mailbox stands leaning in twilight on its concrete post. Tall two-petalled street sign, the cleat-gouged trunk of the telephone pole holding its insulators against the sky, fire hydrant like a golden bush: a grove. (*Rabbit, Run*: 20)

Like any hero just setting out on his journey, Rabbit must feel partly enthralled and partly fearful, because this world is so visibly enchanted. The world in *Rabbit, Run* must be numinous to reflect Rabbit's conflicting emotions and tangled potential– maples must "breathe," telephone wires "sing," the insulators be "giant blue eggs in a windy nest," in order to show Rabbit himself as a pilgrim-saint, a hero in disguise. While the physical environment of Brewer often seems too crushingly narrow for adults, Rabbit remains queerly child-like, at least if vulnerability and inventiveness are child-like qualitites (sic). In a crucial sense, he is still willing to play, to seem to be what he is not, to daydream a new life for himself and then move in to fill its perimeters. He is credulous. At the deepest level of interpretation, Rabbit is the best believer of any of Updike's various heroes, and the kingdom– perhaps eventually that of Heaven, but for now the wide and changeable kingdom of the earth– is his.

*Elizabeth Tallent. *Married Men and Magic Tricks: John Updike's Erotic Heroes*. Berkeley: Creative Arts, 1982.

"Mapless Motion"

Derek Wright*

Twenty years ago the English critic Tony Tanner maintained, as the central thesis of his book *City of Words* (1971), that the fictional imagination of postwar America was as much troubled by the postmodernist novel's dissolution of form as by the constrictive, overdefinitive forms of conventional realism. Tanner linked the erosion of formal distinctions with fears of an entropic universe in which energy was always running down: the abiding anxiety of 1960s writers who discussed entropy (Pynchon, Burroughs) was its homogenizing effect on the universe where all things dwindled to nothing, all things became alike. The waste-making process resulted in a confusion and merging of identities and an eventual dissolving of all things into a blank, formless waste, a perfect homogeneity of nothingness.

John Updike was never of this experimental school of writers but, as Tanner observed, the characters of his early novels discussed these same processes, and the landscapes they inhabited were afflicted by the same cosmic entropy or universal wasting. Conner, in *The Poorhouse Fair* (1959), theorizes about "entropia," and George Caldwell, in *The Centaur* (1963), sees Nature as "garbage and confusion." Harry Angstrom, a tidy man who dislikes waste in his domestic affairs if not in his sexual ones, moves in *Rabbit, Run* (1960) across a terrain of junk heaps, treeless wastes, and derelict houses which become part of a single integrated and indistinct mass (or mess). Even childbirth is seen by Rabbit as an entropic reduction of the universe to the one monochromatic filth: "Janice's babyish black nostrils [widen] to take in the antiseptic smell he smells, the smell running everywhere along the whitewashed walls, of being washed, washed, blood washed, retching washed until every surface smells like the inside of a bucket but it will never become clean because we will always fill it up again with our filth" (159). According to Tanner, doubleness was in Updike's early novels the ultimate defense against entropy and its wasting homogenization of the world (290), and love was crucial in this defense because love involves two in everything: "She was double everywhere but in her mouths. All things double. Without duality, entropy. The universe God's mirror," reflects Piet on Georgene in *Couples* (1968), a novel depicting a complex "universe of twos" (63). Coupledom has continued to be the dynamo of Updike's fictional universe– the chopping and changing of his twosomes in their tireless pursuit of novelty and their adoption of new mirror positions is what keeps their world in motion– and the theoretic importance of love is that it resists the assimilation, the entropic merging, of one identity into another. The idea had some literary currency in the Sixties on both sides of the Atlantic– "What will survive of us is love," Philip Larkin concluded the last poem of *The Whitsun Weddings* (46)– but in the form in which it has come down to contemporary writing it is fraught with fears that ve is itself but another feature of the world's entropy, its every particle inscribed with the process of decay. Here, for example, is Julian Barnes in the "Parenthesis" to his recent *A History of the World in Ten-and-a-Half Chapters* (1989):

> It will go wrong, this love; it probably will. . . .Our current
> model for the universe is entropy, which at the daily level
> translates as: things fuck up. But when love fails us, we
> must still go on believing in it. Is it encoded in every
> molecule that things fuck up, that love will fail? Perhaps it
> is. Still we must believe in love, just as we must believe in
> free will and objective truth. And when love fails, we
> should blame the history of the world. (246)

Moreover, within the context of Updike's fiction, the whole theory of love as an oppositional, antientropic force has always begged the question of whether his female characters are ever allowed sufficiently well- defined and distinct identities to resist being merged into and annihilated by the wills of their dominant males (feminist critics such as Mary Allen have expressed reservations about the bland

and bovine kind of femininity which Updike's women represent). The young Harry Angstrom of the first *Rabbit* novel, for example, thinks his wife Janice so characterless that he actually dreams of her facial features melting away. Caught as he is between entrapment in the world's forms and nightmares of formlessness and fading identities, threatened equally by too much form and too little, Rabbit would seem to be an ideal candidate for the dilemma postulated in Tanner's book. It is arguable, however, that the extremity of his flight from the traps of an over-differentiated world effectively makes him a principal agent in that process of merging and assimilation which annihilates all differences; that Rabbit's "love," because it is not defined by but dissolves form, is itself an entropic force. I propose in this short article to look at some of the novel's permutations, its combinations and oppositions, of form and the flight from it, or of form and space, because it is into space that Rabbit– both in this and the other novels of the trilogy– runs in pursuit of his freedom.

Updike devised for his urban and domestic landscapes in this book an extraordinary rhetoric of constriction to register his protagonist's constant negotiation of clutter in an oppressively commodity-packed world, itemizing objects *ad nauseam* until we feel their accumulated weight pressing upon the nerves and senses of the narrative consciousness:

> Nelson's broken toys on the floor derange his head; all the
> things inside his skull, the grey matter, the bones of his ears.
> . . .seem clutter clogging the tube of his self. . . .The living
> room has the feel of dust. . . .In the kitchen. . .the pork chops
> never taken from the pan, cold as death, congealed grease.
> . . the bag smells of something sweetly rotting . . .the breath
> of steam is like a whisper in a tomb. (80-81)

Rabbit's wife and son, whose "little neck gleams like one more clean object in the kitchen among the cups and plates and chromium knobs" (19), are seen merely as part of this deathly domestic debris of which he must disburden himself. He feels the claustrophobic clutter of his home life closing in upon him "like a tightening net" (14), and, when he tries, in the first part of the novel, to drive out of its suburban equivalent, the outcome of his journey is instructive for the way in which reality is perceived in the book. Hopelessly lost, he stops the car, pulls out his map, and studies its myriad red and blue lines:

> his eyes blankly founder. . . .At once 'Frederick' pops into
> sight, but in trying to steady its position he loses it, and fury
> makes the bridge of his nose ache. The names melt away
> and he sees the map whole, a net, all those red lines and blue
> lines and stars, a net he is somewhere caught in. He claws
> at it and tears it; with a gasp of exasperation he rips away a
> great triangular piece and tears the large remnant in half and,
> more calmly, lays these three pieces on top of each other and
> tears them in half, and then those six pieces and so on until
> he has a wad he can squeeze in his hand like a ball. He rolls
> down the window and throws the ball out. . . . (31-32)

Rabbit's revulsion is against the over-mapped, over-defined world where everything has ben charted and contoured. The paradox is that when there is nowhere you cannot go, there is nowhere left to go: there are no new places, no unmapped territory to light out to. Free movement has been murdered by maps, and there is nowhere for the exbasketballer's (sic) car to move except into preestablished nets, which it has to be forced and squeezed through. Rabbit takes his revenge by screwing the net itself– the map of the road network– into a ball and throwing it out. Unable to get the ball of his car through the available nets, he turns the net into a ball. At a single stroke all imprisoning geometric boundaries have been dissolved.

Rabbit's bid for freedom from the imprisoning nets of the world's forms leads him, however, to the opposite extreme of undifferentiated space. What he seeks is the mapless movement of the player in the pure, uncluttered space of the basketball court; the elegant "motions of grace (sic)" away from the pressures of "external circumstances" in the Pascalian epigraph. In the words of a modern poet, Thom Gunn, "One is always nearer by not keeping still" (12), by a perpetual improvization of movement which never reaches an end. Hence Rabbit's rejection of the garage attendant's advice that "the only way to get somewhere is to figure out where you're going before you go there" (25). This kind of freedom, and its dangers, are defined when Harry wakes up in Tothero's apartment to find that he is about to be taken on a sexual joyride:

> He feels freedom like oxygen everywhere around him; Tothero is an eddy of air, and the building he is in, the streets of the town, are mere stairways and alleyways in space. So perfect, so consistent is the freedom into which the clutter of the world has been vaporized by the simple trigger of his decision, that all ways seem equally good, all movements will put the same caressing pressure on his skin, and not an atom of his happiness would be altered if Tothero told him they were not going to meet two girls but two goats, and they were going not to Brewer but to Tibet. . . .In the vast blank of his freedom Rabbit has remembered a few imperfections, his home's, his wife's, their apartment, clots of concern. It seems impossible that the passage of time should have so soon dissolved them. (42-43)

The key words here are "air," "oxygen," and "space." Rabbit's freedom is conceived as a "vast blank" that vaporizes and renders insubstantial the clutter of the world. But it does so by cancelling out the differences between things, by rubbing out differentials, so that all roads to pleasure seem equally good and, in Rabbit's undifferentiating rabbity sexuality, goats will do as well as girls. Much later in the novel, after being aroused in church by Eccles' wife, Rabbit comes home "carrying something precious for Janice and keeps being screened from giving it to her" (196). It matters very little to his free-floating lust, as it matters little to his animal-namesake's promiscuous, voracious appetite, that the sexual impulse was awakened by another woman. Harry "loves" all women: Janice, Ruth, Lucy Eccles, the waitress in the restaurant, the nurse in the hospital. He tells Ruth, "I am a lover," in the broad abstract sense, and when she mentions her "trade," she seems to be, "in terms of love, so vast" (62), the prostitute's undiscriminating "love" matching his own undifferentiating desire. This unevaluating, nihilistic freedom exults in not having to select, whether sexually, in the case of women, or gastronomically, as in the case of Chinese food, where the constituents are almost indistinguishable, the meat "minced and painlessly merged with the shapes of insensate vegetables, plump green bodies that invite his appetite's innocent gusto" (52). "Innocent" in the sense of undiscriminating and unchoosing, Harry's appetite effects that entropic merging of differences, that rubbing out of identities, which Updike's promotion of coupledom and doubleness were, according to Tanner's theory, meant to resist.

Harry has "the gift of life," old Mrs (sic) Smith tells him, but it is an undirected gift, an unfocused, undefined cluster of reflexes and impulses, or, as his sister Mim tells him in *Rabbit Redux* (1971): "Everybody else has a life they try to fence in with some rules. You just do what you feel like" (317). If he does not have to figure out where he is going it is because he is not really going anywhere. His freedom, as numerous commentators have noted, is flight rather than quest ("all vagrants think they're on a quest at first," says Eccles), and it is unlocatable except in the basketballer's region, the more breathable air of "upward space" (it is significant that the only time that Harry feels close to his wife is when she is floating in the ether after the birth of their daughter, when she is inhabiting the same airy element). After passing the ball on the court, however, Harry remembers that "in effect there was nobody there," and for the shooter at the basket the upward passage of the ball is followed by the dangerous downward plunge into the nothing of space: "He imagines himself about to shoot a long one-hander; but he feels he's on a cliff, there is an abyss he will fall into when the ball leaves his hands" (21-22). During the course of the *Rabbit* tetralogy the experimental quest for authentic sexual experience takes Harry further and further out into this abyss of space. With Ruth in the first novel he senses that he is "out of all dimension" in a "blank sky," liberated from his wife's dull limits into the blank, limitless love of the prostitute, and feels only the latter's "blue-eyed nothing, the nothing she told him she did, the nothing she believes in" (67, 80). In the next two novels the imagery of upward passage modulates from open to outer and, finally, into empty space. In *Rabbit Redux* the 1969 Moonshot is used to chart the orbit of Janice's new free-floating sexuality and to orchestrate a variety of spatial and sexual dockings– Jill and Skeeter, spied by Rabbit in the act of fellatio, look like "an interlocked machine"– and, in *Rabbit is* (sic) *Rich* (1982), Harry's progression to anal sex with the wife of a friend takes him into an ultimate dim ensionlessness: "there is no sensation: a void, a pure black box, a casket of perfect nothingness. He is in that void, past her tight ring of muscle. . . . Where will his come go?" (384).

What is especially problematic about this space-seeking urge to freedom, which reduces travel routes, food, and women to entropized blanks, is that there is a general failure to differentiate between distinct orders of experience, and this leads in the first novel to a confused cluttering of one order with the characteristics of another. Rabbit's early aspirations span a broad spectrum of experience, with sport at one end of the scale and religion and spirituality at the other, and with sex, pivotally, somewhere in the middle. The problem is that the precise nature or identity of the quest keeps inching along the see-saw, shifting its position from a sporting to a sexual, and then to a vaguely spiritual one, refusing to take up permanent residence in any of them. Initially, religion and sex become much entangled (to the extent that Kruppenbach, the thunderous, evangelical Lutheran Minister, is needed to separate the profane and the sacred, nature and supernature). Rabbit goes to Eccles' church not to worship but to be turned on by the Minister's wife and Eccles, although he likes to think of Harry as a kind of "mystic" or "saint" because he "gives people faith," notes how often his "little ecstasies wear a skirt" (105, 117). Rabbit makes a point of worshipfully adoring the bodies of his women and ceremonially undressing them, and "the idea of making it while the churches are full excites him" (75).One of the impressions left by the novel is that the surviving modes of Christianity have become neurotic and repressed, with the result that religious feeling has become displaced and the split religion siphoned off into sexual activity, which has become a substitute for worship. Then, sport and sex contrive to get tied up as explicitly as sex and religion do. Rabbit achieves an almost sexual thrill from a perfect basket, as the ball passes through "the high perfect hole with its pretty skirt of net, the fringed ring that came right down (sic) to your lips"; and the "strings looping the loop set him thinking of "young Du Pont women– (sic) strings of them winding through huge glossy (sic) parties, potentially naked in their sequined sheath gowns," the sheath of the gown becoming a net which the ball passes nakedly through (32-33). From his early sexual conquest of Mary Ann in the gym after a basketball victory, "the two kinds of triumph" have been "united in his mind" (161), and Ruth describes the woman's sexual climax to him as a "falling through," like the netted ball falling into space. "Wonderful women, the way they can join in," Rabbit reflects, conceiving sex as a team game and the woman's pleasure as the spectator's vicarious enjoyment of what is essentially another's experience (71). Later a fellow-basketballer taunts him, in Ruth's presence, with the opinion that "Harry is not a team player" (143). The corollary of this analogic treatment of sex and religion, on the one hand, and of sex and sport, on the other, is that sport and religion also get attached to one another. Tothero speaks of sport as religion, stressing the feeling of the "sacredness of achievement" that has to be inculcated in the six-team (sic) to prepare them "for the greater game of life," while Eccles considers religion in terms of sport, and life as one huge game of golf with God as umpire. One testifies to the deep spirituality of sport, the other to the sporting nature of the Holy Spirit. Harry gives Eccles the feeling that "they are together engaged in an impossible quest set by a benevolent but absurd lord, a quest whose humiliations sting them almost to tears but one that is renewed at each tee" (136), and Harry seeks, through the free, lithe movements of the basketball court, the "motions of Grace."

All three entities– sex, sport and religion– come triumphantly together at the climax of the first game of golf. At the start of the game we find Rabbit vengefully thinking of his golf clubs as his women, confusing his sexual and sporting ineptitudes and blaming his own inadequacy on female stupidity. He then tells Eccles that he has left his wife because "there was this thing that wasn't there," and after some heated exchanges as regards what and if "this thing" is, Rabbit finally tees off and, just as his ball hangs and then vanishes in space, he turns to Eccles and cries "That's *it* (sic) !" This "it" or "thing" that Harry is convinced wants him to find it is, in his understanding, at once sexual, sporting and spiritual.   He automatically assumes that what he is seeking and what is missing from his marital relations has a religious or spiritual dimension and is therefore the province of the priest.   "Well if you're not sure it exists don't ask me," he tells Eccles.   "It's right up your alley.   If you don't know nobody does."   It seems, however, not to be the province of this priest, whose own flirtatious wife is starved for his attentions and who is really, beneath his apparent mockery, deeply curious about the mysterious elixir that keeps Rabbit going.   It "hits Rabbit depressingly that. . .he really wants to be told about it, wants to be told that it is there, that he's not lying to all those people every Sunday" (108).   Then the "it" finally becomes the perfect golf drive, although with the usual metaphysical trappings of air and space.   The ball on the tee is already "free of the ground" like the jumping basketballer; it is then "hung way out" in the air, a "sphere, a (sic) star, a (sic) speck"; and, as the finite opens out into the infinite, it takes "a last bite of space" before Harry utters his exultant cry.

How far Updike succeeded– or intended to succeed– in weaving the spiritual into the secular and the unseen into the seen world, to what extent these analogous orders were continuous with or alternatives to one another, are ultimately imponderables in this early novel, and there is no clear evidence that sexual dissatisfaction is not merely a mask and a perverse pretext for religious questing. Updike has since become famous for the shimmering transcendentalism of his prose, tipped always with a sense of metaphysical dread and punctuated by religious metaphors that seem to hover midway between authorial and narrative consciousness.   It would, of course, be foolish to look in a novel published in 1960 for anything as elaborate or precise as a metaphysical correspondence.   But the vagueness of the analogies between the very different kinds of "upward space" in the novel and the insinuation of a number of qualifying differentials via other characters encourage the view that the conflation of confusion of values is finally the protagonist's rather than the author's doing.   Traditional distinctions and evaluations are constantly restated in defiance of Harry's effortless annihilation of them. Eccles observes pointedly that the physical and spiritual are in fact kept quite distinct in Harry's own devotions; this his Christianity is merely a mystical sense of the numinous and he "has no taste for the dark, tangled, visceral aspects of Christianity, the *going through* quality of it, the passage *into* death and suffering that redeems and inverts these things" (192).   Harry's visceral feelings are reserved exclusively for his sex life.   The episode on top of Mount Judge with Ruth turns out, accordingly, to be a merely pseudoreligious experience in which the sacred is dissolved into an openly oppositional profanity.   The two pilgrims climb barefoot to the summit, and as Harry forces "open the lips of his soul" to receive "truth" at the end of a day "bothered by god (sic)," he has a vision of "cancer-blackened souls (sic)" rising above the rooftops.   But the religious epiphany is abruptly shattered by his question about Ruth's life as a prostitute: "Were you really a whore?" (92-93). Whatever the seriousness of the book's elements of religious parable– the Grail quest, the Mount of Judgment brooding over the cities of the plain, the surname *Angst*rom– its hero remains an ironic and profane pilgrim, not in search but in flight (from boredom), and he runs not in a straight upward passage, but in circles: back to his mother and to his high-school coach, in search of adolescent glory; and, at the end of the book, to and fro between the two women whom he has deserted. His concept of space is nihilistic or unprogressive when realized in material terms: on his car trip he motors sixty miles to travel fourteen. This rabbit runs round in rings.

If form prevails over space and defines limits over freedom in the novel, it is partly because its receiving consciousness is itself an effectively empty space into which the world's forms aggressively ensconce themselves. Rabbit's is basically a nonthinking consciousness– "Into the silence that results he refuses to let thoughts come" (29) – and registers only the superfices of things. It is a mechanical annotator of Brewer and its environs, compulsively recording street names and numbers, prices, and brands of cars and household appliances. Harry's brain is a passive receiver of clutter: "the music keeps coming and the signs keep pointing" until "his brain feels like a frail but alert invalid" (33). Seldom a thinking subject, he becomes at the end of the book a subjectless verb, an agentless action ("Runs"), a runner who disappears into his running. And because his consciousness registers only externals, his vague concept of an invisible force– "something that wants me to find it"– is perfunctorily and ironically indexed to the mundane, concrete visible world which is all that he can perceive. Thus the Sunday churchgoers "seem a visual proof of the unseen world," and their suits and hats are "blooms of faith" that "give substance and respectability to his furtive sensations of the invisible" (74, 190). Dressed to order, spirituality is socialized; the metaphysical made material; faith expressed as fashion. Harry materializes religion as he etherealizes and sacralizes material pursuits such as sport and sex, and the result is that religion becomes simply an index to the materiality of the one world– this world– instead of an otherworldly alternative to it. The "invisible" in any less tangible form is dangerous and threatening, as Rabbit notes ruefully in *Rabbit is* (sic) *Rich*: "He doesn't want to think about the invisible anyway, every time in his life he's made a move toward it somebody has gotten killed" (151). If the novel's religious dimension remains tenuous it is, of course, in part the fault of Updike's style, which pays massive attention to material detail. This style, which habitually gives the descriptive and decorative priority over the interpretative and interrogative, seems at times to live in awe of surfaces and to proliferate the objects of suburban life with an almost hallucinatory fervour. The material world is, simply, too much with us in this book, its inescapable clutter too well done, walling the reader in with detail. The visible is so substantially created that it blots out the invisible, and Harry clings to this material reality, reaching out to touch solid things "to give himself the small answer of a texture" (14).

Tanner suggested in his 1971 essay that Updike succeeded in his early novels in creating not another religious world but only another *narrative* world, an order of mythology and folklore not native to his suburban environment, as substitute and compensation for the transcendental dimension that he really wanted. This element of fiction-making, or fabulation, has persisted in his work over the last twenty years, defining aspiration but without broadening the range of freedoms or extra-empirical access available to his characters, and the numinous edge of Rabbit's character is, in fact, eroded in the more politically and socially-oriented later volumes of the trilogy. From the Grail Quest and Peter Rabbit story of *Rabbit, Run*, the Chiron myth in *The Centaur*, and the various classical sexual gnomes and nymphs in

Couples (1968), Updike moved on to the expansive but no less ironic and sterile mythologies of space travel in *Rabbit Redux*, of a culturally pure Islamic Africa in *The Coup* (1978), and of the Devil in *The Witches of Eastwick* (1984). Although not noticeably reflexive in tendency, these mythological subtexts, like the cross-referencing of sex, sport and spirituality in *Rabbit, Run*, have the air of being too deliberately done and with a self-conscious artfulness which suggests that they finally exist nowhere outside of the protagonal psychology and the fiction in which it is framed. The implication appears to be that only novelistic form is able to accommodate the kind of space and spacious freedom– the uninhibited, uncluttered movement and entropic flight from form– which Rabbit Angstrom yearns for. This mapless motion exists only in purely imaginative, verbal space. Updike's protagonist longs, perhaps, for the kind of freedom– really the artistic freedom of his creator's imagination– which is not available in the kind of novel that Updike writes.

Works Cited

Allen, Mary. *The Necessary Blankness: Women in Major American Fiction of the Sixties.* Urbana: U of Illinois P, 1976.

Barnes, Julian. *A History of the World in Ten-and-a-Half Chapters.* 1989. London: Picador, 1990.

Gunn, Thom. *The Sense of Movement.* London: Faber, 1957.

Larkin, Philip. *The Whitsun Weddings.* London: Faber, 1964.

Tanner, Tony. *City of Words: American Fiction 1950-1970.* London: Cape, 1971.

Updike, John. *Couples.* 1968. Harmondsworth: Penguin, 1969.

_____. *Rabbit is* (sic) *Rich.* Harmondsworth: Penguin, 1982.

_____. *Rabbit Redux.* 1971. Harmondsworth: Penguin, 1973.

_____. *Rabbit, Run.* 1960. Harmondsworth: Penguin, 1964.

*Derek Wright, "Mapless Motion: Form and Space in Updike's *Rabbit, Run.*" *Modern Fiction Studies* 37 (Spring 1991): 35-44.

"'Unadorned Woman, Beauty's Home Image': Updike's *Rabbit, Run*"

Stacey Olster*

> Let me, testing the thin ice, begin as far back in time as my memory can reach, with my maternal grandmother. . . .I still remember the strain on her sharp-nosed face as she stared upward at me while I crouched on a lower branch of a tree. That was one of the things women did, I early concluded: they tried to get you to come down out of a tree. She was afraid I would fall, and that possibility had occurred to me also, so I was half grateful to be called down. But the other half, it seemed, needed to climb higher and higher, in defiance of the danger.

–John Updike, "Women," *Odd Jobs: Essays and Criticism*

"American fiction is notoriously thin on women," John Updike once remarked when asked about how much he sees himself as belonging to an American literary tradition. Asserting "I *have* attempted a number of portraits of women," and contrasting his own inclusions with the notable omissions of nineteenth-century male novelists, he ended by speculating, "we may have reached that point of civilization, or decadence, where we *can* look at women. I'm not sure Mark Twain *was* able to."[1] There is looking, of course– and then there is looking. Harry Angstrom has no difficulty looking at women in *Rabbit, Run*– his gazing at wives and waifs, strangers and sisters, mothers and matrons makes him a consummate voyeur. So able is he to look at women that he even starts looking for them in inanimate objects. "In his head he is talking to the clubs as if they're women," Updike writes, describing Harry on the golf course. "The irons, light and thin yet somehow treacherous in his hands, are Janice. . . .with the woods the 'she' is Ruth," and when "she" betrays him with a shot that goes off into the grass, "the bush is damn somebody, his mother."[2]

A Freudian field day, to be sure, portraying the female as meant to shelter ("Home is the hole" [132]) and the male as meant to reign supreme (the [golf] ball is a "hard irreducible pellet that is not really himself yet in a way is; just the way it sits there in the center of everything" [132]), the passage vindicates the kind of sports therapy that Reverend Eccles undertakes with Harry, based on his diagnosis that "the thing that makes Harry unsteady, that makes him unable to repeat his beautiful effortless swing every time, is the thing at the root of all the problems that he has created" (168). The passage also suggests the root of many of the problems Updike has created for himself with women, particularly with feminist critics who find more to object to in his work than the objectification of women as everything from sports equipment to foliage. Updike conceives of golf as the game "wherein the wall between us and the supernatural is rubbed thinnest." The mystical "it"that a well placed ball can bring (134), what Updike later will specify as "the hope of perfection, of a perfect weightlessness and consummate ease, . . .grace you could call it," is seen as conferring on men the right to transcendent flight, and to condemn women, for all their succoring, to a life of constantly being flown over, a view displayed in all Updike's subsequent fiction.[3]

For most of the critics who cavil against Updike's treatment of women, it is

---

[1]Charles Thomas Samuels, "The Art of Fiction XLIII: John Updike," *Paris Review* 45 (1968): 100.

[2]John Updike, *Rabbit, Run* (1960; rev. and rpt. New York: Alfred A. Knopf, 1970), pp. 131-2. Unless otherwise noted, subsequent page references will be to the 1970 printing and will appear parenthetically after quotations.

[3]John Updike, *Picked-Up Pieces* (New York: Alfred A. Knopf, 1975), p. 98; John Updike, *Rabbit at Rest* (New York: Alfred A. Knopf, 1990), p. 56.

not simply that he portrays his women characters as physically flawed (Mary Gordon's contention), as intellectually limited (Mary Allen's hobbyhorse), as closest to mutts and monkeys.[4] Nor is it only that they are seen as imprisoning men within "a sophisticated Oedipal knot," as Josephine Hendin proposes, so that "getting into a woman means getting back to their mothers' kitchens where there is guilt and frustration for them and hate for any woman who threatens to melt the iced anger that binds them to their mothers."[5] Because Updike subscribes to the notion that "[p]lain realism has never seemed to me enough,"[6] the social and psychological attributes granted to women in his works have spiritual and archetypal reverberations. And it is in fitting women into the dualist metaphysical scenarios that form the plots of his novels, whether as Earth Mothers or Venuses, mainly as of "a different race" (93), that Updike draws the greatest ire, for in doing so he is presumed to imply, as his most intentionally mythological work states, "[t]heir value is not present to themselves, but is given to them by men."[7]

Critics more sympathetic to Updike's designs have tried to exert a degree of damage control in locating a shift in his subsequent novels toward a reconciliation of opposites. Thus, having cited Updike's democratic projection of Venus onto nearly every female character and having centered "*the* nuclear fable" of his life around "the Mother who waits out in Nature," or "Venus in her older, wiser, and more terrifying form," Joyce Carol Oates sees the marriage that ends *Couples* as a breakthrough for Updike, breaking down the divisions between real and ideal love that have characterized Piet Hanema's relations with the opposite sex up to that point. Tracing this confusion of characteristics to a later novel, *The Witches of Eastwick*, Kathleen Verduin sees Updike's endowing women with attributes that

---

[4]See Mary Gordon, "Good Boys and Dead Girls," *Good Boys and Dead Girls and Other Essays* (1991; New York: Penguin, 1992), pp. 18-20; Mary Allen, "John Updike's Love of 'Dull Bovine Beauty,'" *The Necessary Blankness: Women in Major American Fiction of the Sixties* (Urbana: University of Illinois Press, 1976), pp. 97-132.

[5]Josephine Hendin, *Vulnerable People: A View of American Fiction Since 1945* (New York: Oxford University Press, 1978), pp. 90-91. For additional discussion of oedipal themes in Updike's work, see Gerry Brenner, "*Rabbit, Run*: John Updike's Criticism of the 'Return to Nature,'" *Twentieth Century Literature* 12 (1966): 5; Jack De Bellis, "Oedipal Angstrom," *Wascana Review* 24.1 (1989): 45-54; Robert Detweiler, *John Updike* (Boston: Twayne, 1984), pp. 40–2; and Joyce B. Markle, *Fighters and Lovers: Theme in the Novels of John Updike* (New York: New York University Press, 1973), pp. 93-101.

[6]John Updike, *Odd Jobs: Essays and Criticism* (New York: Alfred A. Knopf, 1991), p. 869.

[7]John Updike, *The Centaur* (1963; New York: Fawcett Crest, 1964), p. 177. For perhaps the most explicit statement alleging Updike's presumption, see Margaret Atwood, "Wondering What It's Like to Be a Woman," review of *The Witches of Eastwick*, by John Updike, *New York Times Book Review*, May 13, 1984: 40.

usually define his men– notably, fear of death– as evidence of his "struggling to come to terms with his own tendency toward dualism" in a novel that displays "an honest effort to revaluate a similar dualism, the polarization of the sexes."[8] I would add Updike's more recent portrait of S. deserting husband and home for the freedom of an Arizona ashram as not only reworking a nineteenth-century novel of another author, *The Scarlet Letter*, but as revamping with respect to gender a twentieth-century novel of his own, *Rabbit, Run*. Reviewing that prototypical Updike novel of a man fleeing the nets of domesticity and death from the perspective of his later works shows that revamping need not imply reversal of his earlier treatment of women. His second novel contains the seeds of subsequent emendations. In the difference between the cad and the chronicler, even a cad whom Updike has admitted is "not essentially advanced" over himself,[9] is the difference between the inarticulate literalist for whom, whatever his far-reaching longings, words mean what they say, and the literary imagist for whom language can juxtapose exposition and expose. More to the point, in the juxtaposition of the voices of the men and women in *Rabbit, Run*, Updike questions whether the impulse toward sexual mythologizing is limited to one character, or one author, or bespeaks instead a need to seek in an archetypal Other "a glorious message from the deep" that typifies every human being, regardless of gender.[10]

Any evaluation of Updike's treatment of women must include (even at the risk of repeating a commonplace) some discussion of "More Love in the Western World," the essay in which he addresses Denis de Rougemont's contentions that "'the inescapable conflict in the West between passion and marriage'" lies in a split between the realms of spirit and matter, and that love becomes "not a way of accepting and entering the world but a way of defying and escaping it."[11] Directed

---

[8]Joyce Carol Oates, "Updike's American Comedies," *Modern Fiction Studies* 21 (1975): 463, 467-8; Kathleen Verduin, "Sex, Nature, and Dualism in *The Witches of Eastwick*," *Modern Language Quarterly* 46 (1985): 308. See Verduin's excellent article, pp. 293-4, for a useful summary of feminist criticism of Updike's 1984 novel. For Updike's response to these criticisms, see Mervyn Rothstein, "In *S.*, Updike Tries the Woman's Viewpoint," *New York Times*, March 2, 1988: C-21. I am indebted to Donald J. Greiner's essay, "Body and Soul: John Updike and *The Scarlet Letter*," *Journal of Modern Literature* 15 (1989): 492-3, for calling Rothstein's article to my attention.

[9]*Picked-Up Pieces*, p. 508.

[10]*Odd Jobs*, p. 72.

[11]John Updike, *Assorted Prose* (New York: Alfred A. Knopf, 1965), pp. 284, 285. Nearly every commentator who discusses Updike's view of male-female relations refers to his 1963 *New Yorker* essay on de Rougemont. For particularly good applications of the essay to Updike's fiction, see Robert Detweiler, "Updike's *Couples*: Eros Demythologized," *Twentieth Century Literature* 17 (1971): 237-46; and Victor Strandberg, "John Updike and the Changing of the Gods," *Mosaic* 12.1 (1978): 161-2,

toward an "Unattainable Lady" who, in her idealized state, embodies "'the very essence of what is strange in women,'" yet presents the inherently egocentric lover a crystallization of his past and herself as "alpha and omega, as his Fate,"[12] love in the Western world so confirms the lover in his own sense of importance that the prospects of such an estimable self being extinguished diminish to nought. As Updike explains, "Our fundamental anxiety is that we do not exist– or will cease to exist. Only in being loved do we find external corroboration of the supremely high valuation each ego secretly assigns itself."[13] Simply put, a "man in love ceases to fear death."[14]The caveat is that this most tantalizing of loves must remain the most tremendous of teases; once transferred to the realm of the real, with a woman whose physical imperfections– not to mention mortality– are as certain as those of the lover, the ability of this Doreen Gray to minister to the lover's need vanishes for what she reveals is exactly what he does not want to see. "'[T]o possess her,'" as de Rougemont recognized, "'is to lose her.'"[15] To remain with her is even worse, for mired in her own earthbound condition, she cannot help but drag the lover down as well.

D. H. Lawrence provided perhaps the most literal depiction of that danger in the two drowned bodies dredged from the lake in *Women in Love*, the woman's arms wrapped around the neck of the man in a strangling embrace. Updike comes a close second in the demise he sketches for the grandfather in "The Blessed Man of Boston, My Grandmother's Thimble, and Fanning Island": Trying to jump from a bed he thinks is on fire, he is restrained by the "disproportionate strength" of his sickly wife who "clung to him and in their fall to the floor he died."[16] But, raised in Berks County, Pennsylvania, and not Boston, as a Lutheran not a Calvinist, Updike does not fully inherit the Manichean legacy to which de Rougemont directly traced the "modern Occidental obsession with romantic love."[17] Updike's admiration of Hawthorne for having written "the one classic from the lusty youth of American literature that deals with society in its actual heterosexual weave"[18] is

---

170-2.

[12]*Assorted Prose*, pp. 286, 287.

[13]Ibid., p. 299.

[14]Ibid., p. 286

[15]Ibid., p. 286.

[16]D. H. Lawrence, *Women in Love* (1920; New York: Viking, 1960), p. 181; John Updike, "The Blessed Man of Boston, My Grandmother's Thimble, and Fanning Island," *Pigeon Feathers and Other Stories* (New York: Alfred A. Knopf, 1962), p. 231.

[17]*Assorted Prose*, p. 284.

[18]*Odd Jobs*, p. 858.

tempered by his awareness of the morally conflicted stances in which Hawthorne's "instinctive tenet that matter and spirit are inevitably at war" ("Earth-flesh-blood versus Heaven-mind-spirit") eventuated: an attraction to sensual women that mars the promotion of their ethereal sisters as models of virtue, a rejoicing in the fall of a Dimmesdale as it represents the demise of the Puritan heritage he embodies.[19]

In populating the landscape of *Rabbit, Run* with women who conform to no one (or, more to the point, two) physical type(s), Updike complicates the dualist portrayals of earlier American heroines, just as his tale of Rabbit moving among them, a Lawrencian "son of the morning" (151), complicates the connotations of the choices made by earlier American heroes. This is reflected in the very beginning of the Rabbit tetralogy. When Harry Angstrom opts to leave his wife, in whose overflowing ashtrays he sees a Slough of Despond and whose thinning hair signals an irreversible movement "only going one way, toward deeper wrinkles and skimpier hair" (11), he grants himself honorary membership in the Kiwanis Club of American male characters defined by Leslie Fiedler (in the same year of *Rabbit, Run*'s publication) as fearing "the fall to sex, marriage, and responsibility" that any confrontation between man and woman brings, with all the intimations of mortality that the word "fall" connotes.[20] Yet making his pilgrim's progress from the fat and totally real Janice (as confirmed by her pregnancy) to the fleshy and tempting promise of Ruth (Venus as confirmed by her past promiscuity) provides Rabbit with little relief. The weightiness he resents about Janice's pregnancy is a burden Harry literally carries with him throughout the novel, crippling his basketball playing in the book's first pages, forcing him to see himself an "old man" out of place among "boys" (6, 3), and in *Rabbit at Rest* ballooning into a two-hundred-thirty-pound paunch that leaves him "big-bellied" with a "vague doom" he tries to repress (46). The death's head that peeps through Janice's thinning hair reappears in Marty Tothero's patchy tufts (42) and Jack Eccles's "small-jawed head [showing] its teeth like a skull" (121). Ronnie Harrison's "[f]at and half bald" appearance so oppresses Rabbit that he becomes "obsessed by Harrison's imperfections" (175). Rabbit's car is a "stiff shroud" smaller than his apartment (40); Tothero's Sunshine Athletic Association room is devoid of even a closet whose door Harry must open only halfway lest it hit a televisions set. Ejecting himself from the claustrophobia of living with Janice (emotionally equivalent to being "in your coffin before they've taken your blood out" [215-16]) only projects Harry into the greater claustrophobia of the coffin-like spaces he inhabits without her. With the world of decay Harry has embodied in Janice superseded by signs of decrepitude in the masses, Updike

---

[19]John Updike, *Hugging the Shore: Essays and Criticism* (New York: Alfred A. Knopf, 1983) pp. 77, 78. Donald J. Greiner bases his analysis of *A Month of Sundays, Roger's Version,* and *S.* on Updike's rejection of Hawthorne's division of body and soul. See Greiner, "Body and Soul: John Updike and *The Scarlet Letter*," pp. 475-83, for complete discussion.

[20]Leslie A. Fiedler, *Love and Death in the American Novel* (1960; rev. and rpt. 1966; New York: Stein and Day, 1975), p. 26.

exposes from the start how erroneous is Harry's propensity to limit the threat to one woman or even one gender.

Tothero, Eccles, and Harrison do not sleep with Harry, however (although homoerotic overtures from the first two do cause him discomfort). It is in the sexual relations between men and women that Updike situates the transcendental gamble against death most intensely, sex functioning for so many of his characters "as the emergent religion, as the only thing left."[21] Introduced as the physical opposite of Janice, thick-haired and "pleasingly dexterous" (64), Ruth Leonard appears to be just what the dualist metaphysical doctor ordered. With her large body portrayed in terms of spatial expansiveness, "an incredible continent" (81), she actualizes in the flesh "the broad soft belly of the land" Harry has sought to penetrate on his abortive flight from home (30). When christened "Mrs. America" (70), she even awakens memories of that native land whose piercing historians like Frederick Jackson Turner had lauded at the turn of the century. Unlike Vera Hummel in *The Centaur*, whose deification as "goddess-size" by the Caldwell males is corroborated by a mythic underpinning that enables a physical education instructor to play Venus in gym shorts with no difficulty,[22] Ruth needs something of a makeover before assuming the role Harry assigns her in Updike's more realistic novel. Only when scrubbed of make-up and stripped of diaphragm at Harry's command can her "frozen form" assume the appropriate "pose" Harry desires (82), that of "perfect statue," in the words of the novel's first edition, "unadorned woman, beauty's home image," thus anticipating the women made objects for gazing that populate Updike's later works: the life-size nude encased in bronze in *The Centaur*'s museum; Peggy, in *Of the Farm*, who models sporadically; the wife in "Museums and Women" who is as "fair, and finely formed, and mute" as an eighteenth-century statuette, the mistress whose head and shoulders form a bust before a tapestry; most of the women in *Couples* (Angela, who poses "like Eve on a portal," Marcia, who reminds her lover of a Greek statue, even the Transparent Woman in the planetarium, who makes the Hanema girls think of their mother).[23] The question that must be asked, however, is whose "home image" is she?

Updike has made no secret of his propensity to think of women's bodies in mythologized terms. "The female body is, in its ability to conceive and carry a fetus and to nurse an infant, our life's vehicle," he recently wrote. "Male sexuality, then, returning to this primal source, drinks at the spring of being and enters the murky

---

[21]*Picked-Up Pieces*, p. 505.

[22]*The Centaur*, p. 203.

[23]John Updike, *Rabbit, Run* (Greenwich , CT.: Fawcett Crest, 1960), p. 70; John Updike, "Museums and Women" (1967), *Museums and Women and Other Stories* (New York: Alfred A. Knopf, 1972), p. 12; John Updike, *Couples* (New York: Alfred A. Knopf, 1968), pp. 10, 114, 422-3.

region, where up is down and death is life, of mythology."[24] So, too, does he attribute specific spiritual connotations to specific sexual acts. "Fellatio, buggery— the sexual specifics are important," he stated when discussing the "lifelong journey into the bodies of women" that is advanced over the four Rabbit novels, "for they mark the stages of a kind of somatic pilgrimage that, smile though we will, is consciously logged by most men and perhaps by more women than admit it."[25] Much of this contemporary mythologizing of women is not unique to Updike. Thomas Pynchon's query, "What sort of mistress, then, would Venus be?" underlies the entirety of *V.*, in which mortal versions of the title character become increasingly inanimate, pass through a brief incarnation in a Botticelli painting, and culminate in a chapter that conflates a goddess of sexual love, Astarte; the Maltese word for "woman," Mara; a city of feminine gender, Valletta; and a peninsula in which they all reside that is shaped like the mons Veneris. Norman Mailer's assumption that women "were a step, or a stage, or a move or a leap nearer the creation of existence" than men and hence men's "indispensable and only connection to the future," and his ascribing to the womb an "unaccountable liaison with the beyond," explain his invoking "Sex as Time, and Time as the connection of new circuits" at the end of *The Deer Park*, his proposing the moment of a woman's first orgasm as "The Time of Her Time" in a short story, and his taking Rabbit's contraceptive demand one step further in *An American Dream* by having Stephen Rojack remove a woman's diaphragm himself in the middle of lovemaking.[26]

Refuting the feminist charge that such biological mythologizing of Woman in the abstract occurs at the expense of women portrayed in fiction as all-too-real, Updike remains fully aware of the dangers of sacrificing what Joanne Dobson has called the *"fact* of woman" to the *"idea* of woman." He writes, "The largeness of our mother-myth has a paradoxically dwindling effect upon the women concerned: they must be in all things motherly and become therefore natural processes rather than people."[27] Accusers view very different male authors perpetrating (and perpetuating) very similar American literary crimes: Mary Gordon lambastes Updike for extending in Rabbit the "pattern of moving boys killing females who get

---

[24]*Odd Jobs*, p. 71.

[25]*Odd Jobs*, p. 870. See "An Interesting Emendation" (*Picked-Ip* [sic] Pieces, pp. 438-44) for Updike's discussion of the "swift secularization" of oral sex in recent American fiction and the concomitant rise of buggery in place of the "magical act" he considers fellatio to be (*Picked-Up Pieces*, p. 441).

[26]Thomas Pynchon, *V.* (1963; New York: Bantam, 1964), pp. 193, 429, 434, 438; Norman Mailer, *The Prisoner of Sex* (New York: Signet-New American Library, 1971), p. 47; Norman Mailer, *The Deer Park* (1955; New York: Berkley Windhover, 1976), p. 327.

[27]Joanne Dobson, "Portraits of the Lady: Imagining Women in Nineteenth-Century America," *American Literary History* 3 (1991): 396; *Odd Jobs*, pp. 67-8.

in their way." Judith Fetterley upbraids Mailer for dictating that women "must be killed and killed violently and thoroughly and again and again before the hero is able to break free and head for the West." Comparisons between these two worst offenders, however, show Updike questioning the tendency to mythologize as he delineates the reasons characters continue to portray each other in mythologized terms.[28]

For Mailer, who premises his metaphysics on God being at war with the Devil and every conflict on earth reverberating in that overarching cosmological struggle, the battle he projects onto the bodies of women has ramifications with respect to the ascendancy of creation or decreation. Within this largest of schemata, in which each person is assigned a particular mission, "one of us to create, another to be brave, a third to love, a fourth to work, a fifth to be bold, a sixth to be all of these,"[29] man's venture into the sexual arena demands more than "the adventurous juncture of ego and courage" that confrontation with those who "possess the better half of life already" might entail.[30] It constitutes, quite simply, "the mirror of how we approach God through our imperfections." [31] To the degree that sex advances the cause of God's creation– creation in the most literal sense– the sexual specifics in Mailer's work gain meaning: The difference between anal and vaginal sex is thus denoted as "a raid on the Devil and a trip back to the Lord." For all the rhapsodizing Stephen Rojack does when describing the first orgasm in which "I came up from my body rather than down from my mind. . .and the honey she had given me I could only give back, all sweets to her womb, all come in her cunt," the pleasure he and Cherry experience is less important than the pregnancy in which their act culminates.[32] The Lord, Mailer averred, "was not thus devoted to the absurd as to put the orgasm in the midst of the act of creation without cause of the profoundest sort, for when a man and woman conceive, would it not be best that they be able to see one another for a transcendent instant, as if the soul of what would then be conceived might live with more light later?"[33]

For Updike, who has no doubts about God's omnipotence and openly prefers "a fierce God above the kind God" who is "the more or less watered-down Puritan

---

[28]Gordon, p. 17; Judith Fetterley, "*An American Dream*: 'Hula, Hula,' Said the Witches," *The Resisting Reader: A Feminist Approach to American Fiction* (Bloomington: Indiana University Press, 1978), p. 158.

[29]Norman Mailer, *The Presidential Papers* (1963; New York: Berkley Medallion, 1970), p. 159.

[30]*Prisoner of Sex*, pp. 36, 35.

[31]Ibid., p. 86.

[32]Norman Mailer, *An American Dream* (1965; New York: Dell, 1970), pp. 48, 122-3.

[33]*Prisoner of Sex*, p. 66.

God" that most people now worship,[34] there is no need to invest human beings, much less human sexuality, with the larger sense of mission that Mailer ascribes to them. He who delivers the message that "God gives to each one of us a special talent" in *Rabbit, Run* is a grown man who prances around on television in mouse ears (9). Moreover, the exact processes that signal creation for Mailer signal corrosion for Updike. Harry regains "his old inkling" that "there was something that wanted him to find it, that he was here on earth on a kind of assignment" after experiencing anal sex in *Rabbit is* (sic) *Rich* as "a void, a pure black box, a casket of perfect nothingness."[35] But the procreation that results from genital sex offers little that is any more promising, for in a world in which "[t]hings compete; a life demands a life,"[36] in which, as the opening to *Rabbit, Run* asserts, "the kids keep coming, they keep crowding you up" (3), the birth of the child confirms the death of the parent. "The fullness ends when we give Nature her ransom, when we make children for her," Harry realizes when he looks at the two-year-old Nelson. "Then she is through with us, and we become, first inside, and then outside, junk" (226). Having this early recognized his hierarchal place within "the vertical order of parenthood" Updike proposes (308), Harry remains antagonistic toward the adult Nelson for having "swallowed up the boy that was and substituted one more pushy man in the world,"[37] relenting only when Nelson's own paternity establishes him as a "hostage he's given to fortune," Nelson's thinning hair reminding Harry that "[y]our children's losing battle with time seems even sadder than your own."[38]

What Harry does not realize, until it is too late, is that Nature does not wait to make its point until the pitter patter of little feet has become audible. The same statement about Nature's opportunistic manners appears after Ruth and Rabbit have completed their first act of lovemaking: "Nature leads you up like a mother and as soon as she gets her little price leaves you with nothing" (86). That such a statement appears after the moment of orgasm, an experience Ruth has forgotten she could have, is revealing since it is as "nothing" that Updike portrays that moment of physical sensation. This reflects the attitude of Updike's main protagonist in *Rabbit, Run.* "Yesterday morning the sky was ribbed with thin-stretched dawn clouds, and he was exhausted, heading into the center of the net, where alone there seemed a chance of rest," Harry recalls, comparing the time before he met Ruth to the time after he has slept with her. "Now the noon of another day has burned away the clouds, and the sky in the windshield is blank and cold, and he feels nothing

---

[34]*Picked-Up Pieces*, p. 504.

[35]John Updike, *Rabbit Is Rich* (1981; New York: Fawcett Crest-Ballantine, 1982), pp. 392, 391.

[36]*Pigeon Feathers*, p. 253.

[37]*Rabbit Is Rich*, p. 209.

[38]*Rabbit at Rest*, p. 111.

ahead of him, Ruth's blue-eyed nothing, the nothing she told him she did" (97).

This "nothing" by which Ruth is defined refers, in its most literal sense, to an anatomical absence, the same absence Peter Caldwell discovers when pressing his face against Penny's skirt in *The Centaur* ("where her legs meet there is nothing") and in which he then locates "the secret the world holds at its center."[39] In *Rabbit, Run*, however, this "nothing" also denotes both Ruth's absence of regular employment and the fact that what she does for a living is take money for sexual favors. In fact, in the social world of the novel, money serves as the common denominator of all the women in whose sexuality Harry seeks relief from the base materiality of his daily life, from the whore who takes him into her room in Texas ("Sweet woman, *she* was money" [47]); to Janice, whose father owns Springer Motors; to Ruth, whom he prices at ten cents a pound (72); to, most of all, the Du Pont woman he envisions barefoot beside a swimming pool in France and who symbolizes to Harry the greatest escape of all: "Something like money in a naked woman, deep, millions" (26). More important, within the religious dimension that Updike's works typically seek, money increasingly becomes used by the characters as an index of spirituality. In the most Americanist of senses, the foreclosure of Kroll's department store that had stood "bigger than a church" comes to signify to Harry the forfeiture of divine election: "When the money stopped, they could close down God Himself."[40] With woman now functioning as the place where the spiritual and the sexual meet, no wonder Harry will begin connecting woman as blank with woman as bank: "A blank check. A woman is blank until you fuck her."[41] Therefore, blankness is the condition Harry strives to maintain in women, having already established the "vast blank of his freedom" as a polar– and temporal–opposite to all that stinks of the grave that he has embodied in Janice and their shared apartment (51). He thus loves the fact that Ruth dismisses five former suitors who telephone her at home, for in cutting herself off from her past she encases herself in a perpetual present: "the past was a vine hanging on by just these five tendrils and it tore away easily, leaving her clean and blue and blank" (173). He delights in watching her swim and treasurers how "[c]lean, clean" she looks when in water, for in water her body refuses to sink but keeps floating to the surface of its own buoyancy (142).

Harry's body displays no such buoyancy, though, for it is a leaden inability to sustain an erection that characterizes him as a lover: "it is here he most often failed Janice, by coming too soon" (85). And, as the fate of baby Becky dramatically testifies, bodies in water can only stay afloat for so long. In other words, Harry's

---

[39]*The Centaur*, p. 184.

[40]*Rabbit at Rest*, p. 461.

[41]John Updike, *Rabbit Redux* (1971; New York: Fawcett Crest-Ballantine, 1972), p. 270. For discussions of the linkage between sex and money that is more obvious in *Rabbit Is Rich*, see Detweiler, *John Updike*, pp. 175-8; and Judie Newman, *John Updike* (New York: St. Martin's, 1988), pp. 61-4, 70-6.

desire to endow sex with transcendent properties and envision women as goddesses impervious to time is offset by the denouement Updike attaches to sexual activity that depicts lovemaking between men and women as a temporally bound process. Harry traces that change to his getting married, Janice's orgasms "never as good on their own" bed as they were on the bed borrowed from a friend (41). But since Harry only marries Janice because she gets pregnant, he places the blame on pregnancy for the change in women's sexual potential, when flesh becomes flab, when the "wonderful way they have of coming forward around you when they want it" turns to "just fat weight" (26)– and pregnancy not just for the physical threat of childbirth exposing women to moral harm. Harry "loves women when they're first pregnant" (307), and Updike (no Hemingway in this regard) typically portrays difficult periods of labor in order to highlight the successful deliveries in which they end.[42] But women's pregnancy for Harry later becomes "stubborn lumpiness" when the man who seeks "to bury himself in her" (10, 307) is displaced by a fetus whose destruction of lap prefigures its later displacement of its father. No longer a provider of comfort against fears of death, carrying, indeed nurturing, proof of Harry's inescapable doom inside her body, a pregnant woman to Harry comes to lose all value, and his portrait of her shifts from terms of money to terms of metal: Janice after Becky's birth is a "machine, a white, pliant machine for fucking, hatching, feeding" (234). Unable to grant her even the power of Henry Adams' dynamo, Harry reduces this fallen Virgin to the status of the gadgets he sells, knowing full well, as he will later say of the used gadgets he sells at her father's car lot, that "Metal corrodes."[43]

What Harry experiences as infuriating change, Updike understands as inevitable continuity, a difference encapsulated in the contrast between Harry's experience of Mrs. Smith's garden and Updike's portrayal of it.[44]Filled with trees

---

[42]See, for example, the birth of the narrator's mother in "The Blessed Man of Boston, My Grandmother's Thimble, and Fanning Island" (*Pigeon Feathers*, pp. 239-40), Harry's recollection of Nelson's birth in *Rabbit, Run* (p. 11), and the circumstances surrounding the birth of Nelson's daughter in *Rabbit Is Rich* (pp. 401-2).

[43]*Rabbit Is Rich*, p. 352. Updike's connection of "paternity and death, earth and faith and cars" (*Hugging the Shore*, p. 852) is longstanding and the depiction of used bodies (both male and female) as used metal recurs in much of his fiction. For representative samples, see "Packed Dirt, Churchgoing, A Dying Cat, A Traded Car" (*Pigeon Feathers*, p. 279) and *The Centaur* (pp. 71, 162, 186). In *Rabbit Is Rich*, Nelson will inherit his father's predisposition to judge pregnant women as "[d]efective equipment" (p. 309).

[44]It is in conflating Rabbit's perspective with Updike's and neglecting to consider point of view that feminist critics of the Rabbit tetralogy most often err. Joyce Carol Oates' remarks serve as an especially astute reminder against such misreadings: "the consciousness of a Rabbit Angstrom is so foreign to Updike's own that it seems at times more a point of view, a voicing of that part of the mind unfertilized by the imagination, than a coherent personality" ("Updike's American Comedies," p. 466).

Harry associates with "forbidden estates" (139), the garden surpasses that most forbidden of biblical estates to be "like Heaven" for him (223); yet the immunity from time it promises Harry (signified by his never having to cut his fingernails while working there) is undercut by the testament to time's passage that the portraits inside Mrs. Smith's house display: the disparity between the young woman whose "short puffy little upper lip" looks "so good in a girl" (222) and the gnarled widow in whom Harry finds her incarnated. Viewed within the antipastoral terms in which Updike works, in which the recomposition of plants through photosynthesis and the decomposition of glucose through human respiration are opposing processes,[45] and which, in *Rabbit, Run*, culminate with Rebecca June Angstrom's death in the spring month for which she is named, Rabbit's mythologizing of women as creatures of nature is misdirected from the start.[46] This is particularly the case with his pursuit of the woman who lives on Summer Street. And predicating Ruth's ideality on her purity, cleansing her face of artificial "crust" and coverings (82), and freeing their act from any contraceptive plastics so he can enter her "split pod, an open fold, shapeless and simple" and stretch time "to great length and thinness" (84) prove moot given the way that Updike introduces Harry's amorous approach: "He makes love to her as he would to his wife" (83). Likewise, the very emblems Harry takes as proof that "the world just can't touch you" (109) Updike treats as tokens of his earth-bound vulnerability: the orgasm he enables Ruth to have portrayed as "falling through" (86), an image of descent that prefigures the threat of Skylab falling in *Rabbit Is Rich* and the airplane crashes in *Rabbit at Rest*, all of which signal mortality; the godlike pride he feels at having "made you [Ruth] and the sun and the stars" betrayed by the words with which he appraises his final product, "naked in the shower, her hair hanging oozy with lather, her neck bowed to the whipping water," a Venus de Milo with arms: "I made you bloom" (109).

Even the domination over her to which Harry feels entitled is shown by Updike to be predicated on false premises when being "her master. . . [and] getting on top of her" are rights Harry assumes are his "by nature" (304). Indeed, the moment Harry takes as evidence of his greatest mastery, when he literally gets most "on top of her" having forced Ruth onto her knees in submission, the moment he initiates as a final closing on his property seeing the act she performs as "prov[ing] you're mine," thus confirming once and for all his noncorporeal status in that he stands before her like "an angel waiting for a word" (187), is the exact moment that Updike's images merge together to establish Harry's own coporeality in that he is the only one capable of coming into time with the act of fellatio he forces Ruth to perform. It becomes quite fitting, during this last visit, that his final assertion "of being by nature her master, of getting on top of her" plunges him back into the very

---

[45]*The Centaur*, pp. 142-3; *Couples*, p. 95.

[46]See, in particular, Larry E. Taylor, *Pastoral and Anti-Pastoral Patterns in John Updike's Fiction* (Carbondale: Southern Illinois University Press, 1971), pp. 70-85; and Brenner, pp. 3-14, for detailed discussions of Updike's antipastoral theme in *Rabbit, Run*.

world from which he has sought Ruth's body as refuge: "His hands and legs are suffused with a paralyzing sense of reality; his child is really dead, his day is really done" (304). As he learns later with respect to another kind of possession, "to be rich is to be robbed, to be rich is to be poor."[47]

To a certain extent, Harry does sense Updike's point– that sexuality ends not in resurrection, but in rot. His memory of making love with Janice on her girlfriend's bed is pierced by a recollection of "feeling lost, having done the final thing" (14). The dream he has after first making love to Ruth, which is populated by the women in his family, is permeated by images of metal and "tin-smelling coldness" (88). The icebox, "mottled with the same disease the linoleum has" (88), becomes, in the dream's associative logic, the Pandora's box that causes Janice's skin to slide off her face; it springs from Tothero's earlier description of his wife's skin as clumsily stitched together (54), but it also suggests the particular skin disease of psoriasis that Updike and his autobiographical surrogate Peter Caldwell inherit from their mothers and that a friend of Peter's directly links with sexuality in questioning whether it is syphilis.[48] Yet the dream that instills doubts in Rabbit about the role in which he has cast one woman in particular, indicated when he sees Ruth's "bush a froth of tinted metal" upon awakening (89), engenders no doubts about his mythologizing of women in general. Having "become domestic" with Ruth so quickly (90), he begins looking for a replacement of more refinement. When he meets Lucy Eccles, he immediately casts her as a "fine-grained Ruth" (118), mythologizes her legs spread as "two white gates parted" (232), and invests their relationship (such as it is) with the same qualities of property and ownership with which he previously defined that between himself and her predecessor: "He knows only this: underneath everything, under their minds and their situations, he possesses, like an inherited lien on a distant piece of land, a dominance over her, and that in her grain, in the lie of her hair and nerves and fine veins, she is prepared for this dominance" (240). When the door that Lucy eventually slams in his face indicates he cannot claim these rights, he transfers his sexual impulse, a wish "like a small angel" (243), to a different woman– Janice again– in whose "fullness that calls to him" he starts to envision the fleshiness of others, in whose bent form he sees a body ripe to proclaim as *"Mine, my woman,"* but whose "smeared frantic face" promptly "blots out his pride of possession" (285).

In contrast to the male characters in the works of an author like Mailer, who divide up women by type– fiery Latin brunettes, Marilyn Monroe blonds, Margo Macomber killers– and personify various national traits in those physical aspects, Updike's Rabbit is an absolute egalitarian in that any fertile woman provides grounds (pun intended) for deification. His rotations foreshadow the ongoing square dance that will characterize wife swapping in *Couples*. As a result, Janice is correct and her terminology particularly appropriate when she complains that Harry uses her only as "a pot for his dirt" (251). The resilience Harry continues to display in

---

[47] *Rabbit Is Rich*, p. 351.

[48] *The Centaur*, p. 142.

his pursuit of women may prove to some, as it does to Mrs. Smith, that Harry has the gift of "life" (224), but Updike undermines his efforts at every turn, proving more conclusively that Harry's mythologizing impulses just keep him going around and around in circles that get smaller and smaller as time goes on, and Harry begins revisiting the sites of former failures. If his first pursuit of Janice can be described as nostalgic, an effort by Harry to keep her a girl, "still scarcely adult," even presexually timeless in that her breasts, when flattened against her chest, revert to "tipped softness" (11), his final attempt to make her body keeper of "this little flame" he brings from church is nothing less than desperate (271).

And the women– far from "dumb bovine" creatures whose lack of education Mary Allen equates with a lack of intelligence– recognize the inevitable failure to which mythologizing impulses are doomed. Realizing that for Rabbit "it is not her body he wants, not the machine, but her, her" (79), Ruth recalls how often sex with others was similarly a question of mind over matter. "They couldn't have felt much it must have been just the *idea* of you" (147), she thinks when comparing Harry to the boys she dated in high school and judging as adolescent the quality of Harry's quest. Aware as well of the misogynistic impulse that turning women into "something pasted on the inside of their dirty heads" may reflect (146), suspecting, as the novel's first edition states, "[I]t was like they hated women and used *her*" (123), she fully recognizes what Harry's urge "to crush her" and his need "for pressure, just pure pressure" indicate: "Kill felt more like it," she replies to his pitiful excuse of having given her a "hug" (75, 76). Even Janice, who lacks the vocabulary as well as the experience of Ruth, still knows enough to view with skepticism all attempts to turn sex into a transcendent experience. "What did he and God talk about," Janice wonders after Harry returns from church in a state of arousal, "thinking," like all men, "about whatever they do think about" whenever they need to "[get] rid of this little hot clot that's bothering them" (251).

True, these women indulge in a certain degree of generalizing, if not mythologizing, themselves, as their questioning of men's motives indicates. Ruth's Joycean monologue ends much the same as Molly Bloom's does, with all her previous men conflated into one particular man, as she "forgave them all then, his face all their faces gathered into a scared blur" (148). The difference is that any such mythologizing for Updike's women springs less from sexual difference than from sexual precocity and sputters out in simple boredom: "If they'd just thought, they might have known you were curious too, that you could like that strangeness there like they liked yours, no worse than women in their way, all red wrinkles, my God, what was it in the end? No mystery. That was the great thing she discovered, that it was no mystery, just a stuck-on-looking bit that made them king" (146).Furthermore, unlike Molly Bloom, who comes to a similar conclusion about man's body, his genitals "two bags full and his other thing hanging down out of him or sticking up at you like a hatrack no wonder they hide it with a cabbageleaf," but continues to mythologize woman's body as "beauty of course thats admitted,"[49] the women in *Rabbit, Run* view their own bodies mainly as vehicles for social security.

---

[49]James Joyce, *Ulysses* (1922; New York: Vintage-Random, 1961), p. 753.

Sex for Ruth is work, with oral sex "just harder work" (146). Like any form of labor, it serves as a means for her to establish a particular social position, as her memories of having obliged high school boys indicate: "if you went along with it could be good or not so good and anyway put you with them against those others, those little snips running around her at hockey in gym. . . .But she got it back at night, taking what they didn't know existed like a queen" (146-7). Significantly, "queen" is the very title Harry confers on her after they first sleep together (113). Coming from a family with more money and therefore some social position to begin with, Janice sees sex as providing her with a way of acquiring a different kind of role: "She would be a woman with a house on her own" (250). For both, the antagonists they battle are not men, but women– the high school "girls with their contractors and druggists for fathers" who surround Ruth (147), the mother who humiliates Janice into a state of total inferiority. Thus, whereas women prove essential to men's scenarios, men prove auxiliary to theirs. In Updike's world, women are as much at war with each other as they are with men. More often than not, men who complain about women's dumbness get their ideas from their mothers since the mythology piercing in which younger women indulge threatens the one myth that justifies the power that being "still attached to the cord of his life" enables a mother to wield over her son, making men like Harry feel "they're not even in a way separate people he began in her stomach and if she gave him life she can take it away and if he feels that withdrawal it will be the grave itself" (289).[50]

In the end, neither Ruth nor Janice retains any illusions as to the extended benefits sex can provide. Janice realizes that, after marriage, she still remains "little clumsy dark-complected Janice Springer" (252). Ruth recognizes, as the television show watched by Harry proclaims, that one can be "Queen For A Day" and only a day; having been the victim when younger of locker room talk that refuted any hope of social position, Ruth as an adult looks at sex as a very limited enterprise: "You make love, you try to get close to somebody" (186). Since Updike's book is set in 1959, these thoughts are more appropriate for women than the mythologizing in which Harry, whose later intellectual life will consist of reading *Consumer Reports* on can openers, indulges. To question, as Mary Allen does, "what about work for women?" is to ask the wrong question of a novel set in a period of time in which 34,374,000 out of a noninstitutional population of 117,881,000 defined their role as "keeping house," in which 38,053,000 (or 62.8 percent) of a total of 60,569,000 women did not belong to the labor force, and in which day care for those, like Janice, with small children and few financial resources was not an available option, as indicated by the fact that of the 12,205,000 married women in the labor force, only 1,118,000 (or 18.3 percent) had children under the age of six.[51] For Updike

---

[50]See, in particular, the conversations that Mrs. Robinson and Joey have about Peggy in Updike's *Of the Farm* (New York: Alfred A. Knopf, 1965), pp. 43, 138-41.

[51]Allen, p. 112; United States Department of Commerce, Bureau of the Census, *Historical Statistics of the United States: Colonial Times to 1970*, 2 pts. (Washington, D. C.: n. p., 1975) 1, pp. 127, 128, 134.

to portray women adjusting instead of protesting does not imply endorsement of their options. As the despair he attributes to the drunken Janice indicates, it certainly does not provide evidence that women are, or should be, content with their condition.

It is easy to see these women in *Rabbit, Run* as the literary mothers of a whole slew of women who refuse to take the transcendent risk that in Updike's suburban world is the closest one gets to macho behavior, who in piercing through the pretensions of that risk at every opportunity act as the equivalent of spiritual castrators: Penny in *The Centaur* who treats Peter's mythologizing her as Philyra as evidence that he loves her only in dreams,[52] Angela in *Couples* who shrugs off Piet's designation of her genitals as "heavenly" as nothing unusual,[53] Peggy in *Of the Farm* who likens the sanctuary her mother-in-law proposes to a concentration camp.[54] Such an inability to enter into any form of transcendent thought, to remain conceptually bound to the here and now, may indicate women's imaginative limitations to an author who is devoted to a real/unreal continuum that defines God as "the union of the actual and the ideal" and, in wedding the tangible and transcendental, conceives of all things as "masks for God."[55] For such a charge to hold true, however, one must accept what in many circles has become a myth of authorial intentionality. Working with the text alone provides far less grounds for criticism because the transcendental ideal is never completely espoused in the novel. The appropriately named Doctor Crowe who, in delivering Janice's child, gets closer to the source of her womanhood than anyone else, brings back "nothing to confide, no curse, no blessing" and his eyes do not "release with thunder the mystery they have absorbed" because they witness nothing of mystery to reveal (201). With such confirmation ripping to shreds the basis on which Rabbit has constructed his sexual theology, the ersatz saint, too, falls accordingly. "You're Mr. Death himself," Ruth asserts, after which she lodges her most stinging rebuke: "You're not just nothing, you're worse than nothing" (304). With such an assessment of Rabbit's entire credo, such an inversion of all the emblems that formerly served as testaments to transcendence, the book closes. The "pure blank space" within Rabbit that had signaled his freedom shrinks to an "infinitely small" vacancy (308-9). The selfhood (not to mention sainthood) he had predicated on having a ball– in golf, in basketball, in every sense of the word– is exposed as the

---

[52]*The Centaur*, p. 183.

[53]*Couples*, p. 194.

[54]*Of the Farm*, p. 71.

[55]Updike, *Pigeon Feathers*, p. 249; Samuels, p. 116. Even critics whose stance is not explicitly feminist consider that Updike's failure to have women characters engage in transcendental thought signals a limitation he ascribes to women. See, for example, Bernard Schopen, "Faith, Morality, and the Novels of John Updike," *Twentieth Century Literature* 24 (1978): 533-4.

ultimate negation: "It's like when they heard you were great and put two men on you and no matter which way you turned you bumped into one of them and the only thing to do was pass. So you passed and the ball belonged to the others and your hands were empty and the men on you looked foolish because in effect there was nobody there" (309). Only this time the "nobody" is not Odysseus in disguise, but the cyclops whose faulty vision in Updike's novel turns him into nothing but a cypher.

*Stacey Olster, "'Unadorned Woman, Beauty's Home Image': Woman in *Rabbit, Run.*" *New Essays on Rabbit, Run.* Ed. Stanley Trachtenberg. New York: Cambridge University Press, 1993: 95-117.

"No Place to Run: Rabbit Angstrom as Adamic Hero"

Donald Greiner*

When, at the end of *Rabbit at Rest* (1990), an apparently dying Harry Angstrom thinks the word "enough,"[56] John Updike not only concludes one of the most remarkable achievements in contemporary American literature but also terminates one of the most troubling literary heroes in traditional American culture. To assign heroic stature to Rabbit is to invite controversy, for Harry is often careless with his health, reckless with his family, and heedless of his friends. Yet the extent of his heroism is not to be measured by classical paradigms. Rabbit does not, after all, perform astounding feats of strength and skill. But he does "believe," and he does seek grace in all the connotations of these ambiguous words; and thus in the course of his thirty years of literary life Harry Angstrom personifies Updike's understanding of how, in America, personal aspiration is always compromised by cultural decline. I want to suggest two primary points in the following pages: first, that Rabbit is Updike's variation on the canonical American literary hero, and second, that Updike foresaw Rabbit's defeat even before the publication of *Rabbit, Run* in 1960.

I

Late in *Rabbit at Rest*, Harry looks at his overweight, middle-aged body and sees "an innocuous passive spirit that doesn't want to do any harm, get trapped anywhere, or ever die" (381). Rabbit shares these desires– and their frustrations– with Cooper's Leatherstocking, Hawthorne's Hester, Melville's Billy Budd, Twain's Huck, Fitzgerald's Gatsby, and Salinger's Holden. With Rabbit Angstrom, Updike adds his name to the short list of American authors capable of successfully creating immortal characters who first absorb and then define the national culture.

The list is distinguished, and the novelists on it feature the peculiar brand of

---

[56] I use the following editions: *Rabbit, Run* (New York: Modern Library, 1965); *Rabbit at Rest* (New York: Knopf, 1990).

American literary heroism defined years ago by R. W. B. Lewis: "Tragedy, in American literature, was generated by the impact of hostile forces upon the innocent solitary, who had sprung from nowhere, and his impact upon them" (92). Naming this kind of character an American Adam, Lewis observes that the hero usually takes "his start outside society; the action to be imitated may just as well be his strenuous efforts to *stay* outside as his tactics for getting inside; and if he does get inside, it makes a difference whether he is walking into a trap or discovering a setting in which to realize his own freedom" (101). Although Harry Angstrom cannot think in Lewis's sophisticated terms, he nevertheless intuits Lewis's point: that he is a relative innocent trapped in the American culture of 1950-1990; that he seems to have sprung from nowhere and thus stands outside the accepted norms of the culture; and that his goal– especially in *Rabbit, Run*– is to maintain his freedom by *remaining* outside despite the costs, which are always great. Updike's essential paradox in the Rabbit tetralogy is that Harry is distanced from yet wholly exemplifies his culture. Lewis summarizes what he calls "the matter of Adam" as "the ritualistic trials of the young innocent, liberated from family and social history or bereft of them; radically affecting that world and radically affected by it; defeated, perhaps even destroyed, but leaving his mark upon the world" (127-28).

By the end of *Rabbit at Rest*, in sharp contradistinction to Hemingway's Santiago, who is an earlier version of "American" heroism, Harry is first defeated and then destroyed. Although surely responsible for his own predicament, he is nevertheless at odds with the American cultural malaise that he defines as "Reagan's reign." In *Rabbit at Rest*, as in the other novels of the tetralogy, Updike describes the hairstyles, the inane pop songs, the dismal television programs like *Roseanne*, the physical fitness nuts, and the racial prejudices both to illustrate the uneasiness of the culture that Rabbit would like to flee and to generate sympathy for a character who reflects many of the people who will read the novel but whom those readers will not much like. At age fifty-six, Harry still worries about sex and death, religion and grace, but he is not as certain as he used to be, not as confident. His personal limitation mirrors the national decline as Updike suggests that America is depleted and that dreams are deferred. Looking at the imported Toyotas that have brought him the "easy" life (surely Updike's deliberate contrast with Jay Gatsby's magnificent, pretentious car), Rabbit thinks not of success but of the eerie presence of lurking death.

No longer the hopeful Rabbit of his basketball-playing youth in the Eisenhower 1950s, the Harry Angstrom of *Rabbit at Rest* is similarly distanced from the grace he once pursued with inarticulate fear. Like many Americans of his indulgent generation, he suffers from heart trouble, Updike's physical sign of Harry's spiritual dread. Never well spoken, he continues to define abstractions with the metaphors of sports in an effort to maintain separation from– to stay "outside"– the culture. Golf, he reasons, now has a greater relevance to his life than basketball: starting wide before falling into a small hole in the ground. For all his fear, Angstrom continues his quest to run free of society's limitations. He is Updike's American dreamer, a mundane Natty Bumppo or Jay Gatsby, whose persistent dissatisfaction cloaks a lifelong spiritual yearning.

Despite Harry's transgression of adultery with his daughter-in-law, then, the reader cheers when, in the last movement of *Rabbit at Rest,* he runs one final time–away from complications, away from culture, away from a catastrophe that he himself has helped cause. He no longer runs toward the ill-defined goal of "it" as he does in *Rabbit, Run,* but at least he is on the move, as are Leatherstocking and Huck, "jostling for his space in the world as if he still deserves it" (*Rest* 442). He even returns to the basketball court despite his weight, his age, his heart. In short, he tries, as the solitary American hero always does. But his fear presages the final stillness, and the last word of the tetralogy is "Enough."

    II

    Updike foresaw Rabbit's defeat. Indeed, he prefigured it in a short story and a poem that antedate the publication of both *Rabbit, Run* (1960) and his first novel, *The Poorhouse Fair* (1959). Quite early in his career, in other words, Updike had Rabbit Angstrom in mind– or, at least, an Ur-Rabbit. Initially published in the *New Yorker* for April 9, 1955, before being collected in *The Same Door* (1959), the tale "Ace in the Hole" appeared within six months of Updike's first professional short story ("Friends from Philadelphia," *New Yorker,* 30 Oct. 1954). The poem "Ex-Basketball Player" appeared two years after "Ace in the Hole" in the *New Yorker* for July 6, 1957, before Updike collected it in *The Carpentered Hen* in 1958.

    Both an impressive story in its own right and an early version of *Rabbit, Run,* "Ace in the Hole" touches on the details of popular culture in the 1950s that Updike later stresses in the first Rabbit novel. Fats Domino's "Blueberry Hill" is a hit tune, the jitterbug is the dance of choice, and "ducktails" are the male hairstyle of the day. Fred "Ace" Anderson prefigures Harry "Rabbit" Angstrom as the small-town basketball hero who finds himself on the side-lines after graduating from high school. With the future nowhere in sight, Ace survives on a combination of past memories and present motion. Like Huck floating down the river, Leatherstocking walking west, or Billy Budd sailing the ocean, Ace seeks motion to sustain life. But Updike's irony is apparent: the American 1950s feature diminished heroes and restricted movement. Indeed, throughout his canon Updike suggests a relationship between the loss of space in the United States and the dilution of heroism. The sound of the axes that Natty Bumppo deplores is a staple in Ace's culture. Clearly worried but unable to define his problem, Ace pulls a cigarette from his pack, moves it to his mouth, strikes a match, lights up, inhales, and blows out the flame, all in time to "Blueberry Hill." Yet the motion is deceiving, for like Harry in *Rabbit at Rest,* Ace Anderson is as out of shape as his culture: one half-block sprint and two flights of stairs make him pant.

    Unlike *Rabbit, Run,* "Ace in the Hole" dos not permit Updike the room to fully develop the complex reader response that he nurtures in the novel, a response predicated on the reader's disapproval of the hero's longing to be a basketball star again and the reader's sympathy with the hero's instinct to enjoy life, to lash out at the predictable cultural routine that cramps his easy motion and natural grace. Ace is in danger of becoming what Huck Finn calls "sivilized," and Updike fears the change. What arouses readers' sympathy for Ace is his refusal to give up, the very trait that Ruth attributes to Harry Angstrom in *Rabbit, Run.* Ace is one of the earliest characters in Updike's fiction to experience what will become a general dilemma: how to reconcile the need for freedom with the demands of culture. Like Rabbit, Ace is married, but domestic compromise seems impossible because it suggests a fatal loss of momentum.

So Ace does what American literary heroes have done for two centuries and what Rabbit does throughout four novels: he seeks freedom in motion. Grabbing his wife for a dance, Ace does not so much jitterbug away his problems as keep himself on the move. The crisis will remain after the record stops, but for the moment he can dance within the freedom of the improvised pattern, marking time with the only rhythm he is wiling to acknowledge: "He spun her out carefully, keeping the beat with his shoulders. . . . [H]e could feel her toes dig into the carpet. He flipped his own hair back from his eyes. The music ate through his skin and mixed with the nerves and small veins; he seemed to be great again, and all the other kids were around them, in a ring, clapping time" (*Same Door* 26).

"Ace in the Hole" is not a typical initiation story like *Adventures of Huckleberry Finn* and *Billy Budd*, because the hero neither learns nor becomes disillusioned. Despair may set in later, as it surely does for Rabbit, the result of early fame too easily won, but for the time being momentum is all. Perhaps Ace's mother is too indulgent and his wife too plain. Perhaps his capabilities are limited and his job dull. But none of this is to the point in Updike's first manifestation of the American Adamic hero. Convincing the reader to sympathize with Ace, Updike also persuades the reader to regret the already stalled life of a young man whose joy at graceful movement will join his inability to cope and lead him presently, the reader senses, into the same American cul-de-sac that traps Rabbit, the cul-de-sac from which only death– and four novels of preparation for it– will free him.

Two years after "Ace in the Hole," Updike published the second trial run of the Rabbit tetralogy. The poem "Ex-Basketball Player" is a somber piece of social observation, a quiet commentary on an American culture that cannot sustain its heroes, no matter how mundane they are. Part of the long tradition of poems about the loss of youthful prowess couched in the metaphor of past athletic glory, "Ex-Basketball Player" is a deliberately prosaic rereading of A. E. Housman's "To an Athlete Dying Young." Housman's unnamed hero and Updike's Flick Webb are "runners whom renown outran," but unlike Housman's youthful performer, Flick is not yet forgotten. Still, the memory of Flick's triumphs is Updike's irony: Webb occasionally dribbles an inner tube for laughs, but "most of us remember anyway." He is Updike's solitary, a man outside the society that once idolized him, a hero of motion without space in which to move.

Housman, Cooper, Melville, and Twain may write about depleted heroism, but at least they concede the possibility of heroic action on a grand scale. In Updike's post-World War II America, however, heroic deeds are nearly always local and usually diminished. A few years ago Flick Webb was good, but like the avenue that runs past his high school, he is "cut off." His name foretells the paradox of his fate: natural movement inextricably entangled. Now alone, as American literary heroes usually are, and unassimilated by his culture, Flick sits in a netherworld between the cigars of adulthood and the syrupy drinks of adolescence. Note the pun on "tiers" in the final stanza:

Off work, he hangs around Mae's luncheonette.

Grease-gray and kind of coiled, he plays pinball,
Smokes those thin cigars, nurses lemon phosphates.
Flick seldom says a word to Mae, just nods
Beyond her face toward bright applauding tiers
Of Necco wafers, Nibs, and Juju beads.
(*Carpentered Hen 3*)

III

Ace's "hole" and Flick's "web" become Rabbit's net. "Ace in the Hole" and "Ex-Basketball Player" set the stage for *Rabbit, Run*, one of the great novels in American literature and Updike's first full-length consideration of the way sexual dissatisfaction and marital tension mask spiritual questing in a society that claims to be religious. The imperative voice of the title suggests Updike's sympathetic advice to his hero to break free from confining apartments and mediocre lives, but by the end of the novel, and eventually of the tetralogy, both author and reader know that Rabbit's momentum, his motion, is as stale as the convention he has fled. His defeat already augured in the earlier poem and story, Harry Angstrom has no borders to cross, even though he keeps on running.

Always moving uphill as if questing toward the unseen and thus the unknown, Rabbit has what Updike calls "the beauty of belief" (*Run* 366). A solitary in the midst of Middle America, Harry would not use such terms as "beauty" and "belief," but he knows that something, what he calls "it," is up there. Rabbit's intimations of religion and his pursuit of grace separate him from Ace and Flick and shift him closer to Lewis's definition of the American Adam. Yet a first reaction to Angstrom's haphazard quest is likely to be not admiration but disapproval bordering on disgust. It is not, a reader might argue, that Rabbit intends to cause pain, but that he wrecks the lives of others in a single-minded break for freedom. Updike hopes to convey both the shock and the necessity of Harry's running, for this is a novel of paradoxes. As Updike remarks, "there is a certain necessary ambiguity. I don't wish my fiction to be any clearer than life" ("Desperate Weakling" 108).

In no way can Rabbit call his own predicament clear. Willing to lose his life in the social sense in order to find his individuality, he does not know how to search. Leatherstocking can keep walking west, and Huck can take off down the river, but the highways of Harry's American culture trap him. When he denies his guilt in the burial scene, the reader's dismay at his apparent insensitivity is magnified, but Rabbit senses that the true believer in God need feel no guilt. The faithful need only "cast every care on Thee," which is exactly what Harry does. A believer who cannot define belief, Rabbit feels threatened when family and friends urge him to join their shared expression of guilt for the baby's death, their humanistic ideal that people survive by relying on each other. But Rabbit rejects their appeal to what a theologically astute character in *The Poorhouse Fair* calls "busy-ness," goodness without belief.

Updike's lost America is a nation of lost faith. Updike himself asks the key question about Rabbit in a preface to the 1977 Franklin Mint edition of *Rabbit, Run*: "Rabbit is the hero of the novel, but is he a good man? The question is meant to lead to another– What is goodness?. . .In the end, the act of running, of gathering a blank momentum 'out of a kind of sweet panic,' offers itself as containing a kernel of goodness; but perhaps a stone or a flower at rest holds the same kernel." Updike refuses to answer his question directly, but he implies that goodness is a large part of Rabbit's makeup when he calls him "fertile and fearful and not easy to catch. . .wild and timid, harmful and loving, hardhearted and open to the motions of grace" (n. p.).

Harmful and loving, Updike's hero personifies D. H. Lawrence's famous definition of "the essential American soul," the American Adam, as "hard, isolate, stoic, and a killer" (73). Rabbit's harmful, loving pursuit of grace is especially unsettling because it is a product not of the 1960s, the drop-out decade, but of the 1950s, the so-called tranquil Eisenhower years. As Updike explains in the foreword to the Modern Library edition, "*Rabbit, Run* was written in 1959, in the present tense. The time of its writing contained the time of its action" (n. P.). That is, the songs and news and styles that Harry hears and sees are those that Ace Anderson, Flick Webb and Updike hear and see in the 1950s. The present tense also allows Updike to the primary trait of his character: Harry feels but he does not think. Rabbit reacts to every stimulus as if it exists only in the present, without development from the past or reverberation toward the future. He is Lewis's literary hero, springing from nowhere into the present, affecting the culture before being defeated or destroyed by it. In this sense he is also an extreme product of the hermetic Eisenhower years. Updike comments: "My fiction about the daily doings of ordinary people has more history in it than history books" (qtd. in Samuels 106).

The broader historical context of the Rabbit tetralogy frames the traditional American conflict between the rights of the individual and the demands of society. Probing the complexity of the American experiment, Updike asks the same question that intrigued Cooper, Melville, Hawthorne, and Twain. Should the hero define himself by social convention, or should he indulge his yearning toward individual belief? Harry sees the conflict as either a nine-to-five job and dinner in the kitchen or the freedom to run but with no place to go. Updike calls this clash of values the "yes, but" quality of his fiction: "Yes, in *Rabbit, Run*, to our inner urgent whispers, but - the social fabric collapses murderously" (qtd. in Samuels 100). Although Rabbit is not intelligent enough to realize it, the unsolvable problem that Updike sets him is cultural. The reader may applaud Harry's reluctance to give in, but the reader also shrinks from the pain that his running causes. As Updike explains, "There is no reconciliation between the inner, intimate appetites and the external consolations of life. . . .[T]here is no way to reconcile these individual wants to the very real need of any society to set strict limits and to confine its members" (qtd. in Gado 92).

Rabbit's refusal to allow culture to absorb self may be either the courage not to relent to "sivilizataion"– an intuitive realization that what is right socially may be wrong personally– or it may be individualism bordering on selfishness. But the rightness or wrongness of Rabbit's run is not the issue; rather, the tetralogy urges acknowledging the complexity of the dilemma. The rabbit novels do not offer answers, but they do pose problems; and one problem, as illustrated by the epigraph to *Rabbit, Run*, is how do people find grace when the little demands of living crowd their lives? Ace, Flick, Harry– and Updike– do not know. The epigraph– a quotation from Pascal– reads, "The motions of Grace, the hardness of the heart; external circumstances." Rabbit may be many things, but his heart is not always hard. What he does have are the culturally sanctioned forms of school, family, work, and church, all of which fail him. The epigraph suggests that grace and hardness are in tension and that the relation between social obligation and internal need is determined by the external circumstances of one's life. Culture shapes personality. Social forces clash with the promise of possibilities. The demands of others deny the motions of grace. It is not that culture is malignant or that Harry is a saint, but that neither can prevent the slow disintegration of the other. Updike's negative critics want him to take a stand, to blame either social pressure or individual whim, but to do so is to ignore the ambiguity of Updike's sense of culture. If Rabbit could understand the harmony of Pascal's thought, he would stop running. Rather than wait for the grace that would reconcile both external circumstances and nonspiritual internal needs, he runs. Yet even though he runs, he is the only character to intuit the motions of grace. He cannot translate his intuition into words, but his inarticulate yearning is more valuable than the Reverend Eccles's insistence on demythologizing belief to the level of humanistic cooperation and, finally, compromise.

All Updike's Adamic hero can do is transfer his pursuit of grace to the realm of athletics, where he was once a star with motion and glide. Rabbit's forcing himself into the sandlot basketball game at the beginning of *Rabbit, Run* is Ace's dancing the jitterbug and Flick's dribbling the inner tub writ large. If, in the later volumes of the tetralogy, Rabbit plays less basketball and more golf, he still pursues "it" in the guise of a perfect tee shot. At various times he feels "pinned," trapped by a "shark," "glued-in," "manipulated," and "threatened." In each case the sensation of being crowded challenges the desire for fluid rhythm, graceful action. Significantly, when he tries to renew his stalled momentum at the end of the tetralogy, he does so on a basketball court. To return home to a family in chaos would be to embrace the external circumstances of culture. Like Huck, Harry can't stand it– he's "been there before."

Late in *Rabbit, Run*, Angstrom has what I consider the key insight into both the social dynamic of the entire tetralogy and Updike's sense of American culture as a whole. Deserting the mourners at the grave, Harry sets out on his last but undetermined run, and as he does so he glimpses the conflict between the right way of cultural expectation and the good way of individual need: "On this small fulcrum he tries to balance the rest, weighing opposites against each other: Janice and Ruth, Eccles and his mother, the right way and the good way, the way to the delicatessen– gaudy with stacked fruit lit by a naked bulb– and the other way, down Summer Street to where the city ends" (433-34). Beyond the city lies, to Updike's lament, not Leatherstocking's forest or Huck's river but concrete highways going nowhere. Yet even Leatherstocking and Huck cannot resolve the conflict between the right way and the good way in American culture. They just have more room to run.

The "yes, but" quality that Updike brings to his fiction determines the tone of the Rabbit tetralogy. One feels the urge to say "yes" to the lure of graceful motion, but to do so one must say "no" to the demands of the social contract– often at catastrophic cost. The clash between internal yearning and external circumstances could paralyze a thinking person into stasis, but Rabbit rarely thinks. Relying on feeling and instinct for life, he tries to maintain his momentum through the net. Updike's sympathy– but not his unqualified approval– goes with him.

The irony is that Rabbit is defeated even before he lights out for the territory, as "Ace in the Hole," "Ex-Basketball Player," and the high points of American fiction show. Saying good-bye to Harry Angstrom at the conclusion of *Rabbit at Rest* is like saying good-bye to Leatherstocking and Hester and Huck and Holden and Augie March. It's like saying good-bye to ourselves.

*Donald Greiner. "No Place to Run: Rabbit Angstrom as Adamic Hero." *Rabbit Tales: Poetry and Politics in John Updike's Rabbit Novels.* Lawrence R. Broer Ed. Tuscaloosa, Alabama: University of Alabama Press, 1998.(March 2000): 8-16.

from *John Updike's Rabbit Tetralogy: Mastered Irony in Motion*

Marshall Boswell*

The Rabbit who returns to Mt. Judge endowed with the faith of repetition is essentially the same complex character who prevails throughout the rest of *Rabbit Angstrom*– both a good thing and a bad thing. The various and competing strains that constitute his character have long since elicited strong responses from many readers. By the time Updike published *Rabbit at Rest*, the issue of Rabbit's likability had become something of a literary hothouse argument. On the one hand, Garry Wills used the Rabbit novels to level a direct indictment of what he construed as Updike's selfish, solipsistic middle-class values, which he assumed Updike had transmitted directly into Rabbit. The *Wall Street Journal* went so far as to call Rabbit "an almost entirely unsympathetic character." On the other hand, Louis Menand argued in *Esquire* that Rabbit's selfishness has "an attractive side. . . something about the simple act of running, its loneliness and vulnerability to chance, is eternally appealing," while Hermione Lee, in the *New Republic,* insisted that Rabbit's unsympathetic qualities are redeemed by the fact that "inside his brutish exterior, he is tender, feminine, and empathetic, like Leopold Bloom."[18] The debate even made it onto the editorial page of the *New York Times* in a piece by Brent Staples entitled, "Why So Hard on Rabbit?" This argument dates back to the novel's initial reception, during which *Time* called Rabbit a "hollow hero" and a "desperate weakling," while the *Saturday Review* argued that, despite his irresponsibility, "there is something in this man– call it 'the motions of Grace' if

---

[18] Gary Wills, "Long-Distance Runner," 11-12; Brent Staples, "Why So Hard on Rabbit?"; Hermione Lee, "The Trouble with Harry," 35. For more on the connections between Rabbit an Bloom, see the end of this section.

you choose– that demands our respect."[19]   Clearly, Rabbit is not entirely unsympathetic– as the *Wall Street Journal* would insist– and yet at the same time he stands as no public role model either. What is it about Rabbit that is so unlikable? And what qualities does he possess that redeem him?

His two main shortcomings are his selfishness and what Updike calls his "hardness of heart," a phrase he borrows from Blaise Pascal in a passage that serves as *Rabbit, Run*'s epigraph: "The motions of Grace, the hardness of heart; external circumstances."   Throughout *Rabbit, Run* his selfishness is not only well documented but also repeatedly commented upon. At one point Rev. Eccles tells him, "The truth is, you're monstrously selfish. . .you worship nothing but your own worst instincts" (134/115).His lover Ruth echoes this sentiment when she observes, "He just lived in his skin and didn't give a thought to the consequences about anything" (149/128). Janice's mother calls him "spoiled" while his own father thinks he is "the worst kind of Brewer bum" (163/141). Rabbit's hardness of heart is equally well documented. To take one example: upon returning to Janice after his abandonment, he learns from her that she had not done anything about paying the rent on their old apartment– his old responsibility. Hearing this news he tells her, "The trouble with you, kid, is you just don't give a damn" (216/186). Finally, nowhere in *Rabbit, Run*– or perhaps in all of *Rabbit Angstrom*– is this "hardness" better demonstrated than in the scene devoted to Becky's funeral, in which Rabbit turns to the gathering and, apropos of nothing, snaps, "Don't look at *me*. . .I didn't kill her" (295/253). At moments such as this, it becomes rather difficult to like Rabbit. In fact, Updike seems at times to *demand* that we not like him.

Yet many readers do like him– much like the characters within the books themselves.   Eccles, despite his reservations about Rabbit's selfishness, still declares, "Harry is in some respects a special case" (154/133). He also explains, "There's a great deal of goodness in [him].   When I'm with him– it's rather unfortunate, really– I feel so cheerful I quite forget what the point of my seeing him is" (164/141).   Rabbit repeatedly insists, "I'm lovable," and he is not often contradicted. "Oh all the *world* loves you," Ruth tells him, then adds, "What I wonder is why?" (144/124). Rabbit's answer is not nearly so glib as it might sound on the surface: "I'm a mystic," he proclaims. "I give people faith." Indeed, that *is* Rabbit's power, the source of his magnetism. His energy– what Mrs. Smith calls his "gift of life"– touches those around him in such a way that he gives people faith in their *own* specialness– a gift which, as we have seen, operates as Markle's defining trait of the Updike hero. Rabbit accomplishes this faith-giving task primarily by example– specifically, by the example of his own selfish, hard-hearted insistence upon his own specialness. "If you have the guts to be yourself," he tells Ruth at one point, "other people will pay your price" (149/129). In *Rabbit, Run*, other people do just that. As in the Pascal passage quoted above, "hardness of heart" and "the motions of grace" stand opposite one another as balanced equals. So balanced are they in Rabbit that they become intimately dependent on one another. As Updike tells Jeff Campbell: "[T]here's a way in which hardness of

---

[19] "Desperate Weakling," 108; Granville Hicks, "A Little Good in Evil," 28.

heart and the motions of grace are intertwined. I was struck as a child, and continue to be struck, by the hardness of heart that Jesus shows now and then in the New Testament, advising people to leave their families, driving the money-lenders out of the temple in quite a fierce way. And I think there seems to be an extent to which hardness of heart is tied in with being alive at all."[20]The "grace" that earned the respect of the critic from the *Saturday Review* is inextricably tied to the unsympathetic selfishness that prompted *Time* to label Rabbit a "desperate weakling." Like all things in this zigzagging novel, every "yes" has its "no," every "either" its "or." The judgments of Rabbit as a "desperate weakling" must be taken alongside the assessments of Rabbit as an appealing character of vitality and charm. To isolate one quality over the other– as numerous readers have done– is to miss an essential component of Updike's dialectical vision.[21]

The evocation of Jesus in the above passage is no accident, for Rabbit's role as mystic does make a tidy parallel with this curious reading of Christ's earthy mission. Which is not to say that Rabbit is a "Christ-figure." Rather, he operates as an ironic Christ-like "saint," just as Janice rightly surmises early in the novel. Likewise, Ruth calls him a "Christian gentleman" and Eccles calls him both "a good man" and "a mystic." When Rabbit at one point goes so far as to compare himself to Jesus, Eccles does not contradict him, pointing out instead that Christ "*did* say. . .that saints shouldn't marry" (128/110). Updike reinforces this trope via numerous incidental details, such as the episode in which Rabbit looks at a painting of Joseph and the child Jesus: "the glass this print is protected by gives back to Rabbit the shadow of his own head" (124/107). Rabbit also identifies with the Dalai Lama, who, on the evening of Rabbit's flight to West Virginia (March 20, 1959), has escaped the invading Communist Chinese: "[Rabbit] adjusts his necktie with infinite attention, as if the little lines of this juncture of the Windsor knot, the collar of Tothero's shirt, and the base of his own throat were the atoms of a star that will, when he is finished, extend outward to the rim of the universe. *He* is the Dalai Lama" (50-51/45). To be sure, Rabbit's saintliness, his godliness, is solipsistic– in the passage above he becomes, in a sense, the center of the universe– but such self-absorption is, for Updike, a necessary component of individuality. In his autobiographical memoir, "The Dogwood Tree: A Boyhood," he asserts that his own "subjective geography" is, for him, "still the center of the world."[22] We are all,

---

[20] Campbell, *Thorns Spell a Word*, 278-79.

[21] See Hunt, *Three Great Things*, 42.

[22] Updike, "The Dogwood Tree: A Boyhood." 186. In a related autobiographical passage from *Self-Consciousness*, Updike seems deliberately to invoke both this passage from "The Dogwood Tree" and Rabbit's moment of identification with the Dalai Lama: "I loved Shillington not as one loves Capri or New York, because they are special, but as one loves one's own body and consciousness, because they are synonymous with being. It was exciting for me to be in Shillington, as if my life, like the expanding universe, when projected backwards gained heat and intensity" (30). Obviously, Shillington is the most primordial site on John Updike's "subjective

in this sense, the Dalai Lama.

Solipsism and saintliness: although the two concepts seem entirely alien, Updike conflates them. He does so, in fact, with guidance from Kierkegaard. In *Fear and Trembling*– the one book, it will be recalled, that most changed Updike– Kierkegaard outlines the "paradox of faith" by which "inwardness" takes precedence over "outwardness" and subjective existence surpasses in importance the dictates of human-constructed ethics. It is this version of faith that Updike draws upon to develop his portrait of Rabbit, the saintly rake. Kierkegaard's emblematic figure for the "faith built on a paradox" is Abraham, who, in setting forth to sacrifice his son Isaac, introduced into the world the whole concept of faith. By the standards of any earthly ethical system, Kierkegaard reminds us, Abraham's proposed act of filicide is an abomination. God's intervention does not at all change this unavoidable fact, since Abraham undertook the act with no knowledge of, nor hope for, such an intervention. He went through with the act anyway, for which he earned the distinction as the Father of Faith. Herein lies the "paradox of faith" that, as Kierkegaard argues, "makes a murder into a holy and God-pleasing act, a paradox that gives Isaac back to Abraham again, which no thought can grasp, because faith begins precisely where thought stops."[23] Abraham's faith represents a "teleological suspension of the ethical" whereby "the single individual is higher than the universal"– the "universal" being Kierkegaard's term for objective man-made ethical precepts. Two "absurd" movements govern Abraham's faith: first, he agrees to commit what in human terms is the most atrocious act imaginable, all in obedience to God; second, he undertakes this act in the absurd belief– the "preposterous" belief, Kierkegaard insists– that God, for whom "all things are possible," will return Isaac to him– not in heaven, but here on earth. In other words, faith is the subjective, perhaps even solipsistic, belief in the impossible.

Updike writes of this reading of faith, "Eagerly I took from Kierkegaard the idea that subjectivity too has its rightful claims, amid all the desolating objective evidence of our insignificance and futility and final nonexistence; faith is not a deduction but an act of will, a heroism." Subjectivity is heroic, Rabbit is a saint. But Updike also takes another key component from *Fear and Trembling*, namely Kierkegaard's concept of the Knight of Faith, the ordinary man of subjectivity who, in renouncing the finite in exchange for the infinite, believes wholly in the return, here on earth, of that renounced finitude. John Neary, who also discusses at some length *Fear and Trembling*'s relation to *Rabbit, Run*, writes that Kierkegaardian faith, like the repetition with which it is associated, is "founded in the world of the ordinary: after being negated by the transcendent, the ordinary is returned by an infinitely, absurdly gracious God." Similarly, the Knight of Faith is grounded in the ordinary: he is a man who, on the outside, seems to belong wholly to the world– "no bourgeois philistine could belong to it more"– while inwardly he carries intimate

---

geography."

[23] Kierkegaard, *Fear and Trembling/Repetition*, 53.

knowledge of infinitude.[24]

As Neary points out, "Kierkegaard. . .could almost be describing Harry Angstrom here."[25] Or perhaps Updike, in developing the character of Harry Angstrom, set out to create a Knight of Faith– or at least a Knight of Faith in training. For Rabbit, too, is something of an earthy bourgeois philistine who nevertheless claims to have access to the infinite. "His feeling that there is an unseen world is instinctive," the narrator asserts, "and more of his actions than anyone suspects constitute transactions with it" (235/201).The light behind a circular rose window on the front of a church seems to him "a hole punched in reality to show the abstract brilliance burning underneath" (80/90), while the mere sight of children dressed for church strikes him as "visual proof of the unseen world" (91/99). God's existence is as obvious to Rabbit as his nonexistence is to Ruth. And on his way to play golf– that most bourgeois of all activities– he says to Rev. Eccles: "Well, I don't know all this about theology, but I'll tell you, I *do* feel, I guess, that somewhere behind all this"– he gestures outward at the scenery; they are passing the housing development this side of the golf course, half-wood half-brick one-and-a-half-stories in little flat bulldozed yards holding tricycles and spindly three-year-old trees, the un-grandest landscape in the world– "there's something that wants me to find it" (sic) (127/110). Amid the "un-glamorous" world of Mt. Judge, amid his middle-class pursuits and worldly activities, Rabbit clings to his faith that behind the visible world lies an unseen world that not only redeems all but also includes him. As Nelson sardonically observes about his father in *Rabbit Is Rich*: "such a fool he really believes there is a God he is the apple of the eye of" (325/915). It is a foolish belief, as Updike freely admits, and for that very reason also represents "an act of will, a heroism."

Such heroism would be empty and insignificant if it did not resonate beyond the cave of Rabbit's subjective experience. But resonate it does, if not so much for the novel's other characters then for the novel's readers. In belonging wholly to the world, the Knight of Faith affirms the world, if only insofar as that world has been "returned" to him through the graciousness of God. "He finds pleasure in everything," Kierkegaard writes, "takes part in everything, and every time one sees him participating in something particular, he does it with an assiduousness that marks the worldly man who is attached to such things."[26] Rabbit also performs this act of affirmation; it is, in fact, one of the chief components of his claim as a "good man." In the same way that he reminds those around him of their own specialness by the paradox of his selfish example, so, too, does Updike's careful and meticulous rendering of Rabbit's inner life remind readers of the essential specialness of all

---

[24] Updike "A Book That Changed Me," 844; John Neary, *Something and Nothingness: The Fiction of John Updike and John Fowles, 72;* Kierkegaard, *Fear and Trembling/Repetition*, 39.

[25] Neary, *Something and Nothingness*, 72.

[26] Kierkegaard, *Fear and Trembling/Repetition*, 39.

things. Despite Rabbit's active selfishness, his subjective life is remarkably self*less* and other-directed. Possessed of one of the keenest senses of wonder this side of Leopold Bloom, Rabbit absorbs the world and returns it to the reader bathed in the shimmering light of Updike's incandescent prose.

Both here and in his insistence upon despair, Updike breaks with the existentialists and remains true to his Lutheran roots. The Continental existentialists– Sartre, for example– would argue that Rabbit's "morality" must be judged according to what he does, to the ways in which he asserts his freedom in action. And of course several critics have tried to analyze Rabbit in precisely this manner, David Galloway chief among them.[27] As a Lutheran, however, Updike distrusts a morality based on "works." For him, salvation is based wholly on faith. And as a Kierkegaardian, he is less interested in concrete universals and human ethical precepts than in the absurdity of faith and the primacy of subjective experience. Philosophy does not know what to do with subjectivity because it cannot observe it, which is why Updike is not a philosopher but a novelist: in the novel subjectivity can be rendered and so observed. And it is in subjective experience that he places the highest value– the highest *moral* value, teleologically suspended above the humanly ethical. The Rabbit tetralogy is, among other things, a sustained demonstration of the supreme moral value of subjective experience.

In this respect, Updike affirms the moral philosophy set forth by Iris Murdoch in *The Sovereignty of Good*. Long an admirer of Murdoch's work, he seems to agree with her insistence that the internal, nonobservable motions of the *cogitatio* constitute genuine moral action. He would also agree with her accompanying maxim, "Where virtue is concerned we often apprehend more than we clearly understand and *grow by looking*." Her treatise argues against the idea that morality must be action and that salvation is dependent upon works. Instead, she insists on the ethical sovereignty of subjective experience, on the moral significance of mental concepts, even those concepts that have no external, public correspondence. A decision made but not acted upon, for instance, still carries for Murdoch moral weight. These thoughts, these decisions, are functions of vision, of one's perception of the world, and the moral criterion evoked by these perceptions is precisely this: does one try to view the world "justly and lovingly"? Borrowing the term from Simone Weil, Murdoch places enormous value on "attention," which she uses "to express the idea of a just and loving gaze upon individual reality." This gaze, she believes, stands as the "characteristic and proper mark of the active moral agent." Seeing the world "as it is," and seeing it benevolently, becomes the task of that agent. Before "accurate vision" can be obtained, however, there must be a suppression of self, a freedom from self, or– what for Murdoch is the same thing– a "freedom from fantasy." Fantasy becomes in her system "the proliferation of blinding self-centered aims and images," while "reality" becomes the external world

---

[27] See David Galloway, *The Absurd Hero in American Fiction*, 30-40.

viewed with compassion and a selfless attention to individuality.[28]

Though Rabbit is "self-centered," his gaze is not. The moment he tears up that map and surrenders, he is, in a sense, released from the bindings of self-centered aims, from fantasy, paradoxically because he has embraced the most absurd fantasy of all. Speaking of his own spiritual crisis– which, by his own account, corresponds chronologically to the composition of *Rabbit, Run*– Updike asserts, "After one has conquered this sort of existential terror. . . then one is able to open to the world again."[29]His hero Karl Barth, for instance, was "very open to the world. Wonderfully alive and relaxed." This seeming contradiction between subjectivity and external openness has confused many of Updike's more strident critics, particularly critics of his prose style. Often described as "self-indulgent," the style is in fact anything but. From *Self-Consciousness*: "My own style seemed to me a groping and elemental attempt to approximate the complexity of envisioned phenomena. . .self-indulgent, surely, is exactly what it wasn't– *other*-indulgent, rather." Self-consciousness, moreover, is really, in the hands of a writer, "a mode of interestedness, that inevitably turns outward." By turning outward and honoring the "complexity" of phenomena, Updike insists he is performing a moral, even holy, duty– that of giving praise. This task he designates, in a brief answer to the question "Why Are We Here?" as, more or less, The Meaning of Life: "We are here to give praise. Or, to slightly tip the expression, to pay attention." Meanwhile, in the *Rabbit Angstrom* introduction, he declares, "A non-judgmental immersion was my aesthetic and moral aim. . . .The religious faith that a useful truth will be imprinted by a perfect artistic submission underlies these Rabbit novels" (xiii). Attention expresses gratitude, curiosity about the world is an act of worship, and the writing life constitutes a genuine contribution to this moral endeavor. In a passage that combines subjective faith and Murdoch's "just and loving" gaze, Updike describes his artistic credo: "Imitation is praise. Description expresses love. I early arrived at these self-justifying inklings. Having accepted that old Shillington blessing, I have felt free to describe life as accurately as I could, with especial attention to human erosions and betrayals. What small faith I have has given me what artistic courage I have. My theory was that God already knows everything and cannot be shocked. And only truth is useful. Only truth can be built upon. From a higher, inhuman point of view, only truth, however harsh, is holy."In sum, religious faith, though subjective, is for Updike also contingent upon the outside

---

[28] Iris Murdoch in *The Sovereignty of Good*, 31, 34, 66-67. Updike has written extensively on Murdoch. See the extended sections devoted to her work in *Hugging the Shore* (345-55) and *Odd Jobs* (411-41).

[29] See *Self-Consciousness*, 97-98. "In my memory," he begins, "there is a grayness to that period of my life in Ipswich." In this account, "grayness" represents a nihilistic obliteration of all distinctions between good and evil, life and death. Not accidentally, this period of "grayness" began for Updike on a basketball court: "I was playing basketball. . .and I looked up at the naked, netless hoop: gray sky outside it, gray sky inside it" (97). From this moment of insight emerged *Rabbit, Run*, Updike's dialectical response to that grayness.

world, the material world. Things at rest, he has often asserted, radiate a "quiet but tireless goodness," for (as he affirms in "Midpoint") "the beaded curtain/ of Matter hid an understanding Eye."[30] Subjective faith and selfless outward attention: another inextricable either/or.

"There's a touch of the old artist about old Bloom," remarks Lenehan, a minor character in James Joyce's *Ulysses*, an assessment that applies equally to Bloom's postwar American counterpart, Harry "Rabbit" Angstrom. Quite a large portion of *Rabbit, Run*– and of *Rabbit Angstrom*– takes place inside Rabbit's head in the form of lingering, Joycean internal monologues. And like Joyce, Updike values the internal monologue for its affirmation of subjectivity. Yet this vast exploration of the workings of Rabbit's internal life also demonstrates how rich and just can be the interaction between the interior psyche and external world. Because Rabbit seems to be interested in everything, his perceptions animate all that he sees. His conviction that an "understanding Eye lurks" behind all phenomena further gives everything and everyone he encounters a redemptive sheen.

A few choice examples illustrate this point. While gardening for Mr. (sic) Smith, Rabbit observes of the seeds he plants, "Sealed, they cease to be his. The simplicity. Getting rid of something by giving it to itself. God Himself folded into the tiny adamant structure, Self-destined to a succession of explosions, the great slow gathering out of water and air and silicon: this is felt without words in the turn of the round hoe-handle in his palms" (136/117). Rabbit must feel rather than articulate these lyrical observations, cast as they are in Updike's most self-consciously poetic diction, yet feel them he does, in accordance with Murdoch's conviction that "where virtue is concerned we often apprehend more than we clearly understand."[31] Note how Rabbit takes solace in "giving" the plants to themselves, in his sense of their own individual complexity and self-justified importance.

His first vision of his baby daughter, Becky, elicits similar observations: "The folds around the nostril, worked out on such small scale, seem miraculously precise; the tiny stichless seam of the closed eyelid runs diagonally a great length, as if the eye, when it is opened, will be huge and see everything. In the suggestion of pressure behind the tranquil lid and in the tilt of the protruding upper lip he reads a delightful hint of disdain. She knows she's good" (218/187). Like the previous passage– though without the urge for parable– this description carries beneath it an insistent spiritual throb. By taking in with such attention these visual details, Rabbit discloses the "miracle" of all phenomena and its uncanny sense of being "worked out" by some Transcendent Craftsman. In the process, he is able to "read" the message ("She knows she's good") left behind by that Craftsman, in the same way that David Kern, the spiritually anguished young protagonist of Updike's short story "Pigeon Feathers," "reads" in the intricate detail of a dead pigeon's wings God's infinite concern for all things.

---

[30] Campbell, *Thorns Spell a Word*, 302; Updike, *Self-Consciousness*, 103, 24, 231; Updike, *Odd Jobs*, 864; Updike, "Midpoint," I., 47-48.

[31] Murdoch, *Sovereignty of Good*, 31.

Yet inasmuch as such an approach to perception enlivens Rabbit's dealings with the world and physical phenomena, it does not cloud that approach. If the "truth" is holy for Updike, and if faith gives one the courage to tell the truth, then hardness of heart– inexorably linked with "the motions of Grace"– must also accompany one's comportment through the world. Rabbit best demonstrates both qualities– that is, hardness and Grace– in his observations of people. With regard to the elderly Mrs. Smith, he takes in not only the "tiny brown sockets afflicted by creases like so many drawstrings" that surround her eyes, but also the "cracked blue eyes" themselves which "bulge frantically with captive life." Ruth he also appraises with an unsentimental, fascinated gaze. A large woman– "Chunky, more"– Ruth wobbles a bit in her shoes, a detail Rabbit acknowledges and, in the same breath, redeems by his outwardly directed attention: "Rabbit sees from behind that her heels, yellow with strain, tend to slip sideways in the net of lavender straps that pin her feet to the spikes of her shoes. But under the shiny green stretch of her dress her broad bottom packs the cloth with a certain composure" (56/50). Of Rev. Eccles, Rabbit observes immediately that "there is something friendly and silly about him" (102/88). On the one hand, Eccles has a charming, seductive quality– "this knack," Rabbit calls it– while on the other hand the minister is petty, quick to anger: "Eccles really does have a mean streak. . . .Without the collar around his throat, he kind of lets go" (129/111). Still, Rabbit remains open to Eccles, open to Ruth, open to everyone. Everybody is wild about Harry, and Harry is wild about everyone.

Although the numerous features of Rabbit's character laid out in this section remain consistent throughout the rest of *Rabbit Angstrom*, perhaps no feature takes greater precedence than Rabbit's open, observant response to the world around him. As the completed work rolls on, Harry's role as Updike's Bloomian eye becomes more pronounced, its moral significance increasingly more profound. That Updike had Bloom in mind while writing *Rabbit, Run* seems clear and uncontested enough. Updike says as much in his new Introduction to *Rabbit Angstrom*, wherein he admits that the Joycean influence resounds "perhaps all too audibly," particularly in the novel's "female soliloquies." There are other connections as well. Conceived as a novella, *Rabbit, Run* was originally to be paired with what turned out to be Updike's third and most clearly Joycean novel, *The Centaur*: one novella would borrow the internal monologue device and the other Joyce's "mythic method." Joyce's epiphanic technique from *Dubliners* is clearly invoked in *Pigeon Feathers*– for example, "A & P," the title story, the brief episode "You'll Never Know, Dear, How Much I Love You," which overtly rewrites "Araby"– stories written and published contemporaneously with *Rabbit, Run*. Rev. Eccles has a daughter named Joyce, while Leopold Bloom lives at 7 *Eccles* Street. And so on. As a result of these affinities, many, if not most, of the things said about Joyce's Bloom apply equally to Updike's Angstrom. Craig Raines, in his introduction to the Everyman's edition of *Ulysses*, makes precisely this same Bloom-Rabbit connection. He calls Updike's creation a "fictional character conceived by an admirer of Joyce's average sensual man," yet adds (as praise, I should think), that Rabbit is, "if anything, even more basic a challenge to the novelist's redemptive imagination."[32] Updike's imagination *is* redemptive, and in Rabbit, he meets the extraordinary challenge he set himself at the age of twenty-seven– if not entirely here in *Rabbit, Run*, then surely in *Rabbit Angstrom* as a whole.

*Boswell, Marshall. *John Updike's Rabbit Tetralogy: Mastered Irony in Motion.* Columbia, Missouri: The University of Missouri Press, 2001. 41-53.

---

[32] Craig Raines, "Introduction," xxi.

Rabbit Redux

"Henry Bech Redux"

Henry Bech [John Updike]*

The [New York Times, ed.] Book Review has been fortunate enough to persuade Henry Bech, the hero of John Updike's last book, to interview Mr. Updike on the subject of his newest work, Rabbit Redux. Mr. Bech reports:

Updike's office is concealed in a kind of false-bottomed drawer in the heart of downtown Ipswich (Mass.), but the drowsy locals, for a mere 30 pieces of silver, can be conned into betraying its location. A stuck-looking door is pulled open; an endless flight of stairs, lit by a team of dusty fireflies, is climbed. Within the sanctum, squalor reigns unchallenged. A lugubrious army-green metal desk rests in the center of a threadbare Oriental rug reticulate with mouse-paths; the walls are camouflaged in the kind of cardboard walnut paneling used in newly graduated lawyers' offices or in those Los Angeles motels favored by the hand-held cameramen and quick-tongued *directeurs* of blue movies. On these sad walls hang pictures, mostly souvenirs of his childhood, artistic or otherwise. On the bookshelves, evidently stained by a leopard in the process of shedding his spots, rest repellent books– garish schoolboy anthologies secreting some decaying Updikean morsel, seven feet of James Buchanan's bound works adumbrating the next novel, some daffodil-yellow building-trade manual penumbrating *Couples*; and, most repellent of all, a jacketless row of the total *oeuvre*, spines naked as the chorus of *Hair*, revealing what only the most morbid have hitherto suspected, that since 1959 (*The Poorhouse Fair*, surely his masterpiece) Updike with Alfred A. Knopf's connivance has been perpetuating a uniform edition of himself. Beclouding all, the stink of nickel cigarillos, which the shifty, tremulous, asthmatic author puffs to sting the muse's eyes into watering ever since at the Surgeon-General's behest, he excised cigarettes from his armory of crutches.

Updike, at first sight, seems bigger than he is, perhaps because the dainty stichwork of his prose style readies one for an apparition of elfin dimensions. An instant layer of cordial humorousness veneers a tough thickness of total opacity, which may in turn coat a center of heartfelt semi-liquid. Shamefacedly I confessed my errand– to fabricate an "interview" for one of those desperate publications that seek to make weekly "news" of remorselessly accumulating Gutenbergian silt. Shamefacedly, Updike submitted. Yet, throughout the interview that limped in the van of this consent, as the pumpkin-orange New England sun lowered above the chimney pots of a dry-cleaning establishment seen darkly through an unwashed window, Updike gave the impression of (and who wouldn't?) wanting to be elsewhere. He kept interjecting his desire to go "home" and "shingle" his "barn"; it occurred to this interviewer (the Interviewer, as Mailer would say), that the uniform books, varied in tint and size as subtly as cedar shakes, were themselves shingles, with the which this shivering poor fellow hopes to keep his own skin dry in the soaking downpour of mortality.

I observed, feinting for an opening, that he has stopped writing about Jews. He replied that the book about me had not so much been about a Jew as about a writer, who was a Jew with the same inevitability that a fictional rug-salesman would be an Armenian. I riposted that *he* was a writer, though a Wasp. With the languid shrug of the chronically pained, he bitterly inveighed against the term Wasp, which implies, he said, wealth where he had been poor, Calvinism where he had been Lutheran, and ethnic consciousness where he had had none. That his entire professional life had been spent among Jews and women, that his paternal grandmother had been partly Irish, that he had disliked James Gould Cozzens's last novel, that false loyalties were the plague of a divided Republic, that racism as an esthetic category was one thing but as an incitement to massacre another, etc.

With the chinks in his armor gaping before me like marigolds at the height of noon, I lunged deftly as a hummingbird. Didn't I detect, I asked, in his later work, an almost blunt determination to, as it were, sing America? Would he describe himself, I asked, switching the tape recorder up to fortissimo, as (a) pro-American (b) a conservative? His turtleish green eyes blinked, recognizing that his shell was being tickled, and that there was no way out but forward. He said he was pro-American in the sense that he was married to America and did not wish a divorce. That the American style, and landscape was, by predetermination, his meat; though he had also keenly felt love of fatherland in England, in Russia, in Egypt. That nations were like people, lovable and wonderful in their simple existence. That, in answer to the second prong of my probe, there *were* some things he thought worth conserving, such as the electoral college and the Great Lakes; but that by registration he was a Democrat and by disposition an apologist for the spirit of anarchy– our animal or divine margin of resistance to the social contract. That, given the need for a contract, he preferred the American Constitution, with its eighteenth-century bow to the pursuit of individual happiness, to any of the totalisms presently running around rabid. That the decisions of any establishment, though properly suspect and frightfully hedged by self-interest and the myopia power brings, must be understood as choices among imperfect alternatives; power participates in the weight and guilt of the world and shrill impotence never has to cash in its chips.

I inkled that this diatribe was meant to lead up to some discussion of his new novel, with its jacket of red, gray and blue stripes, but having neglected to read more than the first pages, which concern a middle-aged ex-athlete enjoying a beer with his elderly father, I was compelled to cast my interrogation in rather general terms. Viz.:

Q.: Are you happy?

A.: Yes, this is a happy limbo for me, this time. I haven't got the first finished copies yet, and haven't spotted the first typo. I haven't had to read any reviews.

Q.: How do you find reviews?

A.: Humiliating. It isn't merely that the reviewers are so much cleverer than I, and could write such superior fictions if they deigned to; it's that even the on-cheering ones have read a different book than the one you wrote. All the little congruences and arabesques you prepared with such delicate anticipatory pleasure are gobbled up as if by pigs at a pastry cart. Still, the ideal reader must— by the ontological argument— exist, and his invisibility therefore be a demonic illusion sustained to tempt us to despair.

Q.: Do you envision novels as pills, broadcasts, tapestries, explosions of self, cantilevered constructs, or what?

A.: For me, they are crystallizations of visceral hopefulness extruded as a slow paste which in the glitter of print regains something of the original, absolute gaiety. I try to do my best and then walk away rapidly, so as not to be incriminated. Right now, I am going over old short stories, arranging them in little wreaths, trimming away a strikingly infelicitous sentence here, adding a paper ribbon there. Describing it like this makes me sound more Nabokovian than I feel. Chiefly, I feel fatigued by my previous vitality.

Q.: I'd like to talk about the new book, but the truth is I can't hold bound galley pages, my thumbs keep going to sleep, so I didn't get too far into this, what? *Rabbit Rerun.*

A.: (*eagerly, pluggingly*): *Redux.* Latin for led back. You know Latin: *Apologia Pro Vita Sua.* The next installment, 10 years from now, I expect to call *Rural Rabbit*– you'll notice at the end of this book Janice talks about them getting a farm. The fourth and last, to come out in 1991 if we all live, is tentatively titled *Rabbit Is Rich.* Nice, huh?

Q. (*turning tape recorder down to pianissimo*): Not bad. *Pas mal.* Not bad.

A. (*gratefully, his shingling hand itching*): Thanks. Thanks a lot.

*Henry Bech [John Updike], "Henry Bech Redux," *The New York Times Book Review* 14 Nov. 1971: 3.

"Rabbit Returns: Updike Was Always There– It's Time We Noticed"

Richard Locke*

In 1939 Thomas Mann sent his brother a fan letter. Heinrich's new novel, he wrote, "is great in love, in art, boldness, freedom, wisdom, kindness, exceedingly rich in intelligence, wit, imagination and feeling– a great and beautiful thing, synthesis and resume of your life and your personality." Though fulsome and obviously written in the first flush of enthusiasm for Heinrich's now all but forgotten book, these are the hyperboles that come to mind after reading John Updike's new novel, *Rabbit Redux*. "It must be said," Mann continues, "that such growth– such transformation of the static to the dynamic, such perseverance, and such a harvesting– is peculiarly European. Here in America the writers are short-lived; they write one good book, follow it with two poor ones, and then are finished."

There's truth as well as well-earned snobbery in this observation. American writers do tend to flash and then fizzle. The casualties in our postwar fiction are legion: writers as different as J. D. Salinger and Joseph Heller immediately spring to mind. John Updike knows this well: in an essay on Nabokov he argued that this Russian emigré was the only writer practicing in America "whose books, considered as a whole, give the happy impression of an *oeuvre*, of a continuous task carried forward variously, of a solid personality, of a plentitude of gifts explored knowingly. His works are an edifice whose every corner rewards inspection. Each book . . .yields delight and presents to the aesthetic sense the peculiar hardness of a finished, fully meant thing."

But, keeping this high professional standard in mind, are there any contemporary American writers who are steadily producing distinguished work, not one or two but say a minimum of four full-length books? Who are the novelists who have tried to keep a grip on our experience as we've wobbled along in the past decade or two, the writers to whom we turn to find out something of where we are and what we're feeling, the writers who give the secular news report? I'd suggest that there are five: Saul Bellow, Norman Mailer, Bernard Malamud, Philip Roth– and John Updike himself.

There are, to be sure, many other gifted authors at work, but these five (and possibly Joyce Carol Oates) are wrestling most fiercely with "the novel as history/history as the novel." Barth, Vonnegut, Barthelme, Hawkes are up to something else. In the past two years, Bellow, Mailer, Malamud and Roth have written books that cluster like angry hornets around a few big news items, chiefly the moon shot and racial turmoil. Now, in a surprising return to the hero of his most unequivocally successful novel, *Rabbit, Run*, John Updike plunges Harry "Rabbit" Angstrom, ten years older, into the late 1960's where he tries to cope with sex, fatherhood, marriage, drugs, Vietnam, blacks, the moon shot. And *Rabbit Redux* is the best book of the lot.

Of course to praise Updike on these terms, to place him in the company of the other four, is either an outrage or a truism, depending on who's listening. He began as the darling of the *New Yorker* in the mid 1950's and by the age of 30, in 1962, had published two novels, two collections of short stories, a children's book and a book of light verse. He seemed to have made it as nearly everybody's favorite best young American writer, from Granville Hicks in the *Saturday Review* to Mary McCarthy in Paris, to Stanley Edgar Hyman in *The New Leader*. Yet even then there were qualms. Melvin Maddocks sounded a first graceful note in what became a symphony of critical opprobrium in a few years: "Infinite care is bestowed on infinitely small passions. When the time comes to touch the essential, the writer's grip slips, almost from embarrassment, into rhetoric, and feelings become esthetic sensations."

When Updike's third novel *The Centaur* appeared in 1963, *Commentary*'s editor, Norman Podhoretz, laced into him: Updike, he wrote, is callow, sentimental, cruel, adolescent and fashionably audacious in his treatment of sex, given to self-conscious efforts at verbal brilliance and fake profundity to cover up his lack of substance– "a writer who has very little to say and whose authentic emotional range is so narrow and thin that it may without too much exaggeration be characterized as limited to a rather timid nostalgia for the confusions of youth." When the novel won the 1964 National Book Award it was the kiss of death. Updike's books might be popular, but serious people didn't really have to read them.

In 1965 his short novel *Of the Farm* was almost universally misunderstood and dismissed as trivial. And then in 1968 came *Couples*: a huge best seller, but a critical disaster. It was Alfred Kazin who sealed the coffin: "Among American novelists," he wrote, "John Updike is the college intellectual with genius....I mean someone who can brilliantly describe the adult world without conveying its depths and risks, someone wholly literary, dazzlingly bright, the quickest of quick children, someone ready to understand everything and to describe anything, for nothing that can be put in words is alien to him. But when he describes situations that in life do bring terror to the human heart, his facility reminds one of many other college intellectuals brought up on Criticism, Psychoanalysis, the Death of God. Words become all, and what the words show most is the *will* to be as effective as one is gifted."

Nevertheless, when Updike brought out a collection of stories in 1970 about the imaginary Jewish writer Henry Bech, the critics loved it. Though many had reviled him for trivia, they lapped it up when the literary world they knew and loved became the focus of such elegant satirical attentions. *Bech* (sic) was proclaimed Updike's best book. But almost everybody knew the serious case against him was closed. He was precious, facile, pretentious. When he wrote about rural family life he was too small, they said, except when he dragged in all the high-faluting mythological nonsense in *The Centaur*– which was too big. When he wrote about suburban sexual behavior he was merely sociological and much too long-winded. Only in *Bech* (sic) did he keep his place as a country cousin with a charming eye. But he had nothing to say. Just a boyish cry of "Look ma, no hands" in the prose.

Or so they said. There remains at the very least one large, stubborn fact: in the 15 years since Updike began to write professionally he has published an astonishing range and volume of work that cannot be airily dismissed as the mindless gush of the steady best seller "pro" nor the dreary stream of a genteel "quality author." There are three collections of verse, a large anthology of parodies, essays and reviews, four children's books, four collections of short stories and six novels. This may not in Updike's mind or ours constitute a Nabokovian *oeuvre*, but when one sits down and begins to read through these books the variety and professional effort command respect and critical scrutiny. The publication of *Rabbit Redux* necessitates revaluation of his work.

Updike's three collections of verse– *The Carpentered Hen* (1958), *Telephone Poles* (1963) and *Midpoint* (1969)– have genuine charm and offer the simple delights of wit. Such wit depends, of course, on shared assumptions and social values; the poems are very much on the Harvard *Lampoon-New Yorker* bias and tend to whimsy and worldly word play with a Rolls (sic) Royce ad, a clothes line, cocoa cooling in the cup, a Bendix washing machine. There are more serious poems, including the *apologia pro vita sua* "Midpoint"– which has much thought and confessional emotion obscured behind a picket fence of formal tricks– but on the whole the verse is small, clever, old-fashioned in its classy gleam, no more than it pretends to be. Yet a good light laugh is not to be taken for granted these days.

The anthology of *Assorted Prose* from the *New Yorker*, which appeared in 1965, is more substantial. It opens with a batch of parodies and "Talk of the Town" sketches. Of these Updike once said in an interview "it was playful work that opened the city to me. I was the man who went to boating or electronic exhibits in the Coliseum and tried to make impressionist poems of the objects and overheard conversations." (They might be read as Updike's *Sketches by Boz*.) Then come editorial "Notes and Comments" on subjects of the day and the famous essay on Ted Williams's last baseball game, "Hub Fans Bid Kid Adieu." As sports writing only Mailer's accounts of Patterson and Liston equal it. It's significant that Updike admires most of all Williams's professional discipline and energy; his batting prowess (like Nabokov's literary skill) is a model that Updike at 28 clearly wanted to imitate in his own career. The autobiographical pieces that follow lack bite, as Updike acknowledges in his foreword.

But the most impressive section of *Assorted Prose* is the last, the 17 reviews and literary essays. As a reviewer Updike's great intelligence and technical skill are immediately in evidence. His interests are wide (Beerbohm, Karl Barth, Muriel Spark, Denis de Rougemont), his prose is clear and straight, and his powers of organization and explication are formidable. In recent years he has discussed in the *New Yorker* such writers as Drieu La Rochelle and Alfred Jarry, Kierkegaard, Joyce, Günter Grass, Knut Hamsun, Raymond Queneau. There is an immensely attractive, nonacademic attentiveness to his reviews. At his best he goes right to the human center, the heart of a writer expressed in his art: Borges's cold bibliophilic stoicism, Nabokov's lepodopterist urge to kill and fix the objects of his love. Yet even in his enthusiasms Updike is judicious. He doesn't roll literary logs. He doesn't preen and hasn't a speck of competitive spite. Of American novelists only Mailer, again, though competition incarnate, is his match as a critic. (See Mailer's essays on Henry Miller and D. H. Lawrence buried in *The Prisoner of Sex*.)

As a short story writer, though, Updike often gives the impression of a man who is warming himself up for a longer race. Too many stories feel like expensive limousines idling. The focus shifts away from individual stories, scenes and characters and back to the writer and his verbal skill. He has published four collections: *The Same Door* (1959), *Pigeon Feathers* (1962), *The Music School* (1966) and *Bech: A Book* (1970). The autobiographical *Olinger Stories*– a group of nostalgic epiphanies about growing up in rural Pennsylvania in the 1940's– were plucked from the first two collections and published as a Vintage paperback in 1964. In the preface to this anthology Updike writes that he wanted to capture moments when the "muddle and inconsequent surface of things now and then parts to yield us a gift." Divine grace, he implies, is experienced as a moment of heightened perception and feeling. In the attempt to convey this belief, the stories in their modesty and vulnerability take on a certain hothouse blush. When you're reading them you go along willingly, but when you look back they tend to melt together in a reverent hush of lyrical lissom linguistic curlicues. It is this that so excites the ire of Updike's critics.

But when Updike writes about Bech, the wit cuts both the Olinger pathos and the too easy flow of the more diversified and Cheever-esque *New Yorker* stories. In "Bech Takes Pot Luck," "Bech Panics," "Bech Swings?" and "The Bulgarian Poetess," the prose is light and free and "the silken mechanism whereby America reduces her writers to imbecility (sic) and cozenage" descends o'er poor, caricatured but lovable Bech.

Updike's six novels are of much greater critical interest than his short stories. They fall into three groups: *The Poorhouse Fair*, his first novel, and *Couples*, his fifth– both *romans à thèse*, which work least well; *The Centaur*, his third novel, and *Of the Farm*, his fourth– both novels about Updike's family that draw in unexpected and highly different ways on the same material as the *Olinger Stories*; finally, and most successfully, the two novels about Harry "Rabbit" Angstrom– *Rabbit* (sic) *Run*, Updike's second novel, and its sequel, *Rabbit Redux*, his sixth, which has just been published.

The two thesis novels– *The Poorhouse Fair* (1959) and *Couples* (1968)– were written to make a specific point about society, God and Man. A religious argument hovers in the background and Updike focuses on a group of people as they interact, not on individuals. Above the human comings and goings looms the God of Calvin and Karl Barth, absolutely transcendent, inhuman, "wholly Other," brooding over His Creation, turning the seasons, unexpectedly granting tiny rewards, illuminations, grace. Thus it is the landscape, the changes in weather, the surface of material things, the collective fantasies and feelings of a community that are the chief objects of Updike's attention. His complex metaphors strive to link these elements together. His goal is to achieve a deliberate, generalizing impersonality and distance. But this is what makes *The Poorhouse Fair* so claustral and cautious and makes *Couples* so endlessly detailed and confusing in its characters and affairs.

The Poorhouse Fair is a miniature ballet of crossing and crisscrossing characters, voices, points of view, overlapping feelings and events. Slowly, quietly, the thesis emerges. In a bland totalitarian future America, a group of indigent old people wander around the grounds of a state poorhouse where they're confined and prepare their yearly handicrafts fair for the delectation of the neighboring bourgeoisie. Out of the delicate suite of voices there arises a debate between a 94-year-old religious, patriotic relic of the age of individuality and the "prefect" of the poorhouse, whose ideal of a paradise achieved through secular social reform Updike clearly opposes. The religious backdrop gives the prose a consistently heightened air. One is left with the impression of an infinitely patient intelligence deliberately at work on every filigree that composes this microcosm. I find it claustrophobic. Like some of the stories it does indeed deserve the label "precious."

Yet if *The Poorhouse Fair* is too tight, its cousin *Couples* sprawls. In it Updike delineates the heresies of the "post-Pill paradise" of suburban Massachusetts engineers, brokers, dentists, contractors and their wives, who engage in ritual games of weekend sports, parties and adultery in order to "break back into hedonism" and figuratively form a church, a "magic circle of heads to keep out the night." Updike drowns the reader in detail, blending the characters and their feelings to achieve a generalized effect. But he buries the religious thesis and its intricate symbolic details so deeply that it detaches itself from the realistic surface of the novel and feels willful whenever it's alluded to.

The novel is insufficiently dramatized. Wilfrid Sheed has argued that this slackness is a necessary result of Updike's decision not to play the novel as another suburban sexual tragedy. But there is within the Christian novel another book, a tragedy of a modern Tristan and Iseult. No matter how carefully Updike gets inside this tortuous love affair, he is always reversing gears– because of his over-riding thesis– pulling back to the more impersonal Christian novel about the suburban heretics. He's caught between the secular and the divine, the narrative and visionary, the realistic and symbolic. To keep the narrative of the central love affair going he resorts to awkward melodrama, an abortion, a quid pro quo wife swap, and obligatory confrontation scenes. To stop the reader from simply drifting along through the story he keeps it slow and swells the language and the background details. He continually withdraws from individual psychology and motivation into long shots of the group as a whole, or zooms in so far that individual erotic fantasies are done as revelations of eternal grace, and the language strains.

However, the sociological details of suburban professions and possessions– which were too lightly dismissed by reviewers– are excellent; accurate social observation, even when it's too much of a muchness as it is in this case, cannot be taken for granted. The infamous prose style is not so florid as critics made it out to be; while reading the book you float along quite easily and only start to sink in the lush sexual descriptions where the language is striving for visionary metaphors ("drenched feathers pulled his tip"). Though *Couples* is reputed a dirty novel, it's not voyeuristic; almost all the eroticism is portrayed from inside a character's mind, not outside his body peeping in. Of postwar American novelists only Mailer, again, attempts to write this seriously about sexual feelings. And Mailer in his aggressiveness is far removed from Updike's masculine tenderness.

In short, Wilfrid Sheed's explications of the structure and the symbols and everybody else's outrage are both correct: the book was intended to be much as it is, but as Bech described his own long novel, *Couples* is a "noble failure." It blurs and then fades rapidly from the mind.

Unlike the thesis novels, Updike's two family novels– *The Centaur* (1963) and *Of the Farm* (1965), the first about his father, the second about a mother figure– are enormously readable and unexpectedly varied.

Although *The Centaur* is now commonly regarded as a pretentious mythic allegory piled on top of a tiny boyhood recollection, it is in fact intensely realistic in its rendering of small town Pennsylvania high school days and is filled with energetic narrative and vivid characterization. It is not by any means all written in mythic elevation. There are no less than four modes: one, a third person realistic narrative of three days in the life of George Cauldwell (sic), a high school teacher. Two, his son's first person realistic memoir of these same three days told within a small (but intrusive and unconvincing) framework in the present. Three, the notoriously florid mythological style in which the centaur talks with "milady Venus" or finds himself in a bosky glen; although this tone is intended to serve as an ironic counterpoint to the dominant realism, there is, unfortunately, a patch of it in the first 20 pages of the book which may well have put readers off (in all there aren't more than 10 pages in this style in the entire 300-page book). And four: a brilliant double focus mode, a rapid surrealistic simultaneity of myth and realism that achieves a genuinely Joycean brio. This last is most fully achieved in the book's first chapter which culminates in a breath-taking rapid-fire class room (sic) lecture on the history of the universe. Stanley Edgar Hyman wrote of this chapter, "I can think of nothing in fiction to surpass it since the Nighttown scene in *Ulysses*." This praise is too high but the impulse is right. Nothing in the critical clichés about *The Centaur* could lead one to imagine such an enjoyable comic tour de force of an opening.

But the great triumph of the book is not Updike's technical élan. It is the portrait of the father– the centaur himself– one of the best portraits of Depression man, or the Middle American, in post-war American fiction. Dramatic, self-pitying, generous, fearful, "obsequious and absurd, careless and stubborn," plugging away at a killing job with a violent energy that continually exasperates and embarrasses his loving son, George Cauldwell (sic) is a rural, Irish-German Protestant Herzog. His voice, once heard, is never forgotten.

As for the offending myths, when they spontaneously appear as dim presences at the edge of a realistic character or setting, they do indeed evoke the breathless quality of adolescent emotions and nostalgia. At its worst, the book has a small town Thornton Wilder   wistfulness, but this is rare. The minor mythic correspondences listed in the embarrassing index at the end are arbitrary and easily ignored. But the central metaphor works well: George Cauldwell (sic) is a wounded workhorse giving up his life for the welfare of his son by sticking at a draining job (he does not, as some have thought from the unfortunately lush last pages, commit suicide). But the son, it must be admitted, never convinces on the mythic level. He is not a budding artist, a fire giver, a Prometheus; he is a sensitive, loving 15-year-old, no more. But no less either: there is little of the sugary Olinger mist in *The Centaur*. Rather than exemplifying pretentious self-indulgence, *The Centaur*, read now after the bloom and de cay of black humor and pop absurdity, is a genuine, if much smaller, American son of the my theological novels of Joyce and Mann. It's not offensive in the least; it's an enjoyable and moving book.

Updike's other family novel, *Of the Farm*, is quite short (less than 200 pages) and when it appeared in 1965 reviewers seemed to feel it wasn't "about anything." A 35-year-old New York advertising man and his second wife and her son visit the farm of the hero's mother, recently widowed. In the course of the weekend, the son mows the field, buys some groceries, goes to church, watches over his mother's "spell" of angina and then drives back to New York. But within this tiny frame Updike has written a novel that in its careful description of the agonized incestuous combat between the four characters is a perfect rural Protestant complement to *Portnoy's Complaint*.

Instead of comedy and psychoanalytic hyperbole, Updike chose a chaste Chekovian realism. He dramatizes the crippling exclusive love of mother and son. The most frightening betrayals and sexual drifts are conveyed almost entirely through the dialogue. "I'm surprised at you," says mother to son, "that you would need a stupid woman to give you confidence. . . I look at my son and see a man his father wouldn't recognize. . . Don't mind me, Joey. I'm just a crazy old woman who's gone too long without talking to anybody except her dogs. I thought I could talk to my son but apparently I've presumed." Unscrupulously the mother plays on her illness and approaching death and uses her son's love of his absent children and his first wife to poison his second marriage. After two days at home, the mother has her son at a point where she can ask him outright if he doesn't feel he's made a mistake in remarrying at all, and with subtle sexual appeal and a flattering allusion to their shared superiority, she wraps him in her net. The parallel jealousy of the hero for his new wife's former husband is brilliantly worked out; the more he comes under his mother's sway, the more preoccupied he becomes with his new wife's previous sexual life. The verbal battles between the women are shocking.

In *Of the Farm* Updike writes with a precision that is totally at odds with the received opinion of his style. The book is small the way Flannery O'Connor is small. It is one of the finer American psychological novels, despite its limited scale.

Updike's "Rabbit" novels– *Rabbit, Run* (1960) and its sequel *Rabbit Redux* (just published)-- are his best books. The thesis novels failed because his will and intelligence took the place of emotional force. The autobiographical family novels were full of emotional force yet in the effort to keep it under esthetic control *The Centaur* sometimes became a shade too big and *Of the Farm* a shade too small. But in the Rabbit novels the use of the present tense and the choice of a character who stands at one remove from Updike's personal experience shield him from the overpowering rushes of feeling that result in ornate prose, willful intricacies or problems of scale in his other novels.

In *Rabbit, Run* a young man deserts his wife on an impulse, takes up with another woman, goes back to his wife and then runs off again. When the book first appeared, Richard Gilman described it well: "On one level, *Rabbit, Run* is a grotesque allegory of American life, with its myth of happiness and success, its dangerous innocence and crippling antagonism between value and fact. But much more significantly, it is a minor epic of the spirit thirsting for room to discover and be itself, ducking, dodging, staying out of reach of everything that will pin it down and impale it on fixed, immutable laws that are not of its own making and do not consider its integrity."

Norman Mailer, writing in *Esquire*, greatly disliked Updike's prose but he did concede that "Updike has instincts for finding the heart of the conventional novel" and brilliantly expressed the emotional and ultimately religious intensity of the book: "the merit of the book is not in the simplicity of its problem, but in the dread Updike manages to convey, despite the literary commercials in the style, of a young man who is beginning to lose nothing less than his good American soul, and yet it is not quite his fault. The power of the novel comes from the sense, not absolutely unworthy of Thomas Hardy, that the universe hangs over our fates like a great sullen hopeless sky. There is real pain in the book, and a touch of awe."

What distinguishes *Rabbit, Run* from all of Updike's other work (until the appearance of its sequel) is its dynamic balance between description and narrative energy: as Rabbit escapes from one enclosing situation to another, the pace never flags and yet the physical and psychological details have never been more sharply in focus. The minutiae of the Eisenhower age– the paradigmatic Mickey Mouse TV show, the religious revival, the all-American glamor of high-school heroes, the cramped apartments of small town sweethearts who married too young, the hallowed authority of athletic coaches and parents– all are perfectly there.

But the verisimilitude is more than skin deep. Updike meticulously conveys the longings and frustrations of family life, the interplay of love, tenderness, aggression and lust with self-esteem, the differences of feeling and speech from class to class and generation to generation. The prose speeds along with grace and strength; the present tense has given it dramatic immediacy and yet permitted a rapid flow of psychological nuance. Rabbit's wife, his mistress, the disapproving parents, his old coach, an all too modern Episcopal priest and his wife, the two young children all are brilliantly drawn. Rabbit is caught in the center– a kind of anti-Job who won't abandon the pleasure principle, or a male Madame Bovary who instead of killing himself simply runs away.

Thus, the essential theme of *Rabbit, Run* is civilization and its discontents: the opposing claims of self and society, the sacrifices of energy and individuality that civilization demands. In *Rabbit, Run* Updike pulled against the 1950's, defending the claims of the libidinous presocial self against the smothering complacencies of small town white America. Now in *Rabbit Redux* (that is, Rabbit "returns") he pulls against the 1960's and defends his hero's new commitment to civilization, his longing for social and personal continuity in an age where both are hard to come by.

In the new book Rabbit has greatly changed; it's been ten years since he last ran away. At 36 he's no longer a bounder, but plugs away, like his father, as a linotypist in a local print shop. He sticks to his responsibilities and lives by the old American rules which it cost him so much to learn: family loyalty, hard work, sexual compromise. But in the 1960's such rules no longer seem to apply. "Everybody's the way I used to be," he says.

Rabbit's wife, Janice, has also changed. She is restless, no longer the gloomy stay-at-home. Now she bustles out to work at her father's new Toyota agency, while Rabbit is stuck in his dwindling blue collar trade and is finally laid off as obsolete. Janice, not Rabbit, is the one who has an affair and runs away from home– for much the same reason as he once did. This time he is left behind, the town cuckold, caring for his teen-age son.

Lonely, adrift, Rabbit takes an 18-year-old runaway girl into his house; he becomes her lover and father. The family expands when she brings home another stray: a black Vietnam veteran on the run, who styles himself an agent of apocalypse– and indirectly brings down fire and brimstone on the house. Rabbit returns to his parents' home. Once again he sleeps in his old room, regresses into adolescent fantasies. But in the end his wife decides to let her lover go and comes back to her family. A more complex health and order is achieved.

The action takes place in the summer of 1969, and the Apollo moon shot is used as the organizing image of the book. As Rabbit and his father sit drinking in a bar and he first learns that his wife may be unfaithful, the astronauts are taking off. As Rabbit's life falls apart, Armstrong sets foot on the moon. Everything in the middle sections is in free fall as Rabbit spins around the dark side of the moon. In the end Rabbit and his wife home in like space capsules and, of course, like rabbits in a hutch. The lunar wasteland of contemporary America is everywhere. The tacky houses of the suburban development where Rabbit lives blister the landscape like craters on the moon. Downtown there are deserted lots and empty stores. Desolate shopping centers are lit by burger joints where the drinks all taste like chemical sludge and Luna specials (two cheese-burgers with an American flag on top) are sold. The endless electronic buzz of television fills the air with news reports of rocket launchings and racial turmoil. The young trip out on pot and heroin; their sexual license is bombed out, arid, frozen. All these elements are subtly brought together in the controlling image of space exploration, a journey out into a void and then back to earth.

In *Rabbit Redux*, for the first time in his career, Updike deals in a large way with public subjects: violence, the Vietnam war, black revolution, drug addiction, middle American anger and frustration, hippie life-styles, the moon shot. With great narrative facility he has integrated these volatile elements within a realistic novel of suburban life in 1969. In outline, the book may seem populated with clichés, but on the page they are redeemed by Updike's accurate evocation of people's voices and feelings as well as his description of physical details. Updike has always written about the inner surface of banal experiences; in *Rabbit Redux* he shows highly familiar subjects in all their human particularity.

For example, Rabbit has a series of violent political arguments with his two sexual rivals: his wife's lover and the young black. In *Bech* (sic), Updike wrote "even in an age of science and unbelief our ideas are dreams, styles, superstitions, mere animal noises intended to repel or attract." In the give and take of these debates it is nearly impossible to detach the ideas and political opinions from their psychological, novelistic base. Rabbit gets wild about Vietnam when he feels personally and sexually threatened; he overcomes his fear and dislike of blacks when he himself is an outcast and a cuckold.

The wide range of tones and rhythms in black speech has never been so well reproduced in contemporary white writing. (The apposite comparison is Ralph Ellison's *Invisible Man*.) Bernard Malamud's stereotyped black novelist in *The Tenants* and Saul Bellow's wordless menacing black pickpocket in *Mr. Sammler's Planet* come nowhere near the depth and accuracy of Updike's black characters: a printer, a lowlife singer, the young Vietnam veteran. Although symbolically Rabbit is clearly the "suffering servant"and father, and this young black is clearly the Antichrist– preaching sermons that mix Afro-American history and religious nihilism and administering the sacraments of drugs and sex– this black is portrayed with enormous sympathy and force and is anything but an allegorical cut-out.

In *Rabbit, Run* the hero confronted an essentially static social situation and dove into his inner spaces to avoid it. In *Rabbit Redux* he confronts an unnervingly dynamic social situation that plunges him into outer space– beyond his family, his class, his race and his normal earthbound feelings and behavior. *Rabbit, Run* was a major book about the fifties; *Rabbit Redux* is, like Mailer's *Armies of the Night*, a major book about the sixties– the period when the struggles of the private self became political events and political events broke in on private lives.

Of the writers who are working in a professional way to help us come to some unsteady and evolving understanding of our human and cultural predicament as we slide into the seventies, two in recent years are complementary– Norman Mailer and John Updike. A metaphor might help us here. Mailer is a mountain-climber; Updike a miner. Mailer is heroically scaling the heights– of himself, of ideas, of urban life, of the future, of the sky, the outer spaces. He is aggressive, public, ostentatiously political, outrageously daring, unsparing of himself. Updike is an underground worker, chipping away at banal circumstances and minute feelings, trying to find jewels in a little space. Until this book he was nearly apolitical and even here he carefully grounds his characters' political opinions in their immediate social and psychological conditions. He is tender, not aggressive. His sexual descriptions are not boastful but reverent. His major characters include women as well as men– which is remarkable in American fiction. He is our finest writer about children. He treats his characters with respect; there are no villains.

In an interview in 1966 Updike said, "I like middles. It is in middles that extremes clash, where ambiguity restlessly rules." In an interview two years later he continued

> Everything unambiguously expressed seems somehow crass to me. . .everything is infinitely fine and any opinion is somehow coarser than the texture of the real thing. . . .My work says 'yes, but.' Yes, in Rabbit, Run, to our inner urgent whispers, but– the social fabric collapses murderously. Yes, in The Centaur, to self-sacrifice and duty, but – what of a man's private agony and dwindling? No, in The Poorhouse Fair, to social homogenization and loss of faith, but– listen to the voices, the joy of persistent existence. No, in Couples, to a religious community founded on physical and psychical interpenetrations, but– what else shall we do, as God destroys our churches? . . . Domestic fierceness within the middle class, sex and death as riddles for the thinking animal, social existence as sacrifice, unexpected pleasures and rewards, corruption as a kind of evolution– these are some of [my] themes.

He has never treated them better than in his new novel. In *Rabbit Redux* all is ambiguous, dialectical and yet, finally, novelistically resolved. There are no "Updikean" curlicues of style or yawning gaps between symbol and event. All is dramatized. There are some structural faults, and moments when characters don't ring true. But I can think of no stronger vindication of the claims of essentially realistic fiction than this extraordinary synthesis of the disparate elements of contemporary experience. *Rabbit Redux* is a great achievement, by far the most audacious and successful book Updike has written.

*Richard Locke, "Rabbit Returns: Updike Was Always There– It's Time We Noticed." *New York Times Book Review* 14 Nov. 1971: 1-2, 12-16, 20-21.

"A Special Case"

Brendan Gill*

John Updike has always made it a practice to take immense chances, and his latest novel *Rabbit Redux* (Knopf), is therefore perfectly in character. What could be riskier than to attempt a sequel to a novel that many people had held to be one's best? A novel that not only was a critical and popular success at the time it was published in 1960, but has continued to be praised and to sell vigorously ever since, making any sequel to it a presumptuous competitor. And, finally, a novel of strict and delicate calculation, which seemed– and today continues to seem– complete in itself: not a series of adventures accumulated more or less at random and capable of being added to indefinitely, in the mode of the great comedians (Cervantes, Rabelais, the Joyce of *Finnegans Wake*), but a hermetic sphere of the sort that Henry James considered the ideal shape for a novel, with a surface so closely joined and highly burnished that even the finest pinpoint cannot be found room for upon it. Reading *Rabbit, Run,* one is grateful for every sedulously weighed and placed word, and one feels not the slightest need for another. The book begins and ends with poor Harry "Rabbit" Angstrom running headlong toward an unhappy fate by running in panic away from it. He is only twenty-six, but the days of his glory are behind him. Once a star basketball player, he earns a living, such as it is, by demonstrating a kitchen gadget in five-and-ten-cent stores. He is married to a girl whose mind and body have come to seem mere tiresome souvenirs of the undiscriminating desirousness of youth. Janice, as Rabbit constantly reminds her, is "dumb" and likely to grow dumber. She was pregnant when they married, three years earlier, and Janice is again pregnant and has, ominously, taken to drink. Rabbit abandons her and establishes a relationship with another woman, whom he also gets pregnant. (Careless Rabbit! His nickname, ceasing to celebrate his athletic prowess, threatens to mock his progenitiveness.) Rabbit leaves his mistress and returns to Janice, whom he then abandons for a second time, with consequences that include the death of an innocent. Young as he is, Rabbit is plainly a man at the end of his tether. In the world's eyes, there is little in him worth the effort of saving. Nevertheless, a minister who has been trying to patch things up between Rabbit and Janice, and for that matter, between Rabbit and God, says of him that he is a special case. The subject of the novel is the series of injuries Rabbit does to himself and others in the course of his tormented upward floundering into manhood; the theme of the novel is an acceptance of the soundness of Rabbit's conviction that he is someone of value. "Believe in me," Rabbit begs, not in words. "Help me to find a place among you, whoever I am, whoever you are. I am precious because I exist." It is a modest claim and an enormous one, and we cannot fail to be touched by it, though we honor it at our peril.

Complete in itself– yes, *Rabbit, Run* is certainly that, but the fact is no longer important, save to help measure the boldness of Mr. Updike's gamble. For, against all the odds, *Rabbit Redux* is a sequel that succeeds; it is in every respect uncannily superior to its distinguished predecessor and deserves to achieve even greater critical and popular acclaim. The ease with which Mr. Updike appears to have performed this feat becomes all the more awesome when we note that it amounts not to a single miracle but to a double one: the illuminations of *Rabbit Redux*, cast back upon *Rabbit, Run*, cause it to be seen in a new light, at once brighter and more distressing than the light in which we saw it first. Not a word of the earlier novel is changed, but our feelings about the words have changed; the prospective fate of the twenty-six-year-old Rabbit strikes us as infinitely more poignant than we had guessed it would be, when, encountering him at thirty-six, we discover what the intervening years of running, running, running have done to him. The young Rabbit had been able to say, "If you have the guts to be yourself, other people'll pay your price." He had been wrong to make that boast as he had been wrong about so many things; now he knows better, if only a little better, and his knowledge brings despair. He has learned that being in pursuit of a self is not being oneself, but the pursuit continues, because, though the road grows steeper, there is no other. To most people, he has long since stopped being Rabbit– he is simply Harry Angstrom, a dully trudging sonhusbandfather, tax-payer, drinker, and watcher of TV. He is a linotyper in the printing plant in which his father works; it is a job that he had refused to take in his youth, for the reason, so his father has contemptuously said of him, that he didn't want to get his fingernails dirty. It is also a job that , as cheaper printing processes come into vogue, is about to render him technologically obsolete. To make matters worse, he fears that he may be emotionally obsolete as well; at every turn, he detects signs that he is about to be passed by. Fattening and slowing down as he moves into early middle age, he finds, to his dismay, that his wife daily gains vigor and purpose. For, contrary to our expectations in *Rabbit, Run*, Janice has pulled herself together; it is not she but Rabbit whom the world would accuse of growing dumber. She has taken a job in the automobile agency owned by her prosperous father and has fallen in love with one of the salesmen– a pleasant Greek named Stavros, who gives her far more sexual satisfaction than Rabbit ever has. When she admits to Rabbit that she is sleeping with Stavros, Rabbit does not make an issue of it, and Janice indignantly quits the house: *she* has certain standards of conduct, if he does not. Left in charge of their thirteen-year-old son, Nelson, Rabbit drifts into a miserable affair with a teen-age white hippy waif, Jill; in her train comes Skeeter, a brilliant young black, so revolutionary in his beliefs that he dismisses Bobby Seale as a member of the honky Establishment. Rabbit, Nelson, Jill, and Skeeter set up a kind of accidental commune, sharing experiments in sex, drugs, and intellectual combat, to the anger of Janice, Janice's family, Rabbit's family, and a number of respectable peeping-Tom neighbors. These are the most critical moments of Rabbit's life; never has he struggled harder to come into the world. Anguished and joyful, he stands poised on the brink of gathering every available body, black and white, male and female, into the comfort of his polymorphous-perverse embrace, while overhead his old friend and adversary the Holy Ghost spells out in tongues of fire the welcome message "RABBIT LOVES RABBIT IS LOVED."

Rabbit Redux is a longer, darker, richer, and, in terms of plot, more complex work than *Rabbit, Run*, and it will be wise to break off an account of the novel at this point in order not to deprive readers of the old-fashioned, ever-dash-to-be-cherished pleasure of observing the author weaving together and then separating a score of diverse threads of narrative. How fast his shuttle flies! What glints of gold in unexpected places as the intricate pattern emerges– a pattern which, as in *Rabbit, Run,* convinces us that nothing need ever be added to it and that yet leaves open innumerable ways of continuing it ad lib, volume after volume, well into the twenty-first century. *Redux* in literal translation from the Latin means "led back," and figuratively it means, or can mean, "restored to health," but our last glimpse of Rabbit is far from reassuring; in another ten years, if not sooner, we will be in want of another substantial diagnosis of his case. Marianne Moore has spoken in one of her poems of how we must strive to recover from the disease of ourselves, and in telling us from time to time how it goes with Rabbit Mr. Updike will be telling us how it goes with himself and, indeed, with us. He is one of the novelists from whom we learn much more than we realize at the moment of reading them, so caught up are we in their felicities. In the act of instruction, the Dreisers of this world batter us to our knees with shofars of coarse sound; the Updikes pipe a tune, and such is its sweetness that only afterward do we realize that the words accompanying it were as harsh as they were true. *Rabbit Redux* is more profound than *Rabbit, Run* because Mr. Updike is no longer a dazzling boy in his twenties but a man of the highest intelligence on the threshold of forty, that formidable crossing-over age. He has grown up in the presence of all of us, fearlessly, with poems, short stories, novels, articles, readings, and interviews. It is a difficult thing to practice candor before skeptics, to risk scattering one's spring-morning high spirits before the sourest passersby; Mr. Updike has done so with unabatable zest. We are lucky to have the example of a life so unfaltering in the increase and deployment of its powers, and if, now and again, we miss the prankish young literary showoff and the rumpled, straw-haired, mock-country bumpkin who wore his clothes and spoke his lines, the loss is small next to the possession of a writer looking out upon the world with the freshness of the first time and the comprehension of the ten-thousandth and finding in it much to rejoice at, something to praise.

*Brendan Gill, "A Special Case." *The New Yorker* 47 (8 Jan. 1972): 83-84.

"'The Awful Power': John Updike's Use of Kubrick's '2001' in *Rabbit Redux*"

Jack De Bellis*

"The power of the cinema, the awful power of it."
— John Updike[33]

John Updike's dozens of references to films and allusions to screen actors and actresses reveal not just a passing knowledge of an important aspect of American popular culture but offer verisimilitude and nostalgia, while providing a clever disclosure of character and support for theme. So adept is Updike at using every element of film that even titles on marquees foreshadow and counterpoint his themes. Individual films reveal ironic relations to his images, plots and characters, most suggestively in the use of Stanley Kubrick's *2001: A Space Odyssey* in *Rabbit Redux*, where parallels focus attention on the growth of Rabbit's wife, Janice Springer, and the significance of the black messiah, Skeeter.

Certainly the idea of so consummate a literary stylist as Updike showing a passion for movies must strike some as an amusing irony, yet Updike's enthusiasm for film is well documented. He early intended to work as a Disney animator, but when he saw that his career lay in writing he became anxious to adopt film techniques to fiction, though he eventually became disillusioned with the *nouveau roman*'s employment of the *nouvelle vague*'s devices. Yet from his earliest work, Updike has filled his works with references to films and film personalities in his fiction, poetry and essays. They record nostalgia for the past that modulates into symbolic and psychological revelations. Updike early found in movies a "moral ideal," and a model of "debonair grace." Film contained such "awful power" to captivate and hypnotize that he attributed to *Being There* the answer to his personal question, "Why am I here?"[34]

Dilvo Ristoff has called for a change in the direction of Updike commentary to focus upon scene (the enclosing context of historical fact which suggests psychosocial determinants in character) and away from the concept of the "hero." Perhaps the best novel for such an approach, *Rabbit Redux,* encloses the simple story of a wife's desertion with great events in American life in 1969– the moon landing, the civil rights/black power movements, the Vietnam War, and the sexual revolution. At the same time, Marshall McLuhan prophesied the evolution in human response from the "Gutenberg media" (emphasizing linear thinking) to the "post-Gutenberg media" relying on non-linear thinking (television and film).

---

[33] Charles Samuels. "The Art of Fiction XLIII: John Updike." *Paris Review* 45(Winter 1968): 110.

[34] John Updike, *Hugging the Shore* (New York: Knopf, 1983) 843. Citations to Updike's work after this will be given in parentheses after the quote.

Updike explores this opposition in Harry and Janice Angstrom. In so far as both media gather information, they are the conduits for the facts enclosing the context of action. Since *2001: A Space Odyssey* posits a parallel between the evolution of man through technology and violence, the film provides a suggestive background from which to evaluate the development of the Angstroms' quest for love and quest for self.

To appreciate how thoroughly Updike uses film in this way, consider how marquee film titles underline the action and publicize a character's private attitude. In *Rabbit Redux* this device objectifies Rabbit's fear of social exposure in cohabiting with a hippie and a black militant. Perhaps such a device, akin to the "gimmick" of using imaginary headlines as ways of revealing Rabbit's sense of himself as a social outcast, exemplify how Updike can "convert the gimmick into fine art" in *Rabbit Redux*.[35] For example, placement on the marquee of *10* with other films permits a multileveled pun that radiates throughout *Rabbit Is Rich*: "The four features at the mall cinema are BREAKING AWAY STARTING OVER RUNNING AND 10." Harry thinks, "He'd like to see *10*, he knows from the ads this Swedish-looking girl has her hair in corn rows like a black chick out of Zaire" (*Rabbit Is Rich* 347). As *Rabbit, Run* has shown, Rabbit ran from his family because he no longer felt "first-rate," no longer a "ten." This image of Bo Derek blends with Rabbit's continual fantasies of sex, including curiosity about black women, stirred since he ogled a black waitress in *Rabbit, Run*. This attraction may announce an unconscious resistance to bigotry, as much as marriage, by "running." The marquee's running pun, "STARTING OVER RUNNING," predicts that Rabbit's son Nelson will desert his wife and child in *Rabbit Redux*'s sequel *Rabbit Is Rich* as Rabbit had in *Rabbit, Run*.

In fact, another series of marquee titles ironically comments on Nelson's emulation of his father: "ALIEN MOONRAKER MAIN EVENT ESCAPE FROM ALCATRAZ" (*Rabbit Is Rich* 35). Nelson has alienated his father, and the focus of their strain, Nelson's marriage, is the main event of the novel; like the film the marriage features a fight between the lovers, though the film treats the matter comically. Nelson escapes the prison wife, child and parents, ironically interrupting Rabbit's retreat to a Caribbean isle where Harry and Janice seek a sexual escape in wife-swapping.

Updike's use of the film titles as thematic motifs expands our appreciation of structure while widening our understanding of the implied narrator's view of the characters. Updike also manipulates tone by using film to reveal ironic parallels undercutting his characters. We recognize, while Rabbit does not, that his spouse-sharing in the Caribbean replicates the pornographic cliché he detests in the Rialto's *Babes in Swapland*. His disgust with the decay such films represent contrasts sharply to his own lack of self-recognition, for his priggish attitude is undercut by his own sexual fantasies. Perhaps he fears being robbed of them by having his eroticism made public. Harry is also undercut when he fails to recognize that the

---

[35] Robert Detweiler, *John Updike*, revised edition (Boston: G. K. Hall, 1984) 134.

"Satanism" cursing the family of *Amityville Horror*, which his son Nelson excitedly relates, reflects upon Rabbit's ten-year alienation over the death of his baby (*Rabbit Is Rich* 161).[36]

Turning to films themselves, in *Rabbit, Run* two films counterpoint the seriousness of the action. *The Shaggy Dog* reduces Harry's romantic quest for first-ratedness, while *Bell, Book and Candle* affirms the magical power of love. Harry poises uncomfortably on both the need for self-identity and the need for love. By alluding to the Hollywood fantasy versions of happiness, Rabbit's predicament is shown to be all the more poignant, partly because such fantasies have fed his notions of "first-ratedness."

The Shaggy Dog underlines the opposition of dog/rabbit images in *Rabbit, Run*. Rabbit Angstrom (a "rabbit") has married Janice Springer (a "dog") and the contrast reverberates throughout the novel. This discontent turns comic in *The Shaggy Dog*, a film Rabbit and his mistress Ruth enjoy during their six-week affair. Though Rabbit does not reflect upon this contrast, the reader becomes aware of a parallel between Harry's situation with his estranged wife and the film's antagonist Mr. Wilson Daniels who fears and hates dogs and imagines shooting an invading shaggy dog who becomes the hero. Meanwhile, Rabbit's in-laws try to transform his son into a Springer.[37]

The Shaggy Dog parodies Rabbit's hero's quest, his spiritual groping for the "it" that could make him first-rate again. The dog saves a missile site, rescues a girl from drowning and a baby from a fire. But Harry cannot rescue his drowning baby in *Rabbit, Run*– the image haunts him throughout the sequel– nor in *Rabbit Redux* can he save Jill from burning nor direct the moon rocket Apollo 11 away from the moon, the "big nothing." Only Disney makes modern heroes.

The other film supplying counterpoint, *Bell, Book and Candle*, injects a gothic element into *Rabbit, Run*. When Jimmy Stewart is bewitched by the New York witch Kim Novak, he renounces his fiancée for her, as Ruth bewitches Harry into giving up his family. Unlike Stewart, Rabbit breaks the hold of all the witches and escapes. Other parallels emerge. When the dark pasts of Novak and Ruth are discovered, their lovers flee. As Novak pursues Stewart to her undoing, so Ruth's love of Rabbit weakens the prostitute's protective defenses. Only when Novak's dark past is discovered does Stewart lose interest. Though we may applaud their return to customary human behavior, both women are more unhappy in their

---

[36] As Newman notes, Nelson's interest in the theme of the devil in the house in *The Amityville Horror*, as well as the idea of free fall in *Moonraker*, are each realized at Slim's party. Judie Newman, *John Updike* (New York: St. Martin's, 1988) 69. Newman is particularly insightful in her treatment of Marshall McLuhan in relation to *Rabbit Redux*. Much of my argument is indebted to hers, though I consider film as an "electronic medium" (see Newman 40-62).

[37] The images may be seen as comic relief to the domestic tragedy (see Detweiler 56-57). For a critique of the dog/rabbit opposition, see Jack De Bellis, "The 'Extra Dimension': Character Names in Updike's 'Rabbit' Trilogy." *Names* 36 (March-June 1988): 29-42.

rejection of the unconventional path they had chosen.

Updike uses these films in *Rabbit, Run* to comment on specific aspects of the action. In *Rabbit Redux*, however, Updike traces how the two appearances of Stanley Kubrick's *2001: A Space Odyssey* act as enclosures for the quest theme, with key images which reflect upon the inner worlds of Harry and Janice. The film brackets Janice's infidelity and Harry's exposure to ideas which challenge his comfortable passivity. The arrival of the film and the lunar landing complement each other, creating maximum interest in space flight as a fact and as imaginative stimulation, but they mean very different things to Rabbit and Janice.[38] The Angstroms ostensibly do not seem affected; in fact, Greiner asserts that *2001* is "beyond the comprehension of Janice and Harry, who wonder if the first thirty minutes will bore them."[39] Janice's lover, Charlie Stavros, dislikes it because he does not find technology sexy, but he underestimates the power of the film's imagery to arouse Janice's re-awakened sexual temper. The film can also be seen as a criticism of technology, for the ultimate in computers, HAL, jeopardizes the mission. Only when HAL is "lobotomized" by surviving astronaut David Bowman does Bowman discover the life beyond technology and an end to the union of technology and violence, which Kubrick sees as ineluctably united throughout human history.

The Angstroms select the film as numerous families like them did, to placate their son's enthusiasm for the violence of the apes. Though Janice describes it to her lover as a "silly" movie, divining his objections, the film's imagery provides symbols of her newfound sexuality, which she idly absorbs. Essentially, the film describes Janice's confrontation with the daughter she accidentally drowned, in the image of the film's "star-child," the final development of Bowman's hero's journey. The Apollo 11 moon flight, like Bowman's space flights, underline Janice's running from her family in *Rabbit Redux*. The flights in *2001* provide an objective visualization of her unconscious need for inner journey as well as outer flight. No wonder her affair makes the rest of life, "a kind of movie, flat and even rather funny" (*Rabbit Redux* 53). *2001* stirs Janice deeply because her erotic experience with Charlie has enabled her to embark on her own odyssey, which "makes you think about everything anew" (*Rabbit Redux* 53).

---

[38] Each section of the novel is prefaced by epigraphs from the American-Soviet flights to the moon. The first epigraph, "I've lost you for a while, but now I have you," is Updike's witty announcement of his reunion with his "old friend," as he called him. The last epigraph describes a coupling of Soviet and American crafts as well as the Angstroms who had fled in each book– passed through a test and returned to one another with closer communication and renewal. But it may also refer to the rerun of *2001* at the end of *Rabbit Redux*. With droll irony Updike describes the "docking procedure" of the exhausted, reunited Angstroms. The novel also "docks" with its predecessor *Rabbit, Run*. A film that Harry sees being made in Brewer may well be the film of *Rabbit, Run* (*Rabbit Redux* 184).

[39] Donald J. Greiner, *John Updike's Novels* (Athens: The U of Ohio P, 1984) 68.

But *2001* makes as little impact upon Harry as the moon landing had, with its ambiguous images filled with static. He could make no personal connection to the event, for unlike Columbus, Harry reasons, the Apollo astronauts knew where they were going, yet in the moon landing found nothing. He might have seen *2001* the same way, since the astronauts are apparently rebuffed in their effort to discover why the monolith lured men from the moon to Jupiter, all but one of whom died. Still, he does allude to "best parts" of the picture, so one cannot easily assume he was unaffected by the film.

Stanley Kubrick titled the first segment of *2001: A Space Odyssey* "The Dawn of Man," since it depicted the sudden evolution of ape-men through knowledge transmitted by the black monolith. That knowledge links a murder weapon (a bone) to man's rise, and thus intimately equates technological progress with violence. The famous cut Kubrick makes at the end of this sequence, from the bone tossed in ecstasy into the air to a spacecraft routinely plying its way through airless space on its way to the moon, telescopes human history as the progress of violence. Modern man is more subtle at repressing the link between technology and violence. As Markle notes, the scene "symbolizes the industrial revolution in general, the rise of technology leading to space flight."[40]

As the apes lived in a kind of Eden before the appearance of the monolith provided them with weapons and hence culture, Janice and Harry have lived a virtually sexless life after the death of their baby, in a "pre-sexual" paradise. Janice's dark lover, Charlie Stavros, her "cave bear," provides her with sexual confidence and a mission of self-discovery. When, after stealing kisses with her lover, Janice arrives late at the Rialto during the "Dawn of Man" section, she discovers Harry and Nelson have become alien, the film has set their hair "on fire" and made their ears "translucent red" from the "great exploding screen." These "sparse planets of her life" have already been left behind. The film then validates her intuition.

Janice's journey had begun tragically with the image of her drowned baby in *Rabbit, Run*. The space voyage in *2001* ends with images of the "Star-Child," as A. C. Clarke named it. In the decade between *Rabbit, Run* and *Rabbit Redux* the baby has loomed large between Janice and Harry. At dinner with Stavros before seeing *2001*, Harry could be so casually cruel as to remark to his son, "Your mother's the girl that's good at death." Janice's rejoinder fits the blame: "Tell him who refused to have another child" (*Rabbit Redux* 48). The Star-Child symbolically shows her that Becky is not dead, and the huge image seems to absolve her, in contrast to the accusing baby who seemed to divine that Janice would mishandle her, "this big moon face looking cross at me" (*Rabbit, Run* 203). Beyond the moon, the Star-Child notifies Janice that she may discard guilt and the past and is free to live in the here and now. Recalling her remark to Rabbit about why they went to the movies, we appreciate a retrospective irony: "The movie isn't just for Nelson, it's for *me*" (*Rabbit Redux* 34).

---

[40] Joyce B. Markle, *Fighters and Lovers: Theme in the Novels of John Updike* (New York: New York UP, 1973) 150.

While Harry sleeps, Janice reflects on her lover and the image of the space station while she masturbates, the "great wheel" becoming associated with her feminine sexual symbol and sending her the moon's message: come. She does, though Janice feels she has betrayed her lover by "coming without him" (*Rabbit Redux* 57). Afterward, she lies "awake like the moon," while Harry, like one of the hibernating space scientists of *2001,* sleeps "under the covers with just the top of his head showing."

Though Janice's response to the film's images reflects her sense of a positive personal voyage, images associated with Harry show him to be an impediment to her flight from slavery into love. The last image in Rabbit's mind before sleep at one point suggests connections to his negative odyssey: "he thinks of feathering the linotype keys, of work tomorrow, and is already there." While Janice has learned to live in the here and now, Harry is so stuck in mechanical time that even asleep he prefers work, for the typesetting machine reduces him to a baby: it "stands tall and warm above him mothering" (*Rabbit Redux* 29-30). He has withdrawn grotesquely to his Oedipal phase, and his regression parodies his roles of child, parent, and husband. Harry's image derives from the antique technology whose obsolescence puts him out of a job. Janice is linked to the space station of the future and is bound to sexuality and intuition.

The first appearance of *2001: A Space Odyssey* draws the Angstrom family together for the last time before Janice's defection. They are reunited near Halloween when *2001* returns, "BACK BY REQST."[41] Bracketed by the film, Harry has been exposed to black and white realities through the runaway Jill and the black militant Skeeter. They also function as symbolic emblems of the materials of the linotype which govern his life– white paper and black type, which in turn reflect upon his "linear mode" of stereotyping, typical of Gutenberg man. Unlike the linotype, they test his fidelity and offer a fresh start on his quest.

A "moon child," as Rabbit calls her, Jill corrects Rabbit's mistaken impression that the moon is a "big nothing," for in making love to her as an "earthman" he is able to fight his own war in which sex and death are linked, and humble himself to her. Speaking to Harry and Nelson about the cosmos, she insists it is selfish to deny the possibility of life to other heavenly bodies. Harry merely parrots what he'd read in the Sunday supplements about life existing on Jupiter (unconsciously directed to it by having seen *2001?*) but Jill is concerned with an attitude toward life, not stale scientific theorizing (*Rabbit Redux* 160-61).

Jill's gravest challenge is her "personal" dark monolith, Skeeter, who plies her with heroin so she will provide him with drug-provoked visions of God. Through her, he gains entrance into Harry's impassive life. Like the monolith, Skeeter imports critical ambiguities to the novel. Part of the ambiguity of Kubrick's monolith results from the unknown motives which have governed the monolith

---

[41] The return of the film supports Vargo's insight locating the source of the unusual word "redux" in Dryden's *Astrae Redux,* "return of the star." See Edward P. Vargo, *Rainstorms and Fire: Ritual in the Novels of John Updike* (Port Washington: Kennikat, 1973) 150.

makers, since they appeal to man's violent tendencies and set in motion a civilization based on fear. As Jill tells Harry after he has abused her: "People've run on fear long enough. Let's try love for a change" (*Rabbit Redux* 170). Yet Jill's fears force her to fail in her mission, enslave her to Skeeter and hasten her death. Though Harry feels some responsibility for Jill, his skepticism about Jill's openness to perceptions of God and his resistance to her love reveal the depths of Harry's inability to discover fresh images that might liberate him from his self-imposed paralysis. Unresponsive to the moon, he is enthralled, however, by the monolith.

Like the enigmatic dark monolith, Skeeter raises more questions than he answers, and many of them focus on Harry's capacity to extricate himself from his negative quest. Skeeter's appearances have the same dramatic timing as the monolith in *2001*. He appears first at "Jimbo's Friendly Lounge" offering mysterious Biblically inverted comments about the "offay" Harry, upon whom the blacks subtly rid themselves of Jill. At his second appearance, Harry finds Skeeter has moved in. Taunted obscenely, Harry beats him, but, strangely fascinated, he allows Skeeter to stay. A didactic contrast to Kubrick's laconic monolith, Skeeter lectures Harry on past and modern history, showing how economic and technological forces united to enslave blacks, and how Vietnam, a kind of cosmic "black hole," has brought about apocalypse and placed him in the role of the black messiah. His god-like posture and his cosmic association parallel the monolith emphatically.[42]Skeeter draws Harry to new realizations, and he forces him to confront his own anger, thus brining together Harry's violence and his new sense of history. Skeeter's third appearance occurs when he hides in Harry's car, fearing arrest for Jill's death. Harry allows him to escape, recalling the escape of Bowman into the birth of the Star-Child. When Skeeter leaves him with a mock blessing by spitting in Harry's hand, he seems to have accepted Harry as a disciple. On the cosmic scale, the third alignment of sun, moon and earth accompany the third appearance of the monolith. The celestial images are rendered obscene when Skeeter refers to his testicles as the sun and moon, yet the cosmic imagery reminds us of Janice's masturbatory images and yokes sexuality and the cosmos, as they are blended in the key image of the Star-Child.

In *2001* the monolith appears three times: first on earth, then the moon, then near Jupiter, each time responding to the level of technology man had attained– tool-making, lunar exploration, and space travel. Like the monolith, Skeeter has brought a kind of knowledge at the time when it might be best received. Skeeter offers Harry three illuminations concerning dishonesty in human relations (his pretended indifference to Janice and Jill), indifference to history (his ignorance of his role in continuing a history of oppression), and defensive jingoism (his assumption of American superiority).

Skeeter's own philosophy has developed through similar illuminations: honest response to "sacred texts" like *The Life and Times of Frederick Douglass*,

---

[42] Regarding Skeeter's assertion that he is Christ, Updike remarked that Skeeter: "*says* he is. I think probably he might be. And if that's so, then people *ought* to be very nice to him." John Updike, *Picked-Up Pieces* (New York: Knopf, 1975) 510.

apocalyptic historical awareness of Vietnam, and intellectual conviction that he can unite humanity as the new messiah. As monolith, then, he offers possibilities of discovery akin to the monolith's appearances in *2001*. Jill also tries to educate Harry about himself and history by forcing him to confront his hypocritical capitalist values, as when he beats her for panhandling. Together, Skeeter and Jill show how their own lives are examples of their commitment to a unified theory which the fragmented Harry cannot accept. To him they are aliens, and he refuses to step off the security of his firmament and voyage with them. The irresistible effect of the monolith has met its match in the immovable Harry.[43]

Conspicuous by their absence in *2001* are blacks, the source of Updike's parallels with the monolith. Like the monolith, blacks have been "buried" a long time before making an impact, emerging when humanity's dead-end direction requires fresh inspiration. Harry, like the apes, needs a fresh direction, especially one uniting his own sense of powerlessness to his former vitality. The self-satisfied person "in a sense dies," Updike has remarked, and such a person becomes an "unfallen Adam. . .an ape. . .not a person at all– just an animal with clothes on."[44] Harry's response to Babe's singing at Jimbo's Friendly Lounge shows that, despite his outward appearance of smug indifference, at some level he may be ready to respond to Skeeter-as-monolith.[45]

Even incidental details seem to have correspondences– from the monolith's dark color, to the sounds it emits, and its magnetism. Like the man-ape, Harry needs to touch the strange new force (untypically, he beats the unresisting Skeeter) and get acquainted with its magic. The scientists in *2001* think the monolith has been made by an advanced society, and Skeeter has come fresh from Vietnam. To him Vietnam is the leading edge of humanity's next stage, a black hole through which God means to communicate and appoint his "black messiah." Bowman's last meeting with the monolith apparently brings him a mysterious image of the union of death and birth, though only a reading of Arthur C. Clarke's novel, *2001: A Space Odyssey*, developed from his story "The Sentinel" and primarily written as the film was produced, makes this point clear. Similarly, Harry is left with the enigma of Skeeter, who may have precipitated Jill's death or who may be guiltless. Harry has been extricated from his ape state and carried to personal discovery in Jimbo's, but in the destruction of his house (his symbolic death) he is left in the Safe Haven Motel, possibly an ironic reflection on the Louis XVI room in which

---

[43] Detweiler's view is that, "Harry Angstrom undergoes a quest, a seduction, a conversion, and an education," but it also seems that Harry resists attempts at education (see Detweiler 132).

[44] Samuels 101.

[45] Perhaps Babe's singing of the "tunes that Broadway forgot" finds a complement in the "colossal sacred din of chanting" the monolith emits as the apes approach it. See Penelope Gilliatt, "After Man," *The New Yorker* 44 (13 April 1968): 150. Since Updike has published reviews, stories, articles and poems in *The New Yorker* since 1953, he may have read Gilliatt's review.

Bowman dies/is reborn. Like Kubrick, Updike leaves interpretation to us, with a conclusion as strange as the end of *2001:* "O. K.?"[46] Rabbit's inability to be changed by the black ideologist or the erotic/mystic hippie suggest that he has stepped back toward the apes. Even Jill's mother calls him a "monster," as Tothero had in *Rabbit, Run.* His answer may be close to home, though. Wary of abstractions, he "docks" with Janice at the end of *Rabbit Redux.* Janice has become a Nietzschean "superman" so potent that her sexual energy threatened her lover's life sufficiently to end their affair, but it also brought Charlie back from the dead as she staved off his heart attack. In contrast, Rabbit's sexual escapade with Margaret Fosnacht helps to cause Jill's death. Rabbit's emotional struggles with Skeeter and Jill parallel his inability to find "sense" in Kubrick's film, but Janice's absorption in her passionate affair is an analogue to her openness to the imagery of *2001.* Perhaps from her Harry might absorb her capacity to respond to *2001* the next time it comes around. Harry could not have understood what he was suggesting when he urged her to, "See that space movie again, you slept through the best parts" (*Rabbit Redux* 77). What were the best parts to him? The next time he sees *2001* he may be led further back to rehabilitation.

2001 provides a metaphor for Janice's ascension to Nietzsche's superman stage through Harry's figurative death. The conflict between the astronaut and HAL the super computer parallels the conflict between Janice and her husband. HAL, like Rabbit, fears losing control to the superforce (symbolized by the monolith) and evidently murders five of the crew to protect them, but the commander, David Bowman, in an epic confrontation of hero and beast, outwits HAL and removes his higher reasoning powers. HAL is a hyperbolic reflection of Harry: he has become a machine in order to protect Janice from the awful power of love which leads to death. But Janice, fearing his paralytic guilt might destroy her, outmaneuvers Harry and rediscovers her sexuality. Her life wish overcomes Harry's death wish.

Skeeter had called blacks "technology's nightmare" for having been left out of the Industrial Revolution– Kubrick's cave men who hadn't been affected by the monolith. That same cultural development costs Harry his job at Verity Press by making it obsolete; thus progress toward superman status has left Harry at the middle stage. He has been forcibly removed from the ape stage to the middle world where man is a "rope hung across the chasm" between ape and superman, as Nietzsche remarks. The appearances of Skeeter-as-monolith have not substantially altered his life, for, as Vargo comments,"He needs new rites to lead him out of the darkness of his existence, but he does not search for it."[47] Janice's life may change

---

[46] See the provoking remarks by Margaret Stackhouse which Kubrick called, "perhaps the most intelligent that I've read anywhere." Jerome Agel, *The Making of Kubrick's 2001* (New York: Signet, 1970) 201-05.

[47] Vargo 154.

if, like the HAL computer, Harry symbolically dies to aid Janice's liberation.[48]

Janice's flight has been a struggle for her own "it," a force which lures her to test the unknown within her, just as the astronauts are lured to challenge the unknown at the heart of the universe. Rabbit had also looked to the sky for answers in *Rabbit, Run*, figuring his children as the sun and moon in order to cope with his baby's death. In *2001* the space probe seeks final answers by flying to Jupiter. The film ends with the quester become an embryo, complementing Harry's evolution from baby at the mothering linotype machine to a child asleep with his mother when reunited with Janice at the Safe Haven Motel, like the hibernating astronauts aboard the spacecraft. Harry has not been reborn, but he has been led away from his mechanical self, and healing has begun. Janice, after a brief encounter with a higher but more dangerous form of existence, has returned to the boundary of ordinary humanity. If neither are astronauts nor supermen, neither are they apes.

Perhaps for Harry the "best part" of *2001* was the image of the Star-Child looking ambiguously toward earth, and thus Janice and Harry. For a decade he had harbored a self-destructive guilt for his part in his baby's death. Ruth had called him Mr. Death for his part in it, and she threatened to abort their child. Now the repressed child has emerged in an image reminiscent of the way in *The Scarlet Letter* Dimmesdale's adulterous guilt confronted him as a meteor scarring the night with a lurid red "A." Has he denied it, as the minister did? Or does his quest for his daughter in *Rabbit Is Rich* suggest that he has been affected? We cannot say for certain, anymore than we can settle the meaning of the image which Kubrick left intentionally ambiguous. At the motel Harry is neutral, like "the blank marquees of the deserted movie palaces" (*Rabbit Redux* 397).

Kubrick has carefully employed references to Nietzsche's "Thus Spake Zarathustra" to emphasize the stages represented by the film's action, from ape to modern man to superman. He has underscored this structure by accompanying each of the monolith's three appearances with the first three ascending notes from Richard Strauss's tone-poem "Thus Spake Zarathustra," a triad developed by Strauss specifically to echo Nietzsche's three stages. Though Harry cannot make the ascent, he carries with him a respect for cosmic messages, as his conversations with Jill about cosmology show, that may lead him upward. Apparently Harry had not yet perceived that the theme of *2001*, according to Kubrick, was the search for God.[49] Conceivably, God may speak through such films about cosmic destiny, speak with "awful power." But if Harry didn't comprehend this the night he saw

---

[48] The name "HAL" is popularly believed to have been invented by Arthur C. Clarke as single-letter alphabetical reductions of "IBM." Fortuitously, the names "Harry" and "Hal" originate in "Harold," the covert link suggesting an odd similarity between HAL and Harry Angstrom. The HAL computer was originally called "Athena," another connection to the Apollo 11. Perhaps one of Updike's many inside-jokes, he gives Harry's computer the model number "2001" in *Rabbit Is Rich* 25. Perhaps in his death (if he does die) in *Rabbit at Rest*, Harry at last liberates Janice.

[49] Agel 330.

2001, he might feel comforted by Kubrick's remark: "if this film can be completely understood, then we will have failed."[50]

A decade later, in *Rabbit Is Rich*, Harry inspects photos of Jupiter, the astronauts' destination in *2001*, and finds assurance that, "The planets keep their courses no matter what we do," blending fatalism to a sense of his place in the cosmic design (*Rabbit Is Rich* 463). He now shows an interest in "that movie about Encounters of the Third Kind the way the truck with Richard Dreyfus in it begins to shake all over and the headlights behind rise up in the air instead of pulling off to one side " (*Rabbit Is Rich* 204). In *Rabbit Redux* Harry has had his own "close encounter" which has left him shaken but still unlevitated. Perhaps *Close Encounters of the Third Kind* is "that space movie" that will lead him to get more deeply in touch with himself. His father had found movie-going a prescription for depression: "Forget your troubles. . .go off to a motion picture" (*Rabbit Redux* 354). It might work, especially if the film is *2001: A Space Odyssey*, whose achievement Kubrick characterized this way: "If *2001* has stirred your emotions, your subconscious, your mythological yearnings, then it has succeeded."[51] Since the film had contributed to Janice's self-discovery and Harry had shown himself deeply receptive to it, he may yet feel its "awful power."

Works Cited

Agel, Jerome. *The Making of Kubrick's 2001*. New York: Signet, 1970.

Bernstein, Jeremy. "Out of the Ego Chamber." *The New Yorker* 45(9 Aug. 1969): 40-42, 44, 46, 51-52, 54-56, 58-65.

Clarke, Arthur C. *2001: A Space Odyssey*. New York: Signet, 1968.

Detweiler, Robert. *John Updike*. Rev. Ed. Boston: G. K. Hall, 1984.

Gilliatt, Penelope. "After Man." *The New Yorker* 44(13 April 1968): 150-52.

Greiner, Donald J. *John Updike's Novels*. Athens, Ohio: The U of Ohio P, 1984.

Kubrick, Stanley. *2001: A Space Odyssey*. Screenplay by Arthur C. Clarke. MGM, 1968.

Markle, Joyce B. *Fighters and Lovers: Theme in the Novels of John Updike*. New York: New York UP, 1973.

Newman, Judie. *John Updike*. New York: St. Martin's P, 1988.

Ristoff, Dilvo. *Updike's America*. New York: Peter Lang, 1988.

Samuels, Charles. "The Art of Fiction XLIII: John Updike." *Paris Review* 45(Winter 1968): 84-117.

Taylor, Larry E. *Pastoral and Anti-Pastoral Patterns in John Updike's Fiction*. Carbondale: Southern Illinois UP, 1971.

Updike, John. *Picked-Up Pieces*. New York: Knopf, 1975.

_____. *Rabbit Is Rich*. New York: Knopf, 1981.

_____. *Rabbit Redux*. New York: Knopf, 1971.

---

[50] Jeremy Bernstein, "Out of the Ego Chamber," *The New Yorker* 45(9 Aug. 1969): 60.

[51] Agel 161 (unnumbered).

_____. *Rabbit, Run.* New York: Knopf, 1960.
Vargo, Edward P. *Rainstorms and Fire: Ritual in the Novels of John Updike.* Port
Washington: Kennikat, 1973.

*Jack De Bellis, "'The Awesome Power': John Updike's Use of Kubrick's
'2001' in *Rabbit Redux.*" *Literature/Film Quarterly* 21.3 (1993): 209-217.

"'He. She. Sleeps.': Media and Entropy in *Rabbit Redux*"

Irina Negrea*

According to critic Judie Newman, Harry Angstrom is a Gutenberg man trying to
live in a post-Gutenberg world—a man used to thinking and working in linear and
sequential patterns who is faced with a world that is not linear any more (42).
Newman uses the theory formulated by Marshall McLuhan in order to explain
Harry's confusion and experiences. Roughly at the same time when Updike's novel
is set, Marshall McLuhan revolutionized the world with his "global village" theory
of technology, media, and communication.   The Gutenberg man—the man
habituated to think in linear patterns—is the builder of a visual culture, according
to McLuhan, which has lost the benefits of the "oral and tribal ear-culture" and is
therefore lost himself (*Understanding* 50). The new "electric age" heralded by the
unprecedented development of mass media and technology is supposed to reunite
the post-Gutenberg man with the values and abilities that he had lost, provided he
espouses a new way of thinking, based on instant awareness. A "seamless web of
kinship and interdependence" is created that would unify all senses, and the globe
will turn into "a village," since all man's senses are extended and enhanced by the
implosion of technology (*Understanding* 343). McLuhan's notion of implosion,
applied to Updike's novel, opens new avenues of interpretations.
     McLuhan poses a new way of thinking which is meant to replace the
sequential, linear way of looking at the world characteristic of the Gutenberg era.
The appearance of print on the page has taught the Gutenberg man to think in a
linear way, according to McLuhan, and the technological development imposes a
new way of thinking, based on instant awareness.   In McLuhan's view,
mechanization and printing were characterized by expansion (or explosion), while
implosion seems to be the consequence of the new age of technology. Implosion
is meant to bring people together, to "shrink" the expanse of the world. By using
the extensions of his senses (media), man should be able to turn the earth into a
"global village." In *Rabbit Redux*, Updike explores what happens in the new post-
Gutenberg era.
     Harry Angstrom is a Gutenberg man, not only defined by his profession as a
typesetter, but also by the way he thinks—in straight lines. He is convinced that
"America, it's still the only place," and he clings to the traditional values that give
him the sense of a homogenous, unified world. However, despite McLuhan's

optimism, which affirms the unification of mankind as a consequence of the technological implosion, the America presented in *Rabbit Redux* is far from unified. What the implosion of mass media brings about is entropy, discontinuity, and fragmentation. It is as if McLuhan's theory, when applied, yields the opposite results, as seen in the works of Jean Baudrillard, who argues that mass media starts with implosion as well. Gary Genosko notes that

> For Baudrillard, implosion does not produce the intimacy of the Global Village. The new patterns of inclusive structuration postulated by McLuhan yield their inverse: inertia, silence, indifference. (94)

It is this inertia and entropy that Harry tries to fight in Updike's novel, as everything he believed in crumbles. Implosion brings on simulation, defined by Baudrillard as "a liquidation of all referentials, a question of substituting the signs of the real for the real," the birth of a simulated reality that he calls "hyperreal" (*Simulacra* 2-3). In his quest for a unified and "real" reality, Harry Angstrom fights simulation and the hyperreal, but ends up giving in because what he believes in does not exist any more.

Fragmentation—the breaking apart of a unified, linear, and stable world—is the result of an implosion, of violence, of a rupture that brings about a view of the world similar to the reflection in a broken mirror. Dissolution and entropy follow fragmentation, in a system where, as a consequence, chaos rules. It is only fitting that Updike develops his main motifs through a structure that is not fluid any more, as in *Rabbit, Run*. The division of *Rabbit Redux* into chapters seems to point to an America that is falling to pieces, while Rabbit's life takes on the same trajectory. Although he is unwilling to see it at first, the experiences he goes through, as well as the people he meets, change his perception of the world in the end.

Harry's quest is unraveling against a highly unstable background, even when he is not willing to see it as such. The ironic counterpoint provided by Updike to Rabbit's experience is the American odyssey to the moon, seemingly a successful quest that starts with a blast:

> For the twentieth time that day the rocket blasts off, the numbers pouring backwards in tenths of seconds faster than eye until zero is reached. (6)

It seems for a moment that Updike wants to indicate that there are some (unlike Rabbit) who are able to attain the object of their quest. However, according to Newman, space traveling has a double implication: liberation, but also "the dangers of perishing in a cold void," since even the numbers are going toward zero (60). The moon odyssey represents an important motif in the novel, and the medium through which the characters have access to it is television. A favorite medium for analysis for both McLuhan and Baudrillard, television is definitely proving true that "the medium is the message," adopted by both theorists. Unlike McLuhan, however, who says that the image of the astronaut announces the contraction of the world to the size of a village (*Understanding* 295), Baudrillard takes this formula to the extreme and states that the implosion of information produces a surplus of meaning that is created far faster than the possibility of its incorporation, causing loss of communication and the collapsing of the medium itself. We find ourselves again in the hyperspace, the space of simulacra and of hyperreality (*Simulacra* 80-

2).

The first instance of the rocket blasting is set in a prominent place in the novel—right in the beginning. The contrast between what is shown on TV—the rocket blasting off—and the bar, in which the men "have not been lifted," is telling in the way it dissociates between the artificial reality of the medium (TV) and the reality of the bar, where people encounter their daily problems and try to make sense of their lives (6). Details of the American odyssey to the moon are interspersed throughout the novel. The dangers of losing oneself in the void are real for the astronauts, but also for Harry Angstrom, who is watching them on TV:

> The six o'clock news is all about space, all about emptiness: some bald
> man plays with little toys to show the docking and undocking
> maneuvers, and then a panel talks about the significance of this for the
> next five hundred years. (19)

The reality of the space travel has lost its referent, since it is *simulated* by the man on the news. Loss of referentiality is, according to Baudrillard, one of the defining characteristics of simulacra (*Simulacra* 2). Harry lives in a world that is not "real" any more: the acceleration of information is imploding the meaning, and the loss of reference facilitates the birth of simulation and of hyperreality. In this sense, Rabbit is right to see that the astronauts "see exactly where they're aiming and it's a big round nothing" (19). The void is ruled by entropy, and the technological implosion does not unify people, as McLuhan thought it would.

The presence of the media in *Rabbit Redux* reveals America as a wasteland. According to David Cox,

> The television is at once a magnificent tool of community and spirit in
> its dissemination of ideas and bringing together of people, and at the
> same time a corruptor of images, a suppressor of minds, a glaring
> hypnotic eye that traps people in their homes. (90)

Dissolution is pervasive even at the level of TV programs that (on the surface) have nothing to do with what is happening in the country. For example, Harry's perception of the *Lone Ranger* parody in "The Carol Burnett Show" is continually fragmented. Because he talks to Nelson, he keeps on missing jokes in the show and losing the thread of the story. The introduction of Spanish words in the actor's lines, words that Rabbit misunderstands, represents another discontinuity in his reception of the message, and that affirms once more that the content is not that important, since, as Baudrillard says, its meaning is imploded by the medium. The show itself is a parody of the tale of the Lone Ranger—the mythical figure of the frontier who finds himself weighed down and nagged by his wife. The Lone Ranger is not alone any more, and this puts an end to his quest. It is a mirror of Rabbit's life, who thinks that having a wife and a child hampered his growth and diminished his chances of doing something better, and that it made him settle for less in life. The dissolution of traditional values is pervasive in the show that Harry and Nelson are watching: the Lone Ranger's wife is going to have an affair with an American Indian, and Rabbit feels that "this final gag falls flat, maybe because everybody still thinks of Tonto as incorruptible, as above it all, like Jesus and Armstrong" (21). Rabbit is still willing to believe that there are some values that are not corrupted yet, but entropy and dissolution have become so pervasive that the media reflects them.

The load of information that the media (and especially television) attempts to communicate has as a consequence the implosion of meaning, a fact that McLuhan did not foretell, but to which Baudrillard offers ample space in his analyses of the medium of television. Rabbit is caught in the downward spiral that brings about simulation, and with it, "the artificial resurrection [of reality] in the systems of signs" (*Simulacra* 2). Lost in a system of signs that do not have a referent anymore, Rabbit cannot make sense of what he sees on TV because there is no sense to be made. The coverage of news is, according to Baudrillard, a simulation in itself, since what the viewer sees is not the event itself, but a reproduction of it in a "degraded form" (*Simulacra* 86).

It is what Rabbit gets – a simulation—when he watches the coverage of another event that gets a lot of media attention: the Vietnam War. An important element in the novel, the war is discussed by Harry and—in turn—by Charlie Stavros, Earl Angstrom, Skeeter, and Jill. Willing to believe in his American Dream, Harry supports the war blindly, until he meets Skeeter, a black Vietnam veteran who dispels his romantic notions of Americans as the brave white civilizers fighting a war that is totally just and heroic. Newman points out that when Skeeter tries to tell Harry about Vietnam, he tries to conjure images rather than words: "He tilts his head back as if the ceiling is a movie screen" (224). Trying to convey the images and sounds of war, Skeeter realizes that he cannot do them justice, and that, as Newman says, "Vietnam resists any overall formulation and cannot be parceled up neatly and sequentially" (55). There is a subtle irony here in the way in which Updike treats Rabbit: since Skeeter, who has experienced Vietnam as a fighter, cannot bring himself to accurately convey how the war felt and what it meant, how can Rabbit have a clear, cut-and-dry opinion about a war that he has experienced only in front of the TV?

The imagery of demolition and destruction that is pervasive in Skeeter's words every time he talks about the war points to something that Baudrillard did not account for in his theories: the reality of the experience *as lived*. The Vietnam War got increased television coverage which represented a simulation for the people at home, but not for Skeeter. Updike does not dwell too much on the experienced reality of the war, since he wants to show how TV has distorted Rabbit's perception of the event and how the media in general implodes meaning and kills referentiality. It is interesting that even McLuhan who was an optimist when discussing television and media in general, has found that the coverage of the Vietnam War "has been a disaster because it has alienated people altogether from that war." He states that television

> has begun to dissolve the fabric of American life. All the assumptions—all the ground rules—based on visuality, superficiality, blueprinting, connectedness, equality, sameness—disappear with TV.
> (Media 56)

Experiencing the Vietnam War through what he sees on TV, Rabbit has a distorted and alienated perception of it, naturally different from what Skeeter has seen. Harry takes what he sees on TV as information that would give him an idea about what was happening overseas, but he does not realize that the information lost its meaning and that the event as such is gone, while all that is left is "merely the (flat) encephalogram, only the psychodrama and the TV image" (Baudrillard, *Illusion* 19). Baudrillard takes McLuhan's idea further and states that "INFORMATION=ENTROPY" (*Simulacra* 86). The information that Rabbit gets on TV about the two main events of American history in that year—the moon landing and the war in Vietnam—has lost its meaning in the medium through which it is transmitted. Baudrillard adds that "information in which an event is reflected or broadcast is already a degraded form of this event" (*Simulacra* 86). The reality does not exist any more, since it is replaced by its own simulacrum. This is the main cause of entropy and disorder in Rabbit's world, and it is reflected by Updike through the massive presence of the media in the novel.

If young American men die in Vietnam, on American soil there is a strong reaction to the war that splits the country into two opposing factions, causing violent riots. Harry sees them every day on TV:

> "Windows were smashed, cars overturned, policemen assaulted by the young militants ..." Film cuts of white-helmeted policemen flailing at the nest of arms and legs, ... of sudden bearded faces shaking fists that want to rocket out through the television screen ... [were shown]. (239)

The language used by Updike emphasizes once more one of the main motifs of the novel—fragmentation, enhanced here by the use of body part imagery. The crisis in Vietnam and the riots all over the country suggest that America itself is on a quest, shaken from its post-World War II self-sufficiency, and looking for a way out of chaos. The use of the word "rocket" connects this image with the launch of the moon mission in the beginning of the novel. Updike seems to suggest that they are both aimed at nothingness, at void and entropy.

The way in which Updike develops the main motifs of implosion, entropy, and fragmentation is perhaps most obvious in the texts that Harry works on as a typesetter. Under the reader's eyes lies the proof of the dissolution of the Gutenberg world, the proof that nothing is fluid, linear, or stable any more, as even in a text that seems smooth and flowing, the typesetter (Rabbit) makes mistakes and has to go back and reset a line, or the text itself is constantly interrupted by his breaks and/or Janice's phone calls and his emotional state:

> **Zigzag Electronic Products Inc., Of Seventh and Locust Streets, City,**
>
> Oops.
>
> **Locust Streets, city, revealed to VAT reporters this week that a crucial electronic switching sequence in the on-board guidance and nabifiation computer was the on-board guidance and navigation computer was manufactured by them here, in the plain brick building... (34)**

The structure of the text is continuously disrupted, while the content reflects both the entropy that rules the whole country (as in the article that is shaped like a handgun and relates how three black men were the main suspects in the assault on a white woman), but also rules Harry's whole life. The last article that he tries to set is the one that relates what happened at his house: how it burned down, how Jill died, and how Skeeter was the main suspect. This article is interrupted when Rabbit finds out that he is fired from his job because his expertise has been rendered redundant by the development of technology. It is another discontinuity that adds to the many in the novel. As Baudrillard says, information does not create communication any more, but "it exhausts itself in the act of staging communication" (*Simulacra* 80). The form of the articles that Rabbit sets in type illustrates this implosion of meaning, where the referent is lost and simulation begins. It is as futile to try to gather information from these articles as it is to try to make sense of Brewer's past by gathering arrowheads. Updike makes this clear by the interruptions and mistakes that are introduced in the article about the excavations in Brewer. As Newman points out, "while the item celebrates technological development in terms of an unchecked continuity, it is actually interrupted twice by the pressing demands of the present" (51).

McLuhan optimistically states that the typographic expansion "extended the minds and voices of men" and **brought** them closer together, while spreading "the power that is knowledge" (*Understanding* 170-71). However, Rabbit's work is defined by a profound isolation and a sort of arrested development or even regression, since he feels that the linotyping machine is hovering above him like a mother: "the machine stands tall and warm above him, mothering, muttering, a temperamental thousand-parted survival form the golden age of machinery" (25). At the same time, Harry is alone with the machine when he sets the text that would—ironically—unify people. The form of the language, especially the spelling mistakes and the interruptions, point to another phenomenon analyzed by Baudrillard—the implosion of meaning in language.

Rabbit hears "language collapsing" all around him (128), and this is masterfully realized by Updike in Rabbit's mother's speech. Mary Angstrom is disintegrating under his eyes from Parkinson's disease, which takes control of her body and wreaks havoc:

> "I'm sixty-five," she says, groping for phrases, so that her sentences end in the middle. "When I was twenty. I told my boy friend I wanted to be shot. When I was thirty." (80)

Newman points out that Mom's speech "develops the impression of a sick, over-mechanised America" (48). Her fragmented speech and her fight with her body's uncontrollable movements give Harry another view of disorder in a world that he thought was stable. His mother, the force that gave him life, cannot control what is happening to her. Little by little, Harry's own view takes on the same distortive quality, as in a broken mirror. The fragmentation that has gone as deep as the level of language is exemplified by the movie marquees that jumble the film titles: "2001 SPACE OD'SEY" (12), or "BUTCH CSSDY & KID" (174) and by Rabbit thinking in headlines: "LINOTYPER'S WIFE LAYS LOCAL SALES REP. *Greek Takes Strong Anti-Viet Stand,*" which is also symptomatic of the linear way of thinking that Rabbit still uses in the beginning of the novel (64). Implosion of meaning has descended to the level of language and is followed by entropy. Cox notices a certain "impotence" of language, illustrated by Rabbit's "O.K.'s" and Skeeter's "right's", which contribute to their "frequent misunderstandings" (149).

Harry Angstrom ends by appropriating this vision of the world, of isolation and alienation brought about by the media and the general fragmentation that occurs on a larger scale in America. He has a vision of the post-Gutenberg world when Peggy Fosnacht serves him dinner:

...a casserole of chicken legs and breasts, poor dismembered
creatures simmering. Rabbit wonders how many animals have died
to keep his life going...A barnyard full, a farmfull of thumping
hearts, seeing eyes, racing legs, all stuffed...into him as into a black
sack. (271)

This vision of dismembered creatures that die to keep him alive points two ways:
to Vietnam, where young American men were mutilated everyday in a futile war,
and to Rabbit's microcosm, to his "black sack" that connects unexpectedly but
meaningfully with the void, with the "round nothingness" toward which the
American astronauts make their way.

Toward the end of *Rabbit Redux,* the reader sees Rabbit surrender and
internalize the fragmented view of the world that everyone seems to share around
him. He is slowly turning into a post-Gutenberg man, one who is not "slavishly
dominated by the eye" any more, but one who learns the hard way that the world
around him is not the unified image that he was used to seeing (Newman 41). His
sister Mim has adopted the fragmentary view of the world as well, and she also
practices it. As an aspiring actress who has become a prostitute, she sees herself as
an actress still, but one who performs for "the audience one at a time" (313). Rabbit
comes to share this point of view, most visibly at the end of the narrative. The same
tone of isolation and separation seems to pervade the ending, even though Harry
reunites with his wife: "He. She. Sleeps" (363). It has the same form as his
mother's speech, and it also suggests a sense of loss, passivity, and futility that seem
to invade Harry Angstrom at this stage of his quest. It is another effect of the
entropy that permeates *Rabbit Redux.* Newman also sees it as closing the circle
with the beginning of the novel, as it suggests "the over-and-out of a space
message" (61). While in the beginning of the novel, the TV image prompts the
suggestion of void and loneliness, at the novel's end, it is the reality of life that
gives the suggestion of a space message and of void. The pervasiveness of media
is thus demonstrated by Updike and its influence explored. Rabbit's life seems to
revolve around the TV shows that he watches and the articles that he typesets, while
their meaning seems to be imploded and lost in a chaotic hyperreality in which
Harry fights to find a place for himself and make sense of his life.

Have Rabbit's experiences made him wiser, or have they brought him closer
to the object of his quest? The question still stands. Throughout the book, Rabbit's
"reality instructors"—Charlie Stavros, Skeeter, and Jill, among others—try to make
him change his views on different issues. There is not much hard evidence in
Rabbit Redux that he actually internalizes more than the awareness of living in a
chaotic, post-Gutenberg world. While the readers see the "lessons" and their value,
Rabbit's apparent passivity does not suggest more than his decision to submit to
history and admit to the lack of unity in this world, or in his life. By the end of
Rabbit Redux, Harry Angstrom is appropriating the world as it is: fragmented,
entropic, and meaningless, and this (though a source of sadness for him) can be seen
by the reader as a sign of victory on a quest that seemed futile in the beginning.
McLuhan's optimistic vision of a unified and homogenous global village is thus
challenged by Updike and Baudrillard, who demonstrate that the advent of
developed technology does not unify humans; on the contrary, it depletes

communication of meaning and transforms people into "the terminals of all this communications network." Thus, even our own humanity is losing its referentiality and meaning (*Live* 146). Projected into the cold void of the hyperreal, Rabbit's only solution is to stop trying to look for a meaning where there is none, and give in to the entropy that information causes.

Works Cited

Baudrillard, Jean. *The Illusion of the End.* Stanford: Stanford UP, 1994.

_____. *Simulacra and Simulation.* Ann Arbor: U of Michigan P, 1994.

Cox, David Michael. *An Examination of Thematic and Structural Differences between John Updike's Rabbit Novels.* Ann Arbor: University Microfilms International, 1984. (dissertation)

Gane, Mike, ed. *Baudrillard Live: Selected Interviews.* London and New York: Routledge, 1993.

Genosko, Gary. *McLuhan and Baudrillard: The Masters of Implosion.* London and New York: Routledge, 1999.

McLuhan, Marshall. *Media Research: Technology, Art, Communication.* Amsterdam: G&B Arts International, 1997.

_____. *Understanding Media: the Extensions of Man.* Cambridge, Mass.: MIT P, 1994.

Newman, Judie. *John Updike.* New York: St. Martin's P, 1988.

Updike, John. *Rabbit Redux.* New York: Fawcett/Columbine, 1996.

*Irina Negrea, "'He. She. Sleeps.': Media and Entropy in Rabbit Redux." Negrea's essay was written for this collection of essays.

Rabbit Is Rich

"Updike on Updike"

Henry Bech [John Updike]

An interview conducted, in the New York Times Book Review– as was done ten years earlier on the occasion of the publication of Rabbit Redux– by the tireless Henry Bech.

In the ten years since your hypothetical interviewer bearded the beardless Updike in his Ipswich (Mass.) den, the skittish author has moved some miles inland, to a town without qualities called Georgetown– a nexus of route numbers on the edge of that New England hinterland best know for its bygone Indian massacres. As if to announce his willingness to assume the mothballed mantle of Sinclair Lewis, Updike lives on Main Street. He works, if that is the word, in a former antique shop now crammed with editions of his twenty-odd books in twenty-odd languages, including Finnish, Serbo-Croatian, Hebrew, and Korean. The years have not been terrifically unkind to him; teetering on the verge of fifty, he has retained his figure, which is that of a pot-bellied ectomorph, and his hair, which if not quite silvery is certainly pewter. His complexion has not improved during the Me Decade, and his stammer has grown worse. He gives the impression, reciting his responses into the tape recorder with many a fidget and static pause, of a word processor with some slipped bits; the effort, one feels, of visualizing every utterance in print has somewhat dimpled the flow of language within him, and cast him like a gasping crab onto one dry bank of the onrushing human orality alongside of which literature is just so many irrigation ditches.

However, he is most at home among his own characters, and therefore appeared relatively relaxed with me. I confessed that I had not, due to press of other business, made much headway into his new novel, concerning the adventures of another old friend, Harold C. Angstrom, of Brewer, Pa. I reminded him, though, that at our last interview he had promised that the sequel to *Rabbit Redux* would be, in ten years, a volume entitled *Rural Rabbit*, to be followed, in 1991, with *Rabbit Is Rich*. Updike squirmed and, making sure that the tape recorder was running, stiffly dictated:

A: Well, this novel really has *Rural Rabbit* in it, since he keeps going out into the country to spy on this girl he thinks might be his daughter. Ever since his girl baby drowned in *Rabbit, Run*, Harry has been looking for a daughter. It's the theme that has been pressing forward, without my willing it or understanding it exactly, through these novels.

Q (*primly*): Please, let's not give the plot away. Or do the work of that third, who is among us.

A (*spooked*): Who? Who's that? (*Genuinely alarmed, he darts his scum-green eyes all around the memorabilia-choked shelves of his shabby atelier.*)

Q: The author of the review with which this interview must appear in tandem [*Roger Sale, in the event; he salted his favorable review with so much incidental dispraise as to quite spoil the taste.*) And with whose silent voice we are singing a curious duet, perhaps in grotesque disharmony.

A (*whispering*): Can he hear us?

Q: He or she. I doubt it. Reviewers don't read more than they have to. Anyway, what matters surely is the book itself, in its final thumb-worn library state, stripped of its jacket of publicity and passing financial trauma, a mysterious cloth-and-paper casket waiting to be broken open by the trumpet call of an unknown reader's mind. All else is dross.

A: You've taken the words right out of my mouth.

Q: I know you pretty well. Your theme, in this latest artifact in your habitual ten-point Janson, is inflation, am I correct?

A: Yes, and the trouble with inflation as a theme is that inflation overtakes it. The book was inspired by my sense of outrage at paying ninety-nine cents a gallon for gasoline, and now that would be a steal. Harry is meant to feel rich, but the income I assigned him as of 1979 will within a few years drop him below the poverty line. I fear my sense of the dollar is hopelessly retrograde; I live in a world where you can still buy two sparrows for a farthing. The very price of this novel– who can afford it? My first novel not twenty-two years ago sold for $3.50, and that seemed a lot to ask. There is a terror to all this.

Q (*in Bech's best psychoanalytical manner*): Let's talk about that.

A: Oh, Lordy. The terror of launching yourself into the blank paper. Nelson in this novel hang-glides, and now I see why; a writer hang-glides all the time, out over that terrible whiteness. The abyss is you, your own life, your mind. It's a terrifying thing to exist at all, and an author with every creation tries to exist twice over; it is as when in poker you try to bluff a nothing hand through, and the dark face opposite raises, so you raise him back. And the bookstores– there's terror there, especially this time of year, all those bright books of life fighting it out in their armor of embossed lettering, stacks of them being carted out to make room for the fresh contenders, all these sensibilities the educational system is churning out, dying to describe their parents, their seductions, they keep coming, wave upon wave, and the old sensibilities won't even die off, modern medicine is too good. Who can even spot a trend anymore? Whatever happened to Black Humor, to the Imperial Novel? We live in a coral reef, smothered in a glut of self-regard. And the reviews? There's terror for you, all those muddy paws, even the ones trying to give you a pat–

Q: Yet you yourself are a reviewer.

A (*holding up his muddy paws*): *Mea culpa.* Print is guilt Life is guilt. I believe it.

Q (*smoothly*): And take considerable satisfaction in it all, it would appear.

A (*scarcely chastened*): I've been lucky. My heroes tend to be lucky. But as long as there is one unlucky person in the world, life is grim.

Q: And writing?

A: Makes it less so. I cannot do justice to the bliss that attends getting even a single string of dialogue or the name of a weed right. Naming our weeds, in fact, seems to be exactly where it's at. I've been going out into my acre here (*gestures toward a scruffy meadow visible from his windows*) and trying to identify the wildflowers along the fringes with the aid of a book, and it's remarkably difficult to match reality and diagram. Reality keeps a pace or two ahead, scribble though we will. If you were to ask me what the aim of my fiction is–

Q: I will. I do.

A:– it's bringing the corners forward. Or throwing light into them, if you'd rather. Singing the hitherto unsung. That's applied Christianity, for that matter. I distrust books involving spectacular people, or spectacular events. Let *People* and *The National Enquirer* pander to our taste for the extraordinary; let literature concern itself, as the Gospels do, with the inner lives of hidden men. The collective consciousness that once found itself in the noble must now rest content with the typical.

Q: You've taken the words right out of my mouth.

A: I've been through a lot of interviews.

Q: Yet you say you dislike them.

A: I don't dislike the spouting-off, the conjuring-up of opinions. That's show biz, and you don't go into this business without a touch of ham. But as a practitioner trying to keep practicing in an age of publicity, I can only decry the drain on the brain, the assumption that a writer is a mass of opinions to be trucked in and carted off for his annual six minutes on the pan-American talk show. He is not; he is a secreter of images, some of which he prays will have the immortal resonance of Don Quixote's windmills, of Proust's madeleine, of Huck Finn's raft. As a secreter he must be at heart secret, patient, wicked even. His duty is, in a sense, to turn his back. This is not easy to understand in an era when everybody says "Have a nice day" and even two o'clock in the morning is lit by the phosphorescent glow of money going rotten.

Q: Has the writer's condition changed, do you think, in the twenty-odd years since you took up a pen with a professional purpose?

A: When I began to write, publishers were gentlemen in tweed jackets puffing pipes. Now the only one who looks like that is Hugh Hefner. Publishing houses are owned by oil companies or their cat's-paws, and their interest is naturally in the big strike, the gusher. I don't want to write gushers. I want to write books that are hard and curvy, like keys, and that unlock the traffic jam in everybody's head. Something like $E = mc2$, only in words, one after the other.

Q: And speaking of after the other, what can you tell us about the *Rabbit* book to follow this in ten years?

A: Nothing, except that I hope it exists. I hope, that is, that both Harry and I survive the decade. I have ominous feelings about the Eighties, and it's not just Orwell's book. North America has been by and large an unmolested continent for over a century, and there is a possible perspective from which the postwar decades, decry them though we have, will look as halcyon as the summer of 1914. However, I will hope for the best, and hope to rendezvous with my ex-basket ballplayer and fellow-pilgrim one more time, proving that two plus two equals four.

Q: And in the meantime?

A: I have dreams, I have corners picked out for a web or two. I always am trying to relearn my job, taking into sober account the reproaches of friend and enemy alike and seeking out the great exemplars. I've been reading the late Melville lately, to see what went wrong, if anything. A wonderful man he was, refusing all his life to call the puzzle solved. Let me quote: "Yea and Nay–/ Each hath his say;/ But God he keeps the middle way."

Q (*getting down to business*): Now, I have here a number of more specific and personal questions which–

Tape Recorder: Click.

*Henry Bech [John Updike], "Updike on Updike." *The New York Times Book Review* 27Sept. 1981: 1, 34-35.

"Updike's Rabbit Trilogy"

Thomas R. Edwards*

John Updike became an "important" writer, as we say, with his second novel, *Rabbit, Run*, which was published in 1960 and is still, eight novels and thirteen other books later, one of the his best performances. Since then, Updike's imagination has lingered upon Harry Angstrom, called "Rabbit" in his days of glory as a high school basketball star; *Rabbit Redux* (1971) found him a decade older, beset by the troubles and confusions endemic in America during the late 1960s; and now a third book, *Rabbit Is Rich*, whose opening words are "Running out of gas," shows him middle-aged and slowing down some, in which, once again, we recognize to be the present. One somehow hadn't understood that a series was in progress, and Updike's pleasant surprise suggests that the new work needs to be considered as part of a larger whole.

Rabbit, Run now seems distinctly a novel of the 1950s, if only because it takes so little account of the public terms of life in its time. The setting, a small Pennsylvania city in 1959, is lovingly observed, and the culture of common experience– popular songs, television shows, and the like– is duly acknowledged, but it is Harry Angstrom's sense of self, his inward spiritual being, that draws the novelist's attention and energizes his remarkable lyric style. At twenty-six, with high school, athletic stardom, and stateside military service during the Korean War behind him, Harry, a printer's son, has impregnated, and then married, a girl somewhat above him in the social scheme. Harry and Janice have a small son and another child on the way; they live in a drab walk-up while Harry tries to sell kitchen gadgets and Janice neglects the housework, drinks too much, and nurses her discontent. Harry is on the run throughout the novel: from Janice to Ruth, a good-hearted, overweight prostitute, from Ruth back to Janice when their daughter is born, and eventually from both of them, when Janice accidentally lets the baby drown in the bathtub and Ruth reveals that she's now pregnant too.

This familiar tale, of possessive women and escape-artist men, has little to do in particular with the 1950s in Middle America. It has much more to do with the then rather fashionable religiosity announced by the novel's epigraph from Pascal: "The motions of Grace, the hardness of the heart; external circumstances." Updike intends to look through Harry's apparent human inadequacies, his way of disappointing or hurting those who would love him or at least welcome his love, toward the idea that fascinates the book's rather ineffectual clergyman, Jack Eccles: that (as Harry himself cheerfully reports it) "'I'm a mystic. . . . I give people faith.'" In all the novels, it is suggested– Updike is too canny to insist on it– that Harry, resolutely commonplace in most other ways, has a special spiritual gift, however poorly he understands or articulates it, a persistent sense of what William James in *A Pluralistic Universe* wittily called "a more": "the believer finds that the tenderest parts of his personal life are continuous with a *more* of the same quality which is operative in the universe outside of him and which he can keep in working touch with, and in a fashion get on board of and save himself, when all his lower being has gone to pieces in the wreck."

James's terms are helpful in making out Harry Angstrom. Though his "lower being," the part of him that *ought* to be more observant of what his wife, his lovers, his parents, his children, expect and need from him, does continually go to pieces, he sees at least dimly that "the tenderest parts of his personal life" participate in something more, outside him, and that he can at least hope to save *himself.* At moments of ordinary pleasure– playing basketball or golf, gardening, feeling intimacy with his children, and above all performing the acts of physical love– Harry's life is obscurely but deeply touched by intimations of continuity with some savingly larger presence or purpose, intimations that human time does not erase, as Updike suggests by making Harry's response to his newborn granddaughter at the end of *Rabbit Is Rich* plagiarize from what he felt when he first saw his ill-fated baby daughter twenty years before:

> . . .the tiny stichless seam of the closed eyelid runs diagonally a great length, as if the eye, when it is opened, will be huge and see everything and know everything. In the suggestion of pressure behind the tranquil lid and in the tilt of the protruding upper lip he reads a delightful hint of disdain. She knows she's good. What he never expected, he can feel she's feminine, feels something both delicate and enduring in the arc of the long pink cranium. . .
> (*Rabbit, Run*)

> . . .the baby shows her profile blindly in the shuddering flashes of color jerking from the Sony, the tiny stichless seam of the closed eyelid

aslant, lips bubbled forward beneath the whorled nose as if in delicate
disdain, you can feel in the curve of the cranium she's feminine, that
shows from the first day.
(*Rabbit Is Rich*)

Such reprises are frequent in the Rabbit novels, and they represent Harry's
persisting sense of wonder that the world is as it is and that he himself, just as *he* is,
is always there to apprehend it. It is what makes him so often disappoint the people
around him, and what reconciles them to him, however grudgingly; in his frequent
incapacity for good works, he does "give them faith," though they seldom call his
gift by that name.

Rabbit, Run is a tactfully religious novel whose spiritual implications are
mostly proposed on the sly, by the not very authoritative Jack Eccles. One of the
book's most terrifying moments is when Eccles's helpful, social-worker kind of
ministry is challenged by a fire-breathing old Lutheran pastor: "'If Gott wants to
end misery, He'll declare the Kingdom now.'" For the purposes of a religious
novelist, that's much more like it, and *Rabbit Redux* shows that, a decade later, God
has once again decided not to make that declaration just yet. In the meanwhile,
Harry has returned to Janice and their son, Nelson, lost track of Ruth, taken up his
father's trade of Linotyper, and bought a little tract house in a second-class suburb.
His grim, inflexible mother is dying of Parkinson's disease, and Janice works at her
father's used-car lot, recently adorned by a Toyota dealership, and (it emerges) is
carrying on an affair with Charlie Stavros, her father's best salesman. Around them
all, in 1969, the world is quite visibly falling apart.

Though the religious questions raised by the earlier book continue as an
undertone, *Rabbit Redux* is essentially a political novel of a particular historical
moment. Its four sections bear epigraphs not from Pascal but from the subliminally
bawdy technical talk of space exploration, and even in the hinterlands of
Pennsylvania the abiding subjects are the moon shot, Vietnam, the morality of the
rebellious young, and black revolution. Harry is an unabashed hawk on all such
subjects, to the disgust of trendy Janice and her lover, a decent-minded liberal; but
when Janice leaves him to live with Charlie, Harry allows himself to be drawn into
the black subworld of Brewer, from which he brings home Jill, a runaway young
rich girl, and Skeeter, a bright, articulate, incorrigibly hostile young black drug
dealer and racial messiah, to live with him and poor Nelson. With Jill he extends
his sexual repertory; with Skeeter he samples the pleasures of illegal substances;
with Nelson, who adores Jill and (for good reason) is terrified of Skeeter, he begins
to enact the Oedipal conflict that will persist into *Rabbit Is Rich*. Jill dies when the
neighbors, outraged at such carryings on, burn his house down; Skeeter takes his
nihilistic faith into the wilderness; and Harry and Janice once again come back
together to pick up the pieces of his lower being.

Rabbit Redux seems to me a flawed work, one of Updike's weaker novels, for
several reasons. In it, the pressure of history, which Updike was of course not alone
in feeling in those difficult times, threatens to overpower the individuality of his
characters, who tend to become representative figures, spokesmen, rather than free
dramatic agents. Jill and Skeeter are cartoons of the counterculture; Janice, Charlie,

Nelson, and to a degree even Harry himself seem to have been assigned roles rather than permitted to have experiences (only Peggy Fosnacht, the pathetic, overweight friend of Janice's, with whom Harry has a brief sexual interlude, seems to be fully alive); dialogue inclines toward debate, as in Harry's arguments with Charlie Stavros and Skeeter, where the voices speak less for any personal sense of things than for the public positions that everyone was arguing about at the end of the 1960s. As if aware of a danger, Updike made the book virtually a time capsule for 1969, stuffing it with current news stories, music, advertisements, and products; but the effect is of a theater in which the scenery is more vivid and authentic than the actors themselves. Certainly the book's catastrophe, Jill's violent destruction at the hands of bigots, belongs to a tradition of melodrama one had hoped Updike might disdain.

Both *Rabbit, Run* and *Rabbit Redux* end with images of feeling small and safe within large spaces, an acceptance by the microcosmic self of the macrocosmic "more." In *Rabbit, Run*, Harry, in full flight from the entangling demands of domestic life, thinks "he doesn't know, what to do, where to go, what will happen, the thought that he doesn't know seems to make him infinitely small and impossible to capture. Its smallness fills him like a vastness," and in *Rabbit Redux*, in bed again with Janice like some Ulysses come home to Ithaca, "the space they are in, the motel room long and secret as a burrow, becomes all interior space," and he becomes, in effect, the "microscopic self" of his own penis. At the end of *Rabbit Is Rich*, the small object in a congenial space is not himself but the baby granddaughter in his arms; yet the new novel, however full of problems and anxieties, is governed by the mood of accepted security that its predecessors achieved only after long struggle.

If the first two Rabbit novels are religious and political, respectively, *Rabbit Is Rich* is clearly a story of the economic life. It leaps ahead another decade, to 1979, discovering an augmented Harry, both richer and fatter, in a depleted public reality. In a world that is running out of gas, he is cleaning up, managing his late father-in-law's Toyota agency and selling fuel-efficient cars like crazy. But death is present in this personal Arcadia, having taken not just Janice's father but both of Harry's parents and (he learns from a news clipping) the demonic Skeeter, and he senses its hand on his mother-in-law; on the declining Charlie Stavros; on Thelma Murkett [Harrison, *ed.*], with whom he has encyclopedic sex when he and Janice try spouse-swapping on a Caribbean holiday with friends from the country club; on Peggy Fosnacht, who's had a breast removed; and even on himself, as he begins to feel worrisome twinges in the chest. Not too far away, Three Mile Island is behaving rather oddly.

Yet if disaster hovers around Harry and the nation generally, *Rabbit Is Rich* is a story of disasters averted. No one drowns or burns to death– no one, in fact, dies. Updike teases us into anticipating tragedies that never quite occur. Nelson's repeated fender-benders are not major accidents; Harry's new daughter-in-law falls downstairs but does no lasting harm to herself or her unborn child; Nelson meets and is attracted to a girl who may be his illegitimate half-sister, the child Harry gave Ruth twenty years before, but they don't meet again and the threat of incest passes quietly. At the economic level, Harry's ignorant speculation in the rising gold and silver market leads not to a wipe-out but to a decent gain; he sells too soon, but as they say on The Street, no one ever went bankrupt by making a profit.

Harry's new prosperity is reflected in the quality of his domestic life. He and Janice have stayed together more or less happily for ten years. Their sex life is down a bit but at least adequate; he still wishes she cooked oftener and better, and they occasionally feel hampered by the presence of her mother, whose house they have shared since the fire in *Rabbit Redux*; but their existence is reasonably equable and contented. They have, in fact, moved toward the exurban good life of Updike's *Couples* and *Marry Me*, which for them centers upon the newish country club they've joined, with golf for him and tennis for her and, for both, considerable drinking and a small circle of fairly congenial friends of similar circumstances and outlooks.

This novel's disruptive force is not Harry or Janice but their son. Nelson is now twenty-three, an intermittent student at Kent State, where he has completed seven semesters in five years; at the beginning of the book he is in Colorado for the summer with a vaguely described girlfriend, hang-gliding and bumming around, but presently he shows up in Brewer with what seems to be quite a different girl, strangely determined to go into the automobile business with his father. Harry finds this an appalling prospect– he wants Nelson to finish college, he strongly doubts Nelson's business judgment (during his trial period Nelson takes a snowmobile as a trade-in and starts buying up old convertibles to sell as collectibles), he doesn't want to fire Charlie Stavros to make room for Nelson. But mostly he just doesn't want Nelson around, sensing (quite rightly) that the boy has both a specific hatred of his father for the deaths of Jill and his baby sister long ago and a more general and conventional desire, in effect, to destroy the father and take his place.

Though others keep assuring Harry that Nelson is much like him, the novel makes this seem true only in very limited ways. Nelson too is frightened by the demands of maturity and human obligation, and he too is a "runner," but both his behavior and Updike's occasional incursions into his consciousness reveal not Harry's hopeful interest in the terms of his own life but a cynical, surly, grasping, thoroughly stupid, and unimaginative self-concern that is not like Harry at all. When a second girl (the first was a cover) shows up pregnant, Nelson recapitulates Harry's earlier life, insisting on marrying her against his father's advice, treating her quite badly, and deserting her three days before their child is born. But the parallels are formal only, author's contrivances; Nelson seems to me the one failure in *Rabbit Is Rich*, an irate caricature of the "Me Generation" where there might better be a difficult, confused, vulnerable human presence.

But elsewhere *Rabbit Is Rich* is a strong, secure novel, one of Updike's wisest and funniest. It is as full of the cultural details of 1979 as *Rabbit Redux* was full of those of 1969, but now such details are absorbed into the personal, private texture of Harry's experience. A lovely example is the scene where he and Janice, excited by dreams of speculative profit, make love on a bed heaped with newly bought Krugerrands. (One coin gets lost in the turmoil, but in this novel nothing is irretrievably lost, and it turns up between the mattress and the bed frame.)The effect is not some simple irony about confusion or displacement of desires– they make love not to but *through* the gold, treating the things of this world not as objects but as a medium through which to approach "a more." The incident echoes Harry's fantasy in *Rabbit, Run*, when, fleeing from marriage for the first time, he sees a road sign for Wilmington and "wonders what it's like to make it to a Du Pont"– a conjunction of monetary and sexual possession which he repeats near the end of *Rabbit Is Rich*, flying in a jet over Delaware. Like other details in the Rabbit novels, this owes something to Joyce's *Ulysses*– Harry's covetous image of well-booted Du Pont girls flicking their riding crops is in touch with the more passive fancies of another "plebeian Don Juan," Leopold Bloom, for high-society Amazons such as the Honourable Mrs. Mervyn Talboys. But Harry's version fits into his own cultural geography as neatly as does Updike's delighted perception of how well a famous advertising slogan– "YOU ASKED FOR IT, WE GOT IT"– suits the combination of irrepressible randiness and an almost saintly capacity for sympathy and concern in this particular Toyota dealer.

Rabbit Is Rich is the quietest, mellowest– without derogation, the most middle-aged– of the Harry Angstrom novels. Updike's famous, rather dangerous powers of style remain under control, and small domestic details are trusted to generate and direct action that earlier depended upon larger and more theatrical devices. Here a remarkable literary talent, far from running out of gas, rides smoothly and efficiently in overdrive, getting maximum mileage from minimal apparent effort. Harry himself is in some ways diminished in his middle age; his acceptance of affluence and domestication may mark a falling off of his faith in his own uniqueness, "his sense," as he describes it to Thelma, his newest lover, "of miracle at being himself, himself instead of somebody else, and his old inkling, now fading in the energy crunch, that there was something that wanted him to find it, that he was here on earth on a sacred assignment." But this is also a story of new beginnings, however modest their possibilities: a fine new Celica loaded with options and "charisma"; an elegant little stone house in, at last, the best suburb; hints that Nelson may finish college and come home to his new family and that he may not be quite as hopeless at business as Harry has feared (the convertibles and even the snowmobile do in fact sell), and above all a new granddaughter to engage the feelings the long-dead daughter and the lost son are no longer there to receive.

Imagining a life like Harry Angstrom's brings into play, I think, Updike's strongest fictional gifts, the gifts that function intermittently in *The Centaur* and are radiantly clear in the Olinger stories and in *Of the Farm*. One of these gifts is an illusionless but tender understanding of how families work– how husbands and wives, parents and children, in the name of love and obligation, do unforgivable things to one another and yet may, in the mysteriousness of their felt bonds, achieve some measure or form of forgiveness. Another is a sense of the sanctity of memory, the mind's power to preserve and in a way redeem a life of errors and losses. Harry, in effect, remembers everything; "new" experience acquires its meaning by becoming, in his mind, a celebration of, or an elegy for, something past, a process of "recollection" in which nothing is ever truly lost.

And, I would suppose, Harry matters to Updike because in imagining his fictional character the novelist also honors the memory of his own origins. Harry is almost exactly Updike's age, and the "Brewer" of the novels resembles the area around Reading where Updike grew up. Updike, of course, went off to Harvard, Oxford, and literary stardom, while Harry never went to college but was drafted, got married, and slowly and unsteadily proceeded to a much more modest success. Harry is perhaps a kind of Updikeian anti-self, derived from the envy, and pity, that bright and verbal kids feel for ones whose gifts are mainly physical, the adolescent trope of athleticism and sexuality that the mature imagination never quite outgrows. By now, the two men have little in common except a liking for golf and a vigorous sexual imagination, but in Harry, Updike continues to explore and ponder his own beginnings and where they might have led. Such material, with its sobering depth of feeling, is good for a writer whose seriousness is continually dogged by the shadow of his own marvelous facility.

It seems quite possible that we will get another Rabbit novel around 1990– *Rabbit Is Ruined? Rabbit Raffiné?* But as Dante shows, three is a useful number, and a Rabbit trilogy, if it should turn out to be that, would do nicely for a kind of *Commedia* of the ordinary life in our times. Whatever Updike decides, it is good to know that Harry Angstrom is alive and reasonably well in eastern Pennsylvania, and a pleasure to report that the third installment of his saga is a very fine novel indeed.

*Thomas R. Edwards, "Updike's Rabbit Trilogy." *Atlantic* 248 (Oct. 1981): 94, 96, 100-01.

"Easy Come, Easy Go"

Alfred Kazin*

Rabbit Is Rich, the third of John Updike's romances with his favorite hero, Harry Angstrom (and with Harry's and our acceleration from discontent to dismay), is a brilliant performance. As always, but more soberly and relevantly than in such subjective books as *Couples* and *Marry Me*, Updike revels in his great gifts of style and social – I mean domestic– observation. There have been times in the past when Updike's style was laid across the page like so many layers of marshmallow. How the prodigy loved his style! But here the always summonable Updike brightness, acuity, prancing wit are mostly on the mark. And the mark is inflation, inflated America careening wildly like an overpressured balloon over the pit of the Seventies.

Apart from the helplessness of the characters, just as drugged by the social fix as some kid on Lenox Avenue, Updike's own proud voice rings out with a new steeliness– and pronounced lamentation– about a rich, wasteful, wholly selfish, and hard-talking America whose advantage to a writer is that it is always news. That these brilliant touches will remain news I am not sure. What is sure is that we busy, yammering hedonists have lost nothing but confidence. Here is the scene not far from the Toyota agency that Rabbit took over from his dead father-in-law:

> Fast-food huts in eye-catching shapes and retail outlets of everything from
> bridal outfits to plaster birdbaths have widened the shoulders of this, the old

Weisertown Pike, with their parking lots, leaving the odd old house and its
stump of a front lawn sticking out painfully. Competitors Pike Porsche and
Renault, Diefendorfer Volkswagen, Red Barn Mazda and BMW, Diamond
County Automotive Imports– flicker there FUEL ECONOMY banners
while the gasoline stations intermixed with their beckoning have shrouded
pumps and tow-trucks parked across the lanes where automobiles once
glided in, were filled, and glided on. An effect of hostile barricade, late in
the day. Where did the shrouds come from? Some of them quite smartly
tailored, in squared-off crimson canvas. A new industry, gas pump shrouds.
Among bitter lakes of asphalt a few small stands offer strawberries and early
peas.

I don't remember another novelist noting these "shrouds." If one did, I'm sure
he didn't extend his attention to "Some of them quite smartly tailored, in squared-
off crimson canvas." *Rabbit Is Rich* is more inclusive of the middle-American
mores in a middle-sized town ("Brewer" in 1979), and is wittier about the Middle
America layer, than anything since 1922 and *Babbitt*. That is a book Updike (born
ten years later) wants you to read still; he quotes from the book and parodies
Babbitt's own father-son relationship (a cheerful one on the whole) in the abrasive
gap between Rabbit and his theatrically immature son Nelson.

Sixty years after Sinclair Lewis's one living book, this is where we are now.
Nothing, as they say, has escaped the notice of John Updike, a writer naturally lush
in sensibility but as pitiless of eye as Mencken. Harry, whom we first met running,
running, now stands around old Springer's Toyota agency smirking over "an
average gross mark-up of eight hundred dollars per sale. Rabbit is rich." The six-
foot-three former basketball star now weighs around two-ten, has a forty-two waist,
and *avoids mirrors, when he used to love them.* There is such a line-up in front of
the gas pumps that his mother-in-law had her tank drained dry in front of the hair-
dresser's. A woman lined up for gas had her hip broken, and when her husband
went to her rescue, they were ignored by the crowd rushing to her place.

Rabbit surveys all this (at first) with surface equanimity; he is pulling in over
fifty thou. The walls around the *imitation pine boards* framing the way into his
office are hung with old clippings from his basketball days and team portraits. His
late father-in-law (who would have thought that such a little tense busy bird of a
man *could get it up for a massive coronary*) loved to talk Republican, and *when
Nixon left him nothing to say* he had kind of burst. Harry's face *far behind him,*
with *sleepy predatory teen-age eyes* in the glossy team portraits, exists in his
present face *like the chrome bones of a grill within the full front view of a car and
its fenders.*

Updike pretending to be Rabbit is also very good on the shopping malls
hacked from the former fields of corn, rye, tomatoes, cabbages, and strawberries.
On the downtown wasteland in city after city. On why Barbra Streisand's "Jewish"
voice *and* nose excite the American public. On the Pinnacle Hotel, now a site of
vandalism and terror where once there had been dancing and necking.

Something about spics they don't like to see white kids making out,
they surround the car and smash the windshield with rocks and slit the
clothes off the girl while roughing up the boy. . . .In the park a World
War II tank, made into a monument, points its guns at tennis courts

where the nets, even the ones made of playground fencing, keep getting
ripped away. The strength these kids use just to destroy. Was he that
way at that age? You want to make a mark. The world seems
indestructible and won't let you out.

Rabbit's opening smirk fades page by page. He and wife Janice are reconciled
(you will remember that Janice when drunk accidentally let baby Rebecca drown
in the bathtub), but though active in bed are not really together. Janice has grown
hard, and not just from playing tennis; they are divided by their son Nelson's
dropping out of Kent State and wanting to replace Charlie Stavros, Janice's lover
ten years ago, as sales manager of the Toyota agency. And they still live with
Janice's mother in *her* house.

Standing around all day, Rabbit daydreams of a stone house with exposed
beams, sunken living room. Standing around Charlie, Rabbit sometimes pictures
Charlie being inside Janice. "A man fucks your wife, puts a new value on her,
within limits." Rabbit is less enthusiastic these days about Janice's parts than she
is about his. When he puts aside *Consumer Reports*, April issue, at her urging, he
is encouraged by her avidity but sees "the hateful aged flesh at the base of her
throat." What the New World was to Renaissance cartographers, sex is to Updike.
No one has put so many coasts, bays, and rivers where once there was only silence.
It is all steamy but not exactly stimulating, for Updike's bond to *Babbitt* is that
everything (even the once unthinkable wife-swapping) is now domestic. The details
may startle anyone born before 1932, but the flavor is more of pots and pans, the
bathroom mirror, and even the toilet bowl, than of voluptuousness. And on his
favorite subject Updike's merciless attention and packed style do get in the way.
The thoughts are supposed to be the thoughts of Rabbit, but no husband bored with
making love will be distracted enough to think all this. The voice is the voice of
Updike. "The affair with Charlie Stavros opened her up at about the time of the
moon shot."

> Guiltily he tries to count up how many nights he's given her an orgasm.
> These July nights, you get thirsty for one more beer as the Phillies
> struggle and then in bed feel a terrific weariness, a bliss of inactivity
> that leads you to see how man can die willingly, gladly, into eternal
> release from the hell of having to perform. When Janice hasn't been
> fucked for a while, her gestures speed up, and the thought of Charlie's
> coming intensifies this agitation.

This busy marriage bed finally gets as romantic as the April issue of *Consumer
Reports* as Rabbit responds to Janice's– (sic) new wantonness. The key sentence,
though of course it is not really true, is, "each day he is a little less afraid to die."
Because what this "Rabbit" is really about is no longer running, running out of the
social fix, but the decay that is never so much noticed as when you are looking, *post
coitum homo triste est*, at the beloved's flabby buttocks. Not inflation, not the gas
crunch of 1979, but the dying of the national dream in the emission indeed of
Rabbit's own hope, reflexes, and confidence. A felt lack of continuity is the
pervasive fact. Rabbit keeps looking for the daughter he thinks he had by an old
girlfriend. There is no daughter, or if there is one, old friend will never gratify *him*
by admitting it. Rabbit yearns back to the world of tenderness and solidarity
typified by *his* printer father, and his modest style of life, and by his dead mother's

plainness of speech.

The ominous figures of speech in this book so rich with Updike figures are of the body. Rabbit surrounded by his own girth as well as by his golfing friends (who all talk like TV commercials and newscasters), by the ravages of the city, by the impossibility of Arab sheiks, Big Oil, etc., has no tie to his dropout son Nelson, who delights in damaging Rabbit's car. While willing to marry Pru, whom he has made pregnant back at Kent State, Nelson is sleeping with Pru's friend Melanie, an intellectual and feminist whose interest in him is condescending but unaccountable. There was no daughter, there is not much of a son, and Rabbit making love is aware of wrong smells from Janice's feet.

Death and death and death dominate (in thought) a life outwardly rich and so emancipated that (this time parodying Frank Norris's *McTeague*) Rabbit and Janice make love surrounded by their newly acquired Krugerrands (sic). The wonderful wife-swapping episode turns so domestic that the lady (a neighbor) ends up usefully advising Rabbit about wife and son. Updike and Rabbit are the same age: on the threshold of fifty. Rabbit is running scared. America and Americans in this book are nervously, prematurely apprehensive. Things are out of "control." Everyone knows that society is "crazy," beyond the interpretation even of those who have no cause for complaint, no cause whatever. For they recognize that while they are being led by the nose, events are thrillingly nervous, dramatic, like the news every hour on the hour, like the gallows humor at the club, like the revelations on TV of the great– whose facial expressions are as exposed to us as another body in bed.

Does the fierceness of detail in *Rabbit Is Rich* argue a need to hold on in this horribly evanescent scene? *Babbitt* was about the difference between private illusion and social truth. No illusion is left in "Brewer." Everybody is wise, smart, money-smart; everybody, even the women who gain psychic "equality" by this, talk dirty. Goofy son Nelson finally marries pregnant Pru, as at the end of *Babbitt* Babbitt's son alarms the family but puts new backbone into his Pa by marrying just as he likes. But in *Babbitt* the son gives the father some independence at last; in *Rabbit Is Rich* Nelson knocks a nail into Rabbit's coffin by presenting him with a grand-daughter. Even Updike's most familiar figure of speech, "God," makes a less certain appearance in this book than He usually does. He is unmistakably ticked off as the author of death and, like the salt in the ocean, what gives life (and death?) its taste.

A brilliant book, this, and though a chastening one, what we deserve. And the clearest case we have had for some time that novelists are as much led around by the nose as everybody else these days. Will this book remain "news" as long as *Babbitt* has? Not if the fierceness of detail is there just to hold on to *something* in all this easy come and easy go– this perpetually passing society where you can't even count on empty gas pumps wearing "shrouds."

*Alfred Kazin, "Easy Come, Easy Go." The New York Review of Books 28 (19 Nov. 1981): 3.

"Ordinary People"

Anatole Broyard*

The ordinary doesn't get much attention in serious fiction now. In the 50's, there was a lot of talk about "the literature of extreme situations," and it seems to me that many novelists and short story writers have continued to think of their work as dealing mainly with extreme situations, with people in the throes of metaphysical crisis, rather than with the unspectacular concerns we all more or less share.

In the work of 19th-century writers like Dickens or Hardy, the ordinary man was the cement of society, and as such he occupied a definite place in literature. In the 30's, there were American writers who apostrophized the ordinary man in political or sentimental terms, as if Marx were to dandle a baby on his knee. William Faulkner was one of the great American writers who was deeply interested in ordinary men doing everyday things and who made them interesting to us. In the 40's and 50's in England, Henry Green wrote brilliant novels about ordinary people living and loving and working, and James Hanley, particularly in *Another World*, has also done this in the last decade.

But though there are exceptions, the generalization holds: In modern serious fiction the ordinary man is conspicuous by his absence. In the so-called "revolution of rising expectations," personality too is suffering a period of inflation. Ezra Pound's famous exhortation to "make it new" has been mistakenly applied to character rather than form in fiction, so that, like so many other new things, men and women in novels and short stories today often appear to be trendy, shoddily made, unattractively designed and over-priced.

Fiction seems to be in the grip of an impatience with human nature, which has led some novelists and short story writers to go in, like moviemakers, for "special effects," for eccentricity, anxiety and the grotesque. Just as in movies now almost every other film is a "spoof," so the typical modern novel reads like a spoof of ordinary life.

Though the ordinary man might be supposed to be authentic by definition, some writers insist on stripping away his ordinariness in order to get at what has come to be called the "essential" self, as if there were in each of us a characterological core, beyond circumstance or phenomena, that burns with a hard, gem-like flame. Our fiction also pushes its search for character in the direction of what Robert Penn Warren calls "the dramaturgical self," which I take to mean a self histrionically conscious of itself.

Two years ago in a fine first novel called *The Dogs of March*, Ernest Hebert put in a good word for the ordinary man. Howard, his protagonist, was a down-to-earth guy who lived in a suburb that was suddenly becoming so chic that he felt like a wild animal being driven out of its habitat. His wealthy and influential neighbor was trying to get the town authorities to force Howard to clean up his property, which was dotted with rusting cars and other worn-out pieces of machinery.

To Howard, who was a mechanic, these machines were not ugly, but part of his landscape, part of the natural process of life and death. To him, they were historical monuments, or romantic ruins, as picturesque as a tottering old barn. He was the kind of man who looked forward to having with his son, as soon as the boy was sufficiently experienced, "an intelligent conversation about tires." When Howard admired the moon from his porch, he thought it looked like a dented- (sic) hub-cap.

Now, in *Rabbit Is Rich*, John Updike has written the best book I've ever read about an ordinary man. Rabbit Angstrom is so ordinary that he is a tour de force, almost a patron saint of small-town America. One of the most poignant phrases in 20th-century fiction is E. M. Forster's "only connect," and Rabbit connects all the time, and with everything. He has more genuine contact with people and things than anyone I can remember in recent fiction. In his unabashed love of things, he reminds me of Francis Ponge's remark that things are not the enemies of the self, but its occasions.

At 46, Rabbit is in the middle not only of his own life, but of American life as well. And though he suffers just like anybody else from unfulfilled desires, from all the indignities that flesh is heir to, and from what Ernest Becker called "the panic inherent in creation," Rabbit loves his life. He loves it for its voluptuous, never-ending *specificity*, for the fact that it always provides him with something to do or be, to want or think about.

Rabbit loves his wife because the intricate friction between their two personalities is stimulating to him just as the friction of sex is stimulating. He loves his impossible son in the way an author loves a failed book into which he has put everything.

In *Rabbit Is Rich*, John Updike has almost persuaded me that the ordinary is the last refuge of romanticism, that it is Wordsworth's "speaking presence" in nature. If I could conquer my own impatience with human nature, I'd go out right now and try to make ordinary friends so I could ask them to teach me the secret of happiness and of life– maybe even of literature.

*Anatole Broyard, "Ordinary People." *The New York Times Book Review* 86 (13 Dec. 1981): 43.

"John Updike's Rabbit Saga"

Ralph Wood*

At the beginning of this decade and each of the past two, John Updike has published a novel about Harry (Rabbit) Angstrom, his proto-typical American character who embodies the fears and hopes, the vices and virtues, of our age. Now with the release of *Rabbit Is Rich* (Knopf, 467 pp., $13.95), it is fair to say that Updike's "Rabbit" books are forming an American saga. Indeed, Rabbit Angstrom is becoming as definitive a figure for our cultural consciousness as Mark Twain's Huck Finn, Ernest Hemingway's Nick Adams and William Faulkner's Ike McCaslin. But while these earlier heroes inhabit a world now irrecoverable, Rabbit dwells in our time, in our place. To follow Updike's continuing account of Rabbit's life is to relive our own lives, to see our own era re-imaged and appraised, and to be called to our own self-assessment.

Yet Updike's vision of our world is not something obvious and cheering. It is at once wittily comic and soberly tragic, radically religious and unstintingly secular, almost pornographically sexual but finally committed to married love. No wonder many readers have been perplexed and the critics often unkind. With the approach of Updike's 50th birthday, and with the publication of this his 25th book, it is time to offer an assessment of his work as a whole: to trace his natively Lutheran vision of life as cast by God into an indissoluble ambiguity, to examine his treatment of death and sex as the two phenomena wherein the human contradiction is most sharply focused, to set this new novel in relation to the earlier "Rabbit" books, and to determine what is religiously troubling and compelling about Updike's art.

Updike insists that he writes for no intellectual or cultural elite. "I aim in my mind not toward New York but toward a vague spot a little to the east of Kansas," he says. Middle America is Updike's true subject because middleness is, for him, the heart of the human condition. Bourgeois life is located in precisely the "boundary situation" where the irreducible human duality cannot be denied. We are at once angels and beasts, both material and spiritual creatures, mortal and immortal beings. *The Centaur*, Updike's award-winning novel of 1964, declares our essential doubleness in its very title. Our human heads provide a self-transcending consciousness which no earthly joy can satisfy; yet our equine torsos root us in mortal passions and limits which no heavenly hope can assuage. Nor is there any final reconciliation of the flesh's pull with the spirit's yearning. To be permanently out of phase is, in Updike's lexicon, to be fully human.

When Updike speaks, therefore, of having a primary concern for "suburban or rural, unpolitical man," he is not disdaining interest in our present public crisis. He is declaring his deeper allegiance to the universal struggle which perplexes the human heart regardless of social circumstances, and which an overpoliticized approach to life threatens to obscure. Precisely in this regard Updike is a religious novelist. In his view, it is God himself who renders our existence double, who plants us amid contraries, and who thus ensures the taut oppositions without which life would go slack and lose interest.

Updike's dialectical vision seems to have been shaped decisively by his Lutheran upbringing, and especially by his reading of those two latter-day Lutherans Søren Kierkegaard and Paul Tillich. The Lutheran doctrine of the two kingdoms becomes, for Updike as for Kierkegaard, a way of interpreting the self. That human beings cannot thrive as happy animals, but are both plagued and blessed with a self-reflexive mind, points to God's existence: Someone has set us on this perilous tightwire stretched between finitude and infinity. Updike's characters believe in God if only because of their guilt and anxiety. Their discontent implies that their lives are not godlessly accidental but divinely decreed.

With Tillich, moreover, Updike believes that we must plummet into sin if we are to be truly human. Existence equals fallenness. The plunge into evil is not merely inevitable but necessary, and the apple of iniquitous knowledge must be bitten willfully. "Unfallen Adam is an ape," Updike declares. "The heart prefers to move against the grain of circumstance," he adds in an almost Faustian boast; "perversity is the soul's very life." Updike speaks thus of being "branded with the Cross," for it is the giant X cancelling all swinish adjustment to the world. And faith signifies, for him, a gracious acceptance of our fundamental ambiguity, a steadfast refusal to leap out of the inescapable quandary which our mortality and sexuality force upon us.

Updike's fiction has been obsessed with death ever since his first novel, *The Poorhouse Fair*, described a group of elderly people facing their slow doom in a nursing home. Alone among self-conscious creatures, we humans can anticipate our own death; and this fatal knowledge casts a shadow over the whole of life. Because death calls everything into radical doubt, Updike's characters regard is as the great evil. They tremble not so much at the prospect of pain as at their own annihilation. Their pagan dread of mortality issues in an equally pagan desire for earthly life to continue beyond death. In a sermon devoted ostensibly to the resurrection, Thomas Marshfield, the narrator-priest of *A Month of Sundays*, declares that

> we do not want to live as angels in ether, our bodies are us, us; and our craving for immortality is. . .not for transformation into a life beyond imagining but for our *ordinary* life, the mundane life we so driftingly and numbly live, to go on forever and forever. The only Paradise we can imagine is this earth. The only life we desire is this one.

Updike does not flinch at making God responsible for the deaths that undermine our confidence in the goodness of life. His God is as much hidden as revealed, the worker of terror as well as wonder. On the one hand, the earth is full of a glory that prompts Updike's characters to Lutheran meditations on "the teleologic bias in things." On the other hand, they complain against what Luther called "the left hand of God": the divine bungling that blotches an otherwise splendid creation. Updike's dying President James Buchanan confesses what seems to be his author's own protest: "I am not troubled by the sins of men, who are feeble; I am troubled by the sins of God, who is mighty."

Sexual passion is, for Updike, our chief means of silencing the dread of death. "Only in being loved," he asserts, "do we find external corroboration of the supremely high valuation each ego secretly assigns itself. " Sex is thus bound up with "the Promethean protest" forced upon the human animal who knows it must die. This is what gives sex its "huge but not all-eclipsing" dimension in our lives. It also accounts for Updike's intention to bring sex both out of the closet and off the altar, and thus to reveal sexuality as "a function of, rather than a suspension of, personality."

The problem is that our new sexual freedom, though a valid corrective to the old repression, knows no limits. With the decline of traditional connubial fidelity, once sanctioned by church and state alike, sex becomes a surrogate deity. Indeed, the sexual revolution is a direct correlate of the contemporary eclipse of God. As one of the new amoralists says in *Couples*, these secular swingers "make a church of each other." Adultery is their only sacrament, and they celebrate it with abandon in their "post-pill paradise."

Yet no sooner have these wantons created an earthly heaven from their sexual pleasure than it ends in hellish misery and recrimination. The keenest Updike paradox is that within marriage, sex turns stale and routine but outside it, passion become (sic) demonic and destructive. Only within the bonded love of life-companionship can the vagaries of sexual desire be channeled toward productive ends: children brought to moral maturity, a household established for the good of others as well as one's own, a vocation or career sustained by mutual self-sacrifice. But the spouse who gives sex its moral and spiritual consequence also constricts romantic adventure. And thus does the ambiguity loop endlessly back upon itself.

Marriage, therefore, is a microcosm of the struggle that characterizes all of life: the conflict between the individual and society, freedom and necessity, the head and the heart, faith in God and the impulses of one's own sweet will. Far from the sensualist and pornographer that he is often accused of being, Updike is our premier novelist of marriage. There are virtually no playboys or penthouse girls in Updike's fiction, for the obvious reason that their sex is not significant. He cares only for those unhappy adulterers who cannot leave their husbands and wives as though the marriage vows meant nothing. In marriage the ethical and religious tensions of life are stretched to the breaking point. There as nowhere else we confront the irreconcilable opposites which must be accepted and endured rather than be resolved.

It is in his three "Rabbit" novels that John Updike brings this dialectical vision to its most brilliant expression. *Rabbit, Run* (1960) provided our first acquaintance with Harry Angstrom, the harried and anxious youth yearning to be free from all shackling commitments and responsibilities. He is a former high school basketball hero whose boyhood dream of greatness and glory is withering amid the dullness and mediocrity of adult life. The conformity of the Eisenhower era puts intolerable limits on his sexual fantasies. Rabbit wants to get out, to run.

Like most of Updike's protagonists, Rabbit Angstrom is a version of his creator. He shares not only Updike's eastern Pennsylvania milieu but also the author's stark confessional honesty. Rabbit tells all, and much of his unburdening makes for less than pleasant reading. Yet there is awful truth in Rabbit's cynical thesis that "fraud makes the world go round," and that to submit to it is to bury one's soul. His job as a 26-year-old vegetable-peeler salesman is degrading. His wife, Janice, is turning slovenly with her endless drinking and television-watching. Their baby seems always to be crying. And the sexual exaltation they once knew has been reduced to something routine and predictable. In short, Rabbit has just cause for complaint.

Yet what can he do? Like a latter-day Huck Finn, Rabbit strikes out for his soul's true West– namely, for unfettered sexual freedom. He goes to live with a prostitute named Ruth. But Rabbit purchases his liberty at a terrible price. Drunken Janice, in despair at Rabbit's abandonment of her, lets their infant daughter drown in the bathtub. And the poor harlot Ruth can hardly sustain Rabbit's worship of her as his sexual goddess. Alas, she becomes pregnant with Rabbit's child and prepares for an abortion. Rabbit the romantic thus sets out in search of greater life only to bring death into the world.

Flannery O'Connor once remarked that she had seldom encountered a more convincing portrait of damnation than *Rabbit, Run*. It is far from clear, however, that Updike himself agrees. The narrator so fully inhabits Rabbit's own confused consciousness that we are not certain what to make of him. On the one hand, Rabbit seems clearly condemned for giving full rein to the "urgent inner whispers" which civilized people must hold tightly in check. He is an irresponsible dreamer who will not walk "the straight line of paradox" that makes suffering and sacrifice life-giving rather than soul-deadening.

On the other hand, Rabbit stands strangely justified in his inability to find a middle path between resignation to blighted hopes and the quest for a more intense life, between marital fidelity and sexual vitality. Better, Rabbit reasons, to flee than to conform; better to keep his spirit alive, even destructively, than to let it die in conventionality. Hence the imperative character of Updike's title. Youth that he is, Rabbit *must* run.

For all his Americanness, Rabbit Angstrom is not a typical American figure. Most Americans believe that every problem has a solution. Updike does not, and neither does the Rabbit whom we meet a decade later in the novel of 1971, *Rabbit Redux*. As the title suggests, Rabbit has been "led back," restored to responsibility after suffering the illness of uninhibited youthful desire. But Rabbit's restoration is neither facile nor final. On the contrary, he remains caught in precisely the same paradox which earlier he had fled: the discovery that the deepest human difficulties cannot be resolved.

The 35-year-old Rabbit we encounter in this second novel is a creature driven by the chaos of the `60s into radical self-contradiction. He finds joy and dignity in his job as a linotype operator. Yet he remains discontent with the prospect of upward mobility into middle-class mediocrity. Janice is no longer the dull bed partner she once was, having joined the sexual revolution herself. Yet with liberation also comes experimentation: she has her first affair, and Rabbit takes up with a flower child named Jill, who is young enough to be his daughter. He despises the Vietnam war protesters and black revolutionaries as antipatriotic ingrates seeking only their own aggrandizement. Yet he gives shelter to a nihilistic black political messiah named Skeeter. Rabbit makes splenetic denunciations of the new Narcissus culture, with its endless talk of "self-fulfillment" and "thinking with your whole person." Yet he falls victim himself to "the lovingness of pot" and its soft, sweet world without angles or limits.

Despite his attempts to lose himself in the tribal life of the `60s counterculture, Rabbit cannot. And therein lies his hope. What he painfully learns is that "growth is betrayal," that we abandon those who have given us life, that to live at all is to make choices and commitments which exclude the many roads and selves not taken, that human existence is thus an endless trail of guilt and harm which can be traveled only in perpetual confession and forgiveness.

Rabbit accepts such humbling truths only after venturing into the world of moral and spiritual anarchy, and finding death awaiting him there once more. Amid circumstances that make Rabbit partially responsible, his house burns down with the hapless Jill inside. Rabbit's ultimate reconciliation with his estranged wife is thus far from a return to normality. The last scene reveals them in bed with each other for a change. But the flippant final "O. K.?" does not dispel the shadow that haunts Rabbit's rehabilitation.

Rabbit Redux is Updike's only angry novel. In general, his is a fiction of acceptance, even of benediction. His art is rooted in the largely unnoticed miracle of "things as they are." The decade of the `60s in contrast, was typified by strident demands for a radical alteration, even a wholesale remaking, of the moral and social order. As a novelist pre-eminently of the middle way, Updike seems to have found this era of apocalyptic extremes rather dreary and dead-ended. *Rabbit Redux* is his uncharacteristically testy response to the delusions of the age, and it is not one of Updike's best books.

His latest novel, *Rabbit Is Rich*, marks Updike's return to form: to the depiction of our irrevocable human ambiguity in clear and compelling art. His style is plainer and more straight-forward than usual; elegance is not made to substitute for substance. The present-tense narration of the other "Rabbit" books does not here rush so rapidly forward that we are left wondering how to assess Angstrom's thoughts and deeds. It is a long and leisurely book that deserves to be savored rather than guzzled.

The absence of a social and political Armageddon makes this a more tranquil novel than the previous one. It is Updike's account of the late '70s, when Watergate seemed already a remote event. Inflation and the oil crisis are the only public cataclysms affecting Harry's life. Spiritually, however, it is a stagnant time, as Updike's coarsened diction and blighted commercial landscape reveal. Nor does the outward calm still Harry's inner tumult. Indeed, the novel is comically focused on his troubled status as the prosperous heir of his father-in-law's Toyota dealership.

Financially secure for the first time in his life, Harry is hardly at ease with success. On the contrary, he buys South African gold as a safeguard against the relative worthlessness of Susan B. Anthony dollars. Then he swaps the Krugerrands for silver in fear that the price of gold will fall. But after he and Janice have lugged the satchels of silver from the exchange office to the bank, they discover that the cache of coins will not fit into their safety deposit box. The silver pieces roll wildly about the vault, forcing Harry to carry 300 of them home in his coat and also to ponder the meaning of his new wealth: "to be rich is to be robbed, to be rich is to be poor."

Nor is it merely inflation that reminds Angstrom of his fundamental insecurity. The once-lithe athlete is now growing paunchy at age 44. Not only is America running out of gas; so is Harry. He is more death-conscious than ever, thinking constantly of the corpses that stare up at him from the ground. And in a poignant bedroom scene, Harry confesses to Janice that they are caught in the inescapable paradox of life: "Too much of it and not enough. The fear that it will end some day, and the fear that tomorrow will be the same as yesterday."

There is, however, a good deal of the old romantic flame yet alight in Harry. He is still willing to strike out sexually for the territories. The carnality in this new Updike novel is thus rawer than ever. But it is also a funnier and sadder kind of sex. Angstrom keeps thinking of *Consumer Reports* when he ought to be concentrating on erotic matters. He pours his Krugerrands over his naked wife in the hope that their new money will arouse them as their old passion increasingly will not. But the spouse-swapping at the end is treated with none of the quasi-religious seriousness found in *Couples*. There is no attempt to deny what is silly and tragic and nihilistic about it. With the middle-aged banking down of the body's fire, Harry is learning that it is better to suffer the "daily seepage" than to let life rush out in a single foolish passion; better to stay at home than to run. Despite his often murderous thoughts about her, Harry is bound to Janice by all the trouble they have endured and survived. They are ineluctably *married*, and for better more than worse. The presence of Angstrom's elderly mother-in-law also serves to remind them that their lives are not merely their own. Harry still chafes, of course, at the way the world is enclosing him ever more tightly. But his rage lacks its old bitterness and desperation. The surprise dawning on him is that his "inner dwindling" contains a new freedom, and that to be obligated is oddly to be liberated.

The main obstacle to Harry's reconciliation with midlife decline is his own progeny. Nelson is still living at home, has not finished college, and has got his girlfriend pregnant. The son's irresponsibility is exceedingly irksome to the elder Angstrom. And when Nelson tries to prove himself as a salesman at the Toyota agency, by marketing old gas-guzzling convertibles, the results are at once uproarious and pathetic. In a fit of fury at his father's repeated humiliation of him, Nelson smashes the ancient clunkers, thus sending Harry into even crueler attacks on the boy's many failures.

Harry is all the angrier because he sees that Nelson is repeating his own sorry history: the son is the father one generation removed. Finally Harry comes to confess the humbling truth. "I don't like seeing you caught," he blurts out to Nelson. "You're too much me." This freely acknowledged guilt marks Angstrom's real progress. It is evident even in the final scene, where Harry is holding his new grandchild and complaining that she represents another nail in his coffin. But he is also obviously pleased to be cuddling the first member of the next Angstrom generation. Life in the ongoing "Rabbit" saga thus has not merely gone 'round; it has moved at least a small pace forward. And Updike has brought his epic American character a very long way indeed: from Rabbit the scared and solipsistic youth fleeing life's limits to Harry the middle-aged grandfather reluctantly accepting life's essential ambiguity. Rabbit Angstrom has come of age.

Rabbit's gradual spiritual advance is the product of Updike's natural religion: his conviction that God is discovered, if at all, in the irresolvable dialectic of human existence. The world remains too ambiguous a place for Updike to call its underlying principle *sola gratia*. Faith must stand in permanent conflict with doubt, joy with sadness, comedy with tragedy, the revealed with the hidden God. This deity remains, moreover, a kind of Archimedean point wherewith Updike's characters get leverage on life. Only as God is posited over against the world is there any check upon the omnivorous ego, any validation of its enormous self-importance, any growth beyond mere animal self-absorption.

This existential belief that God ensures the world's final duality sets Updike off from Karl Barth, despite his supposed allegiance to the Basel dogmatician. Theologically, what is missing in Updike's fiction is precisely Barth's vision of life not as an endless conflict of opposites but as the realm of God's redemptive victory over them. It is perhaps too much to demand of fiction that it make an orthodox declaration of faith. But it does seem fair to ask that a writer, especially one with Updike's profound Lutheran sensibility, not decadently celebrate the absence of final solutions, nor nihilistically relish the agony of contraries.

Updike escapes such severe allegations whenever his fiction moves beyond the deadly antithesis of self-canceling polarities. *Rabbit Is Rich* makes such an advance. Harry Angstrom is indeed caught in the hard passage from youth to age, and he negotiates the narrow divide between the angels and the apes with only uncertain results. Yet he is not the same Rabbit we first met in 1960. Though often cowardly and cruel, he is also forgiving and forgiven. Though still obsessed with vague romantic longings, he now sees that he must live in the muddled midground between pleasure and responsibility. And while there may be no joyous prospect of Rabbit's redemption, he has at least come to affirm the goodness of his God-ordained condition. In my view, therefore, John Updike is our finest literary celebrant both of human ambiguity and the human acceptance of it.

*Ralph Wood, "John Updike's Rabbit Saga." *The Christian Century* 99 (20 Jan. 1982): 50-54.

"The World of Work: *Rabbit, Run, Rabbit Redux* and *Rabbit Is Rich.*" From *John Updike*. N.Y.: St. Martin's, 1988. Chapter 3: 32-78.

Judie Newman*

Published at roughly ten-year intervals, the novels which constitute the *Rabbit* trilogy (*Rabbit, Run* (1960), *Rabbit Redux* (1971), *Rabbit Is Rich* (1982)) appear to differ somewhat in their major emphases (respectively religious, political and economic). As Updike has also announced his intention to complete a tetralogy, critical discussions of the overall form of the work must inevitably remain tentative. None the less, the trilogy coheres internally around one major organising theme: that of the relation between individual and society, particularly expressed as the instinctual, sensual and libidinous dimensions of the human being in conflict with social constraints which are politically and economically determined. Freud's analysis of society as founded upon repression is important in this connection, though Updike is no naive Freudian and clearly contests Freud's understanding of religious faith as an illusion. For Freud the methodical sacrifice of libido to work and reproduction *is* culture. Because the lasting inter-personal relations on which civilisation depends presuppose that the sex instincts are inhibited, there is therefore a fundamental opposition between sex and social utility, and a high price in individual happiness which must be paid for the benefits of civilised life. Most work requires that energy be directed away from direct sexual satisfaction, to produce the gains of technical civilisation, a process arguably exacerbated in modern society in which desire is over-controlled ('surplus repression') in order to maintain men as cogs in the industrial machine. In the trilogy Updike introduces this central conflict in *Rabbit, Run*, proceeding in *Rabbit Redux* to examine the potential sensual liberation of the individual, freed from toil by the new technology, and finally in *Rabbit Is Rich*, analysing the ways in which society may deform and exploit the instincts by the creation of mass fantasy, in order to repress once more. Work, technology and sex are therefore the three major strands braided together throughout the trilogy.

*   *   *   *   *   *   *

In the first section of [*Rabbit Redux*], *Pop/Mom/Moon*, Updike carefully establishes Harry Angstrom as Gutenberg Man, sensually deprived and passively dependent upon the machine. A social conformist and ardent supporter of state intervention in Vietnam, Harry lives his life by outdated rules, values order and neatness, and is isolated from his fellows to the point of racism. Sex has lost its charms for him, he no longer plays contact sports, and exists in a standard suburban locale on a diet of ersatz TV dinners. Stooped by a decade as a linotyper, Harry appears in the opening scene with 'a weakness verging on anonymity' (4/9). Confronted by Pop's news of Janice's adultery, Harry adopts two diversionary strategies to avoid getting the message, each of them linked to technology. Initially Harry turns away from the sound of Pop's voice towards the soundless image on the TV screen, repeatedly broadcasting the Apollo moon shot. Profoundly unmoved, Harry shares his reaction with the other drinkers: 'They have not been lifted, they are left here' (7/12). In a second programme, quiz-show entrants contend for an eight-foot frozen-food locker. Together with the iced drinks and air-conditioned chill of the bar, the pervasive cold imagery suggests a parallel with the state of human beings, as emotionally frozen, left behind by the new technology. Harry's father, however, also a printer, glories in technology, seeing himself as one of the little men who have been 'a piece of grit in the launching pad' (11/16). When Harry turns the conversation once more away from Janice towards his mother's illness, Pop declares his faith in medical technology. According to him, Mom should 'put herself in deep freeze' (8/13), until scientists discover a miracle cure. Harry is less optimistic, reflecting ironically upon the fact that Pop, the anonymous little man, survives, while Mom, 'the source of his life' (12/16), is failing. The two remaining members of Harry's family are also dwarfed by the machine. Back home Harry listens with one ear to Nelson extolling the delights of Billy's new machines (hi-fi and mini-bike) and takes refuge in television. When Janice puts in an appearance, Harry reaches out to caress her, but thinks instead of 'feathering the linotype keys, of work tomorrow, and is already there' (27/29). Tactility, emotional closeness, oral communication yield to the attractions of the machine and the demands of the working timetable.

At the Brewer *Vat*, a conservative rag specialising in racial innuendo, crime stories and jingoism, Harry is seen setting an item with [*sic*] also celebrates technology: BREWER FACTORY TOOLS COMPONENT HEADED TOWARDS MOON. Carefully rearranging the spaces and columns of the item to avoid a 'widow', an awkward gap in the lines, Harry revels in the warmth of the press's hot-lead processes. The machine appears here as if eroticised, able to meet all the individual's emotional needs. It stands, warm and 'mothering' above him. It is also described as a baby (30/31). Unlike Harry's own child its demands are few and once they are met 'obedience automatically follows' (31/31). With the machine, in contrast to Janice, 'there is no problem of fidelity. Do for it, it does for you' (31/31). Accosted once more by Pop at the coffee-break, Harry is grateful to return to the machine, personified here as 'pleased he is back' (31/33). Mother, wife, child, the all-enclosing machine 'fits right around him' (31/33). While the message Harry sets celebrates the new electronic technology (the machine part is in the space rocket's navigation computer) Harry remains trapped within the mental set of typographic attitudes: obedience, docility, dependence.

When watching television with Nelson, Harry had enjoyed a comic skit in which the Lone Ranger's wife, disenchanted with her husband's concentration on his work, takes Tonto as a lover. While Harry ignores the obvious parallels with his own situation, he is momentarily drawn to consider Tonto as a member of an oppressed minority. Rather in McLuhanite terms he speculates on Tonto as a Judas to his tribe. Whereas in the past he had accepted that Tonto was simply on the side of right, that law and order belonged to the white man, Harry is now much less certain. 'Where has the side of right gone?' he wonders. When, however, he figures as Paleface to Stavros's Tonto, in the ensuing scene in the Greek restaurant, Harry reverts to type. Janice characterises Harry and Nelson as 'Ugly Americans', insular, imperialistic and hostile to other cultures. Harry notes only that Janice and Stavros are sitting too close together 'to his printer's sense' (48/47), leaving awkward space on either side of them and creating a 'widow'. In the ensuing argument over Vietnam, described here as 'one more Cherokee uprising' (49/48), Harry defends America as order, opposed to darkness and chaos, and as a source of technological bounty. Stavros sums up his view of American benevolence in an image which associates America, Mom and the mothering machine: 'We're the big mama trying to make this unruly kid take some medicine' (46/45). While Janice and Stavros linger over delicious Greek food, Harry and Nelson are impatient to see *2001: A Space Odyssey*, a film which also celebrates technological evolution. Stavros is uninterested: 'I don't find technology all that sexy' (42/42). In the event the film also makes little impact on the Angstroms. Eclipsed by the confirmation of Janice's adultery it merely numbs them (51/49), providing a means of avoiding emotional confrontation.

Where Harry seems to be stranded in the typographic world, Janice's affair with Stavros appears to open up new vistas. The Greek restaurant with its tasty food, handwritten menus and extended Greek family in the background suggests possibilities of sensual reintegration and social retribalisation. Harry has already noted Janice's use of Stavros's slang, hearing 'We're the big mama trying to make this unruly kid take some medicine' (46/45). When Stavros arrives in the restaurant Janice also adopts a new set of theatrical gestures (41/41). While Janice and Stavros linger over delicious Greek food, Harry and Nelson are impatient to see *2001: A Space Odyssey*, a film which also celebrates technological evolution. Stavros is uninterested: 'I don't find technology all that sexy' (42/42). On her return from the movie, Janice lies awake, masturbating beside Harry. Her long interior monologue, verging on stream-of-consciousness, is non-sequential, free-flowing and centred, somewhat evidently on feelings. For Janice, what originally attracted her to Stavros was than [*sic*] he allowed her to tumble out her thoughts in any way (53/51) as opposed to Harry, whom she sees as rule-bound. Compared with the sensual intensity of her love affair, the rest of her life now appears like 'a movie, flat and even rather funny' (53/51). As the reference to electronic technology suggests, the opposition between sensual Janice and deadened Harry is not, however, entirely clear-cut. While ostensibly rejecting the work ethic, celebrating her body as sexual plaything, Janice also mentally accuses Harry for not having awakened her sensuality, on the grounds that 'It was his job to call it out' (56/54). Irony cuts both ways here. When Janice loses concentration she thinks in terms of getting on with the job in hand: 'This is silly. This thinking is getting nowhere' (56/54). Ominously, in her sexual encounters with Stavros, Janice often relies on a mental image of Mom to provoke orgasm. In addition her comment here on her solitary orgasm, 'it's always best when you do it to yourself' (56/54), suggests sensual isolation rather than integration. When Harry finally confronts her, Janice attempts to fend him off with the terms of her working vocabulary– bills of lading, customs forms, franchises– just as she had earlier used 'working late' as a cover for play.

Janice's eventual confession seems at first to confirm Harry's earlier intuition that 'the news isn't all in, a new combination might break it open, this stale peace' (6/11). For a moment cracks appear in the cut-and-dried surface of Harry's life. Janice makes him see that 'there were rules beneath the surface rules which also mattered' (68/63). Yet though the couple now make love several times in the light, the visual and mechanical emphasis remains relentless. Janice celebrates daylight love ('Don't you love seeing?' (69/65)), but in the event their sexual encounters are illuminated by a soundless TV set, flickering bluish images across them, transforming Janice into desert sand, Harry into 'a barren landscape lit by bombardment' (70/65). Janice's hasty touches are subordinate to the 'flickering touch' of the set. The fragile possibility of a new development in their relationship collapses under the threat of the visual. Harry is aghast to discover that rumours are flying: 'It's all over town. Talk about daylight' (73/68). His fear of exposure to the power of the eye is vividly suggested when he imagines that his news will be headlined in the *Vat*: **LINOTYPER'S WIFE LAYS LOCAL SALESMAN**. Passively, he hands Janice over to Stavros, 'as long as I don't have to see the bastard' (78/72). Turning away from Janice's scrawled farewell note, Harry picks up the phone book and searches out

   Stavros Chas 1204 Eisenhwer Av.

Rather than telephone, however, he contemplates this different typographic item, 'as if to see his wife, smaller than a pencil dot, crawling between the letters' (86/79). Print still dominates Harry's perceptions, and he remains trapped within the domination of the eye.

Consigning his wife and her lover to the printed item, Harry retreats into two excursions with parents, each of which draws attention to him as a figure in transition between two stages of technological development. The first, a baseball game attended with Janice's father, foregrounds the inevitability of Harry's evolution. For once the game bores him: 'the spaced dance of the men is white fails to enchant, the code. . . refuses to yield its meaning' (83/76) as a national ritual the game reflects McLuhan's theories. Harry notes that the players are 'speciliaists like any other' (83/77) in a game in which each player seems intent upon a 'private dream of making it' (83/77). In *Understanding Media* McLuhan analysed the reasons for the change in popularity in America, from baseball to football. Just as technologies are extensions of the animal organism, so games are extension of social man. Their relative popularity reflects American social evolution, from baseball, an elegant image of a specialised, individualist society, to the new social centre, football, a non-positional and decentralised sport, in which players can switch to any role in the course of the game. Significantly, Nelson, who later takes up football, is unmoved by the baseball game, missing TV's running commentary and commercials.

From the outdated national ritual, Harry moves to a more personal celebration, Mom's birthday, which coincides with the triumph of new technology in the moon-landing. Contemplating an array of possible gifts in a drugstore, he discards a Sunbeam Clipmaster and Roto-Shine Magnetic Electric Shoe Polisher, in favour of a Quikease Electric Massager. He comments that 'It is life. Life is a massage' (90/82). Evolving in response to technology, Harry appears to adopt the McLuhanite message in its least affirmative form. The entire final scene of the section amplifies the dehumanising consequences of the new technology. Far from becoming a global village, Brewer has been transformed into a ghost town; everyone is indoors watching the moon shot on television. Mom's appearance develops the impression of a sick, over-mechanised America. Her speech, disrupted by drugs, is no longer linear but robotic, broken up by random pauses. 'The doctor. Wants me up. I had to bake a cake. Earl wanted' (93/85). The reader has to remove the full-stops and reconnect the sentences to make any sense of her utterance. Her blank gaze reminds Harry of a 'blackboard from which they will all be wiped clean' (93/84), suggesting the loss of humanity involved in the loss of language. Unable to show Nelson any affection.[*sic*] Mom is reduced to massaging his head with the Quikease.

In the background the computerese banalities of the spacemen carry a similar message of human expression disintegrating and impoverished by technology. An astronaut speaks:

> I was trying to get time sixteen sixty-five out and somehow it proceeded
> on the six-twenty-two before I could do a BRP thirty-two enter. (96/87)

Lost amidst references to torquing angles, recycling and gravity align, Harry finds that the technological terms make the voice quite incomprehensible. Nelson and Harry adopt space language themselves: 'We better rendezvous with our spacecraft.' 'Negative Pop.' (99/89) But they remain to watch the moon-landing only in order to avoid returning to their empty house. Nelson and Pop promptly sleep through the broadcast, while Harry misses the vital phrase 'one small step for a man, one giant leap for mankind', hearing only 'something about steps' (99/90) obscured by crackle. The medium in fact completely obscures the message, and the degree of viewer participation is minimal. Visually the TV screen provides data in excess, but the actual event, spacewalk, seems no more real than preceding simulations, and electronic letters have to spell out that **MAN IS ON THE MOON**. Harry's final comment, as Mom massages his head refers equally to the moonshot and to Janice's flight: 'I know it's happened but I don't feel anything yet' (100/90). The section closes therefore on a note which suggests that old and new technologies are equally dehumanising, fostering similar degrees of dependence and emotional deadness. Harry remains poised between two alternative social and technological states, in each of which his identity is attenuated and his feelings benumbed.

Harry's feelings are to some extent reawakened in the second section of the novel, *Jill*, which examines two particular aspects of McLuhanism, the need for sensual reintegration on a human level, and the backward looking, essentially cyclic structure of McLuhan's thought. Initially the section involves a retreat from all technology, and especially from the primacy of the visual. At the beginning Harry recognises the dreary sameness of his repetitive existence: 'He was lying down to die, had been lying down for years. His body had been telling him to'(103/93). As a result he responds to two invitations, from Peggy and from Buchanan. Harry's encounter with Peggy signals the rejection of the visually dominated in comic terms. Repelled by her wall eye, Harry makes a polite comment on the view from her picture window, only to find that Peggy is offering a different vista, up her skirt. Peggy hates machines and invites Harry to consider that 'You think with your whole person' (110/98). To round out her message Peggy outlines Harry's shape in the air. Attracted, Harry steps into the body-shape she has drawn with her gestures and is rewarded by her gumdrop-textured kiss. The incipient sensual reintegration is immediately interrupted however by their two sons, squabbling over a broken machine, the minibike.

The mood broken, Harry hesitates over a synthetic Lunar Special in the dazzling brightness of Burger Bliss, but turns away to Jimbo's Friendly Lounge, a black bar which is presented as a dark, non-visual but intensely synaesthetic locale. Music flows here, against a background of 'tickled mutterings' and the 'liquid of laughter' (114/102). All Harry's senses are immediately engaged. He drinks a Stinger, and sucks slowly on a joint, shared with Babe, who caresses his hand until 'his mind is racing with his pulse' (116/104). Sounds are also foregrounded. Buchanan parodies Harry's linear, linotype expression, giving the syllables of the parody 'an odd ticking equality' (116/103), describing Harry as a former 'ath-e-lete', and 'expert lino-typist' at 'Ver–i–ty Press'. In contrast the black voices, richly textured in accent and slang, hint at hidden meanings below the surface, in particular their desire to pass Jill on to Harry on the grounds that she makes them too 'visible' (130/115) to the police. Under the influence of dope Harry feels himself expanding 'to include beyond Jimbo's the whole world with its polychrome races' (132/117). The recorded music of the jukebox yields to Babe's interconnected medley of show tunes, flowing into each other and into older songs from an earlier unmechanised America, running back through ragtime to the cyclical vision of time in the words of Ecclesiastes, 'A time to be born, a time to die' (125/111). The whole episode appears to celebrate both social and sensual reintegration, and a cyclic return to an original Golden Age. Although Harry also feels continually threatened at Jimbo's, he becomes less passive, and is able to turn to meet the threat of muggers on the bridge hone. Where previously Harry had distanced his fears, tending to cast them mentally in imaginary headlines (**AUTOPSY ORDERED IN FRIENDLY LOUNGE DEATH**) he now faces up to the threat rather than retreating into automatic visual defence mechanisms. Appropriately the movie house in the background has replaced *2001* with *True Grit*, also a celebration of physical courage and of an older set of American values.

Jill's presence in the Angstrom home is also originally presented in positive terms, as marking a separate peace, a retreat from the mechanical, and a rekindling of the senses. Jill banishes TV, substituting guitar music and discussion. Her healthy cooking restores Harry's 'taste for life' (171/150) and she uses music and poetry to draw the family together. When Jill improvises the ballad of her life to guitar accompaniment, Harry is at first aloof ('Don't rhyme on my account') but finally drawn in to the oral performance, following Jill's 'Narrangansett Bay' with an 'ole', and applauding with Nelson (175/152). In the oral sex which follows Jill becomes responsive to Harry's touch, her deadened emotions also reawakening. Without multiplying examples, it is fairly clear that both parties are, in auditory, oral and tactile ways, being 'led back' or 'restored to health' in the figurative meaning of *redux*. The new sensuality even extends to Mom, whose latest drug, L-dopa, eroticises her, making her feel perpetually lovey-dovey.

In addition the fresh sensual reintegration is accompanied by a renewed religious emphasis, also couched in McLuhanite terms. Jill, now clean of drugs, had originally been attracted to them as a source of religious visions. She expounds a playful, non-utilitarian view of the cosmos, in which the planets 'don't have to be used for anything' (161/141). In strong contrast to the anonymous surroundings of the Angstrom home, Jill propounds a vision of man as 'a mechanism for turning things into spirit and spirit into things' (159/139). For her, man's best creations, whether artistic or technological, are not anonymous but personal, bearing the mark of the craftsman's feelings. She argues that the artist expresses 'whatever he feels when he makes his mark' (159/139) leaving his feelings exposed 'like fingerprints, like handwriting'. Significantly, her own note to Harry is signed, not with her name but with ideograms and drawings, reproduced as such in the text. While skeptical, Harry is not dismissive. Jill's new non-competitive ethic enables him to avoid confrontation with Stavros over Janice, and the machine also appears to be losing its dominance. Returning eagerly home from the press, Harry comes across a film crew making a movie in Brewer, notes their 'heightened reality' and registers his own existence critically as 'dim' (184/161).

Harry's peaceful evolution into a richer sensual and spiritual world does not go unchecked for long, however. Another typesetting scene strikes a sourer note, undercutting the preceding positive images of a return to older values, and emphasising the illusory quality of any such return. Harry is setting an item concerning local excavations which have uncovered artefacts from the past, from the wall murals of a speakeasy, to old pictorial signs and Indian arrowheads. The historical evolution of Brewer from Indian trading post, through a colonial period when George Washington slept there, to the first iron mines and industrialisation, is briefly sketched. While the item celebrates technological development in terms of an unchecked continuity, it is actually interrupted twice by the pressing demands of the present. It is time for the return to school, pleasantly envisaged by Harry as 'beginning again and reconfirming the order that exists' (193/168). Buchanan, however, approaches Harry in the coffee-break, and 'touches' him for twenty dollars, for his children's back-to-school expenses. A second interruption, from Janice, arranges for Nelson to buy new school clothes on Saturday, rather than visiting Valley Forge with Jill. When Harry finally returns to the machine he is so out of control that he garbles three lines and finally sets one complete line of gibberish. On one level the errors indicate that his working habits of order and control are being disrupted by his emotions, messing up the established order. On another the message (handcrafted artefacts, an idealised American past) is undercut by its medium, print. The boss's anger that Janice has phoned during working hours also draws attention to the fact that Harry's life is still structured in terms of the school timetable and work, his time segmented into coffee-breaks and work shifts. The two interruptions pointedly undercut any notion of beginning again or returning to an American Golden Age. Buchanan's touch is strictly commercial. Harry hands over twenty dollars in exchange for Jill, much as if his relation to the blacks was merely the equivalent of trading with the Indians. There is no going back to Valley Forge. Nelson will buy silk neckties instead. Harry is left silently contemplating the out-of-date calendar in the office, an image of his own situation. Jill's alternative culture, with its non-materialistic, sensual and idealistic overtones is too fragile to withstand the power of the established order. When Jill does visit Valley Forge, she returns, high on drugs, having noted only George Washington's sleeping pills.

The implicit suggestion that American idealism fails, delivering man to the drug and the machine, is developed and made explicit in the character of Mom. Though L-dopa has to some extent restored her health, it has also sapped her will. Mom relates a series of frightening dreams in which she feels crowded by things, sees her children as corpses, and finds a dead man in the icebox. In contrast, however, to these familiar images of emotional deadness amidst materialism, the worst of her dreams projects a McLuhanite nightmare of the future. In the dream, people are reduced to puddles on hospital tables, connected by tubes to machines with television patterns on them, while Pop rejoices in the background, as he had earlier rejoiced over health insurance: 'The government is paying for it all' (196/171). Mom's dream pictures human beings as docile servo-mechanisms of the new machines, which feed upon them under the aegis of the state. Harry's bitter comment, 'That's not a dream. That's how it is' (196/171), indicates how far he has progressed form his earlier belief in state and technological benevolence. At the same time Harry also distances himself from Mom, angrily rebutting her suggestion that he abandon Janice and Nelson, to get free. Mom is interested only in her son, the generation of the past. 'Her tyrant love would freeze the world' (197/171). From his earlier flight, in *Rabbit [sic] Run*, however, and from the death of his daughter, Harry has learned that 'Freedom means murder' (198/172). Unwillingly Harry recognises that change is inevitable. The clock cannot be turned back to a world without Nelson or Janice. Already the maples outside his parents' home have been mutilated to protect electric wires. The American individualist ethic now reminds Harry only of the death of John F. Kennedy, suggesting that his society offers only two alternatives, murderous freedom or passive, drugged well-being. Harry returns, however, to his responsibility, his son, noting in the background that the movie house is now playing **BUTCH CSSDY & KID**.

The section closes with a sexual encounter between Harry and Jill that effectively rings the knell of their relationship. Making love in front of the 'mother planet' of the TV screen, the pair figure as 'moonchild' and 'earthman', the space vocabulary and the presence of the electronic medium dramatising the extent to which they remain trapped within the machine. Jill is now actually 'spaced out' on drugs, and as a a result her dilated pupils emphasise her enormous eyes. Eroticism fails here. Jill is described as 'an angry mechanic' (202/176) working to arouse Harry, who only manages to complete the act by imagining a machine in Jill's belly. The fragile separate peace of an alternative cultural settlement collapses with the return of Nelson, laden with the excessive purchases which Janice has charged to Harry. From now on, as Harry realises, 'It's war' (203/17 *sic*]). The phrase has a special relevance. In *War and Peace in the Global Village* McLuhan discusses the consequences of the damage done to the American sense of identity by the new technology, noting two specific reactions. In the first, 'rear-mirrorism', the past is re-emphasised in an attempt to recover the older self-image. Alternatively McLuhan envisages war as a reaction to a threatened sense of self, an attempt to reassert identity in new terms. On the failure of Jill's past-oriented values, the novel moves forward to explore this alternative possibility.

In the third section of the novel, *Skeeter*, the emphasis shifts from the individual and religious aspects of McLuhanism to its social and political implications, in particular the notion of renewed human solidarity in a media-created global village. Where Jill essentially looked back to an older set of values, Skeeter's historical theology turns the clock forward, towards apocalypse rather than Golden Age. Importantly, Skeeter is also cast in McLuhanite terms. When he describes the blacks as the future, 'We're what has been left out of the industrial revolution, so we are the next revolution' (235/203), he paraphrases McLuhan's belief that 'backward' or minority cultures, which do not have to retrain literate and mechanical minds into electronic workers, have an inherent advantage over the obsolete typographic states, and are thus the wave of the future. By sheltering Skeeter, a fugitive, Harry definitively breaks the rules and stands out against the law, which he now describes as serving only a ruling elite. Skeeter, a Vietnam veteran, also ends Harry's passivity, challenging him to fight, physically, and provoking a series of verbal confrontations. At the printing plant Harry is rewarded by the return of Buchanan's 'touch', and by Farnsworth's acknowledgment that they are 'brothers in paternity' (219/191). Cheered by his sense of interracial male brotherhood, Harry is able to slam the phone down on Janice's next interruption and to finish setting the type-item of this section without error.

In contrast to Jill, Skeeter reintroduces both books and television to the Angstrom home. In a series of structured discussions he puts the Angstroms through a short course in Afro-American history, with selected readings from his sacred texts. Skeeter obtained the books while serving in Vietnam, and his comment, 'They love us to read, that crazy Army' (226/197), connects linear reading with military regimentation. In *his* readings, however, the readers skip to and fro between different texts, and importantly they read aloud. Updike calls attention here to the personal voice, each distinctive, as opposed to the anonymity of print. Jill reads in an unnaturally high 'nice-girl-school' voice, Nelson stumbles over words but slowly gains confidence. The readings shake the parody out of Skeeter's voice, while Harry reads 'thrillingly' (247/213) as a black. The reading ends with Skeeter's comment, 'Makes a pretty good nigger, don't he?' (247/214), as the four gather to watch *Laugh-In*. The television skit, in which black Sammy Davis and white Arne Johnson appear 'like one man looking into a crazy mirror' (247/214), reinforces the impression that Harry and Skeeter are brothers under the skin, brought together by the new medium.

For Updike's readers the typographic form of the readings also carries its own messages. The selections are set in smaller italicised type, squashing more words to the line and creating a cramped and old-fashioned impression, in marked contrast to the more spacious typography in which the main events of the novel are set. Where the preceding sections were largely divided into uniform sub-sections, the *Skeeter* section substitutes a series of unconnected scenes, separated by asterisks, undated and of variable length. Less clearly sequential, these short sections undermine the earlier realist texture of the novel, suggesting a less linear reading and inviting Updike's readers to make connections for themselves.

Skeeter's own monologues explicitly recognise the deficiencies of linear narrative in relation to two topics, Vietnam and God. When Skeeter tries to describe Vietnam he tilts his head back 'as if the ceiling is a movie screen' (257/222), allowing a series of visual impressions of the war to flash across his memory. These visual images, however, are not enough to communicate the entire experience. Moving through the sounds and tactile sensations of war, Skeeter recognises that he is still selling his own experience short. Vietnam resists any overall formulation and cannot be parcelled up neatly or sequentially: 'There isn't any net to grab it all in' (258/223). While Skeeter's vision of the war as necessary apocalypse and total sensual experience, in which racial distinctions are dissolved, makes its own ironic comment on McLuhan's sensual and tribal Utopianism, the medium here is McLuhanite. Skeeter's associative, loosely structured monologue communicates fully to Harry who is left wanting to know and to understand in more depth. In religious terms Skeeter sees himself as New Messiah and Black Jesus, in a violent and barbaric second coming. Ironically, however, his Messianic visions are described as descending form the same source as his memories of Vietnam. As Saviour, he says, 'I've come down' (263/227), pointing to the 'movie screen' in the ceiling. While Harry remains somewhat skeptical about this vision of media-induced religious rebirth, Skeeter's multi-media readings and monologues do educate him out of the worst of his racism, and free him to confront both his own exploited status, and his class hatreds (249/215). For all Skeeter's menacing qualities Harry learns enough form him to stand up to this [*sic*] racist neighbours, just as Nelson fights off their children who call him 'Nigger Nellie'.

The contradictory and ambiguous aspects of the characterisation of Skeeter become very evident, however, in two scenes. In the first, Harry's neighbours Showalter and Brumbach, the one in computers, the other an assembly worker in the steel plant, accost Harry, demanding that he eject Skeeter. Up to this point in the novel Harry's neighbours have been very much an offstage presence. Here he is surprised suddenly to notice a mail truck collecting torrents of letters from a mailbox which he always imagined went unused. In the encounter Harry remains cool, noting that the two men's roles, negotiator and muscleman, reflect 'an age of specialisation and collusion' (289/249). The fact that Skeeter, like Brumbach, is a

Vietnam veteran cuts no ice at all, however. While Skeeter's presence alerts Harry to the existence of his surrounding neighbours, the message they deliver is a nakedly racist threat, and the eventual outcome hardly suggests the solidarity of the global village.

In the second scene, a trip to the country, Skeeter's bold rhetoric contrasts with his evident dependence on the machine. When the car breaks down, he is fearful, vulnerably conspicuous, his claims that 'blacks are everywhere' merely empty threats. Rescued by an old-fashioned mechanic, Skeeter adopts a slavish Uncle Tom flattery in the taxi home:

> Yo' sho' meets a lot ob nice folks hevin' en acci-dent lahk dis, a lot ob
> naas folks way up no'th heah. (271/234)

Unlike typographic man, Skeeter has many voices, but is ultimately just as dependent on the roles and resources which he ostensibly decries.

On the individual, emotional level two further episodes emphasise the extent to which Skeeter's rhetoric is also dehumanising and self-serving. In the first Skeeter asks Harry to read to him form Frederick Douglass's account of his life as a slave. Harry complies to protect Nelson form Skeeter's violence: 'if he reads the boy will be safe' (280/241). Beyond the protective 'white island' of the page, Skeeter celebrates sensuality in the 'dark abyss' of the living room. Telling Harry to 'sing it', he strips naked 'to hear it with my pores' (282/243). He proceeds to masturbate, begging Harry to read on: 'Do me one more.' 'It's not the same, right? Doin' it to yourself.' In fairly obvious terms, Skeeter ignores the message here in favour of self-massage, inducing Harry to adopt the role of slave for his own gratification.

The implication that Skeeter is as isolated within his individual reality as the Earlier Harry is confirmed in a darker sense in the ensuing scene in which he forces Jill to enact the role of sexually abused black slave-girl. Here the swapping of black and white roles, the oral emphasis, imply exploitation rather than human solidarity. While Skeeter has taught Harry to resist, to fight back, he has also induced Jill to 'shoot', in her case drugs. Jill's steady decline has run in tandem with the developing relationship between Skeeter and Harry. Her cooking has deteriorated into part-burnt, part-frozen offerings and her drawings are now 'linear, arrested' (265/229). The terms in which Harry registers the scene emphasise that Skeeter and the new media enslave as much as their predecessors. Illuminating the couple with a lamp, Harry is reminded, in the first flash, of the printing process, with Jill as white paper, Skeeter as inked plate. The pair appear to him as an interlocked machine. In addition the couple are framed in the blue rectangle of the picture window, a screen. The image of window as screen is developed when Harry changes the screens for storm windows, lovingly cleaning them until 'four flawless transparencies permit outdoors to come indoors. The mirror is two-way' (306/264). Unfortunately this proves all too much of a two-way process. There is a face at the window. The trio's activities are all too open to the viewer at the screen, rumour has broadcast them and they are exposed.

Skeeter's apocalyptic rhetoric and his celebration of multi-media experience culminate in 'the fire this time', the arson of Harry's house, an act of war on the part of his neighbours reasserting their white identity. The fire is announced telephonically by a voice which, initially, may or may not be Skeeter's. The medium here, too cool by half, carries a violent message. Skeeter, who has previously cultivated a 'cool', hip expression, is in reality 'hot', on the run from the police. When the fire explodes, with a sound like an APM in the war, his solidarity crumbles and he reverts to his past basic training. He simply flees, abandoning Jill to the flames. Skeeter has previously celebrated Vietnam as all-inclusive brotherhood and sensual experience. Now Jill is brought from the ruins in a body bag identical to the army's, as badly burned as a napalm victim, unidentifiable as white or black.

Skeeter's comment, 'The war is come home' (334/286), contrasts, however, with the neighbours' reactions. McLuhan's description of Vietnam as the first television war in which the public can be present at the event and participate in it is horribly parodied here. The onlookers at the fire remain as impassive as if they were actually watching events on television. Arriving at the scene Harry is reminded of the crowd watching the earlier moviemakers in Brewer. Now at the centre of events, Harry still feels 'peripheral, removed, nostalgic, numb' (319/274). None of his neighbours come forward 'to sparkle on the bright screen of his disaster' (330/283). The drama is on the ground, with Nelson, who struggles with the police but eventually submits, 'relieved to be at last in the arms of order, or laws and limits' (326/280). Both the firechief and the watchman guarding the house are deliberately non-committal, uninvolved. It is not the firechief's usual beat and he feels no special responsibility. Covering his notepad with his hand 'as if across the listening mouth of a telephone receiver' (327/281) he coaches Harry in the right responses to his question-and-answer series. The pair collude to obscure the question of responsibility for the fire. Entering the ruin, in which only the televison set remains undamaged, Harry is told by the watchman that he will not be responsible for Harry's safety: 'Far as I'm concerned you're not there. See no evil is the way I do it.' Harry's response, 'That's the way I do it too' (331/285) underlines his own withdrawal into neutrality. While he avoids accusing his white neighbours, while he assists Skeeter in his escape, his last sight of Skeeter, receding into the distance, framed in his rear-mirror, strikes him as 'oddly right' (337/289). As the image of rear-mirrorism suggests, Skeeter, the apparent voice of the future, is travelling backwards, reverting to past patterns of behaviour (basic training), as caught in the confusions of his self-image as Jill and Harry.

The final section of the novel, *Mim*, opens with Harry typesetting the account of his own tragedy, a message which cannot be subordinated to its medium. The item remains unfinished, however, interrupted this time not by Janice but by the boss who fires him. The *Brewer Vat* is to go offset and be printed form film in Philadelphia, bypassing hot metal processes entirely. A few men will be retrained in computers, but the new technology makes Rabbit redundant. Reduced to dependence on his father's state pension, Harry returns to his tribe, to be welcomed by Mom in terms which are heavily ironic. For her, he is worth 'a hundred doses of L-dopa' (350/300).

The appearance of Harry's sister, Mim, extends the moral that McLuhancy leads to emotional deadness, dependence and state control. A would-be actress who has become a whore, Mim's large inhuman eyes and abrupt laugh suggest to Harry that a coded tape is being fed through her head, producing 'rapid as electronic images, this alphabet of expressions' (352/302). While Mim's large nose has kept her off the screen, she admits to fulfilling the fantasies of others: 'I take on the audience one at a time' (360/309). When Mim did act in Hollywood it was in Disneyland, dressed in colonial costume, leading tourists around a replica of Mount Vernon. She repeats the performance for her family, her jerky robotic gestures accompanied by a sweetly slow idiotic voice: 'The Fa-ther of our Coun-try was himself nev-er a fa-ther' (362/311). Her own father's affirmative comment, that Disney kept America from Communism during the Depression, reinforces the image of the electronic media as propaganda and control. Mim tells Harry that she has learned to manage and manipulate others, but is herself under gangster control, featuring in her publicity pictures in the role of slave-girl. While the family enjoy the excursions Mim organises to see *Funny Girl*, Mom comments that the film obscures the fact that its heroine was also involved with gangsters. In addition, though ostensibly enjoying sex, Mim has evolved a set of survival rules for living in the new human desert of the West, limiting her erotic performances to three repetitions. Stavros's comment, that in bed Mim's 'thermostat' switched off immediately, leaving him with the sensation of handling rubber, underlines her lack of emotional responsiveness. At this point in the novel Harry is similarly benumbed. His only sexual activity is masturbation, and even then he gains satisfaction only through grotesque fantasies. 'Real people aren't exciting enough' (378/324). He has better luck 'making a movie that he is not in', imagining Mim and Stavros together.

The extent to which the quasi-religious McLuhanite Utopia also fails is explicated in relation to Nelson and Janice. Nelson's reaction to the fire is to blame Harry. Not having been raised to believe in God, 'Blame stops for him in the human world' (325/279). His face 'crazed with some television of remembrance' (350/300), Nelson takes refuge instead in composing a scrapbook on the fire. Its format, which includes news-clippings, doodles, peace-signs, musical notes, Tao crosses and fuzzy Polaroid snaps of the ruin, ironically imitates the form of McLuhan's *The Medium is the Massage*, a similar assemblage of different typographies, headlines, drawings and photographs. It offers Nelson little solace. Janice's decision to leave Stavros, while partly the result of Mim's intervention, also highlights the insufficiency of a life lived entirely in secular and physical terms. When Stavros suffers a near heart attack, Janice recognises that he, too, needs things to be orderly. Importantly, medical technology fails here. Janice is too flustered to find the nitroglycerine tablets, and offers him cold pills instead. Understanding that they are 'beyond chemicals', she feels that she must 'make a miracle' and exorcise the 'devil' within Stavros (386/330). Though Stavros survives, his illness makes the point to her that while 'spirits are insatiable. . .bodies get enough' (388/332). The sensual joy of her relationship is not merely devalued by the example of Mim, but also revealed as insufficient in itself.

Although Janice and Harry are reunited at the close of the novel, the symbolic terms in which their reunion is described leave the final position unresolved. In the course of the novel, different sensory images have been unpacked, revealing the double-edged quality of sensuality, in personal and political terms. At several points Jill and Harry are described as drowning. While Harry survives, surfacing at the point of the novel where the US/USSR ban on underwater weapons is announced, Jill goes under, like Mary Jo Kopechne at Chappaquiddick. Fire imagery includes the warmth of human relations, the 'hot' media, napalm, and the burning of the house. The term 'cool' ceases to be affirmative when extended to frozen human beings. Space travelling, floating free may imply liberation and technological triumph, or the dangers of perishing in a cold void. In each case the elemental imagery may be read in two different directions offering messages of opposed types.

At the close of the novel Harry and Janice's communications are similarly ambiguous. Although they succeed in reading each other's silences on the telephone, they are less successful face to face. Harry's attempts to convey by gesture to Janice that she should show the suitcase to the motel clerk are interminably protracted. Contemplating their ruined home, now defaced by the contradictory messages, swastikas and peace signs from the same spray can, Harry feels that it all 'adds up to no better than the cluster of commercials on TV' (395/338). In the Safe Haven Motel the couple switch off the television and ignore the advertised attractions of the Magic Fingers massage, but their delicate manoeuverings towards each other are presented in space metaphors. They are 'slowly revolving, afraid of jarring one another away' (396/339), 'slowly adjusting in space', while Harry lets Janice's breasts 'float away, radiant debris' (406/347). The suggestion that Harry 'redocks' here, returning from the void to human contact, is undercut by his comment that he and Janice are made for each other as companion killers. Each flight into freedom has had murderous consequences, for Rebecca in Janice's case, for Jill in Harry's. The last sentence of the novel, 'He. She. Sleeps. O. K.?', while suggesting that over-and-out of a space message, is also uncomfortably close to the robotic voice of Mom. The reunion here is neither a new beginning nor a blessed return, in McLuhanite terms. Any such suggestion is undercut by the contradictory ways in which the fictional message can be read. The novel closes, therefore, on a note of interrogation. While Gutenberg Man has been satirically exposed, while some aspects of the McLuhanite and countercultural synthesis have been treated sympathetically, the electronic Utopia remains an illusion, and the couple are left in transition. Typographic man may find such an irresolute ending unsatisfying. For the informed reader, however, Updike's refusal to accommodate to the desire for a final 'adding up' or ordered closure, whether linear or cyclic, is entirely appropriate.

Where *Rabbit Redux* focuses upon technological evolution, *Rabbit Is Rich* explores economic change. From its first sentence, 'Running out of gas' (3/7), the novel refers outwards to the rise in oil prices, the American energy crisis of 1979, the declining power of America abroad, challenged by the hostage crisis in Iran, and inwards to the apparently failing physical energy of Harry Angstrom, whose obsessive concern with death expands the frame of reference towards a vision of life as entropic decline. In quite explicit terms the novel questions American systems of values. While rabbit is rich materially as the prosperous part-owner of the Toyota franchise, a member of the Flying Eagle Country Club, with savings to boot, he is poor in human terms, impoverished in spirit and in his relations to others.

In order to suggest the paucity of Harry's values, Updike draws on three major organising metaphors: anal and libidinal atitudes to money, media fantasies, and information as capital. Readers of *Rabbit Redux* will be familiar with the image of the media as propaganda, purveying a fantasy American Dream. In addition, in an extension of McLuhan's thesis, information figures as capital. Given that money is the supreme medium, extending man's grasp from the nearest to more distant staples, it is readily replaced in the next development by the movement of information, so that money merges with informational forms of credit, in this case, particularly, in terms of inside financial information as a capital resource. The third major metaphor treats the fantasies of homo economicus in overtly psychological terms. One dimension of the novel has offended several reviewers, the crudity of the hero's language and the overt sexual and anal detail. Rarely in a novel, with the possible exception of *Tender is the Night* or *Portnoy's Complaint*, have so many major events taken place in bathrooms. The scatological emphasis is relentless from the most common expletive ('shit') to the imagery of waste and waste products, Harry's fascination with male homosexual practices, and his rectal sex with Thelma. An early image establishes connections between energy and waste in both human and economic terms. Stavros is reminiscing about the gas-guzzlers of the past:

> When you took off the filter and looked down through the inlet valve
> when the thing was idling it looked like a toilet being flushed. (11/14)

This imagery of waste forms a vital part of Updike's analysis of the power of money in the novel, and necessitates a brief digression into psychoanalytic theory.

The connection between faeces and money has been exhaustively discussed by modern psychoanalytic thinkers, who have developed Freud's original insights in various directions. While it is not within the scope of the present study to engage with these debates in detail, the connection seems an important one.[52] Essentially, the crux of psychoanalytic theories of the anal character of money lies in the idea that faeces are the child's first autonomous product and first material possession, exposing the child also to the power of parents and providing the first opportunity to exercise power over surroundings. By being taught to be clean the child recognises the power of his environment and realises that it is necessary to subordinate self to others. Rewards are obtainable from parents for prompt discharge, and defecation in itself offers auto-erotic pleasure. Alternatively the child may discover that faeces retention provides an opportunity to challenge parents and that such retention may intensify pleasure. In *Three Essays on the Theory of Sexuality* Freud argues that there are four successive stages in the development of sexuality: the polymorphous, oral, anal and genital. Focusing on the 'anal neurotic', the adult who has become arrested in the anal stage, or who has achieved the genital stage so weakly that he later reverts to psychic infantilism, Freud argues that the traits of this character conform to three basic types. Firstly unmodified anal eroticism may express itself openly through coprophilia, homosexuality, or the

---

[52] Readers are referred for a fuller discussion to Ernest Bornemann, *The Psychoanalysis of Money* (New York: Urizen Books, 1976).

desire for rectal coitus. Alternatively the instinct may be sublimated, creating an acquisitive, thrifty, miserly character for whom savings replace faeces. Lastly, in reaction, the anal instinct may express itself in an obsessive concern with order and cleanliness, as opposed to dirt, creating an over-conscientious, rigid character type.

Many different types of activity may be understood in terms of Freud's analysis. Getting rid of objects of value may have a libidinous emphasis, as in selling with a profit, pleasurable wastefulness, or gambling. Conversely, hanging on to objects of value, avarice, or collecting, may provide a similar source of pleasure. The small child's delight in moulding clay, making mudpies, or playing in sandpits has also been understood as an expression of the desire to manipulate and handle his 'treasure'. While later theorists (Ferenczi, Abraham, Jones) have contextualised Freud's theories as belonging particularly to bourgeois capitalism with its emphasis on thrift, regular hours and ordered performance, the equation of gold and faeces is also widespread in very different cultures, in folklore (the golden donkey, the goose that lays the golden eggs), in superstitions (bird-droppings on the head are lucky) and in language. Given Updike's linguistic background, he may have noted the high incidence of scatological metaphors for money in colloquial German. English-speaking readers are probably familiar with such expressions as 'to do one's business', 'to make a pile', 'to be tight-assed' (mean) or 'liquid' (in funds), 'to be up shit creek' (in money difficulties) or to possess 'filthy lucre'. Although capitalism may not have created the anal character, it has been argued that it has raised to a high degree of prominence a type which is relatively rare in other social systems. Updike has an illustrious predecessor in calling attention to the connection. In *Our Mutal [sic] Friend* Dickens employs the central metaphor of dirtmounds to focus the economic nature of an earlier society.

While Harry Angstrom is not a case study in neuroticism Updike uses the perceived connection between faeces and money in order to illuminate the flaws in Harry's system of values, and the links between money and fantasy. Within this concept even quite minor events in the novel take on a deeper significance. Harry is fascinated, for example, by cars, which have a magical and erotic significance for him. To Mim they are 'shitboxes' (239/221), while to Nelson they are worth acquiring only as 'collectibles'. At the car lot the employees work 'all the shit hours' (264/249), in contrast to Nelson who sees his college degree as 'horse poop' (327/301). Lyle, Slim and the Reverend Campbell are homosexuals. Slim is also a 'stuffer' for the electric light company, putting bills in envelopes– an image which conjoins money, anality and eroticism. Even the erotic activities of the major characters involve sex either in or from the rear (Webb and Cindy, Thelma and Ronnie, Harry and Thelma, Janice and Harry, Nelson and Melanie). In addition, a dominant stylistic feature of the novel, the hero's tendency to catalogue his environment in excessive detail, may be understood less as a documentary approach to Middle America in all its facticity than as an expression of the relentless desire to collect, store up and incorporate information. Importantly, this phenomenon is not limited to Harry. When Pru bombards Nelson with letters packed with information on her pregnancy, Nelson complains that she even tells him 'when she's taken a crap practically' (150/140). It is within this complex framework of associations that certain key plot events and image patterns take on their full resonance.

The opening of the novel foregrounds information as Harry's main capital asset. At the car lot a young rural couple present themselves: 'We chust came in for some information' (14/17). Harry meets the request to excess, bombarding his auditors with mileage figures, technological detail and brand names. The reader is similarly stunned by the description of the Corolla's four-speed synchromesh transmission, fully transistorized ignition system, power assisted front disc brakes and locking gas cap, and the steel-belted radials, quartz crystal clock, and AM/FM stereo of the Celica GT Sport Coupe. The overload of information here is also accompanied by its falsification. When Harry tries to sell the economy model, the Corolla, he quotes *Consumer Reports* approvingly, and argues in favour of rapid turnover: 'Who in this day and age keeps a car longer than four years?' (15/18). Seconds later, listing the features of the more expensive Corona, the *Consumer Reports* experts are described as in error in their mileage figures. When the luxury model, the Celica, is the focus, Harry reverses direction again to emphasise its investment value: 'That old Kleenex mentality of trade it in every two years is gone with the wind' (16/19). Harry has an abundance of information here but it is both contradictory and relies on a libidinal emphasis. 'Picking a car is like picking a mate' (16/19) in Harry's view and he puns happily on Japanese currency: 'When trade-time comes you get your yen back' (16/19). Harry's own 'yen' in the affective meaning of the term is also prominent. The girl who accompanies the prospective purchaser is the daughter of Ruth, Harry's erstwhile lover, and may even be Harry's own child. On the test drive Harry becomes obsessed with this possibility, feeling 'the sudden secret widen within him' (23/25).

In the novel Harry is persistently established as a man who is obsessed with inside commercial knowledge, an avid reader of *Consumer Reports* and a keen listener to Webb Murkett's investment advice. In human terms, however, Harry has the wrong information. While he treasures his erotic or financial secrets, other secrets are withheld from him. He is, for example, the last to discover that Nelson has impregnated Pru, though Janice and her mother swiftly discover this fact. One scene specifically highlights Harry's lack of human information. On a wet evening he is studying *Consumer Reports* while Nelson reads up on the motor industry. As Harry explains the mechanics of car financing in exhaustive detail, he keeps trying to discover what else Nelson has on his mind. Is he sleeping with Melanie? When the subject becomes more delicate, extending to Jill, Harry retreats briskly into accounts of the best four-slice toaster, and fails to see the underlying message in Nelson's cross-questioning on the subject of Stavros's capabilities. When Nelson criticises his father for being 'uptight', Harry listens eagerly, 'thinking this might be information' (119/112), but he lacks the hidden clue which would make everything clear. In each major plot event Harry is similarly the last to discover the right information. He treasures the secret of his Krugerrands and his house, unaware that Janice has already spilled the beans to Nelson. Janice and her mother arrange to fire Stavros and introduce Nelson into the business without Harry being aware of the machinations afoot. Melanie proves a red herring, merely a cover for Pru. Much of the comedy of the novel depends upon Harry's lack of awareness. At Pru's wedding, for example, he notes the gaeity of Campbell and Slim, and assumes that Slim and the organist, fingering each others' shirts, are discussing clothes, failing to see that they are all 'gay' in quite another sense. Harry never suspects that Thelma is attracted to him, though it is crystal clear to Janice, as is his yen for Cindy. Even the wife-swapping in the Caribbean is a surprise to Harry, though the other parties have consulted each other and allocated partners in advance. Finally, Harry never discovers whether Annabelle is his daughter. When he mentions the possibility to Janice, she comments astutely that 'you always want what you don't have instead of what you do' (72/69). Annabelle, unlike the real Nelson, remains a fantasy child. In the final confrontation with Ruth, Harry offers financial support, but is refused in horror, in terms which put his fantasy in its place: 'When I think of you thinking she's your daughter, it's like rubbing her all over with shit' (448/413). This is one secret which money cannot buy. The various revelations of the plot suggest that while Harry hoards his own fantastic secrets, he is blind to other information which is both more important and more real.

It is essential to note that the reader is placed in the same position. Updike makes careful use of proleptic imagery which reveals its true meaning only on a second reading or with hindsight. When Harry sympathises with the young couple, 'I think it's a helluva world we're coming to where a young couple like yourselves can't afford to buy a car or own a home' (23/25), the remark points ahead to anticipate Pru and Nelson's difficulties. When he refuses Nelson a job at the lot because Jake and Rudy are married men 'trying to feed babies on their commissions' (100/95), he little thinks that Nelson is soon to be in the same position. Harry's cosy relation with Stavros has been comfortably accepted, 'When a man fucks your wife, it puts a new value on her' (12/15), but when Webb Murkett does likewise the remark rebounds. While prolepsis often places Harry in an ironic light, the reader is also implicated. Readers may think, for example, that the clipping concerning Skeeter, last seen near Galilee, came from Ruth who lives nearby. When Nelson sees beyond Melanie to 'a more shallow-breasted other' (131/123), the reader has to assume that the absent female is Jill. Pru has not yet been introduced. Hindsight provides an ironic frame, but in the experience of reading, hero and reader advance toward knowledge at the same pace, establishing a strong empathetic relationship which creates a degree of sympathy for Harry. The reader is thus continually invited to consider which information is more valuable, the affective or the economic, the secret fantasy or the human reality.

Since *Rabbit Is Rich* is the third volume of a trilogy, the reader also benefits from hindsight of another type, informed by prior knowledge of Harry's preceding disasters. Harry draws attention to this aspect of events when discussing *Jaws II* with Cindy: 'D'you ever get the feeling everything these days is sequels? Like people are running out of ideas' (403/371). In plot terms, Nelson's impregnation of Pru, his absorption into the family business and his later flight from domestic responsibilities, suggest that the past conditions the present and that its horrors are merely repeated by the second generation. Nelson clearly mimics the earlier Harry's racism, and after an initial flirtation with vegetarian, mystical Melanie, a similar figure to Jill, marries a woman who is in appearance strongly reminiscent of Mom Angstrom. In addition a succession of media images offer two alternative interpretive frames for the family events of the novel, as pleasant repetition or as reenacted horrors. Harry exists in a world dominated by media fantasies. At the country club his crowd act loudly and boisterously, modeling their behavior on TV beer commercials. The bronzed Murketts hug each other, 'framed as if for an ad' (172/160) against the background of Mount Pemaquid. In his car Harry listens to pop music, particularly the John Travolta theme song, which recalls the dominant feeling of the preceding summer, with 'every twat under fifteen wanting to be humped by a former Sweathog in the back seat of a car parked in Brooklyn' (33/35). The imagery suggests that in economic terms corporate capital reproduces itself by controlling desire to create new consumer wants and a mass market. Harry's own Toyota franchise depends upon a similar creation of mass fantasy in its advertising campaign ('Oh what a feeling!').

Within this general framework two specific media-genders are counterpointed. The women of the novel revel in television soap opera. Harry's antagonistic discussions of past horrors, with Nelson, are repeatedly interrupted by Janice and her mother, wiping their eyes from an episode of *The Waltons, The Jeffersons* or *All in the Family*. At several points an ironic counterpoint is established between screen image and Angstrom family. When, for example, Nelson returns to demand money and a job, with attendant complications, Mrs. Springer retreats into a re-run episode of *All in the Family* in which a character's old girlfriend also asks for money. As Nelson and Harry clash over the job at the lot, Janice interrupts, laughing at herself for being so carried away by *The Waltons*, when 'It was in *People* how all the actors couldn't stand each other' (120/113). In each case the women are watching re-runs, and in each case the repeated screen image of American Happy Families is undercut by the real conflicts in the Angstrom home. Harry dislikes the TV series, Nelson is equally irritated as Pru succumbs increasingly to pregnancy and the lure of afternoon soaps. Nelson does enjoy one episode of the series *Charlie's Angels*, laughing empathetically as huge automobiles collide in slow motion. When, however, Nelson acts out the fantasy, demolishing the convertibles, the climax is registered not in the slow motion of fantasy, but as comically fast. Far from enjoying a fantasy triumph, Nelson sobs in Harry's arms, while Harry repeats the slogan, 'Oh what a feeling' (170/158). The episode undercuts the advertisement much as the preceding slogan 'You asked for it we got it' suggested ironically that, in the oil crisis, America got what it asked for in a less affirmative sense. Although Harry has been scornful of the fantasy family image, hating to see the Pittsburgh football team win because their image depends upon 'all that Family crap' (269/248), he has been too swift to discount the force of real human emotion, as opposed to commercial mass fantasy. As he comments, 'Funny about feelings. They seem to come and go in a flash and yet outlast metal' (163/153).

In opposition to the female soap opera an alternative image of the family as horror obsesses the men. At Nelson's wedding, Harry notes the Reverend Campbell emerging from the vestry as if 'from a secret door like in a horror movie' (242/224). For Harry the wedding is selling Nelson down the river. He has previously imagined Pru's father as a 'sorehead who wants to strangle his daughter and put her in the potato bin' (230/213), and his memories of rural horror stories, incest and murder, as related in the *Brewer Vat*, undercut the cosy image of the rural past now on show to tourists at the Albrecht Stamm Homestead in Brewer. Nelson's image of the family is vividly suggested by his fascination with the *Amityville Horror* film, in which an ordinary home is occupied by the devil. Nelson repeatedly describes his past as a horror story, and was initially attracted to Pru by her 'horror stories of her own growing up' (315/291), beatings, rages and tangled family tensions. Nelson's exaggerated image of his father coincides with a remembered picture of an ogre in a children's book, with blubbery lips and hairy face: 'That's how he sees Dad these days (361/333). When Nelson repeats his griefs to Pru, however, she dismisses them as no worse than other people's experiences. As they talk Nelson observes a framed print of a goateed farmer in his room. In the past the print had seemed 'a leering devil' (318/293), but is now 'merely foolish, sentimental'. For all their overt hostility the two men are intimately connected through their shared fantasies, and both have to learn to see the reality instead.

At Slim's party fantasy and horrors merge, undercutting the exaggerated image. Nelson's hostility to pregnant Pru had previously led him into reverie about freefall parachuting in *Moonraker*. At the party the couple argue in a room filled with grotesque pornographic images of women and boys. Mesmerised by these obscene pictures, moving 'from one horror to another' (335/309), Nelson lets Pru slip away from him, and takes refuge in the bathroom, fascinated by an album of Nazi pornography. Images of horror precede the actual accident, when Pru slips from Nelson's grasp and freefalls down the stairs. In the event, disaster is averted. Pru does not lose the baby, but merely breaks an arm. In the action of the novel melodramatic horrors repeatedly threaten but fail to materialise. There is no death (despite the frailty of Stavros and Thelma), no financial ruin, and such accidents as do occur are mostly minor automobile scrapes. Nelson does not commit incest with his sister, though the possibility hovers, and even the wife-swapping culminates in cosy chat about children. Neither of the mass fantasies is therefore confirmed. The careful alternation between the two media frames, soaps and horrors, keeps the reader from assessing the events of the novel in terms of mass fantasy, undercutting the image of American Happy Families, while refusing to cater for the opposite suggestion of America as horror. In the finial pages of the novel Harry watches the Superbowl on television, particularly the half-time show with its orchestrated American propaganda. 'Sentimental Journey' is sung, followed by dancers flashing tinfoil solar panels, singing 'Energy is people'. Harry turns away from the television, however, to his granddaughter who is described in exactly the same terms as Rebecca in *Rabbit, Run*, 'She knows she's good' (467/429). This is a real child, neither the daughter of fantasy nor a remembered horror from the past. Where the Superbowl dancers celebrate naive patriotism, Harry's final comment refers less affirmatively to the Iranian hostages: 'Fortune's hostage, heart's desire, a granddaughter. His. Another nail in his coffin. His' (467/429). The new child reminds Harry of the past, of failing energy, of death and yet also of fulfilled desire. In a sense, Harry has given hostages to fortune, his family, and emerges from fantasy only at the end of the novel when he realises their true value. While the novel points towards a humanist message in which human beings are more important than money, it is not itself a sentimental journey. Any such reading is checked by the continual undercutting of soap opera and mass media imagery.

Harry takes some time, none the less, to appreciate the real bases of his fortune. Initially his attitude to his family appears to be entirely conditioned by his economic position. In particular his sexual life has been affected by his new wealth. Although he is rich because of Janice's inheritance, having money has made him feel 'satisfied all over' (49/49) leading to an energy crisis all his own. Of recent years his sexual interest has begun 'to wobble, and by now there is a real crisis of confidence' (49/49). Nelson's return wakes Harry up once more. He tells Janice that 'It's great to have an enemy. Sharpens your senses' (125/117). Where Harry is miserly, Nelson is wasteful, a continual drain on his father's resources, landing him with car repair bills, an expensive wedding and Pru's hospital charges. In the course of the novel Harry evolves from anal hoarder to pleasurable spender, an evolution assisted by Nelson who tells him that 'Money is shit' (169/157).

Two key scenes establish the libidinal associations which money has for Harry. In the first, money and sex are intimately conjoined. Acting on Webb's inside information on the money market, Harry takes his savings from the bank and converts them into Kruggerands [*sic*] at a shop in Brewer. The terms of the description here are explicitly anal. 'Fiscal Alternatives' is situated opposite a shop which sells 'dirty magazines for queers' (210/195) and looks itself as if it might be 'peddling smut'. The coins come in plastic containers with round lids which suggest tiny toilet seats: 'Bits of what seemed toilet paper were stuffed into the hole of this lid to make it fit tight' (211/195). Hiding the coins away Harry moves through two memories, one of surprising Nelson, massively phallic in the shower, the other of catching his father, vulnerably naked: 'such white buttocks, limp and hairless, mute and helpless flesh that squeezed out shit once a day' (212/197). As the two memories suggest, Harry, endowed with his gold, feels a renewed sexual power, distancing himself from the image of the aging father. Nelson, who has just spent an evening with the Reverend Campbell, is now under threat. Harry enjoys his son's irreverent comment on the homosexual pastor's continual description of the Church as the Bride of Christ: 'What does he do, fuck the church up the ass?' (213/197). The repeated anal references precede the scene, reminiscent of a similar luxuriation in gold in Norris's *McTeague*, in which Janice and Harry make love amidst the Krugerrands. The gold here appears to recreate Harry's sense of sexual identity and to recharge his batteries. Imitating funerary rites (pennies for the ferryman) Harry positions two coins on his eyelids, and then removes them, 'a dead man reborn' (216/201), tumescent amid scattered gold. The scene also dramatises the extent to which Janice is the foundation of Harry's fortune. Balancing coins all over her, he cautions her to lie still: 'If she laughs and her belly moves the whole construction will collapse' (218/202). Harry has previously enjoyed Janice's 'new sense of herself as a prize' (188/175), commenting that there is 'nothing like fucking money'. When he is summoned home by Janice to meet Pru her guarded tones make him think that she is being held hostage. Nelson, who is in a sense holding Harry to ransom, is also associated with the Iranian hostages: 'Khomeini and Carter both trapped by a pack of kids who need a shave and don't know shit' (354/327). Harry's private fantasy assertion of his sexual power is thus imagistically connected with political and economic realities. While the couple's love-making is ecstatic, the description, in financial terminology, is highly ironic. Coins spill between Janice's legs as Harry's 'interest compounds' until, after the final 'payoff', the spent hero engages in a comically panic-stricken hunt for a lost coin. When Harry later converts his hoarded gold into silver, darker suggestions undercut the preceding pleasurable enactment of his deepest fantasies. The anal emphasis recurs. Janice asks, 'How liquid is this silver?' and the coins are brought in by Nelson's homosexual friend Lyle. Sorting the coins, Janice titters, and Harry understands why: 'playing in the mud' (368/339). Unlike the Krugerrands, however, the silver is less magically attractive, consisting of old coins which have already been sifted for collector value. They are also extremely heavy, so that handling them is less a pleasure than a chore. Perversity and grotesqueness pervade the scene. Lyle squints at Harry as if the latter had bought 'not only the massage but the black-leather-and-whip trick too' (368/339). Sweating and struggling to the bank, Janice figures as a gross image of maternity, cradling her sack as if it were a baby, in an ironic image of reproductive capitalism in action. In the bank the Angstroms attempt to stuff their safe deposit box, but finally have to abandon their efforts, apologising to the teller for having 'loaded it up with so much crap' (374/345). Where the gold appeared magically erotic, the silver is described in terms which associate it with dirt and death. Although Harry feels a furtive rush of desire for Janice in the bank vault he speedily realises that it is 'Not a good place to fuck'. The safety deposit box is described as sliding into the wall like a coffin in a vault. As they leave the bank Harry feels only loss:

> His silver is scattered. . . .It's all dirt anyway. He glimpses the truth that
> to be rich is to be robbed, to be rich is to be poor. (375/346)

In the movement between the two scenes Updike conveys Harry's dawning realisation that money is not magical treasure, life-giving in erotic terms, and that death undercuts the physical and materialist fantasy in which he lives. Material riches rob him of human emotions and render him poor in spiritual and psychological terms.

It is important to note that Harry's fantasies are not purely the product of individual neurosis but are representative, a point indicated in the evening spent at the Murketts', which generalises his position. Just as Webb Murkett has access to financial inside information, his job as a contractor provides him with superior plumbing fixtures. Harry is enchanted by the guest bathroom with its Popeye toilet paper, monogrammed towels and furry seat cover. The bathroom is so sparklingly clean that it appears to be unused. Its furnishings, catalogued over some two pages, emphasise an obsessional concern with the display of order and cleanliness. When, however, Harry opens the medicine cabinet its contents hints at darker secrets. The ostensibly relaxed Murketts have a battery of medicaments to hand, including Maalox for stomach ulcers and Preparation H for haemorrhoids. Harry's comment suggests his growing awareness of the connection between money and anality:

> Carter of course has haemorrhoids, that grim over-motivated type who
> wants to do everything on schedule ready or not, pushing, pushing.
> (285/263)

Back in the living-room, entranced once more by the ostentatious Murketts as living embodiments of the American dream, Harry's thoughts turn libidinous. Are the pellets for erotic use? 'Everybody loves an ass. Those wax bullets in the yellow

box– could they have been for Cindy? Sore there from, but would Webb?'
(286/264)   In the background money and secrets recur. Murketts, Angstroms
and Harrison form the inner circle of the party, while the Fosnachts are outsiders.
Ronnie Harrison, who depends for his living as an insurance agent on the threat of
death, spends part of the evening bombarding Ollie Fosnacht with financial
information, humiliating him just 'to see how much garbage he could eat'
(295/275). Peggy, unaware that Cindy is a Catholic, commits a social gaffe in her
attack on the Pope, the result of not having the information on Cindy which the
others share.

When Peggy blocks the guest toilet, mopping up her tears with Kleenex, Harry
goes upstairs to use the domestic facilities. Money and Cindy are on his mind in
almost equal proportions. Urinating he fills the bowl with gold. 'His bubbles
multiply like coins' (302/278), as he thinks of his savings. Upstairs Harry
discovers Polaroid photographs of Webb and Cindy having sex. At the party the
Murketts have been embracing 'like a loving pair advertising vacations abroad'
(298/275), posing as the ideal couple of fantasy. In the late afternoon light of the
photos the couple again appear 'golden' (307/283). Closer observation, however,
reveals the flaws in the image. Although this section of the novel was published as
an excerpt in *Playboy*, the images are actually designed to undercut the mass
libidinal fantasy. Posing as if for a centrefold, Cindy is described as a grotesque,
truncated object. Because of the camera angle her face is out of focus beyond her
drooping breasts, her chin is double, and her feet, in the deficient perspective, look
enormous. A second snap catches only her buttocks and their Cyclopean 'eye'.
Squinting, Harry deciphers a fuzzy background as Webb's chest, a bulge as Cindy's
face, Webb's pot-belly, feeble erection and 'shit-eating expression', but the overall
effect left by the photographs is distinctly unenticing. Webb and Cindy are
considerably less 'golden' than they would like to appear, and while Harry is
excited he is also repelled by the over 'dirtiness' of the images. In response Harry
reverts to his own secrets: 'He tries to discipline what he has seen with his other
secrets. His daughter. His gold. His son' (308/284). Only the thought of Nelson is
sufficient to bring him back to earth.

Back again at the party Harry spots the two remaining Polaroids. Importantly
Webb has used only two exposures to picture his children. Earlier Harry had noted
that Webb's display of coulour photos had captured the children of his previous
marriages but had been edited to exclude the wives, represented only by an
amputated hand or arm in the background. Webb had previously described to Harry
how he drove his adult children away, breaking off all contact. In the two Polaroids
the son stands 'sadly' on the patio, the daughter squints foolishly, menaced by her
father's large shadow. On one level the scene draws a parallel between Webb and
Harry, each neglecting their real children to focus upon fantasy images, and
abandoning mature wives in favour of child-women who are purely the objects of
male desire. Mass fantasy has clearly affected Webb's emotional life to its
detriment. Though Harry is still in transition at this stage of the novel, the episode
suggests that human responsibilities (here, Nelson) form a necessary discipline, and
that human affections and emotions are more complex than the one-dimensional
centrefold image allows. Later, emerging from fantasy, Harry finds a stack of old

pornographic magazines in his new house. Though he flicks through the centrefolds to reveal the slow widening of the models' legs, until full pubic display is permitted, he remains quite unmoved. The sexual secret is not everything. The girls' genitals merely 'act as a barrier to some secret beyond' (458/421). In the Caribbean vacation this beyond figures prominently as the last of Harry's fantasies is definitively exploded.

At the Murketts' Harry had announced, 'I want to go to the Caribbean. But first I want to go to the bathroom. Bathroom, home, Caribbean in that order' (301/278). Later events reverse the sequence as Harry travels to the Caribbean, indulges in bathroom activities with Thelma, and returns home. On One level the vacation is part of his evolution from saver to spender, following as it does upon the purchase of the house which wipes out his savings. Each of Harry's previous holidays reflected his economic position, from his childhood trips to the shore, the outings of the poor, to his holidays in the Poconos, dependent on Janice's parents. The vacation in the islands is the ultimate fantasy, enjoyed by rich Americans in a protected enclave, fenced off from the background of Caribbean poverty.

In the plane, rising above the material world below, Harry has a fleeting religious intimation: 'God, having shrunk in Harry's middle years. . .is suddenly great again' (390/359). Beneath the new constellations of the Caribbean, however, Harry's spending takes on a less spiritual guise. When Janice worries about the size of their final bill Harry is sanguine.'[sic] The expense in his mind is party [sic] of a worthy campaign, to sleep with Cindy' (396/364) . Harry's pleasurable wastefulness almost produces its desired libidinal reward. After he loses $300 in the Casino, Cindy approaches him beside the sea, and it seems as if their moment has come. The pair are immediately interrupted by the news that Ronnie Harrison is 'burning up the crap table inside' (400/368). Though Ronnie ends up only a few dollars ahead, it is in fact he who gains Cindy, described here as Webb's 'treasure to barter'. The wife-swapping deliberately organises human sexuality in terms of exchange values. Webb cautions that it must not be repeated, and must be purely sexual, non-romantic (407/375). While Ronnie, star of the crap table, gains Cindy, Janice chooses Webb, entranced by his commercial 'bullshit'.

The faecal suggestions in the two images are developed in Harry's anal intercourse with Thelma. On one level the scene is highly ironic. Harry is bitterly disappointed in his allocated partner. In the event, though, the night with Thelma proves oddly liberating. Initially Harry's desire is merely to get through the evening, to save his energies for Cindy on the following night. In the Harrisons' bathroom the thrifty emphasis recurs. Harry contemplates the conspicuous consumption evident in their toiletries, from the pressurised ozone-eating shaving cream, to the monster toothpaste and new razor: 'Harry can't see the point, it's just more waste' (411/379). When Thelma appears, however, clad in cocoa bra and black panties, which she discards into a 'dirty pile' of laundry, Harry finds her more enticing than he had imagined, and eagerly accepts her sexual offer. But when this event occurs, the fantasy is demystified. Penetrating Thelma, Harry feels, 'There is no sensation: a void, a pure black box, a casket of perfect nothingness' (417/384). The terms refer back to the safe deposit box, and to funerary caskets, rather than to treasure trove. When Harry finally enacts the fantasy underlying his behaviour, he sees through it to the emptiness at its centre. Thelma's impending death from lupus also has a symbolic resonance. Lupus, a tubercular skin condition, is a consuming disease, hence its name, and connects to other images of greedy consumption in the novel. At home with death, Thelma reawakens Harry's `sense of miracle at being himself' (419/386). Their long conversation, centred on their children, emphasises that Harry has not reverted to psychic infantilism, but has conquered it, reassuming his role as a father. Thelma points out that to young girls like Cindy he is `just an empty heap of years and money' (420/386), whereas to her he is both real and unique. When, the next morning, Harry discovers that he must return home, Nelson having gone missing, his reaction is mixed. Though irritated at missing Cindy, he also feels that in a way `this is a relief' (426/392). Listening to Janice's tale of woe, he is infuriated by Webb's knowing comments, hating `people who seem to know; they would keep us blind to the fact that there is nothing to know. We are each of us filled with a perfect blackness' (425/391). Sexual and commercial secrets are exploded together, as false knowledge, companion voids. Beneath the plane the riches of America are now distanced and irrelevant. Harry had previously imagined the American South as a land of wealth, butlers, and above all attractive women. Now, `the possibility of such women is falling from him' and he prays silently and turns to Janice. The night with Thelma is assessed as `in texture no different from the dream. Only Janice is real' (427/393). Weeping, exchanging expressions of love, the two clasp hands, floating above the revealed void.

Events do not of course conclude on such an unambiguous potentially `soapy' note. Harry returns to both a new beginning and new responsibilities. Though Nelson is no longer perceived as a threat, though Mrs Springer appears to have shrunk in size, Thelma is not so easily shaken off. At the close of the novel she sends Harry a clipping, an account of a Baltimore physician who killed a goose on a golf course. The story is told several times in the novel. When Harry first hears it on the radio, he understands it as involving the mercy-killing of an injured bird, rather than `murder most foul' and re-tells the joke at the club. Thelma later uncovers a clipping of the story in a syndicated column, in which a Washington doctor is described as beating the goose to death as he was about to sink his putt— a very different version. When Harry sees geese on Ruth's pond he wonders if the doctor killed the bird because of the `little green turds' which geese leave on the fairway. In the final version the doctor has been fined $500 and is described as having `cooked his own goose' (454/418). The evolution of the story accompanies Harry's own evolution, alternatively emphasising false information, anality and financial loss in a series of different media versions which recast the event as joke or horror. Potentially the story suggests that in sleeping with Thelma, Harry has cooked his particular golden goose, Janice. Thelma is in love with Harry and is unlikely to respect the terms of the exchange. Indeed, the Angstroms' first day in their new home is soured by the preceding night's party with the gang. None the less when Janice voices her unease, Harry defuses the threat, hugging her to him and reassuring her that the Harrisons are as ordinary as they are, and that he will never run again. Reflecting, Harry remembers a Princeton Professor's theory that `in ancient times the gods spoke to people directly through the left or was it the right half of their brains' (462/424), a system which later broke down. The reference (to Julian Jaynes, *The Origin of Consciousness in the Breakdown of the Bicameral Mind*, (1976) suggests that Harry has begun to perceive, for all his materialism, the existence of a possible human relationship to a greatery [*sic*] mystery.

Though Updike is too realistic to convert Harry wholesale at the end of the novel, the image of Harry's new house also suggests a compromise between saving and spending, between past materialism and a dawning realisation of other possibilities. Updike draws here upon Thoreau, whose *Walden*, particularly the 'Economy' chapter, describes the author's symbolic house-hunting and his withdrawal from a materialist world to a simplified existence at Walden Pond. Throughout *Rabbit Is Rich* reference is made to Thoreau, and to images of rural simplicity (the Poconos vacation, the woodchuck which Nelson swerves to avoid, Melanie's horror of animal food). While the poverty of Ruth's rural home, with its rusting buses, fallen fruit, and general atmosphere of decay, undercuts any pastoral moral, Rabbit finally occupies a small house, which is curtainless and stripped to its essentials, like Thoreau's, and looks out on a small ornamental pond and squirrels. The conclusion of the novel suggests, if tentatively, that Harry has transcended the worst of materialism, to perceive with Thoreau that the only standard of value lies in vital human experience, as opposed to the complexities of civilisation which stand in the way of significant life. Though the things of the world have not been cast off, they have been reassessed and placed in relation to a potentially spiritual if muted conclusion.

*Newman, Judie. *John Updike*. N.Y.: St. Martin's, 1988. Chapter 3: "The World of Work: *Rabbit, Run, Rabbit Redux* and *Rabbit Is Rich*." 32-78.

Rabbit at Rest

"So Young!"

Joyce Carol Oates*

With this elegiac volume, John Updike's much-acclaimed and, in retrospect, hugely ambitious Rabbit quartet - *Rabbit, Run* (1960), *Rabbit Redux* (1971), *Rabbit Is Rich* (1981) and now *Rabbit at Rest* - comes to an end. The final word of so many thousands is Rabbit's, and it is, singularly, "Enough." This is, in its context, in an intensive cardiac care unit in a Florida hospital, a judgment both blunt and touchingly modest, valedictory and yet enigmatic. As Rabbit's doctor has informed his wife, "Sometimes it's time." But in the nightmare efficiency of late 20th-century medical technology, in which mere vegetative existence may be defined as life, we are no longer granted such certainty.

Rabbit at Rest is certainly the most brooding, the most demanding, the most concentrated of John Updike's longer novels. Its courageous theme - the blossoming and fruition of the seed of death we all carry inside us - is struck in the first sentence, as Harry Angstrom, Rabbit, now 55 years old, more than 40 pounds overweight, waits for the plane that is bringing his son, Nelson, and Nelson's family to visit him and his wife in their semiretirement in Florida: he senses that it is his own death arriving, "shaped vaguely like an airplane." We are in the final year of Ronald Reagan's anesthetized rule - "Everything falling apart, airplanes, bridges, eight years . . . of nobody minding the store, making money out of nothing, running up debt, trusting in God."

This early note, so emphatically struck, reverberates through the length of the novel and invests its domestic-crisis story with an unusual pathos. For where in previous novels, most famously in *Couples* (1968), John Updike explored the human body as Eros, he now explores the body, in yet more detail, as Thanatos. One begins virtually to share, with the doomed Harry Angstrom, a panicky sense of the body's terrible finitude, and of its place in a world of other, competing bodies: "You fill a slot for a time and then move out; that's the decent thing to do: make room."

Schopenhauer's definition of walking as "arrested falling" comes to mind as one navigates Rabbit's downward plunge. There is an angioplasty episode, recounted in John Updike's typically meticulous prose, that is likely to be quite a challenge for the hypochondriacs and physical cowards among us. (I'm not sure I met the challenge - I shut my eyes a few times.) There are candid and un-self-pitying anecdotes of open-heart surgery. We come to know how it probably feels to suffer not one heart attack but two, how it feels to strain one's "frail heart" by unconsciously (that is, deliberately) abusing one's flabby body.

A good deal is made, in the Florida scenes, of the American retired elderly. Rabbit thinks, with typical Rabbit crudeness, "You wonder if we haven't gone overboard in catering to cripples." A former mistress of Rabbit's named Thelma (see *Rabbit Is Rich*) reappears in these pages as a lupus sufferer, soon to die, not very gallantly described, when they kiss, as smelling faintly of urine. There is an AIDS patient who exploits his disease as a way of eluding professional responsibility, and there is a cocaine addict - Rabbit's own son, Nelson - whose dependence on the drug is pushing him toward mental breakdown.

The engine that drives the plot in John Updike's work is nearly always domestic. Men and women who might be called ordinary Americans of their time and place are granted an almost incandescent allure by the mysteries they present to one another: Janice Angstrom to Harry, in *Rabbit Redux*, as an unrepentant adulteress; a young woman to Harry, as possibly his illegitimate daughter, in *Rabbit Is Rich*; and now Nelson to Harry, as his so strangely behaving son, whose involvement with drugs brings the family to the edge of financial and personal ruin. Thus, though characters like Janice, Nelson and, from time to time, Rabbit himself are not very sympathetic - and, indeed, are intended by their resolutely unsentimental creator not to be - one is always curious to know their immediate fates.

John Updike's choice of Rabbit Angstrom, in *Rabbit, Run*, was inspired, one of those happy, instinctive accidents that so often shape a literary career. For Rabbit, though a contemporary of the young writer - born, like him, in the early 1930's, and a product, so to speak, of the same world (the area around Reading, Pa.) - was a "beautiful brainless guy" whose career (as a high school basketball star in a provincial setting) peaked at age 18; in his own wife's view, he was, before their early, hasty marriage, "already drifting downhill." Needless to say, poor Rabbit is the very antithesis of the enormously promising president of the class of 1950 at Shillington High School, the young man who went to Harvard on a scholarship, moved away from his hometown forever and became a world-renowned writer. This combination of cousinly propinquity and temperamental diamagnetism has allowed John Updike a magisterial distance in both dramatizing Rabbit's life and dissecting him in the process. One thinks of Flaubert and his doomed fantasist Emma Bovary, for John Updike with his precisian's prose and his intimately attentive yet cold eye is a master, like Flaubert, of mesmerizing us with his narrative voice even as he might repel us with the vanities of human desire his scalpel exposes.

Harry Angstrom, who tries to sate his sense of life's emptiness by devouring junk food - "the tang of poison that he likes" - the very archetype of the American macho male (whose fantasies dwell not, like Emma Bovary's, on romance, but on sports), appears as Uncle Sam in a Fourth of July parade in *Rabbit at Rest*, and the impersonation is a locally popular one. Rabbit, who knows little of any culture but his own, and that a culture severely circumscribed by television, is passionately convinced that "all in all this is the happiest . . .country the world has ever seen." As in *Rabbit Redux* he was solidly in favor of the Vietnam War, so, as his life becomes increasingly marginal to the United States of his time, in ironic balance to his wife's increasing involvement, he is as unthinkingly patriotic as ever - "a typical good-hearted imperialist racist," as his wife's lover put it in the earlier book.

Rabbit is not often good-hearted, however, living as he does so much inside his own skin. Surprised by his lover's concern for him, he thinks, funnily, of "that strange way women have, of really caring about somebody beyond themselves." From *Rabbit, Run* to *Rabbit at Rest*, Rabbit's wife, Janice, is repeatedly referred to as "that mutt" and "that poor dumb mutt," though she seems to us easily Rabbit's intellectual equal. A frequent noun of Rabbit's for women is unprintable in this newspaper; a scarcely more palatable one is "bimbo." As a younger and less coarsened man, in the earlier novels, Rabbit generates sympathy for his domestic problems, but even back then the reader is stopped dead by his unapologetic racism ("Niggers, coolies, derelicts, morons").

In *Rabbit at Rest,* an extreme of sorts, even for Rabbit, is achieved when, at Thelma's very funeral, he tells the dead woman's grieving husband that "she was a fantastic lay." Near the end of the novel, it is suggested that Rabbit's misogyny was caused by his mother! (Of course. Perhaps women should refrain from childbirth in order to prevent adversely influencing their sons?) It is a measure of John Updike's prescience in creating Rabbit Angstrom 30 years ago that, in the concluding pages of *Rabbit, Run*, Rabbit's ill-treated lover Ruth should speak of him in disgust as "Mr. Death." If Mr. Death is also, and enthusiastically, Uncle Sam, then the Rabbit quartet constitutes a powerful critique of America.

Of one aspect of America, in any case. For, behind the frenetic activity of the novels, as behind stage busyness, the "real" background of Rabbit's fictional Mt. Judge and Brewer, Pa., remains. One comes to think that this background is the novel's soul, its human actors but puppets or shadows caught up in the vanity of their lusts. So primary is homesickness as a motive for writing fiction, so powerful the yearning to memorialize what we've lived, inhabited, been hurt by and loved, that the impulse often goes unacknowledged. The being that most illuminates the Rabbit quartet is not finally Harry Angstrom himself but the world through which he moves in his slow downward slide, meticulously recorded by one of our most gifted American realists.

Lengthy passages in *Rabbit at Rest* that take Rabbit back to his old neighborhoods - "hurting himself with the pieces of his old self that cling to almost every corner" - call up similar nostalgic passages in John Updike's autobiographical novel *The Centaur* and his memoir, *Self-Consciousness*, as well as numerous short stories and poems tasked with memorializing such moments of enchantment. This, not the fallen adult world, the demoralizing morass of politics, sex and money, the ravaging of the land, is the true America, however rapidly fading. The Rabbit novels, for all their grittiness, constitute John Updike's surpassingly eloquent valentine to his country, as viewed from the unique perspective of a corner of Pennsylvania.

After Rabbit's first heart attack, when he tells his wife of an extraordinary sight he has seen on one of his drives through the city, pear trees in blossom, Janice responds, "You've seen [it before], it's just you see differently now." But John Updike has seen, from the first.

*Joyce Carol Oates. "So Young!" *The New York Times Book Review.* 30 Sept. 1990: 1, 43.

"Why So Hard on Rabbit?"

Brent Staples*

Harry Angstrom is dead after three decades as the fidgety, flinching hero of John Updike's Rabbit novels. We met Harry in *Rabbit* (sic) *Run,* in 1960, a beautiful, brainless guy in his 20's, mourning the loss of high school basketball stardom, already experiencing that loss as the hand of death itself.

We say goodbye now, three novels later, in *Rabbit at Rest,* where, fat and 55, Harry has retired with a fat-eating habit that finally blows his heart to pieces. In between passed an uncommon private life woven through public events from the time of Ike through the rule of Reagan.

Harry is receiving a brutal send-off. Gary Wills's savage, humorless obituary in *The New York Review of Books* condemns him for a lack of "moral heft." *Esquire* makes Harry's excess poundage a metaphor for all that ails the nation. The *Wall Street Journal*'s assessment: He was "an almost entirely antipathetic character."

Rabbit wasn't perfect, but these criticisms of him are excessive. They also say more about discontent with the American self than they say about the novels.

Yes, he cheated on his wife. He drove off in a panic when family politics got dicey. His relationship with his only son was a ruin to the last, and he was mute when he could have repaired the damage. None of these sins, however, are mortal. Many readers know them. Why, then, this bum's rush? There are several likely explanations.

Class Snobbery– directed at a retired auto salesman who lacks a college education.

Fat. Rabbit would have been better liked if he had joined a health club, got sleek and worked up death-defying strength.

Television. TV propaganda infiltrated Harry's person, circumscribing his world. Rabbit therefore invites the scorn of the truly sophisticated, who claim to watch only a little public television and the occasional episode of *Thirtysomething.*

Advertising. The ads washed over Rabbit, particularly the ones for the Toyotas that he sold for a living– like "Oh, What a Feeling!" and the smoky voice of the woman, crooning, "I love how you set me free, Toyota!" Small wonder that he drove off when he felt the emotional pinch. Inevitably, he gave up and went back home– where has wife and his child reminded him of his own mortality, looming ahead.

Failed Escape. This is probably the principal (sic) beef against him. That Harry stayed put is anathema to the video age, when anybody can be everywhere at once and selves are shed several times an hour. Harry's press would be brighter if he had fled Brewer, Pa., dumped Janice and the kid, and turned up at poolside on the Coast– tan, in shades and squiring a teen-aged bride. This would be called "roguishness," and would bring burlesqued winks all around.

Harry dealt as best he could with the fundamental issues: the painful lack of fit with loved ones; how to live bearably in a skin that is lent to us only briefly. For his thoughts and experiences in these directions, Rabbit will be missed.

*Brent Staples "Why So Hard on Rabbit?" *The New York Times* 140 (5 Nov. 1990): A-20.

"Reading at Rest?"

Ed Christian*

Reading's own John Updike (or should I say Shillington's own?) is, in the opinion of many literary critics, America's finest living writer. In his new novel, *Rabbit at Rest* (Knopf, 512 pages, $21.95). Updike returns once again– and perhaps for the last time– to the city of his youth.

To call Updike Reading's own is, of course, to bestow upon ourselves a dubious compliment. Art, even the most beautiful art, is the distillation not of sweetness and light, but of suffering. No suffering, no art.

Yes, Reading influenced John Updike, but his repeated return to our green hills– in person, in reminiscence, in stories, and in novels– suggests that his memories are bittersweet, his fondness tempered by regret.

To the rest of the country, Updike's Brewer is a composite of everything good and bad about small city, post-industrial America. To us, Brewer is here, it's home, and every wart Updike paints on it itches and burns when chafed.

Some of us may not like the Reading we see in *Rabbit at Rest.*

Others, more realistic and reconciled, may share the feelings of the poet Ted Kooser, who, looking at himself in the mirror, said, "Good dog, old face. Good dog."

We may be homely, but we're home.

Although the book stands well on its own, *Rabbit at Rest* is the fourth and final volume of a series about ex-high school basketball star Harry "Rabbit" Angstrom. The series follows him at decade-long intervals frm 1959, when he is 26, to 1989. The earlier novels are *Rabbit, Run, Rabbit Redux,* and *Rabbit Is Rich.*

Rabbit at Rest finds our hero, now 56, long retired from the Toyota dealership that his wife, Janice inherited from her father. Plump, bored, and boring, he spends his winters in Florida with his wife while their son, Nelson, runs the car lot.

Rabbit has a mild heart attack while rescuing his drowning granddaughter and goes to the hospital.

In the spring Rabbit and Janice return to Brewer/Reading. Rabbit has a coronary artery widened; refuses to renew an old affair with Thelma Harrison, a high school friend's wife; and discovers that his son has embezzled more than $200,000 from the dealership to keep up a cocaine habit.

Nelson agrees to enter a rehabilitation program rather than face prison. While he is gone, Rabbit has a brief affair with his wife, Pru.

As the summer ends, Thelma dies of lupus, the Toyota company finds out about the embezzlement and revokes the family's franchise, Janice neglects a very threatened Rabbit while studying real estate, and Pru tells Nelson and Janice about her coupling with Rabbit.

Again Rabbit runs, this time to his condo in Florida.

There he challenges a young black man to a game of basketball, but suffers a massive heart attack while sinking the winning shot. As the book closes, Rabbit, in intensive care and unable to tell anyone about his final success on the court, decides that death isn't so bad. He is at last at rest.

As Rabbit lies dying, Janice thinks of her husband, "He had come to bloom early and by the time she got to know him. . .he was already drifting downhill."

Here, in a sentence, is Rabbit's tragedy. Although Rabbit is never quite forgotten by his admirers, his days of glory are over at 18.

Updike has said that all of his books have at their centers some sort of moral dilemma. It would be simplistic to say that Rabbit symbolizes the immorality of idolizing high school athletes, forcing them to a physical prime at the expense of their mental development, yet Rabbit's life is undoubtedly blighted by sports.

Where most successful people have trained in their youth for a lifelong career and mature relationships, Rabbit has trained for basketball, and he is never much good at anything else, though he tries to use sex as a substitute.

A superficial reader might question the moral stance of a man who writes novel after novel about the perils of suburbia: adultery, alcoholism, failed parents, failed children, the frantic filling of empty lives with possessions.

Updike, though, is an intensely compassionate author. He makes us care for his characters, no matter how unattractive they may be.

Rabbit's ex-lover Thelma Harrison expresses Updike's moral purpose when she says, "You make your own punishments in life, I honest to God believe that. You get exactly what you deserve. God sees to it."

Through four volumes, in generation after generation, Updike shows us Rabbit and his family lying awake in beds of their own making. Amidst the beauty of the earth and the joy of life, they stew in a poisonous brew of passion and their past.

Another aspect of Updike's moral stance is seen when the narrator says, about Thelma, "The affair has enriched her transactions with God, giving her something to feel sinful about, to discuss with him (sic)."

Updike believes, in the theological sense, in grace. If we "sin boldly," we are more likely to suffer greatly, and through that suffering be called to reformation. It's the old idea of God loving the worst sinners best because they give his grace the greatest scope.

Rabbit's sister Mim says of her parents, "I suppose their hearts failed in the end but so does everybody's, because that's what life is, a strain on the heart."

Rabbit's heart fails him in the face of that strain. To a happy reader, his strenuous life may seem appalling rather than appealing, and this is good.

To the reader who knows Rabbit's struggles firsthand, though, his suffering can lend strength and the determination to avoid Rabbit's sad fate.

Rabbit tells another ex-lover, "I've had some physical problems lately and they give me the feeling I've walked through my entire life in a daze."

He's right: He has. But we, Updike suggests, shouldn't.

Interspersed with the sad story of Rabbit and his family are many descriptions of this area and its people. Many events in the book are set in Mount Judge, which is a fictionalized version of Mount Penn.

Updike writes:

Empty to him as seashells in a collector's cabinet, these plain domiciles with their brick-pillared porches and dim front parlors don't change much; even the slummier row houses such as he and Janice lived in on Wilbur Avenue when they were first married are just the same in shape, climbing the hill like a staircase, though those dismal old asphalt sidings the tints of bruise and dung have given way to more festive substances imitating rough hewn stone or wooden clapboards, thicker on some facades than others, so there is a little step up and down at the edges as your eye moves along the row.

Reading becomes Updike's Brewer, and he describes it well:

Brewer was his boyhood city, the only city he knew. It still excites him to be among its plain flowerpot-colored blocks, its brick factories and row housing and great grim churches all mixed together, everything heavy and solid and built with an outmoded decorative zeal. The all but abandoned downtown, wide Weiser Street which he can remember lit up and as crowded as a fairgrounds in Christmas season, has become a patchwork of rubble and parking lots and a few new glass-skinned buildings, stabs at renewal mostly occupied by banks and government agencies, the stores refusing to come back in from the malls on Brewer's outskirts.

The street names and places in *Rabbit at Rest* are sufficiently similar to places we know for us to take a special pleasure in reading about them.

And residents of the Reading area, where the summertime humidity is "like being wrapped in warm washcloths," will, of course, find it especially interesting.

(Residents of Shillington might prefer Updike's autobiography, *Self-consciousness: Memoirs*, which is available in paperback and fondly recalls many familiar places and friends.)

Flying Eagle Country Club, where Rabbit plays golf, reminds us of Flying Hills Golf Club. Springer Toyota is on "Route One One One," which is rather like Lancaster Avene Route 222.

Rabbit and Janice live in a little limestone house among mansions in Penn Park at 14 ½ Franklin, a block and a half from Penn Boulevard. There is, in fact, a Franklin Street similarly close to Penn Avenue in West Reading, though a home with that number would have to be a houseboat in the Schuykill River. The neighborhood described fits much of Wyomissing.

The site of Brewer High School, on Linden Street, is reminiscent of Reading High School, on 13th Street.

Updike writes, "Of pale-yellow brick and granite quoin, it clings to the greening mountainside like a locust husk."

Thelma Harrison lives in Arrowdale, which was once Arrowhead Farm. This calls to mind Laureldale and Cherokee Ranch.

Updike writes, "The split levels with sides of aluminum clapboards and fronts of brick varied by flagstone porchlets and unfunctional patches of masonry facing. *Rabbit at Rest* is now among Updike's best novels. The writing, as usual in Updike's work, is breathtaking. The insights into American life are astonishing.

*Ed Christian, "Reading at Rest?" *The Reading* (Pa.) *Eagle* 11 Nov. 1990: F-1, 2.

"Rabbit Runs Down"

Ralph C. Wood*

It is tempting to thank John Updike, if not also God, for relieving our misery by putting Rabbit Angstrom out of his. The final installment of Updike's tetralogy takes Angstrom to his fated end, and it is no giveaway of the plot to say so. The novel's only mystery is how and when rabbit will go into the dark. But there is no surprise that our most antinomian literary hero sins his way to the grave. Rabbit has been a destroyer from the start. He has always followed the impulses of his own sweet will, letting neither God nor anyone else stanch his carnal and spiritual promptings.

Now a 55-year-old retired Toyota dealer afflicted with a failing heart, Angstrom remains a terrible hurricane of a man, one who can still flatten other people's lives. After almost drowning his granddaughter Judy in a Florida boating mishap, Angstrom cuckolds his son Nelson and then abandons his wife, Janice. One final time, Rabbit runs. Yet nowhere does Updike censure his self-seeking, other-forsaking rogue. After all, Angstrom does no crime against life that life would not first do unto him.

There being no Christ to judge or forgive him, no community to sustain or check, no vocation to fulfill or frustrate, Rabbit faces death with all that is left: an egotheistical eroticism. When God dies, Updike believes, only sex remains alive and divine. In one of his last meditations on the meaning of it all, Angstrom declares his own unrepentantly hedonic creed: "One thing he knows is if he had to give parts of his life back the last thing he'd give back was the fucking . . . . A lot of this other stuff you're supposed to be grateful for isn't where it matters."

Why not give thanks— with Garry Wills and a host of hostile critics— that so dreadfully shallow a character has at last been put down? The answer, if we are honest, is close at hand. Rabbit Angstrom is one of us: the average sensual man, the

American Adam, the carnally minded creature whom our moralistic religion and politics cannot encompass. Rabbit offends so many because he embodies such unpleasant truth.

As the only animal for whom sex is not a joyless act of procreation, we humans are caught in a tragic bind: our glory is also our shame; our blessing, our curse. We are animated with bodily desires that require ethical control, even as they cannot be confined within a purely ethical life. Updike seeks thus to instruct his American audience in the rudiments of carnal reality. And it is his considerable literary accomplishment to have rendered this tragic vision palpable and convincing.

For those who have followed Rabbit Angstrom's previous peregrinations– we can hardly call them his "progress"– *Rabbit at Rest* is riveting. It lets us roam backward into the fields of Harry's youth even as it drags us inexorably to his death. With consummate artistic skill, Updike recapitulates the major events in Rabbit's life. In place of a clumsy exposition scene, Updike's narrator has Rabbit recall, at surprisingly appropriate times, the myriad events, people and places that shaped his life.

The novel is as much about the past as the present. Everything current is connected to something distant. Hence Rabbit's constant remembrance of things past: his fading stardom as a high school basketball hero in Mt. Judge, Pennsylvania; his youthful marriage to the store-clerk Janice Springer; their many sexual felicities and infidelities; the deaths that each so horribly caused in their own house; their moral enmeshment in the lives of their friends and families, especially their elderly parents and their own son Nelson; Rabbit's jobs as a typesetter and car dealer, and now Janice's belated career in real estate; their financial prosperity during the boom of the '70s, when they bought vacation homes in Florida and the Poconos; now their fear of economic ruin amidst the coming Depression.

Updike is sometimes called the chronicler of our culture, the one writer historians will consult to find out what life was like in the latter half of the American century. I doubt this judgment, if only because the density of Updike's catalogs– brand names, highway numbers, advertisement jingles, specificities of dress, localities of fauna and flora– will require endless footnoting. Good American that he is, Updike writes for the present more than the future. It is we who have ourselves lived through these 40 tempestuous years of America (sic) history who will keep returning to the Rabbit Angstrom tetralogy. In letting us join Rabbit's scurrying life, Updike enables us to absorb the ethos of our time, to breathe the air of our distinctively American culture, above all to remember and so discover who we are.

Rabbit discovers that he is a man in rapid demise. He tries to face his death with a typically American determination to live for the moment. Thus we find him still skidding forward in the jumpy present-tense narration that Updike pioneered in 1960 with *Rabbit, Run*. Yet Angstrom is far more reflective than he was then. Rabbit not only runs; he also remembers and judges. There is an aphoristic quality to his mind. Now that his life has come full circle, he has acquired more than physical pounds; he has learned a hard-bitten wisdom as well. "Everything falling apart," Rabbit laments, "airplanes, bridges, eight years under Reagan of nobody minding the store, making money out of nothing, running up debt, trusting in God."

Rabbit blames his family's calamity on the badness of the times. Surrounded by so great a cloud of troubles, who could have done much better? Rabbit is enraged, for instance, that his son has turned out to be such a failure, a cocaine addict who has pilfered the profits from the family's once-thriving Toyota dealership. Yet in his frenzy of accusation against Nelson, Rabbit remembers that he has hardly been a moral exemplar himself. Nelson is indeed Rabbit writ small: the son who repeats, on a lesser scale, the faults of his father: vagrancy, irresponsibility, egomania.

But just as Rabbit proves more than a mere wastrel, Nelson is revealed as more than a dopehead: he seeks and finds a cure for his drug addiction. Updike discloses the dark truth that the generations do not progress so much as stay in the same place. We do not see further than our forebears because we are not mounted on their shoulders. All the forward fury is, in fact, a way of standing still. Rabbit has his fatal heart attack at the same place where we met him three decades ago: trying one final time to win on the basketball court.

The discovery that our lives go around in a circle is the center of Updike's tragic vision. He is our great elegist of the heart-break that life inevitably brings: the grim news that we are finished before we have barely begun, and that our lives are but brief candles rocketed into the void. Harry voices this perception by way of an analogy to the fount of all our wisdom— neither Scripture nor the church but television:

> TV families and your own are hard to tell apart, except yours isn't interrupted every six minutes by commercials and theirs don't get bogged down into nothingness, a state where nothing happens, no skit, no zany visitors, no outburst on the laugh track, nothing at all but boredom and a lost feeling . . . .
> His whole life seems . . . to have been unreal, or no realer than the lives on TV shows, and now it's too late to make it real, to reach down into the earth's iron ore and fetch up a real life for himself.

Lacking any guide outside himself, Rabbit has recourse to the only thing he knows to be real: his own sexuality. This is no mere cultural or religious limitation, as if Rabbit might have done better with a Harvard degree and an active life in the Lutheran church. What Rabbit has to rely on is all that, in Updike's view, anyone can rely on. In *Couples*, his notorious novel of 1968, a character named Freddy Thorne declares Updike's own position. Thorne says that we dwell in "one of those dark ages that visit mankind between millennia, between the death and rebirth of gods, when there is nothing to steer by but sex and stoicism and the stars."

In the absence of God, Eros and Thanatos are the only engines left to drive the human machine. The closer Harry approaches death, the more he is obsessed with his own carnality. He lies distraught in the Florida sand after being rescued from death's double assault— a heart attack during a boating accident where he almost killed his granddaughter. Instead of turning his mind to Last Things, Harry looks up at the spandex crotch of his daughter-in-law's bathing suit. Alone in a North Carolina motel in final flight from his Pennsylvania family, Harry masturbates "to show himself he is still alive."

In perhaps the most chilling scene of the whole novel, Rabbit grants Thelma

Harrison, his dying and lupus-ridden ex-mistress, one final grope at his penis. Sex, she has taught him, is the true soul food. It is the one remaining means of establishing our momentary worth, as we see ourselves reflected in the mirror of the other who desires us even as we desire her or him. His high-toned critics to the contrary, Rabbit is right. We are troubled by his perpetual moral adolescence not because it is so foreign but because it is so akin to our own. Rabbit is a man of the flesh, fleshly. He can be dismissed only by moralists who believe Rabbit needs merely to do the right thing.

To say that Rabbit Angstrom is one of us is not to issue an imprimatur on his thoughts, words or deeds. And to commend Updike for making us see ourselves in this scoundrel is not to baptize him as a Christian writer. He calls Christianity his "curious hobby, firm but dusty." Like Harry himself, Updike confesses only that he cannot "*not* believe." God has always been present in Updike's work chiefly through his absence, as a felt void which once was filled and which may yet be filled again. God was for Updike the God of Job and Jeremiah, the absconding God of the cross. God's refusal to rescue the drowning baby Rebecca-- in the terrifying scenes near the end of *Rabbit, Run*– is so palpable that he could be rightly accused of truancy.

But now God seems hardly to exist at all. The drug-recovered Nelson offers a godless grace before meals in the name of "Peace. Health. Sanity. Love." Harry himself can affirm only that God "is like an old friend you've had so long you've forgotten what you liked about Him . . . the closer you get [to death] the less you think about it, like you're in His hand already." This proves alarmingly true. In the near-fatal boat accident, Rabbit and his granddaughter tack desperately back to shore. They comfort themselves not with the assurances of faith but with the triviality of television commercials: "Coke is it," Judy sings, "the most refreshing taste around, Coke is it, the one that never lets you down, Coke is it, the biggest taste you've ever found."

One suspects that Updike is not merely recording our contemporary godlessness but judging it to be inevitable. Yet there are hints of another way, the way not of Rabbitic self-indulgence but of eschatological self-surrender. Angstrom himself remarks the absence of nuns at the Catholic hospital where he undergoes angioplasty:

> Vocations drying up, nobody wants to be selfless any more, everybody wants their own fun. No more nuns, no more rabbis. No more good people, waiting to have their fun in the afterlife. The thing about the afterlife, it kept this life within bounds somehow, like the Russians. Now there's just Japan, and technology, and the profit motive, and getting all you can while you can.

In his more reflective moments, Rabbit admits the sinister thing about sin: it always seems justified. Rarely do we commit overt, self-conscious acts of evil. The crooked heart always has excuses that even God will understand. Harry occasionally glimpses the truth that we are creatures far more sinning than sinned against, far more fallen than tragic. He confesses, at least once, that his plight lies not in his sorry situation but in his own "failure or refusal to love any substance than his own."

Rabbit's confessed egomania is at its worst with women. Updike himself is often accused of being the most egregious of male chauvinists. I would argue that this is not the case. It is more to the point to say that he is an unapologetic advocate of heterosexual love. Romantic regard for members of one's own gender is, for Updike, a terrible refusal of the other– and perhaps also of the Other. Men and women who can love their opposites reflect the love of a God whose ways and thoughts are drastically not our own.

Yet heterosexual love has its peril, as Updike knows all too well. Rabbit candidly names it: the stream of gratitude runs more generously from women to men than from men to women. He could never love his mistress Thelma, he adds, as she loved him. He expresses a poignant exaltation in that "strange way women have, of really caring about somebody beyond themselves." Though Updike has not discerned it, there is a deep link between such womanly other love and the selflessness of nuns and rabbis and ordinary believers in God. Scripture knows the theological root of romance as well as ethics when it declares that we love because we have first been loved.

Now that Rabbit is tragically at rest, perhaps Updike will show us a more excellent way. We will not soon forget Harry Angstrom, if only because he so realistically reflects our carnal condition. But something surprising has happened: Nelson and his wife, Pru, have been reconciled in spirit as well as flesh. Having long been aliens in bed, they are seeking to have a third child as an affirmation of their new life together. Would that Updike might make this love the start of a new, more redemptive tetralogy.

*Ralph C. Wood, "Rabbit Runs Down." *The Christian Century* 107 (21 Nov. 1990): 1099-1001.

"Rabbit's Run"

Thomas M. Disch*

I must begin by confessing a fondness for the character of Harry Angstrom that has little to do with literary discrimination. I think of him the way soap opera fans are supposed to regard the characters on the programs they watch, as though he were a real person, a distant but beloved member of the family, and I feel the same say-it-isn't-so sense of loss, at the end of his tetralogy (and of his life), that made Sherlock Holmes's fans implore Conan Doyle to restore their hero to life. Except that I know the rules for serious literature and medical science don't work that way, and that nothing can be done for Rabbit's heart. Rabbit is dead.

It has, therefore, been distressing to read reviews of *Rabbit at Rest* that speak of Harry Angstrom with the kind of contumely usually reserved for pro wrestling villains. Donna Rifkind of *The Wall Street Journal* declared Rabbit to be "an almost entirely antipathetic character." Bruce Bawer in *The New Criterion*, while having good things to say about the Rabbit books ("Tense, taut, and suggestive . . . a fine example of that demanding genre, the acute, fluent study of a not very acute or fluent protagonist") came down on Rabbit for possessing "a crippling sensibility" and being "an odious character" and, overall, someone derelict in his sense of duty.

The most unremitting critic of Rabbit, however, was Garry Wills in *The New York Review of Books*, who both deplores Rabbit as an implausible and unconvincing character *and* belabors him for his sins, as though he had been plucked living from the decades' headlines. "Though he is supposed to have been the local star [of his basketball team]," Wills marvels, "we hear of no college or semi-pro scouts interested in him. He plays no pick-up ball with young adults–just one pathetic game, in his street clothes, with some unwelcoming teenagers. He does not attend games, or even watch them on TV. Harry's dreams of basketball are a satiric device stuck onto his character rather than an expression of a real athlete's love of the game." Rabbit is also reprehended for thinking in "purple passages," though he "is not a reader." Rabbit's pro-war opinions in *Rabbit Redux* are held to be an expression of "the reactionary dandyism [John Updike] shares with Tom Wolfe and William Buckley." But Rabbit's worst sin is that he constantly serves as Updike's dopplegänger : "Rabbit even has Updike's teeth, and his habit of finding lost food in them." Wills seems to believe that Harry Angstrom is not a fictional character at all but John Updike in disguise, and thus doubly reprehensible:

Harry's creator has lost track of what he originally meant him to mean. Rabbit loves the feel-good Reagan years; but, as usual, it is Updike the aesthete who speaks through Harry the slob: "The guy [Reagan] had a magic touch. He was a dream man. Harry dares say, 'Under Reagan, you know, it was like anaesthesia.'"

As to Rabbit's plausibility and consistency as a character, I would put him on a par with Mr. Pickwick or Leopold Bloom: one of the great originals, a type at once profoundly self-consistent and always full of surprises. He is also, again like Pickwick or Bloom, emblematic of his class, his country and his era. By the time he leads the 1989 Mt. Judge Fourth of July parade in the costume of Uncle Sam, he really has come to embody the spirit of America. In Updike's allegory, this is both a tragic and a comic fate, for Rabbit is now overweight, out of shape and just about ready to self-destruct because his arteries are "full of crud." However, he accepts his condition with a characteristic blithe grace, goes on eating the junk food that is killing him and at the end of the parade has one of those epiphanies Updike's critics seem to think those of his low station aren't entitled to:

> closer to the front [of the parade], on a scratchy tape through crackling speakers, Kate Smith belts out, dead as she is, dragged into the grave by sheer gangrenous weight, "God Bless America"– ". . . to the *oceans*, white with *foam*." Harry's eyes burn and the impression giddily– as if he has been lifted up to survey all human history– grows upon him, making his heart thump worse and worse, that all in all this is the happiest fucking country the world has ever seen.

That passage nicely illustrates the fundamental magic trick of the four Rabbit books, the mix of high diction and demotic speech that conveys Rabbit's most fleeting perceptions in speech that flickeringly is and is not his. In "dead as she is" you can hear a kind of redneck affirmation, but "sheer gangrenous weight" is not intended as precise verbal stream-of-consciousness; rather, it is Updike's own rendering of the image in Harry's mind, just as the parenthetical phrase splitting "the impression giddily" and "grows upon him" is not meant to echo Rabbit's own rhythms of speech but to imitate the giddiness it describes, and to set up the final marvelous affirmation, which *can* be understood as direct quotation of Rabbit's subvocalized thoughts.

It's clear from Wills's review that his mental wiring doesn't accommodate Updike's alternating current. Wills is simply unable or unwilling to read Updike's prose; to him it's "stylistic solipsism" and "Keatsian images." *Real* ath-a-letes, Wills would have us believe, love the game and don't go soft, and real men don't see the world as something continuously fresh and beautiful. However, it is at the very root of Rabbit's character (and Updike's inspiration) that he experiences the vicissitudes and the trivia of a representative middle-class life with the finely tuned sensual intelligence of his creator. Bawer is mistaken in supposing Rabbit is "not very acute or fluent." Rabbit simply applies his acuity and fluency to ends Bawer deems unworthy. In Bawer's estimation Rabbit is constantly guilty of thought crimes. By way of demonstrating that Rabbit is "remarkably obnoxious," Bawer offers two quotes: "It gives him pleasure, makes Rabbit feel rich, to contemplate the world's wasting, to know that the earth is mortal too" and, "The great thing about the dead, they make space." For having such thoughts Rabbit forfeits, according to Bawer, any claim to "our interest or empathy."

Such philosophical commonplaces in the context of a poem would raise no eyebrows. Why it is particularly reprehensible for Rabbit to have such thoughts is because he has established himself as a representative figure. It won't do for All-America to be irreverent about Death. Rabbit's progressive disillusionment in the course of the tetralogy, his careless amorality and rabbity philandering, and now, in this last volume, his utterly secular and *untroubled* approach to death– these are what have given such offense to Rabbit/Updike's critics, and such delight to his admirers.

Rabbit is not intended as a "role model." In many ways Nemesis punishes him for his sins quite severely in *Rabbit at Rest*. His son avenges himself for decades of emotional neglect by bankrupting the family's auto business to pay for his cocaine habit. Rabbit's much-put-upon wife cooperates gleefully in accelerating the family's downward mobility. And Rabbit's lechery finally gets him into a real pickle. The beauty of the story– its central delicious irony– is that despite all Nemesis can do, Rabbit somehow escapes without hurt, and his dying words to his distraught son are, "Well, Nelson, all I can tell you is, it isn't so bad."

Surely one of the reasons I've enjoyed these books so much is that I see myself and "my people" mirrored in them as in no other work of American fiction I've read. Most literary accounts of middle-class life, from Flaubert to Sinclair Lewis, have been satirical and dismissive, while popular fiction sentimentalizes and sanitizes Middle America out of recognition. Updike's Rabbit and the landscape he inhabits more closely resemble the world I've witnessed during the time span of the four novels– 1959 through 1989– than any other work of American literature I know. And it does what art can in the way of redeeming the world it represents by valorizing its commonplaces. For me that makes the Rabbit tetralogy the best large-scale literary work by an American in this century (including the many-volumed magnum opuses of Dos Passos, Dreiser and Faulkner), and Updike the best American writer. Someone has finally written, albeit inadvertently and in the form of a tetralogy, the Great American Novel.

I'm a little surprised to find myself so far out on a critical limb, since I don't have a similar high regard for the rest of Updike's *oeuvre*. He is often prolix, especially on the subjects of religion and sex. When his fiction mirrors his own circumstances too closely, it can be plain boring. But in the Rabbit books his gifts found their perfect focus in a character who is the mirror of our age. Here he is, on page 10 of *Rabbit, Run*, watching Jimmy the Mouseketeer giving his viewers a lesson in class consciousness as he explains what the Greeks meant when they said "Know Thyself," concluding his lesson by pinching his mouth together and winking:

> That was good. Rabbit tries that, pinching the mouth together and then the wink, getting the audience out front with you against some enemy behind, Walt Disney or the MagiPeel Peeler Company, admitting it's all a fraud but, what the hell, making it likable. We're all in it together. Fraud makes the world go round. The base of our economy.

This is exactly the Rabbit who will later defend Reagan by likening him to anaesthesia. If Wills is right in thinking this is Updike the aesthete speaking through Harry the slob, the implication would seem to be that the *real* Harry Angstroms of the world take Reagan, and Jimmy the Mouseketeer, at face value; that when they vote for Reagan or Bush they are being the guileless dupes of the media and credulous believers in ads that insult a moron's intelligence. That's a dismal thing to suppose. I'd rather believe in Updike's America, where Harry Angstrom knows Reagan is a fraud, and is a fraud himself, and votes for him in a spirit of friendly collusion. At least in Updike's world it's possible to have something to talk about with your neighbors, a common ground, a shared reality.

Fraud is the governing principle of Rabbit's and Reagan's America. *Rabbit at Rest* opens in the fool's paradise of a Florida retirement colony, where the retirees while away their declining days in a parody of childhood, playing at sports and puttering at handicrafts. Rabbit golfs enough now to satisfy even the stringent athletic requirements of Garry Wills, and off the course his conversation rarely strays from those two mainstays of manly discourse, sports and cars, except with those he knows well enough to discuss what really concerns him, which is now, and always has been, sex.

But in every one of these categories, Rabbit's life (and so America's) is a hollow shell that, like his heart, is "full of crud." His first heart attack is brought on when, having rented a sailboat he can't operate, he has an accident that almost kills his granddaughter. Aerobically, his golf game is a sham, since he rides a cart about the course instead of walking it. At the end of the book he ruptures his heart after taking on a black teenager one-on-one at basketball. So much for the world of sports.

The third volume of the series, *Rabbit is* (sic) *Rich*, already got much mileage out of the irony that the model American earns his living from a Toyota dealership. In *Rabbit at Rest* Nelson has taken control of the dealership, and with the collusion of a gay accountant dying of AIDS he creates a miniature version of the S&L crisis. The scene in which a representative from Toyota headquarters appears to announce that the franchise is being withdrawn is cruel and tasteless and a precise scale model of Japanese-American relations in A. D. 1989:

> "Arways," [Mr. Shimada] says, "we in Japan admire America. As boy during Occupation, rooked way up to big GI soldiers, their happy, easy-go ways. Enemy soldiers, but not bad men . . . .Japanese very humble at first in regard to America. You know Toyota story. At first, very modest, then bigger, we produce a better product for the rittle man's money, yes? You ask for it, we got it, yes?"

So much for the great American product, which has figured at the center of he Rabbit tetralogy from the now classic set-piece in *Rabbit, Run,* when Rabbit, spooked by a sudden unaccustomed attack of self-awareness, flees Mt. Judge and his marriage and drives off for nowhere until he stops short, caught in the highway system, as in a net: "The names melt away and he sees the map whole, a net, all those red and blue lines and stars, a net he is somewhere caught in." In *Rabbit at Rest* there is a matching set-piece as Rabbit again finds himself on the road, taking the sum of America from its roadside garbage and radio broadcasts. But this time, "The dashboard lights of the Celica glow beneath his line of vision like the lights of a city about to be bombed." This time,

> Rabbit fumbles with the scan button but can't find another oldies station, just talk shows, drunks calling in, the host sounding punchy himself, his mouth running on automatic pilot, abortion, nuclear waste, unemployment among young black males, CIA complicity in the AIDS epidemic, Boesky, Milken, Bush and North, Noriega, you can't tell me that– Rabbit switches the radio off, hating the sound of the human voice. Vermin. We are noisy vermin, crowding even the air. Better the murmur of the tires, the green road signs looming in the lights and parabolically enlarging and then whisked out of sight like magicians' handkerchiefs.

So in Updike's last analysis, the automobile is revealed as a kind of incarnate death wish– and that may be, as well, its place in history, once the greenhouse effect kicks in. This sense of the nation and the planet spinning out of control or hurtling to ruin is omnipresent in *Rabbit at Rest*, and what most distresses Updike's critics is that, to quote the line that Bawer particularly comminates, "It gives him pleasure. . . to contemplate the world's wasting." But if Updike is to be reprehended for his tragic vision, what of Shakespeare or Sophocles?

As for sex, that has always been Rabbit's strong suit, the source of his most blissful insights and his major difficulties. Always until now. Rabbit continues to be sexually active but no longer at fever pitch. There is a valedictory air to his couplings. And that may be what most aggrieves his critics– that he's old and fat and tired out and finally dead without any angel chorus of redemption, with scarcely a tip of the hat to the decorous Protestant God who loomed so large in the first volume. In this regard, Updike's writerly genius has triumphed over his penchant for theologizing. Indeed, in the way of other archetypal literary figures, Rabbit seems to have an ampler spirit than his creator. It may be that in the mirrored relation between Rabbit and Updike, it is Updike who derives from Rabbit, not vice versa; that in the process of inventing Rabbit he discovered his own larger nature. One of the most painful sadnesses at the end of *Rabbit at Rest* is the sense that Updike is saying goodbye to us, much as Shakespeare says goodbye in *The Tempest*. Surely nothing he writes in the future can hope to exceed or match the greatness of the Rabbit tetralogy. It's all over now. Rabbit is dead.

Now, it's America's turn.

*Thomas M. Disch, "Rabbit's Run." *Nation* 251 (3 Dec. 1990): 688, 690, 692, 694.

"The Trouble with Harry"

Hermione Lee*

When *Rabbit at Rest* was recently published in Britain, John Updike made an appearance on television. Smiling urbanely in a solid tweed jacket, and looking like a priest disguised as a banker, he seemed to identify uncomplicatedly with Harry "Rabbit" Angstrom as a "good person"– "good enough for me to like him." In *Rabbit, Run*, we were told, he acted out Updike's unfulfilled desire to have been a six-foot-three basketball hero. In *Rabbit Redux*, he reflected Updike's own "conflicted" conservatism. In *Rabbit is Rich*, his own happiness. In *Rabbit at Rest*, his mixed feelings of being worn-out and ill-at-ease and yet still in love with his country.

An epitaph for Rabbit? "Here lies an American man." This neat formulation went unchallenged by his interviewer, but probably Updike's statements as a smiling public man should be distrusted. For what goes on in the Rabbit books is much stranger than he makes out. Rabbit is certainly solid and "real," a very thick fictional entity. Part of the joke of the name (more easily recognized, I suppose, in 1960, when people still read Sinclair Lewis) is its echo of Babbitt, whose idea of the ideal citizen ("At night he lights up a good cigar, and climbs into the little old bus, and maybe cusses the carburetor, and shoots out home") is one of the epigrams for *Rabbit Is Rich*, the smuggest book of the four. When Rabbit supports Nixon and Vietnam in *Rabbit Redux*, or hangs around the wife-swapping clubhouse types in *Rabbit is Rich*, he seems a stable enough piece of the American booboisie, a spokesman (though in a language he would never use himself) for the American dream: "America is beyond power, it acts as in a dream, as a face of God. Wherever America is, there is freedom, and wherever America is not, madness rules with chains, darkness strangles millions. Beneath her patient bombers, paradise is possible."

But Rabbit as ideal citizen has always been a problem. His years of glory as a 1940s high school basketball champion in Mt. Judge, a suburb of Brewer, Pennsylvania, are well past by the time the first book begins, when he is 26. Right from the start, then, he is looking back on lost virtue. What takes place inside his continuing present is mostly dismal, squalid, or banal. In *Rabbit , Run*, trapped by parents, parents-in-law, local minister, and his miserable small family, Rabbit runs out on his alcoholic wife, Janice, who accidentally drowns their baby while their small son Nelson looks on. Then Rabbit leaves his pregnant mistress Ruth (a lapsed hooker) and returns to Janice. Ten years on in *Rabbit Redux*, the book of the `60s, Janice goes off to have an affair, and Rabbit takes Jill and Skeeter, a rich lost hippy girl and her black revolutionary friend, into his house. Teenaged Nelson observes their sexual and political skirmishing. One night (while Rabbit is next door making love to the mother of Nelson's best friend) the house is burned down by racist neighbors, and Jill is killed. In the `70s Rabbit gets "rich" in his wife and mother-in-law's Toyota business. He buys gold, and he and Janice make love covered in Krugerrands, but out there in Carter's America the gasoline is running out and the hostage crisis is running on.

Now, in *Rabbit at Rest*, the greedy Rabbit of the Reagan years has become hugely overweight. On a quarrelsome family holiday in Florida, where he and Janice now have a condominium, he takes his granddaughter out sailing and has a heart attack and an operation– not a bypass, which terrifies him, but an angioplasty, to unclog his arteries from all "the old grease I've been eating." Meanwhile the wretched Nelson is stealing from the Toyota franchise to feed his cocaine habit and is beating up his wife, and Janice is becoming increasingly independent. (Rabbit "preferred her incompetent.") Nelson's secrets come out and she gets him to a rehabilitation center, from which he emerges talking in an "aggravating tranquilized nothing-can-touch-me tone." But Rabbit alone refuses to be cured of junk food and irresponsible desires, and out of the hospital he finds himself unexpectedly making love to his daughter-in-law. When she tells on him, he runs away to Florida, where, after a last pathetic attempt at a basketball game with a group of black kids, Rabbit has another, probably terminal, heart attack.

Rabbit reaches the climax of his career as "an American man" in *Rabbit at Rest* by playing Uncle Sam in his hometown July Fourth parade, his heart Babbittishly thumping at the feeling that "this is the happiest fucking country the world has ever seen." Are we supposed to take this seriously? The episode has an uneasy tone, partly ironic (his goatee is coming unstuck with sweat, he is having to stay back from the lead car in the parade "so Uncle Sam doesn't look too associated with the police"), but also embarrassingly mawkish, as Rabbit's eyes burn at the strains of "God Bless America." Even here, Rabbit's Babbittry is not stable or comfortable: like the disastrous family barbecue he decides to have in Florida, "it sounds ideally American but had its shaky underside."

When Rabbit starts out, in *Rabbit, Run*, making the journey south that the older Rabbit finally completes, he stops at a wayside café and looks around at the other customers. They all seem to him to "amplify his strangeness." "He had thought, he had read, that from shore to shore all America was the same. He wonders, is it just these people I'm outside, or is it all America?" There are times when Updike wants to put him inside, to make the overweight ex–sports-champ car salesman a voice for the American dream, a paradigm for an American era. In *Rabbit at Rest* he seems to be doing this more, but it's equivocal.

The analogies between a Rabbit reduced by illness, who has lost domestic authority and is being pushed out of the Toyota business, and America under Bush ("we're kind of on the sidelines. . . doing nothing works for Bush, why not for him") are explicit enough to be acknowledged by the other characters, and by Rabbit himself. There's no doubt that Rabbit's compulsive junk snacking, Nelson's addiction, the ruin of the business, even granddaughter Judy's compulsive flicking between TV channels ("an impatient rage. . . a gluttony for images") are meant as figures for American waste and greed: "Everything falling apart, airplanes, bridges, eight years under Reagan of nobody minding the store, making money out of nothing, running up debt, trusting in God."

This would just be dull, post-Reagan disapproval (sometimes it *is* a bit dull) if Rabbit weren't so oddly ambivalent. He is the emblem of the obnoxious age, but he is also outside it, minding about it, alienated by it. A lonely Rabbit. Nelson and Janice are more at home in America than Rabbit, and he distrusts the language they use. "Faux," he notices, seeing tourist signs on Route 27 for museums and antiques ("Old, old, they sell things as antiques now that aren't even as old as he is, another racket") is itself a false word: "*False* is what they mean." Rabbit spends a lot of time skeptically listening to (brilliantly travestied) "faux" languages, from Nelson's rehabilitated sermons on low self-esteem and Janice's women's group pieties, vindictively ridiculed ("all those patriarchal religions tried to make us feel guilty about menstruating"), to the health-speak of heart surgeons ("For my money, not to keep beating about the bush, the artery bypass is the sucker that does the job") and waitresses ("it's wonderful if your going macrobiotic seriously and don't mind that slightly bitter taste, you know, that seaweed tends to have"). These languages are all about getting yourself cleaned up and becoming a better product. Unlike everyone else in the novel, the salesman Rabbit is losing faith in sales talk.

And in other American myths, too. Harry and Janice take their bored grand-children on a tour of the Edison house in Florida (one of the novel's dazzling set pieces), but Harry doesn't buy the guide's sickly spiel about Edison as "the amazing great American." "It was all there in the technology, waiting to be picked up," says Harry. "All this talk about his love for mankind, I had to laugh!" Edison was just another greedy American consumer. Money is all anything is about. When they close Kroll's, the big downtown Brewer department store, "just because shoppers had stopped coming in," Rabbit understands that

> the world was not solid and benign, it was a shabby set of temporary
> arrangements rigged up for the time being, all for the sake of the money.
> You just passed through, and they milked you for what you were worth.
> . . . If Kroll's could go, the courthouse could go, the banks could go.
> When the money stopped, they could close down God Himself.

God Himself another American artifact, and no one to trust, after all.

And so Updike has it both ways. Harry is Uncle Sam, but he's also Ishmael. He is all too American and he is alienatedly un-American. He fits in with that long line of Hs, from Huck to Holden to Humbert to Herzog, who carry the freight of American history but are outside of it, looking on. But there is a difference. Harry lacks charisma.

Who likes Rabbit, apart from his author? Sexist, dumb, lazy, illiterate (he spends the whole novel not finishing a book on American history), a terrible father (for Nelson he's "a big dead man on his chest"), an inadequate husband, an unreliable lover, a tiresome lecher, a failing businessman, a cowardly patient, a typically "territorial" male: What kind of moral vantage point is this? Here is Rabbit, for instance, shaking hands with a dying homosexual:

> Squinting, Harry takes the offered hand in a brief shake and tries not to think of those little HIVs, intricate as tiny spaceships, slithering off onto his palm and up his wrist and arm into the sweat pores of his armpit and burrowing into his bloodstream there. He wipes his palm on the side of his jacket and hopes it looks like he's patting his pocket.

This awful joke brilliantly caricatures the lowest common denominator of reactions to AIDS, implicating readers who pride themselves on being too liberal and informed to think like this. There is even a kind of charm to the episode, in Harry's anxiety not to offend, and in the gap between what his mind and his hand are doing. The charm of Rabbit, such as it is, has to do with the distance between this feelings and his behavior, or with his own surprise at what he seems to be like:

> Though his inner sense of himself is of an innocuous passive spirit, a steady small voice, that doesn't want to do any harm, get trapped anywhere, or ever die, there is this other self seen from the outside, a six-foot-three ex-athlete weighing at least two-thirty. . .a shameless consumer off gasoline, electricity, newspapers, hydrocarbons, carbohydrates. A boss, in a shiny suit.

What redeems Rabbit is that, inside his brutish exterior, he is tender, feminine, and empathetic, like Leopold Bloom, the more intelligent and complex character who inspired him. Lying in the hospital, he "thinks fondly of those dead bricklayers who bothered to vary their rows at the top of the three buildings across the street. . . these men of another century up on their scaffold." Sometimes, eating meat, he can even imagine how it felt to be that animal before it was killed, can apprehend "the stupid monotony of a cow's life" in the taste of beef. He is curious, inquiring, not bigoted– or at least his bigotry is benign, as in his Protestant envy of the chosen people: "Harry has this gentile prejudice that Jews do everything a little better than other people, something about all those generations crouched over the Talmud and watch-repair tables, they aren't as distracted as other persuasions, they don't expect to have as much fun." It must be a great religion, he thinks, "one you get past the circumcision."

This is affable and easy-going compared with that other long-running fictional American, Nathan Zuckerman, who is unable to make light of prejudice in Rabbit's way. They are opposites, of course: famous author vs. obscure salesman, relentlessly eloquent taboo-breaker vs. muddled consumer, thin Jew vs. fat Protestant. The nearest thing to a Roth character in the Rabbit books is Skeeter, who speaks with all the rage and the obsessive energy of a black Portnoy. Yet both Angstrom and Zuckerman are heart cases. In *Rabbit, Run* Harry's unforgiving mother has been taught at church that "men are all heart and women are all body," and Harry's heart, where "guilt and responsibility slide together like two substantial shadows," beats loudly through the book. Now it is clogged, vulnerable, a second self exposed. In *The Counterlife*, Nathan's (and/or his brother Henry's) hearts are their manhood; only a heart operation will renew their potency. Maybe this coincidental anxiety about heart disease is just an inevitable phase for middle-aged male American writers. But both, in their dramatically different fictional ways, are speaking about the difficulties of life as an American man. To "have a heart" is to be unmanly; and both feel acutely the dangers of being unmanned, whether by surgery, loss of libido, feminism, or oblivion.

Zuckerman, though, like Herzog or Humboldt, speaks his author's language, whereas Rabbit doesn't sound like Updike. This makes life easier for Updike, since people don't go around accusing him of losing his Toyota franchise or making love to his daughter-in-law. But it also adds to our sense of Rabbit's unmanly helplessness– he seems to be caught inside a language that is strange to him, but by which he is defined. It is a virtuoso operation, even to those readers who feel, inappropriately I think, that Rabbit is being socially condescended to by his author. But what is it for?

It's quite clear that Updike can write in any version of American he chooses. Why has he returned so often, in between novels of immense erudition and sophistication like *Roger's Version*, to this elaborate, even perverse match of dumb subject and lyrical, fastidious text? The voice of the Rabbit books, so unlike Rabbit's, is wise, mournful, elegiac, telling us wry truths: "Life is noise," or "Within a hospital you feel there is no other world," or "We grow more ins and outs with age." Rabbit as Everyman? That's easy enough. But the voice does something stranger still. Everything it looks at– and how much it looks at!– changes its shape as it gets put on the page. This is the most metaphorical prose writing in American fiction, except for Melville's.

And like Melville's, Updike's metaphors are born of that old American transcendentalist desire that the things of this world should stand for something, and not be mere junk. "And some certain significance lurks in all things," Melville's Ishmael hopes, "else all things are little worth, and the round world itself but an empty cipher." In the debate over belief in *Roger's Version*, the god-fearing computer scientist complains about the arguments of a skeptical Jewish bacteriologist: "This is all metaphor." "'What isn't?' Kriegman says. `Like Plato says, shadows at the back of the cave.'"

Rabbit's Platonism makes us see everything as meaningful, but also as shadowy and strange. His heart, of course, has the star role as shape-shifter: it can be a fist, an amphitheater, a drum, a galley slave, a ballplayer waiting for the whistle. But the solid world outside is also undone by images of floating and drowning, so that Rabbit's tumble into the Gulf of Mexico, an incident itself rich with metaphor ("Air, light, water, silence all clash inside his head in a thunderous demonstration of mercilessness"), spills out into the rest of the book as a figure for his mortality: "His heart floats wounded in the sea of ebbing time."

No object, no creature, is too ordinary or too technical to be subjected to metaphor. Things used to being treated figuratively– birds, trees– get a new treatment, always cunningly connected to what Rabbit might observe: birds call "like the fluttering tinsel above a used car lot," a pink dogwood blooms "like those old photos of atomic bomb-test clouds in the days when we were still scared of the Russian." Even Harry's uncircumcised hard-on makes an American poem: "You can feel the foreskin sweetly tug back, like freezing cream lifting the paper cap on the old-time milk bottles."

Updike is rightly admired for the dazzling thinginess of the Rabbit books.

British readers of *Rabbit at Rest* especially love getting so much American stuff, and praise Updike most for "his meticulous taxonomy" of "the material nature of the world" and for his "everywhere saluting and memorializing American super-abundance." Where Updike is dispraised by British critics, it's for doing too much American materialism, "pigging out" on it, just like Rabbit. But such a criticism misses the point. For Updike, as for Rabbit, there is no such thing as too much of what is called (in *Roger's Version*) "the irrepressible combinations of the real." Rabbit's last word, "Enough," is carefully preceded by "Maybe."

But whether it is too much or enough, Updike's America is surely there: Brewer and its suburb, Mt. Judge, are accepted as Pennsylvanian places historically surveyed from the 1940s to the 1990s. Neither reader nor author feels any embarrassment about identifying Brewer as Reading, Berks County, Pennsylvania. Like William Carlos Williams's Paterson, Rabbit's Brewer is a real, recognizable place– and it keeps posing the question of whether there are no ideas but in things.

Still, how peculiar these metaphor-laden, metamorphosing, cluttered landscapes are! Nobody can "do" the strangeness of American places better, not David Lynch or Sam Shepard or Nathanael West or Don DeLillo. Look at the lovingly horrified attention he gives to what for anyone else would be a non-space, the corridor outside the Angstroms' door in "Valhalla Village," 59600 Pindo Palm Boulevard:

> The corridor is floored in peach-colored carpet and smells of air freshener, to mask the mildew that comes into eery closed space in Florida. A crew comes through three times a week, vacuuming and the rug gets lathered and the walls worked once a month, and there are plastic bouquets in little things like basketball hoops next to every numbered door and a mirror across from the elevator plus a big runny-colored green and purple vase on a table shaped like a marble half-moon, but it is still not a space in which you want to linger.

Rabbit's final run through Southern poverty and north Florida theme parks to this out-of-season condo is a masterpiece of verisimilitude; but this is verisimilitude hovering on the borders of the surreal. When Rabbit turns the key into the empty apartment, "There are no cobwebs to brush against his face, no big brown hairy spiders scuttling away on the carpet." But even without tipping it over into American Gothic, this place, with its shell collection and its formica and its fake-bamboo desk and its dead TV screen, is scary enough: "a tight structure hammered together to hold a brimming amount of fear."

Florida is made for surreality, but even in solid old Brewer, Pennsylvania, there is something untrustworthy about the landscape. Updike has Rabbit drive through his "boyhood city" over and over again, minutely noting the changes from industrial energy to postindustrial decay and renewal: mills turned into factories, railroads into garbage dumps, music stores into running-shoe emporiums, churches into community centers, hotels into Motor Inns. Defunct movie houses and retitled restaurants haunt Rabbit's wary vision of the present: "Johnny Frye's Chophouse was the original name for this restaurant on Weiser Square, which became the Cafe Barcelona in the Seventies and then the Crepe House later in the decade and now has changed hands again and calls itself Salad Binge." And in the course of this poetry of naming, appearances come adrift.

So Rabbit's memory, which cuts a deep, narrow slice into the American past, fuses with the narrative's metaphors to make an elegy for our world. Even the tastelessly caricatured Japanese Toyota representative, who has come to pass stern judgment on the Angstroms American mismanagement of the franchise ("Too much disorder. Too much dogshit."), ends up sounding like Tasso, in a transformation only Updike could bring about: "'Things change,' says Mr. Shimerda (sic): 'Is world's sad secret.'" *Il mondo invecchia, E invecchiando intristisce.*

If everything is flux, what becomes of our selves? Rabbit's sensuality, materialism, greed, and fear-- his ordinariness-- have been necessary to Updike because they embody so powerfully his discussion of the soul's relation to the body. Because Rabbit is so fleshy and gross, so tender and frightened, he brings home the human condition. In *Roger's Version*, whose debate on science and belief could be read as a chilling scholastic commentary on the Gospels according to Rabbit, Roger considers the heresy of Tertullian, who believes "that the flesh cannot be dispensed with by the soul," and will be resurrected. An Angstromian version of his proposition would read: "Dear Flesh: Do come to the party. Signed, your pal, the Soul." Roger can see the attraction:

> In our bodily afterlife, are we to know again ulcers and wounds and fevers and gout and the wish for death?. . .And yet, my goodness, pile on the cavils as you will, old hypothetical heretic or pagan, we do want to live forever, much as we are, perhaps with some of the plumbing removed, but not even that would be strictly necessary, if the alternative is being nothing, being nonexistent specks of yearning in the bottomless belly of *nihil.*

Under surgery, Rabbit is queasily aware of the peculiar relationship between the self, the soul, "the me that talks inside him all the time," and "this pond of bodily fluids and their slippery conduits." Where does the "me" that talks go, if it is separated from its home of flesh? Rabbit has a terrible fear of falling into the void. The Lockerbie disaster preoccupies his imagination, very much as space travel did in *Rabbit Redux.* The dread of the unsleeping universe is picked up from that novel; in *Rabbit Redux* he thinks: "The universe is unsleeping, neither ants nor stars sleep, to die will be to be forever wide awake." Here, again: "Stars do not sleep, but above the housetops and tree crowns shine in a cold arching dusty sprinkle. Why do we sleep? What do we rejoin?"

Rabbit resents the little space he has to occupy, penned round within the limits of his life. But he hunkers down into it too, like a creature in his burrow. Outside is what met the passengers on the plane over Lockerbie. "It is truly there under him, vast as a planet at night, gigantic and totally his. His death. The burning intensifies in his sore throat and he feels all but suffocated by terror." His fear is our fear; Updike makes us know it.

*Hermione Lee, "The Trouble with Harry." New Republic 203 (24 Dec. 1990): 34-37.

"Rabbit Rerun: Updike's Replay of Popular Culture in *Rabbit at Rest*"

Stacey Olster*

Fifty-five years old, toting two-hundred-thirty pounds, and wallowing in semiretirement, Harry Angstrom has decided to take up books in *Rabbit at Rest*, so fulfilling an intention that a wall-to-wall carpeted den has inspired at the end of *Rabbit Is Rich*. Not just any books does this newly literate Rabbit read, though– no potboilers or murder mysteries or harlequin romances for him. Harry, as befits his paterfamilias status of grandfather, has taken to reading history, "that sinister mulch of facts our little lives grow out of before joining the mulch themselves" (44), and this last volume of John Updike's tetralogy shows Harry studiously progressing through Barbara Tuchman's *The First Salute*. Given the fact that the heart attack that Harry suffers early in the novel provides him with an opportunity to see his own proverbial history pass before his eyes, this desire to review the past is all to the good. In Harry's case, however, the past that he reviews on that occasion is one that lends itself, quite literally, to re-viewing. Sunfishing with his granddaughter when the attack occurs, and aware of his need to deliver the child to safety, Harry asks the girl to sing to him in order to keep him awake at the tiller. Judy quickly exhausts her repertoire of nursery rhymes and shifts to television jingles, and when pressed for as yet unused material, she comes up with songs from *The Wizard of Oz, Snow White,* and *Pinocchio*, "children's classics Rabbit saw when they were new, the first time in those old movie theatres with Arabian decors and plush curtains that pulled back and giant mirrors in the lobby" (*Rest* 140), and she and Harry glide safely onto shore.

Judy's familiarity with the songs of those classic movies stems from the videotaped versions she has watched over and over again in her home since, as *Rabbit Is Rich* depicts, the theaters for which Harry nostalgically yearns have been turned into porno palaces well before her birth, and, as *Rabbit at Rest* adds, even their pleas for historical restoration have themselves succumbed to time, mere shingles whining ELP AVE ME. Unfortunately, the substitutes that have taken their places offer little in compensation due to artifacts they show that provide still less in the way of innovation. We're no longer off to see the Wizard, just cruising on *The Love Boat*; not wishing upon a star, merely "Stayin' Alive." "D'you ever get the feeling everything these days is sequels," Harry responds when asked if he has seen *Jaws II*. "Like people are running out of ideas" (*Rich* 377).

And not just ideas. Whether it be gas, as the opening to *Rabbit Is Rich* asserts, or gumption, as the entirety of *Rabbit Redux* illustrates, the America that Harry Angstrom is meant to mirror is in steady decline in Updike's novels.[53] And not just

---

[53] Critics who have noted this decline of America that Updike portrays in the Rabbit novels conceive of it in different terms. For representative samples, see Larry E. Taylor's discussion of antipastoral elements (74-75), Donald J. Greiner's account of 1960s social collapse (65), and Gordon E. Slethaug's overview of American history since

according to Updike. Tuchman's "View of the American Revolution" that Updike has Harry reading in *Rabbit at Rest* is a view of an American empire succeeding a British empire that succeeds a Dutch empire, all of which suggests a view of empire as an inevitably declining state of affairs. Yet Harry, for all his good intentions, cannot warm to such an intellectual view of history or to such a distant period of time: in point of fact, they put him to sleep. The only periods of America's past in which he can immerse himself thoroughly are those through which he himself has lived. Likewise, for all his ranting about global events and crises in American foreign policy, the concerns that touch him personally are contained more in the popular than the political, specifically, within those same artifacts of popular culture to which his own weakening heart has responded. To him, as Updike writes, "[t]he movie palaces of his boyhood, packed with sweet odors and dark velvet, murmurs and giggles and held hands, were history. HELP SAVE ME" (*Rest* 184). What Harry does not realize, however, is that the very history he would wish to save has contributed to his own state of exhaustion, a condition in which even his forbidden dreams are but "intensely colored overpopulated rearrangements of old situations stored in his brain cells" (*Rest* 472), summer reruns for his autumnal years, turning him not so much into a rabbit redux as a rabbit reduced.

That the America of the Rabbit novels has seen steady decline is no secret to any reader of Updike's works, although the particular empires on the rise have shifted in accordance with world politics and economics. Thus, the threat that communist aggression poses in the first two novels is replaced by the leverage that oil grants the Middle East in the third and the edge that technology affords Japan in the fourth. That Updike cites Tuchman's book in *Rabbit at Rest*, however, and that he quotes so extensively from it, is significant in that the long-range view of empire that she traces comes linked to hypotheses about the inevitability of imperial decline in general and about the potential for eventual decline in America specifically. As a passage that Updike quotes at length reveals, early dreamers were well aware of the potential problems that the American landscape presented with respect to maintaining sovereignty: *Climate in the New World, according to a best-selling French treatise translated into Dutch in 1775, made men listless and indolent; they might become happy but never stalwart. America, affirmed this scholar, 'was formed for happiness, but not for empire'* (86). Compounding this lethargy induced by climate was the enormity of a continent that required both conquest and consolidation: "*According to one school, America was too big, too divided, ever to become a single country, its communications too distended for the country ever to be united*" (*Rest* 86; Tuchman 77).

Two hundred years later, Harry Angstrom provides perfect proof of the impotence to which lethargy leads: rich from the sales of Toyotas, and "so fucking *happy*" that he offends those around him, he tries to picture what will turn him on

---

the nation's inception (249-251). The most extensive discussion of Harry Angstrom as American representative may be found in Dilvo I. Ristoff's *Updike's America*, predicated as it is on the set of Rabbit novels constituting "a story of middle America as much as it is Harry Angstrom's" (8).

and finds "he's running out of pictures" (*Rich* 124, 129). As such, he serves well as exemplar of all those "soft, lazy Americans" whom the Japanese see as "over the hill" (*Rest* 37). Yet the country of which he is a reflection, which both literally and figuratively is "running out of gas" as well, has not lost power from the kind of divisions that distended communications promote. Nelson's cross-country journey makes no impression on him at all because, as he puts it, "the country's the same now wherever you go" (*Rich* 70). And why should it seem very different to him when shopping malls screen the same movies and television sets broadcast the same shows, when, in short, the communication networks in America not only avoid divisiveness but actually promote homogeneity? Because the same networks also cater to that desire for happiness that Tuchman cites as so threatening, the unity that might increase power has here only led to its diminution. "Television's tireless energy," Harry realizes in a more astute moment, "all this effort to be happy, to be brave, to be loved, all this wasted effort," yields just "the saddest loss time brings, the lessening of excitement about anything" (*Rest* 114).

By the time he reaches middle age, Harry's observations about the changes in American life form a litany of loss. He may wonder "what's the point of being an American?" Without that cold war that "gave you a reason to get up in the morning" to count on (*Rest* 442-443, 353), but the absences that pierce his heart most deeply he expresses with respect to less monumental things. Where have all the Chiclets gone? "Have they really gone the way of penny candy, of gumdrops and sourballs, of those little red ration tokens you had to use during the war?" (*Rest* 97). "Whatever happened to the old-fashioned plain hamburger? Gone wherever the Chiclet went" (*Rest* 100). What ever [sic] happened to movie stars? "Where did they go, all the great Hollywood bitches?" (*Rich* 65-66). What even happened to nuns? "[B]lended into everybody else or else faded away" (*Rest* 272). At best, Harry can recoup his losses by salvaging the particular item lost, as evidenced, for example, by the junk food he tends to favor, peanut bars that recall the fresh, hot nuts he bought as a child from vendors in Brewer. More often, his reclamation of the past is wholly imaginative, a sentimental journey evoked by song to those times when "[l]ife was not only bigger but more solemn" (*Rest* 326), when Franklin D. Roosevelt was President, when Ronald Reagan shot Japanese fighters from airplanes, when Harry himself saved his little sister Mim from falling, from a sled, from a bike, from any heights of danger (*Redux* 176, *Rich* 211, *Run* 22, 24-25).[54] Because Harry also remains aware of the limitations that his time-bound position in history presents, that being born in 1933 has placed him at the end of an

---

[54] Harry's nostalgia, then, is not primarily for the Eisenhower era in which his own adolescent athletic career soared, as some critics claim (Robert Detweiler [37], Joseph Waldmeir [19], Donald Greiner [69]). Directed more toward childhood, as both Kathleen Verduin (255) and J. A. Ward (38) recognize, the period it enshrines is one at least a decade earlier. For Updike's memories of what it was like to listen to Jack Benny on "those little late-30's radios," see Robert Boyers (55). For Updike's account of the effects that watching old films of Bing Crosby and listening to "a honeyed bit" of Doris Day have on him now, see *Self-Consciousness* (245).

American epoch, "as the world shrank like an apple going bad and America was no longer the wisest hick town within a boat ride of Europe and Broadway forgot the tune," his nostalgia is not for a time of power and perfection, "decades when Americans moved within the American dream, laughing at it, starving on it, but living it, humming it, the national anthem everywhere" *(Redux* 114). Rather, his nostalgia is for a period of time when individual heroism was possible so as to aid an America in time of need. "You're what made America great," Charlie Stavros tells Harry. "A real gunslinger." Harry himself is more precise: he dreams of when he can have his very own silver bullet *(Redux* 49, 263).

As Ariel Dorfman has pointed out, the 1930's witnessed the emergence of many "superbeings"– the Lone Ranger, Superman, Batman, Green Arrow, Green Hornet, Flash Gordon– who acted as "representatives of the average citizen" during a period of time in which the average American citizen felt less than in complete control (115-116).[55] More than in any one popular protagonist, however, Harry locates the greatest of such beings in a purveyor of popular culture: "*That Disney, he really packed a punch*," he thinks after hearing the last of Judy's songs at sea *(Rest* 140).Harry's father goes even further. In his view, "it was Disney more than FDR kept the country from going under to the Commies in the Depression" *(Redux* 315).No wonder Harry, at age twenty-six, still approaches Disney products with reverence, watching a grown man cavort in Mouseketeer clothes on television because "he respects him," moved to silence when that man wearing mouse ears gives advice in God's name (and years before the PTL) *(Run* 12).And no wonder that a loss that pains him to grief years later is the loss of that very same spokesman. "Where are they now?" he muses, when reminded of Annette and all her cohorts. "Middle-aged parents themselves. Jimmie died years ago, he remembers reading. Died young" *(Rest* 110).

An extreme reaction, perhaps, but not an isolated one or one restricted to those of little insight or intelligence. Citing Mickey Mouse as having been his "first artistic love and inspiration" and admitting that his first ambition was to be an animator for the cartoon's creator, Updike himself recalls the ubiquity of the Disney enterprise: "in that pre-television Thirties world, the world of the movies and the world of the popular press were so entwined, and the specific world of Walt Disney so promiscuously generated animated cartoons and cartoon strips and children's books and children's toys, that it all seemed one art" *(Self-Consciousness* 242, 105; "Art of Fiction" 88). Others, too, have testified to the impact that those Disney products wielded. According to Robert Feild, "no one will ever know to what extent *The Three Little Pigs* may be held responsible for pulling us out of the Depression," but its porcine heroes taunting a Big Bad Wolf in 1933 "contributed not a little to the raising of people's spirits and to their defiance of circumstances" (60-61). *Fortune* magazine declared Mickey Mouse "an international hero" one year later, "better known than Roosevelt or Hitler, a part of the folklore of the world" (Heide and Gilman 57). Winston Churchill, legend has it, even went so far

---

[55] For an account of The Lone Ranger's origins at the hands of George Trendle, a Detroit businessman, see Andrew S. Horton (570).

as to make Franklin D. Roosevelt see *Victory Through American Power*, Disney's 1943 film on long-range bombing, as a means of convincing the United States to adopt a similar strategy (Maltin 64).

More noteworthy than Harry's fascination with the world of Disney is the faith he continues to maintain in it despite the falseness it engenders, both with respect to the mass culture it epitomizes and the nation whose impulses it symbolizes. Mim blatantly announces to her family that her Las Vegas specialty is "milk[ing] people," but her memories of having worked at Disneyland evoke just eager queries from her father about how close she came to the grand guru himself, her wobbly rendition of Lincoln's Gettysburg Address inspiring "[w]hat kind of work did Disney have you do," her saccharine tour guide's spiel of a model Mt. Vernon eliciting "you ever get to meet Disney personally" (*Redux* 313-315). Harry, to his credit, actually connects Walt Disney and the MagiPeel Peeler Company that he himself represents as linked in fraud together, the "base of our economy" (*Run* 12), but this equation of his early years lasts hardly as long as it takes for him to make it. More typical of those few connections he makes between American commerce and American popular culture is a response he exhibits toward the end of *Rabbit at Rest*. Running, yet again, from the scene of another Pennsylvania domestic disaster– this time, the discovery of his one-night fling with his daughter-in-law-- Harry gets into his car to drive to Florida, a southern flight that echoes the one that has initiated his aborted travels three decades earlier. Listening to the songs of his youth on the radio, much like he has on that first trip, which have now become (like Harry himself, one may speculate) Golden Oldies, and struck by the fact that singers like Roy Orbison are now being joined into the fold, he realizes "that the songs of his life were as moronic as the rock the brainless kids now feed on, or the Sixties and Seventies stuff that Nelson gobbled up." From his resentment comes the subsequent recognition that the motive force behind all such music is greed: "It's all *disposable*, cooked up to turn a quick profit. They lead us down the garden path, the music manufacturers, then turn around and lead the next generation down with a slightly different flavor of glop" (*Rest* 460-461). And the sense of betrayal that this recognition evokes, he associates, in turn, with the feeling that the closing of Kroll's department store, "where you could buy the best of everything," and its extended consequences have elicited during his adolescence: "If Kroll's could go, the courthouse could go, the banks could go. When the money stopped, they could close down God Himself" (*Rest* 461). But not Disney, as the next lines make clear, for the claims of fakery that Harry's proximity to Disney World causes him to cast upon those second-string amusement parks that "hold out their cups for the tourist overflow" leave the master showman inviolable (*Rest* 462).

This is not to say that Disney's media remain invincible, however, for media empires, like all those other empires mentioned in Tuchman's book, have lives of limited duration. The Lone Ranger who filled Harry's young head with dreams of silver bullets no longer rides roughshod over radio airwaves; he just gets ridiculed on Carol Burnett reruns (*Redux* 29-30). The hero with the "right stuff" today, Deion Sanders, hits home runs and scores touchdowns and calls himself Prime Time– as well he should if his impact is to reach those up-and-coming acolytes who, as Charlie Stavros puts it, "grew up on television commercials" with the box "the only mother they had" (*Rest* 470, *Rich* 250). From those first scenes of Janice staring at its flickering "blank radiance" of particles in 1959 (*Run* 213), Updike has been attuned to the power that television can wield. His later works compound power with presence. Whether as news source in *Rabbit Redux* (for the Vietnam War, SDS riots, the trial of the Chicago Eight, the moon shot) or news promoter in *Rabbit Is Rich* (Iranians outside the Teheran U. S. Embassy, that "cocky little" Pope on his way to Yankee Stadium [256], the plucky Dalai Lama doing the talk show circuit), whether as white noise (Ma Springer's Pennsylvania hometown companion) or silent chaperon (for Harry and Janice, Harry and Jill, Harry and Pru), television remains ubiquitous. Indeed, so strong has its impact now become that interference with its operations is perceived as tantamount to blasphemy– no matter what or who the source of interruption, as reactions to an NFC playoff struck by foggy weather indicate: "The announcers. . .seem indignant that God could do this, mess with CBS and blot out a TV show the sponsors are paying a million dollars a minute for and millions are watching" (*Rest* 163).[56]

Considering the fact that the black-and-white box first invented by RCA had become, by 1976, a commodity ninety-eight percent of which was imported from Japan, this growth in television's power epitomizes the shift from American to Japanese power that *Rabbit at Rest* assumes as a given. Clyde Prestowitz, Jr., in fact, has gone as far as to find no advance as significant or endowed with as many ramifications as Japan's "conquest of the television industry," its illustration of American manufacturers turning themselves into distributors of goods produced abroad making it "the quintessential example" of the process known as "hollowing" (200-201). Considering the additional fact that it was the United States that licensed the necessary technology to Japan, for monochrome sets in the 1950s and, again, for color in 1962, the nation that first wooed Asia to maintain its own preeminence in global affairs ends up hoisted by its own petard. Dwight D. Eisenhower's 1962 remark that "Only Americans can hurt America" takes on significance beyond the demagogic (*Assorted Prose* 106).

Living in "The Era of Corolla," as the Toyota ads proclaim (*Rich* 403), Harry adapts to the times: just as he and Janice have exchanged their Falcon for a Celica and a Camry Deluxe Wagon, they now have his and her SONYs, his in that same den in which he reads Tuchman's account of falling empires, hers in the kitchen to watch while cooking dinner. So, too, does Harry change with respect to the degree of appreciation he accords the medium, from early contempt in *Rabbit, Run* to an incorporation of it as a veritable lifeline, "its wires com[ing] out of the wall behind him, just like oxygen" when hospitalized in *Rabbit at Rest* (294). And functioning as a conduit of information between Harry and the outside world, television *does* serve as a data lifeline. "I don't have prejudices, just facts," he declares (à la Jack Webb) when discoursing on Italian business practices. "The Mafia is a fact. . . .It

---

[56] Disney himself realized he no longer could buck the trend to television: the man who, in 1950, turned down one million dollars to televise his cartoon shorts out of a belief in their "timeless" theatrical quality decided, four years later, to produce a *Disneyland* series of his own (Maltin 20).

was all on *60 Minutes* (*Rest* 259).He also knows that "[s]lave ships, cabins, sold down the river, Ku Klux Klan, James Earl Ray" comprise the principal facts of black American history: "Channel 44 keeps having these documentaries all about it" (*Redux* 116). What he does not know, however, is the degree to which his source has skewed his sight.[57]"More and more in middle age the world comes upon him like images on a set with one thing wrong with it," Updike writes in *Rabbit Is Rich*, and so it does (67). Whereas at thirty-six Harry imagined just the past in television terms, picturing the paraphernalia with which Skeeter has shot up Jill with dope "from having watched television," at forty-six he perceives the present with the same predisposition, watching Nelson crash cars in the back of Springer Motors, "expect[ing] it to happen in slow motion, like on television," and surprised when it happens "comically fast" (*Rich* 158). So conditioned has he become by fifty-five that he envisions events that have not yet occurred– and that do not, in fact, *ever* occur– with respect to the formulae the medium dispenses: waiting for the plane bearing Nelson and his family to land at Florida's Southwest Regional Airport, Harry "imagines the plane exploding as it touches down, ignited by one of its glints, in a ball of red flame shadowed in black like you see on TV all the time" (*Rest* 10).

    To the extent that all the Angstroms rely on television as a source of information, Harry is not unique. "All I know about cocaine is what's on *Miami Vice* and the talk shows," Janice cries when confronted with the fact of her own son's addiction; if limited in this area because "they don't explain very much," she has nobody to blame but herself for preferring drama to documentary (*Rest* 148-149). Nor is Harry unique with respect to the influence the medium has had on his capacity for independent thought. The idea of dropping televisions on Southeast Asia instead of bombs may not originate with Janice in *Rabbit Redux* (Harry suspects Charlie Stavros), but it does suggest a way in which those hearts and minds desired by American strategists could be won with much less bloodshed (288-289). What distinguishes the effect that television has had on Harry is less the degree to which it has influenced his independence of thought, for Harry has never been much of an intellectual, and more the way it has diminished in scope the very nature of that thought, for this is a man who had pictured a "quilt-colored map of the U. S." emerging from the head of a sleeping God after hearing of the "American dream" for the first time (*Redux* 106).

    When assessing this capacity for the expansive, it is important to remember

---

[57] As Judie Newman astutely remarks, "the content of particular news items is less important that the fact that Harry is continually bombarded by them" (40). Whereas Detweiler and Ristoff also note the fact of television's impact on Harry, Detweiler with respect to its effect upon a "Gutenberg man" more comfortable with the linearity and sequence of print (136-137), Ristoff with respect to its being one of those "forces of scene" that guide the passive Harry into action (8, 71-72), neither one pursues his point as far as it merits. For the most sustained discussion of the impact that television has on Harry, and one whose McLuhanite analysis approaches the issue from a different perspective than my own, see Newman's excellent chapter on "The World of Work," particularly 40-70.

that Harry, and Janice as well, take their original codes for conduct from a different visual medium: film.[58] Harry after a heart attack takes his cues for cool from "Bogey at the airport in Casablanca [1942], Flynn at Little Big Horn [*They Died With Their Boots On,* 1941], George Sanders in the collapsing temple to Dagon, Victor Mature having pushed apart the pillars [*Samson and Delilah,* 1949]" *(Rest* 172). Janice acting casual in a convertible he casts as Liz Taylor in *A Place in the Sun* [1951]; Janice talking tough he treats like Ida Lupino *(Rich* 64-65). Films all made between that 1938 to 1954 period in which Updike describes himself as having gone to the movies "pretty intensely," and upholding the quality of "debonair grace" he considers "a moral ideal," they typify the kind of films he finds "now all gone to scatter and rumpus in the fight with television for the lowest common denominator" *(Hugging the Shore* 843).

As representing that "lowest common denominator" within the Angstrom household, Nelson portrays perfectly the shift in sensibilities in which a shift from movies to television has resulted. Looking at him dressed in a purple paisley robe, and reminded of what rich people wore in the movies of her youth, Janice mourns the reduced sense of aspiration that differentiates his generation from hers:

> Robes, smoking jackets, top hats and white ties, flowing white gowns
> if you were Ginger Rogers, up to your chin in ostrich feathers or was it
> white fox? Young people now don't have that to live up to, to strive
> toward, the rock stars just wear dirty blue jeans and even the baseball
> players, she has noticed looking over Harry's shoulder at the television,
> don't bother to shave, like the Arab terrorists. When she was a girl
> nobody had money but people had dreams. *(Rest* 143)

Nelson, in contrast, experiences no sense of diminution because he experiences no change. Growing up with Mighty Mouse instead of Mickey Mouse *(Run* 194), he finds "the screen of reality" too big for him as a teenager and actually "misses television's running commentary" *(Redux* 80) . Having learned about John F. Kennedy from watching *PT 109* on TV *(Redux* 78), his adult ideas of glamour derive from actors so reduced in stature by the box that they need *People* magazine scandals to make them at all interesting *(Rich* 265). Harry may accuse Nelson and those his age of having had "[e]verything handed to them on a platter" and "think[ing] life's one big TV," but if television is the medium that gives them this message, its platter of leftovers provides very little, filled as it is with nothing but "ghosts" *(Rich* 150). The shows that Nelson watches most often are reruns.

Used to the size of the silver screen instead of SONY's meager inches, Harry fights the diminished sense of expansiveness to which television contributes. Nowhere is his resistance displayed more clearly than in the media with which he measures America's pursuit of new frontiers. "Well, nobody was going to the moon much these days," Updike's narrator admits in 1979 *(Rich* 85), and, as critics have noted, given the nonevent that the televised moon shot is portrayed as having been

---

[58] See, as well Updike's repeated remarks about his original cinematic conception for *Rabbit, Run* and his deliberate choice of present tense to approximate the temporal manner in which we experience film ("Art of Fiction" 109-110; *Hugging the Shore* 850; "Why Rabbit Had to Go" 1).

ten years earlier, how high the lyrical moon was when actually conquered remains a subject for conjecture.[59] Yet Harry, who "was always worrying about how wide the world was, caring about things like how far the stars are" (*Redux* 332), still tries to see space as expansive. He may think of *Alien* and *Moonraker* when Nelson's friend Melanie describes "a world of endless possibilities" because he has just seen those films advertised in a nearby movie complex, but he does not think of *Battlestar Gallactica*, which he (sic) just seen the week before (*Rich* 90, 31, 44). He may shoot space invaders in video parlors in Florida, but he still finds the computer screen too small for him to score a single point (*Rest* 107). Yet with the continual thrust for the smaller a trend he cannot reverse, the media with which he gauges the expansive get (sic) progressively smaller in turn. He thinks of films when the trend is toward television, he thinks of television when the trend is to video, with the result a compounding of media formulae that turn his original gaze at the stars into a starcast glaze, as his overdetermined perception of the *Challenger* disaster illustrates: "And wasn't that the disgrace of the decade, sending that poor New Hampshire schoolteacher and that frizzy-haired Jewish girl, not to mention the men, one of them black and another Oriental, all like some Hollywood cross-section of America, up to be blown into bits on television a minute later?" (*Rest* 458).

As the example of the *Challenger* also indicates, the shift in prominence from one media to another has ramifications with respect to America's grandiosity itself. "Even John Wayne" has died, Harry notes at the opening of *Rabbit Is Rich* (7), although the man who, in Joan Didion's words, "determined forever the shape of certain of our dreams" (30), had already been reduced to parody from *Red River* to *True Grit* a decade before (*Redux* 127). The President with movie magic and his own "dream distance" is replaced in *Rabbit at Rest* by one whose publicists have turned him into "a beer commercial," with the prospects of one who, "like God," might "know nothing or everything" shrinking to the reality of another who "knows something, but it seems a small something" (*Rest* 61, 295). With the freedom that comes with being an American now defined as the freedom to watch whatever television shows he wants, it is no wonder that Harry's standards for excellence have shrunk to the level of quiz shows by the time he hits middle age: "That Vanna! Can she strut! Can she clap her hands when the wheel turns! Can she turn those big letters around! She makes you proud to be a two-legged mammal" (*Rest* 384, 430).[60]

---

[59] For the most complete discussions of Updike's portrayal of the televised moon shot, see Charles Berryman (121-124) and George Held (333-341).

[60] In 1968, Updike noted the difference that television had made in its audience's capacity for engagement: "Where we once used to spin yarns, now we sit in front of the T. V. and receive pictures. I'm not sure the younger generation even knows how to gossip" ("Art of Fiction" 115). In 1989, he reiterated his diagnosis with the greater force that twenty-one more years of media overload warranted: "Our brains are no longer conditioned for reverence and awe. We cannot imagine a Second Coming that would not be cut down to size by the televised evening news, or a Last Judgment not subject to pages of holier-than-Thou second guessing in *The New York Review of Books*" (*Self-Consciousness* 216).

Satisfied by so little, we do turn into a "nation of couch potatoes," as Harry realizes, lulled so easily into the complacency that precedes collapse (*Rest* 485). This, of course, has been a function that television has performed in Harry's domestic sphere of (non) influence for years, from those early days in which *Queen For A Day* made for "a kind of peace" between the errant Harry and his erred against wife (*Run* 181), to the weeks when *Laugh-In* joined a runaway rich girl, a resentful adolescent, a messiniac (sic) black radical, and a flag-waving linotyper in communal harmony (one cooking, one washing, one drying, one tidying), to the months when *Days Of Our Lives* turned Ma Springer, Janice, and pregnant Pru into a maternal triumvirate: Mom-mom, Mom, and Mom-in-the-Making. Yet short-circuiting sources of conflict also subverts genuine causes for concern. Janice worries more about Bryant and Willard getting along on the *Today* show than she does about "that evil pockmarked Noriega" who "just won't leave" Panama (*Rest* 309-310). Little Judy watches news of the Pan Am 103 explosion with impatience, "believ[ing] that headlines always happen to other people" (*Rest* 79). And Harry, horrified at first by the Lockerbie disaster and "shocked" at his ability to imagine Nelson's plane in flames with "just a cold thrill at being a witness," eventually follows suit when he hears of later airline crashes: "The plane in New York skidded off the end of the runway and two people were killed. Just two. One hundred seventy-one died in the Sahara. A caller in London gave all the credit to Allah. Harry doesn't mind that one as much as the Lockerbie Pan Am bomb. Like everything else on the news, you get bored, it gets to seem a gimmick, just like all those TV time-outs in football" (*Rest* 10, 501).

More than a conditioned response to sensory overload, this detachment that television cultivates increasingly renders Harry emotional service as the events that it neutralizes have greater personal reverberations.[61] Watching the landing on the moon on television at the same time that he tries to discuss the most recent break-up of his marriage, he acknowledges, "I know it's happened, but I don't feel anything yet" (*Redux* 93). Feeling "peripheral, removed, nostalgic, numb" at the sight of his home going up in flames, he finds the graffiti that memorializes its wreckage "add[ing] up no better than the cluster of commercials TV stations squeeze into the chinks between programs" (*Redux* 278, 342). And fleeing from his last familial fiasco, and realizing that "TV families and your own are hard to tell apart" (the laugh tracks of one and ennui of the other notwithstanding), he comes to a final conclusion about his own degree of authenticity: "His own life seems. . .to have been unreal, or not realer than the lives on TV shows" (*Rest* 468-469).

By this time of his life, this is a detachment for which Harry desperately yearns, for the show that has left the greatest impact on his consciousness has been the "Rabbit Angstrom Show," on which he has seen his heart surrounded by specks

---

[61] For examples of the diametrically opposed critical position that debate over Updike's own degree of detachment has generated, see Terrence A. Doody (204-220) and Robert Alton Regan (77-96). Whereas Doody's notion of reification ascribes to Updike the objectivity of a camera lens (209), Regan's neo-Kantian analysis applauds the subjective eye that perceives the picture (81-84).

of plaque that look like Rice Krispies (*Rest* 271, 273). Whereas reading about the detouring of his blood that the angioplasty he is to undergo will entail makes Harry think back to film, to "those horrible old Frankenstein movies with Boris Karloff" (*Rest* 269), watching what is happening to him on an actual monitor forces him to shift his thoughts to terms of television– which is all for the best. Aware as he is that his heart is to lie "dead in its soupy middle" while a machine does the living for him, and angry that such "Godless technology is fucking the pulsing wet tubes we inherited from the squid" (*Rest* 270, 274), Harry *needs* to conceive of the procedure as a television program, needs to hear his doctors talking with "those voices on television that argue about the virtues of Miller Lite," needs to wonder whether the experience will be discussed on Oprah, needs, in short, to combat "a wave of nausea" with "a test pilot's detachment" and so keep the entire experience "as remote from his body as the records of his sins that angels are keeping" (*Rest* 273-275). The proximity of death simply makes it too frightening for Harry to conceive of himself in any other way.

The reruns that his family watches, then, do not bore him with prepackaged dialogue because they provide proof of continual recycling. Anniversary newscasts of Chappaquidick and the Manson murders do not disgust him, for he sees them as "full of resurrected footage" (*Rest* 372). And Toyota ads virtually inspire him, showing "men and women leaping, average men and women, their clothes lifted in cascading slow-motion folds like angels' robes,. . .leaping and falling, grinning and then in freeze-frame hanging there, defying gravity," because their defiance of gravity contains within itself the prospects of defying those other natural laws that draw us earthbound (*Rich* 328). Whereas imagining himself a television star once confirmed his own sense of being special (*Redux* 325), Harry now takes pleasure at thoughts of being one with the ordinary. He takes hope from those programs in which "a nation of performers, of smoothly talking heads, has sprung up under the lights, everybody rehearsed for their thirty seconds of nation wide attention" because the celluloid immortality that levels all their *Unsolved Mysteries* into one collective fantasy is an illusion to which Harry himself can subscribe (*Rest* 339).

In the past, it was religion that relieved the fears from which these wanna-be stars all suffer. In Updike's view, it is still religion that caters to the need for "Being a Self Forever," as his essay bearing that title affirms, only religion "construed, of course, broadly," not just as organized faith, "but in the form of any private system. . .that submerges in a transcendent concern the grimly finite facts of our individual human case," be it "adoration of Elvis Presley or hatred of nuclear weapons," "a fetishism of politics or popular culture" (*Self-Consciousness* 226). As it turns out, the closest that Harry comes to the immortality that celebrity inscribes combines both a fetishism of politics and a fetishism of popular culture. His being cast as Uncle Sam in a Fourth of July parade has little to do with klieg lights, cables, or monitors of any sort, but it does enlist every other form of American popular culture to conflate age, class, and, most of all, time. An impersonator resurrects John Lennon, a tape recorder revives Kate Smith ("dead as she is"), and as "God Bless[es] America" before a "recycled" crowd of all the people whom Lennon imagined "living for today" and Harry had lamented as lost within his high school past, Harry, too, is rerun as Rabbit, "a legend, a walking cloud," who, as national symbol, is further "lifted up to survey all human history" (*Rest* 368-371). What Harry surveys when he removes his costume is a sight he would just as soon avoid: a "boss, in a shiny suit" personally, a "shameless consumer of gasoline, electricity, newspapers, hydrocarbons, carbohydrates" politically (*Rest* 381). It may be hard these days, even for Updike, to transform the country his character reflects into anything more than a "big Canada" that "doesn't much matter to anybody else" (*Rest* 358). But Harry's assumption that the "beyond where some celebrities like Elvis and Marilyn expand like balloons and become gods" is beyond him does not necessarily follow (*Rest* 483). He may feel relieved at America's not having to act "the big cheese" anymore and he may sign off on his own saga with a weary "Enough" (*Rest* 358, 512), but his own renunciation does not consign him to that other beyond "where most shrivel and shrink into yellowing obituaries not much bigger than Harry's will be in the Brewer *Standard"* (*Rest* 483)– unless four volumes bearing his name are equivalent to a standard obituary. It may not be Graceland, but it is still a form of grace all the same.

Works Cited

Berryman, Charles. "The Education of Harry Angstrom: Rabbit and the Moon." *Literary Review* 27 (1983): 117-126.

Boyers, Robert, et al. "An Evening with John Updike." *Salmagundi* 57 (1982):42-56.

Detweiler, Robert. *John Updike*. Boston: Twayne, 1984.

Didion, Joan. *Slouching Towards Bethlehem*. 1968. New York: Touchstone-Simon, 1979.

Doody, Terrence A. "Updike's Idea of Reification." *Contemporary Literature* 20 (1979): 204-220.

Dorfman, Ariel. *The Empire's Old Clothes: What the Lone Ranger, Barbar, and Other Innocent Heroes Do To Our Minds*. New York: Pantheon, 1983.

Feild, Robert D. *The Art of Walt Disney*. New York: Macmillan, 1942.

Greiner, Donald J. *John Updike's Novels*. Athens: Ohio UP, 1984.

Heide, Robert, and John Gilman. *Dime-Store Dream Parade: Popular Culture 1925-1955*. New York: Dutton, 1979.

Held, Charles. "Men on the Moon: American Novelists Explore Lunar Space." *Michigan Quarterly Review* 18 (1979): 318-342.

Horton, Andrew S. "Ken Kesey, John Updike and The Lone Ranger." *Journal of Popular Culture* 8 (1974): 570-578.

Macnaughton, William R., ed. *Critical Essays on John Updike*. Boston: Hall, 1982.

Maltin, Leonard. *The Disney Films*. New York: Bonanza, 1973.

Newman, Judie. *John Updike*. New York: St. Martin's, 1988.

Prestowitz, Clyde V., Jr. *Trading Places: How We Allowed Japan to Take the Lead*. New York: Basic, 1988.

Regan, Robert Alton. "Updike's Symbol of the Center." *Modern Fiction Studies* 20 (1974): 77-96.

Ristoff, Dilvo I. *Updike's America: The Presence of Contemporary American History in John Updike's Rabbit Trilogy*. New York: Lang, 1988.

Slethaug, Gordon E. "*Rabbit Redux*: 'Freedom is Made of Brambles'." Macnaughton 237-253.

Taylor, Larry E. *Pastoral and Anti-Pastoral Patterns in John Updike's Fiction*. Carbondale: Southern Illinois UP, 1971.

Tuchman, Barbara W. *The First Salute: A View of the American Revolution*. New York:

Knopf, 1988.
Updike, John. "The Art of Fiction XLIII: John Updike." With Charles Thomas Samuels. *Paris Review* 45 (1968): 85-117.
_____. *Assorted Prose*. New York: Knopf, 1965.
_____. *Hugging the Shore: Essays and Criticism*. New York: Knopf, 1983.
_____. *Rabbit at Rest*. New York: Knopf, 1990.
_____. *Rabbit Is Rich*. 1981. New York: Fawcett Crest-Ballantine, 1982.
_____. *Rabbit Redux*. 1971. New York: Fawcett Crest-Ballantine, 1972.
_____. *Rabbit, Run*. Greenwich: Fawcett, 1960.
_____. *Self-Consciousness: Memoirs*. New York: Knopf, 1989.
_____. "Why Rabbit Had to Go." *New York Times Book Review* 5 Aug. 1990: 1, 24-25.
Verduin, Kathleen. "Fatherly Presences: John Updike's Place in a Protestant Tradition." Macnaughton 254-268.
Waldmeir, Joseph. "It's the Going That's Important, Not the Getting There: Rabbit's Questing Non-Quest." *Modern Fiction Studies* 20 (1974): 13-27.
Ward, J. A. "John Updike's Fiction." *Critique* 5.1 (1962): 27-40.

*Stacy Olster, "Rabbit Rerun: Updike's Replay of Popular Culture in Rabbit at Rest." *Modern Fiction Studies* Spr. 1991: 45-59.

from *John Updike's Rabbit at Rest: Appropriating History*
Chapter Four: Debt Crisis and the Japanese Invasion

Dilvo Ristoff*

> That is what I am also trying to do: to say what is changing in the
> United States– through imagination, to tell the truth about the U.S.
> –John Updike, *Conversations*

Waking up from the Reagan anesthesia also meant waking up, among other things, to the reality of foreign debt. As Rabbit appropriates Bush's plight, America is emblematized in the Springer Motors dealership or, as Rabbit calls it, "the lot." The lot becomes a microcosm of America, plagued by debt to foreigners– completely at the mercy of foreigners– and administered by "scatterbrains" who, like Janice and Nelson, "will just drift along deeper and deeper into debt like the rest of the world" (431). Edward Vargo's finding among Updike's manuscripts at Harvard's Houghton Library of a note reading "Natl deficit = Nelson's debts" verifies that Updike intended us to see the lot as a symbol standing for America (32).

Although Nelson insists that they owe very little money and, moreover, that Springer Motors has been underfinanced for years, Rabbit cannot help expressing his fears that the country has been taken by foreigners and that Americans are losing control: "We are drowning in debt! We don't even own our own country any more" (417). Earlier in the novel, Nelson predicts that in ten years the Japanese will "have bought the whole country. Some television show I was watching, they already own all of Hawaii and half of L. A. and Nevada. They are buying up thousands of acres of desert in Nevada!" (37).[62] We should recall that the Japanese presence in the United States became highly visible to common citizens precisely during the *Rabbit Is Rich* days of the seventies when the gas-saving Toyotas looked like salvation. The threat of Japanese economic power in the eighties, however, achieves added presence through numerous dramatizations on television. These dramatizations are obviously themselves an expression of the economic phenomenon in action. It may be worth recalling that as early as 1987 America's foreign debt was eased by the borrowing of $1 trillion from the Japanese and others. The fear of the Japanese buying into America can be found in a large number of documentaries broadcast during the years 1987-1989. These documentaries stress that Japan is not only lending money to the United States but also buying into every sector of the American economy. Japan is buying government bonds, stocks, Hollywood studios,[63] ballpark franks, record companies, computer chips, financial services, real estate, high-rise buildings, and universities, from Tennessee to California to New York. Furthermore, in 1989 Mitsubishi bought a majority share in the corporation that controls the Rockefeller Center in the heart of New York City.

A similar "scare documentary" was seen by Rabbit. His fears can be explained in part by the fact that America was throughout the decade the country in the world with the highest rate of foreign investment by far (Goyal C1). Some more visible materializations of this investment were the Japanese purchase of buildings in downtown Los Angeles, their buying of traditional American corporations, their presence in Hollywood, and as the *New York Times* edition of

---

[62]Nelson probably watched ABC's *20/20* documentary called "Buying Hawaii" which was aired on July 8, 1988, although many similar documentaries were aired as early as February 1987. A more recent and shorter report was aired by ABC on October 31, 1988, about Japanese control over major American cities, specifically citing Los Angeles. During their presidential campaign, Michael Dukakis and George Bush presented opposing views of this Japanese presence; the former expressing serious concern over foreign dominance, the latter claiming that markets need to be open. The population interviewed also showed ambivalent feelings, much like Rabbit's, some claiming that their jobs depended on the Japanese, others saying that there ought to be some restrictions on foreign investment.

[63]Of the five major Hollywood studios, three were purchased by foreign money in the 1980s or early nineties: Universal Pictures, later MCA, was taken over by the Japanese company Matsushita in 1990; Twentieth Century Fox was bought in 1985 by Rupert Murdoch and became a part of his Australian-based News Corporation Ltd.; and Columbia was purchased by Sony in 1989. The other two studios were saved by national mergers and acquisitions: Warner Brothers benefitted from the merger of Time, Inc. and Warner Communications, Inc. (WCI), forming one of the largest communications companies in the world; and MGM, after selling its library to Turner Broadcasting System, merged with United Artists to form MGM/UA. In 1989 Quintex Corporation of Australia failed to obtain MGM/UA.

August 2, 1989, reported, their buying into ailing United States campuses[64] (having already bought part of a campus in Oregon and created the Salem-Teikyo University in Salem, West Virginia, among other aggressive initiatives).[65]

The lot as a microcosm of America operates in Rabbit's mind as a prefiguring of national economic disaster— a disaster caused by increasing national and international debt and by reckless spending. Springer Motors's loss of the Toyota franchise due to debt and poor administration is but an emblem or an omen of what Rabbit perceives might happen to his country.

Rabbit is definitely not alone in his concerns. From January 1987 to December 1989, over seventy documentaries were aired on American television dealing with the Japanese presence in America. The questions raised by these documentaries are frequently announced in their titles: "American Game, Japanese Rules," "Losing the Future," "Washington Debt," "Japanese Investment in the U. S.," "The Newest Japanese Export," "Semi-Conductors— Japanese Hegemony?," "Buying Hawaii," "U. S. Versus Japan on Copyright Differences," "Biotechnology— Will We Rise to the Japanese Challenge?," "America's Sellout," "Another Japanese Invasion," "Should Japan's Buying Spree Scare Us?," "Could a Bust on Wall Street Begin in Tokyo?," and "Who Owns America?" Each and every program poses enough questions to scare the most self-reliant American: How dangerous is Japanese domination of the microchip market? How will the trillion dollar loan from Japan be paid back? Is the Japanese buying spree good for America? Are the Japanese buying America's security? Will America win or lose? Will the Japanese dominate the market in high-definition television? These and other similar questions are so prevalent and so frequently asked in the national media that the historical references we find in Updike's text become in comparison little more than the tip of the enormous underlying ideological iceberg which composes the scene— a scene whose fear and xenophobia impregnate all agents, agencies, acts, and purposes.

Mr. Shimada, the Toyota representative, not only informs Rabbit of the cancellation of the franchise, but he also lectures him about the proper ways to conduct business. As we can see from the excerpt below, however, Mr. Shimada is not lecturing to Rabbit, the individual— he is lecturing to the American nation:

> In recent times big brother act rike rittle brother, always cry and comprain. Want many favors in trade, saying Japanese unfair competition. American way in old times. But in new times America make nothing, just do mergers, do acquisitions, rower taxes, raise national debt. Nothing comes out, all goes in— foreign goods, foreign capital. America take everything, give nothing. Rike big brack hole. (390)

What Mr. Shimada is saying can be read as the Japanese version, with a Japanese accent, of what concerned the Reagan and Bush administrations in relation

---

[64]It is probable that Rabbit is referring to the *Business World* documentary called "Japanese Course at Brigham Young" aired on August 21, 1988.

[65]In *New York Times*, August 2, 1989.

to foreign trade throughout the decade. Japanese trade restrictions were the main topic of many high-level meetings between officials of the two countries, with officials frequently voicing their complaints about Japanese trade practices. Considering the date Mr. Shimada makes his observation to Rabbit (i. e., in the first week of August), we could assume that he is referring to the Bush administration's manifest intention of citing Japan for unfair trade practices, expressed in late April 1989. The intention to file a complaint and to impose trade sanctions against Japan was the subject of television programs such as "Japan in Crisis" and "Japan and Unfair Trade Practices": the first aired on ABC's *Business World* on April 30, 1989; the second on *Business World* on May 7, 1989. Just as Mr. Shimada's bill to Rabbit covers a period ranging from November 1988 to May 1989, we may assume that these particular references are again only the visible part of the immense iceberg of the trade war. In fact, historical evidence confirms that one of the high points of the trade war occurred as early as March and April 1987 when America imposed trade sanctions on Japanese products containing semi-conductor chips. High tariffs were imposed on these products as an attempt to curb reported Japanese dumping practices and to protect American industry. As the trade war heated up, Japanese officials came to Washington for trade peace talks and negotiation on the marketing of microchips. Thus Mr. Shimada's reference to America as "rittle brother" who "comprains" all the time and wants special favors in trade has as its source not just one incident but the whole spirit of the American economic scene in the 1980s. It should be recalled that the trade deficit was extremely high throughout the decade, having increased from $24.2 billion in 1980 to $107.9 billion in 1984 to $152.1 billion in 1987. By 1989, the first year of the Bush administration, the trade deficit had come down to $109.6 billion. Similarly, the national debt increased steadily during the Reagan-Bush years, starting at $1 trillion in 1980, increasing to $2.8 trillion in 1989, and reaching $4 trillion in 1992. It is not surprising, therefore, that Rabbit has the feeling that America is no longer American and that the country is drowning in debt and at the mercy of foreigners.

Mr. Shimada's reference to "mergers" also deserves a few comments. It finds its clearcut rock-bottom equivalent in ABC's *Business World* documentary aired on March 15, 1987, called "Takeover Fever and Merger Mania"[66] and in the over two hundred fifty mergers and acquisitions which occurred during 1989, many of them involving foreign capital. Mr. Shimada's view that America is at a point where all goes in and nothing goes out, like a "big brack hole," speaks directly to the fears of middle America in general in those days– a fear aired on all major television networks and materialized in such programs as "Foreign Investments in the U. S.,"[67]

---

[66]Major question asked by the program: "Are mergers good for the economy?"

[67]Aired on February 1, 1987 (ABC's *Business World*).

"U. S. Debt,"[68] "U. S. Trade Deficit,"[69] and "Foreign Goods & U. S. Debt,"[70] just to name a few of the most popular. The questions asked in these broadcasts invariably suggest that the United States is being financially infiltrated by foreign countries, exporting jobs and money, and allowing itself to be dangerously flooded by foreign money and foreign goods.

Should Americans take foreign investment as a demonstration of confidence in their country? Should they be happy about it, or should they feel threatened by an imminent takeover? Rabbit has difficulty dealing with this uncertainty, especially because he seems to share Mr. Shimada's assumption that instead of being afraid of foreign competition and blaming others for their increasing economic problems, Americans should reexamine their own inadequate ways of conducting business. He has seen what Nelson's drug use, Lyle's AIDS, and poor administration overall have caused on the lot. The Angstroms' dealership, therefore, as a microcosm for the country, seems to be a perfect target for the outpouring of Mr. Shimada's petulance and impertinence.

The American trade deficit reached such critical heights during the Reagan years that in 1988 Congress enacted the Omnibus Trade and Competitiveness Act, authorizing the government to retaliate with high tariffs on Japanese imported goods if the Japanese restrictions on imported goods were not removed. Aware that economic interdependence required a solution which would benefit both countries, the American government devalued the dollar in relation to the Japanese yen to make American products more competitive, and Japan was persuaded to set voluntary quotas in its automobile and steel exports to the United States. But as Peter Levy notes, "the American appetite for Japanese goods remained very high. By 1989, Honda had become the best-selling car in America, and Japanese electronic goods, from videocassette recorders (VCRs) to stereo components, gained an even greater share of the American market" (214). Japanese-American relations improved only with the breakout of the Gulf War when Japan proved to be a financially useful ally.

Trade deficit and budget deficit also concerned the International Monetary Fund (IMF), which registered its complaint in April 1989. The American administration's projected budget deficit for that year was $162 billion, and the trade deficit was an estimated $135 billion– $35 billion less than it had been in the previous year. Both deficits were considered by the IMF to pose a danger to the growth of the world economy. By September 1989 the Bush administration could claim a small victory in its fight for trade deficit reduction. It announced that in July, because of the decline in imports, the trade deficit fell to $7.5 billion– the

---

[68]Aired on April 26, 1987 (ABC's *This Week*).

[69]Aired on September 13, 1987 (ABC's *Business World*).

[70]Aired October 4, 1987 (ABC's *This Week*).

lowest in four-and-a-half years.[71]

Mr. Shimada's speech is then constructed as a Japanese answer to well-known problems that Americans were facing at the time. Mergers and acquisitions were rampant to the extent that the terminology suffused even the movies. In *Working Girl*, for example, a marriage proposal is made by saying "Let's merge," and the acquisition of a major radio network succeeds because of the threat of a supposedly imminent Japanese takeover. Although Mr. Shimada blames poor administration for America's present predicament, he tries to find a deeper and more meaningful explanation for this dire situation. As he continues with his lecture, he identifies as its ultimate cause the imbalance between the way Americans value discipline and freedom. For him, America is failing because there is too little *giri* (order, responsibility, obligation) and too much *ninjo* (freedom, human spirit). In America these two forces are said to receive disproportional value, *giri* having lost its relative importance. That is the reason why Toyota sees as its role the creation of "irands of order in oceans of freedom" (392). While blaming the *national* attitude for the present predicament, Shimada is also blaming Nelson and Nelson's father, who spends half the year "in Frorida, enjoying sunshine and tennis, while young boy plays games with autos" (393). In other words, America's methods are failing because American citizens are placing excessive value on what has historically been one of the most precious of America's assets– individual freedom. Freedom has been pushed to such extremes, he believes, that it is leading Americans into self-indulgence, selfishness, and lack of group order. Again, Rabbit and America are regarded as one.

Rabbit's humiliating experience with Mr. Shimada and his disappointment at losing the Toyota franchise are briefly replaced by optimism when Janice suggests that they could reopen the lot as a family business, as it used to be before the Japanese and their money came in: "The idea of rebuilding the lot from scratch. . .excite[d] him" (398). In another demonstration that he sees himself as sharing the problems and concerns of the nation, Rabbit appropriates the hegemonic national attitude when considering the possibility of the lot's economic revival: "So they owe a few hundred thousand– the government owes trillions and nobody cares" (398). If the country can make it, so can Springer Motors.

What could be a solution for the lot could also be a solution for the country, and vice versa. But the idea of the whole world in debt and nobody paying– the United States, Mexico,[72] Brazil,[73]–is troubling and difficult to follow. International

---

[71]In *New York Times*, September 16, 1989.

[72]A special report on Mexico's foreign debt called "Debt Reduction for Mexico" aired on PBS's *Washington Week in Review* on July 28, 1989.

[73]In 1987 Brazil suspended all payments on its foreign debt, arousing concern whether the huge third world debt could lead the American bank system to a crisis. On March 1, 1987, the documentary "Brazilian Debt" was aired on PBS's *Adam Smith*. On September 27, 1987, the *Business World* documentary "Third-World Debt" discussed the

relations have become too complex for Rabbit, operating in mysterious ways; business has become so elaborate that he does not trust himself to analyze the books of Springer Motors, especially now that Lyle has their accounts on computer diskettes. Somehow the global economy, with its intricate national and international network of operations, currency devaluations, tariffs, taxes, loans, interest rates, and mortgages, plays tricks which are transferred right into his home.

It is necessary to recall that throughout the year Secretary Nicholas Brady and Japanese delegates had been discussing ways of reducing the foreign debt of third world countries. The over $1.3 trillion debt owed by these countries was crushing their economies and threatening international economic stability. The idea was to ease this debt by providing financial support or indirect guarantees of interest payments to banks which accepted a reduction of the principal or of the interest rates on the loans made to third world countries. Mexico, Venezuela, and Brazil were the countries which would most likely benefit from this agreement. For Rabbit this is equated to having somebody else pay your debt for you; and this was precisely the resistance the plan met, for banks thought it would encourage debtor countries to avoid engaging in strong programs of economic recovery to meet their commitments. For the banks, up to the point of interruption of debt-service payments, it was more convenient to simply continue receiving payment of interest rather than the principal. This is one of the curious ways in which the historical scene is appropriated by Nelson in the novel. When Rabbit complains that everybody owes and nobody seems to have to pay, Nelson explains that the debt of the lot with Toyota has already been settled with a loan from:

> "Brewer Trust. A second mortgage on the lot property, it's worth at least half a million. A hundred forty-five, and they consolidated it with the seventy-five for Slim's five cars, which will be coming back to us pretty much as credit on the rolling inventory we were maintaining with Mid-Atlantic Motors. As soon as they took our inventory over to Rudy's lot, don't forget, they started owing us."
>
> "And you're somehow going to pay back Brewer Trust selling water scooters?"
>
> "You don't have to pay a loan back, they don't *want* you to pay it back; they just want you to keep up the installments. Meanwhile, the value of the dollar goes down and you get to tax-deduct all the interest. We were underfinanced, in fact, before." (418)

To Rabbit's despair, Nelson, the unreliable former drug addict, seems to have it all worked out, much in accordance with what came to be called Reagan's "voodoo economics" and much in tune also with the creditors of third world debtor countries. Nelson's statement is dated August 28, 1989, a piece of information which only adds to his irresponsibility; for at this precise moment the dollar, which had been falling since 1987 and making American products more competitive in the international market, was on the rise against the West German mark and the Japanese yen–unlike it was in December 1988 when Nelson complained to his

---

meeting of international bankers in Washington, D. C. Debt repayments were at the top of their agenda.

father about how expensive the "gas misers" or the "tidy little boxes" the Japanese call cars had become: "That's what hurts. The lousy dollar against the yen" (36). We could call Nelson a clever gambler, for he does not seem to be economically illiterate, but the precise placement of his statements in time adds to the identification of his behavior as irresponsible.

How much further into debt will Nelson drive them? Rabbit's feeling is that the Nelsons of America have already placed a second mortgage on the country– a country which he realizes is no longer his, as the lot is no longer his. Foreigners are everywhere– Japanese, Koreans, Italians, Mexicans, Cubans, Africans– all of them placing demands, giving orders, and complaining.

Rabbit's fear and xenophobia find their justification in the American scene of the 1980s, or at least in one possible reading of this scene. The massive presence of foreign money in America during the decade could be considered reason enough for fanning the flames of any nationalist. As David H. Blake and Robert S. Walters tell us in 1987:

> From 1973 to 1985 foreign direct investment in the United States increased from $20.5 billion to $183 billion. There is already more direct foreign investment in the United States than in any other country. The leading sources of foreign direct investment in the United States, by country of origin, are the United Kingdom, the Netherlands, Japan, Canada, Germany and Switzerland, respectively, and they account for almost 75 percent of the total. (92)

Rabbit, a common man, may not be aware of the statistics and of the specifics the data seem to reveal. Blake and Walters's observations may be startling to most Americans, even to American intellectuals. That the major portion of foreign money invested in the United States is not Japanese does not seem to match the national perception. Nor does it match Rabbit's perception, for whom, since the late seventies, it has become difficult to conceive of the lot or of America without the Japanese. What Rabbit seems to notice more, despite his professional respect for them, is the foreignness of the Japanese, their otherness. He views the Japanese much the same way as he views blacks and Mexicans, with the difference that they have money. His perception then comes less from the statistical evidence of foreign presence in the country than it does from the way this presence interferes with the life of white America and threatens to jeopardize its centrality. In this respect, considering Rabbit's white, Anglo-Saxon, Protestant cultural tradition, it is easy to understand why he would perceive non-central Europeans as posing a greater threat.

Even in hospitals Rabbit cannot avoid foreigners. At the hospital in Florida Rabbit's nationalism and xenophobia manifest themselves again as he gets irritated with Doctor Olman– an Australian who, according to him, keeps attacking America: "If he doesn't like the food here, why doesn't he go back where he came from and eat kangaroos" (172). The irony of it all is that a foreigner is taking care of his very heart, his "typical American heart" (166).

Rabbit's enthusiasm to restart the business according to old American ways, national and independent, meets with reservations from Janice. As she sees it, they should not rush into things, for "everything is in flux" (398). To which Rabbit replies as usual: "I'm too old for flux" (398). The ongoing struggle finds its expression in the pain of readaptation and throughout the Rabbit novels becomes an endless fountain of tension between the protagonist and the world in which he lives.

Concerns like these which point to the death of an era and the birth of another find Rabbit unprepared. His mind, like the minds of middle Americans, is boggled by what is happening to the world and especially to his country. He finds it hard to understand the beginning of the end of communism; the end of the Cold War; the invasion of America by so many different races, colors, cultures, languages, and nationalities; the extensive inter-nationalization of the American economy, with all these "scare documentar[ies] about foreigners buying up American businesses" (114); and the transformation of America into the leading debtor country. Somehow the death of the era is also the ominous foreshadowing of his own death, on its way to get him. But Rabbit is still moving, walking to "forbidden"places in the country, asserting his rights and insisting that he is not quite dead yet.

   *Ristoff, Dilvo. *John Updike's Rabbit at Rest: Appropriating History.* New York Lang, 1998, pages 62-73.

"*Rabbit at Rest*: The Return of the Work Ethic"

Judie Newman*

Writing in 1988, I argued that the Rabbit trilogy cohered around one major organizing theme, that of the relation between individual and society, particularly expressed as the instinctual, sensual and libidinal dimensions of the human being in conflict with social constraints that are politically and economically determined. Updike quite clearly--though not naively-- draws upon Freud's analysis of society as founded upon repression. To recap: for Freud, the methodical sacrifice of libido to work and reproduction *is* culture. Because the lasting interpersonal relations on which civilization depends presuppose that the sex instincts are inhibited, there is therefore a fundamental opposition between sex and social utility, and a huge price in individual happiness that must be paid for the benefits of civilized life. Most work requires that energy be directed away from direct sexual satisfaction, to produce the gains of technological civilization, a process arguably exacerbated in modern society in which desire is overcontrolled ("surplus repression") in order to maintain men as cogs in the industrial machine. In the Rabbit trilogy, Updike introduced this central conflict in explicitly Freudian terms in *Rabbit* (sic) *Run*, proceeding to examine in *Rabbit Redux* the potential MacLuhanite sensual liberation of the individual, freed from toil by the new technology, and in *Rabbit Is Rich* the ways in which society may deform and exploit the instincts by the creation of mass fantasy in order to repress once more.

   The reader who turns to *Rabbit at Rest* will find few immediate surprises. Work, technology, and instinctual indulgence remain the central organizing concerns of what is now a tetralogy. Once again Updike stages the Freudian psychomachia of society as opposed to instinct, dramatizing both the gratifications and the failings of the American Dream. But with one major difference. In *Rabbit at Rest*, in contrast to the libidinal economy of scarcity in the preceding volume, desire is overindulged, actively encouraged by a society intent on keeping its members unquestioningly inside the American myth. In the America of *Rabbit at Rest*, notions of play, games, leisure, and holiday occupy center stage, together with their commodification in the leisure industries, whether official or unofficial. The novel opens in the emblematic locale of Florida, as Nelson arrives for a short vacation with his father, now in enforced retirement and entirely at leisure. The legitimate attractions of Deleon– golf, theme parks, cinemas, and bingo– are shadowed by commodities equally productive of engineered happiness. While Harry has been over-indulging in food and play, Nelson has been acting on the same imperatives. Ironically, in the subsequent action, it is Nelson's permanent holiday of crack cocaine addiction that triggers Harry's return to work to safeguard the family business (an image that unites the forces of work and reproduction) and the forcible reassertion of the work ethic in the shape of Mr. Shimada, who terminates the Springer Motors Toyota franchise on the grounds that they all "play" too much. Despite the pleasurable emphasis of their advertising slogans ("I Love What You Do for Me, Toyota" [375]),[74] Toyota technology demands the sacrifice of individual happiness to the corporate culture.

In broad strokes, the plot clearly indicates Updike's continued interrogation of the Freudian repressive hypothesis. The ambivalent role of technology in liberating/enslaving the protagonists is emphasized in the chemical technology of crack cocaine, which almost ruins the family as both an emotional and financial entity. In a parallel plot, medical technology offers Harry physical salvation (a choice between angioplasty and a coronary bypass) but reduces him to a soft machine, a spectator on the activity of his own heart, displayed on a television screen, "a typical American heart," "tired and stiff and full of crud" (164). Both male protagonists appear to end the novel in a state of newfound happiness, but an apparently commodified one. Nelson, born-again in a narcotics clinic, substitutes faith for his addiction, but in a form that has such a mechanistic emphasis that it appears as merely a means of reducing the individual to conformity. Harry is last seen floating in a morphine haze after a massive heart attack. The two have apparently swapped places, with Nelson, sober and abstemious, at the bedside of his father, who is described as floating "in a bed of happy unfeeling" (504). In the outcome, the indulgences of each of the two men represent less the lineaments of gratified desire than a surrender to the death instincts, a return to a pain-free state of nonbeing.

As a result, the novel interestingly reverses the structure of its predecessors. In *Rabbit, Run*, Harry's indulgent holiday from virtue with Ruth is ended by the death of his daughter and a return to family and repression. In *Rabbit Redux* the

---

[74]*Rabbit at Rest* (London: André Deutsch, 1990). All subsequent references are from this edition.

excursion with Jill and Skeeter again closes with death and a return to the family, as well as a job in the family business. In *Rabbit Is Rich* an actual excursion (to a Caribbean playground) brings Harry into metaphoric contact with death and nothingness (the sexual encounter with Thelma, terminally ill of lupus) and returns him, chastened, to the fold. (He is last seen holding his new granddaughter in his arms.) *Rabbit at Rest*, however, begins in leisure, then makes a brief return to the world of work, only for Harry to restage his original "run" once more, this time definitively, returning to die on the basketball court in Florida as the circle of the tetralogy closes upon him.

In this connection, the political dimension of the novel is worth foregrounding. In Updike's work, economic forms and fictional form continually interact. The structural reverse reflects America's own self-identified reverses, its position of global domination under threat from the new "Asian tiger" economies. When Nelson plans to replace the Toyota franchise with a shop selling jet skis, expensive toys for a leisured society, Harry argues caution in the face of imminent Depression: "We don't have any discipline! We're drowning in debt! We don't even own our own country any more!" (411). Nelson's view is that nobody works for necessities anymore, that the profit is in toys and fads, in other words that work has become play– and conversely, play is work. In Mr. Shimada's analysis, the United States has opted for a society based upon instinctual gratification and has lost its technological lead as a result. After a preliminary polite conversational skirmish with a sales-woman on the subject of playing tennis (in his heavily accented English he appears to be asking her if she *prays* [381]), he delivers an authoritative verdict: "Toyota does not enjoy bad games prayed with its autos" (387). Extolling the virtues of discipline, Shimada notes the American lack of happiness in indulgence and places the blame firmly on too much freedom, too little order, and on both Nelson's and Harry's games: "Not just son. Who is father and mother of such son? Where are they? In Forida enjoying sunshine and tennis" (387). Mr. Shimada's speech is entirely consonant with Updike's description to Iwao Iwamoto of the change in values in America, as opposed to the image of Japan that reflects the Freudian hypothesis: "We picture Japan as a very efficient and orderly place, with everything it is place and very industrious. And any industrious people have repressed a great deal in terms of pleasure-seeking, or feeling, even. One of the phenomena that I've noticed in my lifetime has been a loss of the sense of the urgency to work" (Iwamoto 122). Expanding to his theme, Updike noted that for his own father work had a sacred importance (he had to work or his family would starve), whereas Updike's own sons did not take work so seriously: "I think this creates a kind of vacuum which has to be filled with other things– with romance, or sex, or even games" (122).

In the novel, Updike inscribes this particular opposition of indulgence/achievement in global political terms, as the cold war (the ultimate image of repression, at home and abroad) comes to an end, and America finds itself liberated into insignificance, consigned to the sidelines "like a big Canada" (352). In its political dynamics, baldly stated, the novel appears to argue straightforwardly in favor of repression in the service of an older American code of family values, the work ethic, technological progress, and the right of America to global domination.

But Updike is never quite as simple as this. The plot of *Rabbit at Rest* is very carefully engineered in order to strike a series of variations on the central theme; the reader's experience is thus of a finely nuanced succession of debating points scored with or against the Freudian hypothesis, together with its political agenda.

   Rabbit at Rest divides into three long sections, FL (Florida), PA (Pennsylvania), and MI (Myocardial Infarction): the latter's substitution of a coronary for a place-name converts the whole of America into the site of one giant heart attack. In the opening sequence Harry is poised between two alternatives–play as death or pain as life. Florida, where life is a "perpetual vacation" (41), has necrotic rather than erotic overtones, the airport terminal (aptly named) offering large windows onto the runways, "so if there's a crash everybody can feast upon it with their own eyes" (7).Chewing peanut brittle, Harry, unwittingly feasting on his own death, meditates obsessively on other deaths (Max Robinson, Lockerebie, Roy Orbison) and on a culture that is, in his view, in terminal tailspin: "Everything falling apart, airplanes, bridges, eight years under Reagan of nobody minding the store, making money out of nothing, running up debt" (9). When Harry scares his family by getting lost in the terminal, Nelson's comment foreshadows the end of the novel: "'Suddenly we looked around and you weren't there.' Like Pan-Am 103 on the radar screen" (25). In conversation with his father, Nelson had derided the values of the work ethic, the Toyota emphasis on rules and discipline and the absence of creativity. His grandfather's era had allowed for more freedom: "Grandpa was a dealer. . . .He loved to make deals. . . . It was fun. There was some play in the situation" (8). The conversation is set in Deleon named for Ponce de León, the "discoverer" of Florida, but pronounced by the local people "Deal ya in" conjoining the imagery of finance and play, commodification and game. Just like his father, Nelson promptly gets "lost," in quest of a different kind of dealer, to supply his habit. The losses attendant on indulgence are foregrounded in the Florida sequence, which moves from minor "missing persons" incidents to a near-fatal accident to Judy, the potential heir to the curse of Rebecca and Jill, and to Harry's heart attack.

   The theme is firmly established in an extended sequence that concerns Harry playing golf, a game in which his losses are dual– the game itself, and twenty dollars to his opponents. The dialogue of the scene continually contrasts play (the game, the foursome's comments) with death and pain. Conversation ranges over politics, drug addiction, disease. The central theme is stated by Bernie Drechsel: "There are two routes to happiness. Work for it, day after day, like you and I did, or take a chemical shortcut." In his view it is unsurprising, given the state of the world, that kids take the shortcut cocaine, described as "instant happiness" (57). Immediate gratification, rather than the long haul, is Nelson's choice, and by implication, America's. Nelson describes the experience of cocain as "feeling no pain" (147), and in this he is not distinct from the political choice of his father's generation. "Rabbit like Reagan. . . .Under Reagan. . .it was like anesthesia" (61). Bernie (his memories of heart surgery still fresh) cautions: "When you come out of anaesthesia, it hurts like hell" (61). Bernie and his Jewish friends, fellow adherents of the work ethic, represent a set of values in which repression in the service of work and family is primary. "The soldier in Harry, the masochistic Christian, respects men like this. It's total love, like women provide, that makes you soft and does you in" (63).The Jewish/Christian opposition dramatizes, however, an alternative way of reading the work/play dynamic, reminiscent of that developed in *Rabbit, Run* between good works and grace, Eccles and Kruppenbach. For Bernie golf is "just a game" (5), not, as Harry intermittently sees it, "infinity, an opportunity for infinite improvement" (65). Ironically, Harry loses the game because he is hampered by repressed emotion, following a family row: "I couldn't get my ass into it, I couldn't release. I couldn't let go," he explains (68). In *Rabbit, Run*, Updike had suggested the possibility of reading Harry's playfulness less as social irresponsibility than as presocial innocence, instinctual openness, even spiritual grace– values lost to social man. Though the connection between play and grace is only vestigially developed in this initial game, it recurs in the game with which the novel closes.

In general terms, however, in the Florida sequence, play features repeatedly as pain or loss. Harry remembers holidays as "Torture" (48), though he himself promotes an "educational ordeal" (50), a visit to the Edison house, in preference to an excursion to the attractions of Disney. The house displays grounds full of exotic trees, apparently a triumph for nature and indulgence. (The eye lingers on the sloth tree and the apparently immortal banyan.) Nature, however, is firmly subordinate to culture here. All the trees had been imported in the search for a substitute for rubber. The Edison house proclaims technological triumphalism, a monument to the invention of the storage battery, phonograph, toaster, waffle iron, and other examples of the type of technology that has liberated the Angstroms into leisure. They remain bored, irritated, or impatient and retire speedily to McDonald's, where bingo is available in one corner. While Janice (about to become a career woman when the business collapses) watches *Working Girl*, Harry and Roy play a video game: *Annihilation*. Roy's attention span is too short to enjoy a long movie. He had already left *Dumbo* halfway through, before events turned upbeat. Presciently Harry points out that "it all works out. Roy, you should have stayed to the end. If you don't stay to the end the sadness sticks with you" (100). Both grandchildren, however, appear constitutionally incapable of the long haul. In front of the television, Judy continually channel-surfs, possessed by "a gluttony for images" (78) almost as devouring as her grandfather's appetite for snacks. Judy's television-watching offers an apt image of the fashion in which the Angstroms are being formed and molded by the mass fantasies disseminated by the media. Family dinner in the "mortuary calm" (31) of Valhalla Village is dominated by technological play, bingo numbers blaring from a loudspeaker. Harry can see Judy speak, and Pru's mouth move in response, but the sound track is that of the bingo caller. When Judy watches television, her attention is held, if not for long, by a film, *The Return of Martin Guerre*, the tale of a man who usurps another man's wife and family. Harry rather enjoys the idea: "There ought to be a law that we change identities and families every ten years or so" (84). As well as an in-joke for the knowing reader (the tetralogy appears at ten-year intervals), the comment is proleptic. In the event, Harry will take over Nelson's job and, for one night, his wife. Judy's channel-surfing vividly reveals the instability of the family in an America dominated by exchange values. In *Rabbit Is Rich* the wife-swapping episode introduced the notion of individuals as mere counters in emotional barter. Now whole families are interchangeable: "Faces, black in *The Jeffersons*, white in *Family Ties*, imploringly pop into visibility and then vanish" (77).

In the pursuit of easy happiness, the Angstroms risk dehumanization. Harry's bedtime reading, identified by Stacey Olster ("Rabbit Is Redundant") as Barbara Tuchman's *The First Salute*, restates the problems of the novel in broader historical terms: "Fantasies about America produced two strongly contradictory conclusions that in the end came to the same point of injecting some caution into the golden dreams. . . .Climate in the New World. . .made men listless and indolent, they might become happy but never stalwart. America. . .`was formed for happiness, but not for empire'" (*Rest* 85). Harry's reaction to this admonitory comment is telling. Hilariously, as he drifts off to sleep, he surfs the page much as Judy surfs the channels, transforming Tuchman's solid history into sexual double entendre: "Expectation of lucrative commerce. . .tangled issue. . .increased tension. . .neutral bottoms. . .French vigorously" (86).

If channel-surfing features initially as an image of technological short-circuiting of emotional affect in a society that sacrifices the long perspective to immediate gratifications, it takes on a different guise in the incident, Sunfish sailing in the Gulf, in which Judy and Harry almost die. Libidinal pleasures, with the implicit threat to family cohesion, culminate in a real threat, in the surf of the ocean itself. Harry has been offered a cheap deal on the hire of a Sunfish by the son of one of his golf partners, Gregg Silvers, a "holiday facilitator" (116) who makes his living out of the leisure industry. Harry notes that beneath his perpetual tan he is older than he at first appears: "He shouldn't still be horsing around on the beach" (118). In the locker room, immediately prior to embarking, Harry had been meditating on the opposition of natural pleasure to social repressions. Roy is circumcised. Harry is not. He wonders whether, had he been less sexually responsive, he might have been a more dependable person. "From the numb look of his prick Roy will be a solid citizen" (118).On the beach the immensity of the ocean, its "raw glory," entrances him, especially in contrast to the "hemmed in"nature of his own native state. Pennsylvania is remembered as a land "dingy with use," a *worked* nature, where even the wild patches "had been processed by men" (119). Out in the Gulf, however, one puff of wind is enough to capsize the boat. Play almost does result in death, as commodified pleasure is transformed into an encounter with nature red in tooth and claw. Struggling heroically to save his granddaughter's life, Harry suffers a heart attack that is presented as life-giving pain: "Joy that Judy lives crowds his heart, a gladness that tightens and rhythmically hurts, like a hand squeezing a ball for exercise" (132). Although in agony, Harry "feels good, down deep" (138), rescued from anaesthesia into life. Singing to keep Harry from lapsing into unconsciousness, Judy can at first only remember snatches of television commercials. "It is like switching channels back and forth" (139), though her attention seems to linger, appropriately, on "Coke is it!" But slowly her voice strengthens, and the songs increase in length, as she returns to those of the past, children's classics from the movies of the Depression years. As play becomes a desperate struggle to survive, a long haul back to the safety of the shore, it is only Judy's existence that prevents Harry from giving in to death.

In the aftermath, Pru attempts to retranslate the event back into a lighter vein, suggesting that instead of being trapped, Judy was merely hiding from Harry "as a sort of game" (159).The suggestion registers a truth of a kind. A game that had got out of hand almost did kill Judy, and *will* kill Harry. American free play, unrestrained indulgence, poses a threat to Judy's survival, whether directly (the crack dealers who threaten to kidnap Nelson's family) or, more generally, in the attenuated human relationships and lack of responsibility of a generation that no longer puts its children's welfare first. Nelson's squandering habits have already consigned Judy to outgrown clothes and a shabby home; more legitimate entertainments have produced a child whose gluttony for a rapid succession of images forms a parallel to her grandfather's snack-damaged heart. Harry's heart may be physically endangered. The hearts of his family risk underdevelopment, their emotions attenuated by media substitutes.

In the hospital Harry has two television screens to watch: his own heart on a monitor, and a football game. Nature has again thrown a spanner in the cultural works; the game is almost invisible as a result of a sudden fog. Television coverage has been reduced to the sideline cameras, and spectators at the game can see even less than Harry, drugged to the eyeballs in a hospital bed. The game cannot be abandoned– it is costing the sponsors a million dollars a minute. As an image of America it could hardly be more telling.[75] Nobody knows what is really going on; there is an unbridgeable gap between real action and media image. The crowd "rumbles and groans in poor sync with the television action, trying to read the game off the electronic scoreboard" (161).They are actually present, but their understanding and reaction is attuned only to the media. In contrast to the spectators, Harry, his vision less clouded as a result of his brush with death, goes beyond the commodification of America into a deeper sense of ludic existence. "The game flickering in the fog, the padded men hulking out of nothingness and then fading back again, has a peculiar beauty bearing upon Rabbit's new position at the still centre of a new world" (162).

Harry's is a lone intuition, however, amidst a plethora of images of bodily commodification. Around him the image of his heart– damaged, struggling, real– is juxtaposed with television commercials, notably one for Gallo wine (gallows humor here), which sells the product on the basis of an erotic plot line, as customer and liquor saleswoman date. "'It was perfect,' the girl in the commercial sighingly says. . ..[Y]ou can see that they will fuck, if not this date the next. . .all by the grace of Gallo" (165). Janice ("a channel that can't be switched" [168]) hangs equally starry-eyed on the jargon of the heart specialist, intent on restoring the physical process to smooth function without any awareness of the emotionally calcified hearts around him. Judy, channel-surfing again, pauses only on images of physical violence. Bruce Lee's kung fu kicks alternate with the surgeons's plans to violate Harry's body, fading into nude bodies, and a film in which a man changes into a werewolf. On screen, bodies metamorphose painlessly, instantly interchangeable,

---

[75]A very similar image of a fogbound game as national symbol (baseball in this case) occurs in Anne Tyler, *Ladder of Years* (London: Chatto and Windus, 1995), 131ff.

in the fiction of play that is American culture. The implication is that the next generation will have precious few desires to repress– they are easily, if unsatisfactorily, gratified by a form of media play that sidelines reality in a fog of mystification and commodification. Bodies and hearts have become only constructed products. America is no longer simply surrendering to pleasurable emotion as opposed to sacrificing all to the work ethic. It is confusing the two, turning all forms of emotion into marketable product, all play into work. In a real economic sense, America *capitalizes* on family affections, while simultaneously deforming them to commercial ends. Even more disturbingly, Roy has learned from his experiences (as he demonstrates by painfully yanking out his grandfather's nose tube) "the idea of inflicting pain to show emotion" (313). In this he is distinctly representative of the underside of the American Dream, his actions generalized in Charlie Stavros's comments on punk fashion: "Pain is where it's at for punks. Mutilation, self-hatred, slam dancing. For these kids today, ugly is beautiful. That's their way of saying what a lousy world we're giving them" (237). Harry's implicit choice of pain as opposed to political and emotional anesthesia has both its representative and its darker side.

Back in Pennsylvania, Harry embarks on a period of convalescence and treatment that restores his heart in both physical and emotional senses– angioplasty repairs the muscle, and the near-death experience sharpens his emotional take on the world. The extent to which he has come to his senses (sensually and sensibly) is underlined in the description of Pennsylvania. The return to his native state carries suggestions of a return to an older, less befogged condition in which Harry is able to disentangle libidinal pleasure from the mystifications of America, to see its attractions and its dangers. The question posed for the reader is whether this is an advance on the earlier state of anesthesia. Emotion is restored– but potentially redemonized. No longer tired of life, Harry appears to yield to sensual gratification, committing, in the act of adultery with his daughter-in-law on which the sequence closes, the one act of sensual indulgence that is, even is the permissive 1990s, utterly taboo. Harry returns to Pennsylvania in the spring as blossom erupts about him, "a sudden declaration of the secret sap that runs through everybody's lives" (179). Cruising through town, his eyes rest on women in running tights ("Young animals need to display" [182]), on a young Hispanic girl in a lilac party dress, decorated with a cloth rose ("She is a flower" amid "a swarm of boys" [183]), and a half-naked boy kissing his girl, all of them representing "lives that are young and rising like sap" (184). The emphasis on the irrepressibility of nature is continued in Harry's memories of Mary Ann ("his to harvest" [185], her underpants described as "stuffed with her moss" [184]) and in his awe-stricken reaction to a street of pear trees in bloom, their heart-shaped leaves bending into one another to form an enclosure almost as enchanting as Mary Ann's, over his head.

This America– an America of happy indulgence– contrasts with Harry's later experience, particularly in his relationship with Thelma. Thelma (relocated in a new housing development that is skimpy on trees, and decidedly not representative of natural overabundance) has loved Harry only within the masochistic framework of Freudian repression, sin, and guilt. (She understands their relationship as having "enriched her transactions with God" [193] by giving her something to be guilty about.)A conventionally good housewife and mother, Thelma's secret affair with Harry embodies the Freudian economy, in which family and work take precedence over sensual gratification. The latter has not been lacking (Harry remembers Thelma's plush sofa with needlepointed scatter cushions and lace antimacassars as conveniently positioned for oral sex). By bringing Harry news of Nelson's cocaine habit, however, Thelma transforms a potentially erotic tryst into characteristic sadness: "Why don't you like me to make you happy? Why have you always fought it?" As Harry admits, "We've never been exactly set up for a lot of happiness" (200). A second factor also comes between Harry and consummation—has own fear of AIDS, a new and powerfully repressive element in the dynamic relation of eros to culture. As the plot develops it transpires that Nelson's associates in the scam that ruins the Angstroms are two gay men, both of whom are to die of AIDS. If the national, political reference to the Japanese has disquieting elements, the sexual politics of the plot are even less reassuring. Because of unrestrained indulgence in "unnatural," nonreproductive desires, the family business totters. Racial and gender betrayal are both potentially present in the plot. Everything appears to support the Freudian case for repression as necessary for social health. Indeed, when Nelson attacks Pru, Harry features entirely as the voice of order. Nelson's attack is described as a typical product of a society that is glutted by images and which expresses its emotions by violence. Nelson felt "like a monster or something had taken over my body and I was standing outside watching and felt no connection with myself. Like it was all on television" (258). When Nelson takes refuge in psychobabble and therapy-speak, Harry asserts an older set of values: "We can't expect society to run our lives for us. . . .There comes a point when you got to take responsibility" (265).

Harry's angioplasty also appears to register Freudian imperatives, if in quasi-religious guise, as the opposition of grace/good works shadows that of pleasure/toil. He reflects that the hospital is no longer run by nuns. Vocations have dried up, and the days of deferred gratification are over: "No more good people, waiting to have their run in the afterlife. The thing about the afterlife, it kept this life within bounds, somehow, like the Russians. Now there's just Japan, and technology, and the profit motive, and getting all you can while you can" (269). In a wonderfully apt phrase, Harry telescopes God, the cold war, and sexual repression in one image. Now the Iron Curtain is coming down on all counts. Angioplasty enacts Harry's worst nightmares, of invasion and violation. In the process he becomes, successively, a soft machine, a media product, a woman, and a gay man. Harry has persistently resisted surgery on the grounds that it constitutes an unnatural violation. "You, the natural you, are technically dead. A machine is living for you" (266). When Charlie Stavros objects that "You're just a soft machine" (234). (sic) Harry silently resists, envisaging himself as "a vehicle of grace" (235). Opting for angioplasty rather than open-heart surgery, he is horrified to discovery that the process is carried out under local anesthetic, and that he can watch it all on television. As "The Rabbit AngstromShow" unfolds (on several television screens in the operating theater and the monitoring room), Harry observes the catheter snaking into his heart and wonders "if this is what having a baby is like, having Dr. Raymond inside you? How do women stand it, for nine months? Not to mention being screwed in the first place. Can they really like it? Or queers being buggered?"In his view, "godless technology is fucking the pulsing wet tubes we inherited from the squid, the boneless sea-cunts" (270). Indeed, his voice is now high, "as if out of a woman's throat" (271). Even worse, imagistically, the act is not located in the vaginal so much as the alimentary realm. Harry repeatedly describes the plaque in his heart muscle as if it were food debris– "Rice Krispies" (270), for example. The operation involves a catheter expanding (a balloon inflates) in order to clear the artery of its blockages and open up a larger internal space. The description is clearly tumescent. Harry sees "a segment of worm thicken and swell, pressing the pallid Rice Krispies together" (270). Because of the injected dyes, his only other sensation is that of "knifelike sweet pressure in his bladder" (271). To add to his complete humiliation, the two doctors agree that the procedure has been entirely successful, in tones reminiscent of a beer commercial, "like those voices on television that argue about the virtues of Miller Lite" (271). Even worse, it transpires that, without even recognizing it, Harry has had a heart attack anyway, or as the surgeons put it, "some new Q waves and. . .an elevation of the creatinine kinase myocardial enzyme, with positive MB bands" (281). The language of the heart offers its own mystifications, its own forms of exploitation.

It is his perception of the violation of his masculinity, his individuality, and his heart that motivates Harry's adultery with Pru. In committing this particular act, Harry marks a decisive division between his own desires and state-sponsored indulgence. Incest with one's in-laws is not generally a feature of the plot line of soap opera: this is an event that cannot be reassimilated into the comfortable schmaltz of American "family values." It is, as far as Harry is concerned, a purely libidinal event, in opposition to both Freudian repression and the commodified gratifications previously on offer to him. The encounter takes place while Janice is out taking an exam as part of her return to the world of work. Janice has already sacked Nelson from the car lot; temporarily he has been sacrificed to the business and removed from the family group. Both Janice and Thelma are no loner objects of libidinal fantasy. Janice, converted to power dressing and hulking shoulders, is now "electric, businesslike" (292), resembling a television newscaster. Bearing news of Nelson's embezzlement, she appears to be wearing contact lenses, tears "prepared for him during the station break" (292). Her language lends her a pre-programmed quality, with her need to "process" after all the "trauma" (298). Thelma, meanwhile, has herself become a soft machine, dependent on the process of dialysis for life, with a permanent shunt attached to her arm.

In contrast, the sexual encounter, in the spare room that is permeated with the green, wet fragrance of leafy trees, overtly draws upon suggestions of natural spontaneity and innocent emotion. In the past, before Nelson (safeguarding the domestic structure) cut down the great copper beech tree that shaded the room, Harry experienced the sound of rain in its leaves as the most religious experience of his life. He still associates nature with grace and innocence, in the realm of the presocial. In bed, Harry places Pru's hand on his erection with a gesture that "has the presexual quality of one child sharing with another an interesting discovery" (341). To the accompaniment of the affective fallacy– crashing rain, thunder and lightning– Pru disrobes "as if in overflow of this natural heedlessness. . . lovely much as those pear trees in blossom. . .were lovely. . .a piece of Paradise" (341).

The irony here is that, although Harry is spontaneous, Pru is not. Indeed, she has chosen quite consciously to sleep with Harry in order to safeguard her own family unit. Before their encounter, Harry and Pru spend the evening on the sofa watching television, particularly *The Cosby Show*, in which Harry admires Phylicia Rashad's wide smile, "implying that indecency is all right in its place, its wise time, as in one of those mutually ogling Huxtable snuggles that end many a Cosby show" (332).Judy however, interrupts, switching to the image of a huge turtle "determined to defend its breeding grounds" (332). Unknown to Harry, Janice is planing to sell their house, in order to pay the debt to Toyota, and move back in with Nelson and Pru. Watching *Unsolved Mysteries*, Harry had been struck by the fluency of the witnesses; America has become "a nation of performers" (334). It does not strike him that Pru is one of them, even when she joins him, scantily clad (but equipped with condoms), laments her enforced sexual abstinence, and huddles close to him while carefully checking his capacities ("Does Janice say you can't fuck? What did your doctor say?" [340]). Describing the ruin of her life, Pru wails, "I had my little hand of cards and played them and now I'm folded" (339). But in fact she is playing with considerable skill: both in the sexual game (Harry feels "expertly used" to provide two orgasms), in the finely calibrated performance that he never suspects of being a role, and in the long-term strategy of which it is a part. In America play has a use value, as Pru demonstrates, defending her breeding grounds.

Harry's ignorance also carries a political point. Shortly before leaving the hospital Harry had met Annabelle, the woman who may be his daughter by Ruth. Annabelle had left Brewer for an independent life but has now returned to live with her mother. She contrasts with Harry's sister, Mim, remembered as "a leggy colt of a girl dying to break out of Brewer, to kick or fuck her way through the fence" (283). Once out, Mim never came back to the fold. Harry then has a peculiar dream in which Ruth appears to be living with him and Janice, and his embrace of her is "semi-permitted, like an embrace of a legal relation" (288). The house in which they are living is the Springer house, the polka dots on Ruth's dress are the pear blossom. Harry reflects that "two men for a woman and vice versa is just about right, just as we need two kinds of days, workdays and holidays" (302), underscoring the connection between the adulterous triangles of the tetralogy and the work/holiday opposition. As the dream suggests, on some unconscious level, Harry is aware of Janice's plans– though he converts them into erotic fantasy. Again he is politically typical. His ignorance is that of a nation fed on dreams, which now wakes up to economic and affectional scarcity. Remembering Reagan, he comments, quite unselfconsciously, that Reagan "had that dream distance; the powerful thing about him as President was that you never knew how much he knew, nothing or everything" (291). Harry's own situation reveals, however, that ignorance is not bliss. The dream of happiness for all, guilt-free and permitted, has terminated. Harry may happily envisage sharing himself with two mistresses; he does not envisage being forced by economics to include a son, daughter-in-law, and two kids as well.

Where the Florida section of the novel ended with an encounter with nature which was a corrective to mass fantasy, the Pennsylvania sequence closes with an encounter that is much less "natural" than Harry thinks. Pru is almost as much an actress as Phylicia Rashad. As the final section of the novel reveals, Harry gets his manhood back only in illusion– and in the service of Pru's economic ends. In addition, at the car lot he discovers that technology has "screwed" him economically as well as physically: Nelson has exploited the computerization of the bank to extract five car loans in the name of a dead gay friend. When Harry marches in a Fourth of July parade as Uncle Sam, a role for which he is apparently fitted by his service during Korea and his past as a sports hero, his masculine strutting is rather belied by his appearance. The wig makes him look like "a very big red-faced woman" (357). Citizens keep asking him for directions, "because he is dressed as Uncle Sam and should know," but he has to admit that "he doesn't know anything" (359). This is a "holiday and liberty" occasion– in American terms *the* holiday celebrating liberty– and the crowd that turns out to celebrate the American Dream appears to Harry "younger, more naked, less fearful, better" (365), the roads lined by "a cheerful froth of flesh" (364) creating in him the impression that "this is the happiest fucking country the world has ever seen" (366). (The erotic emphasis is relentless.) Harry's own happiness, however, is drug-assisted. It is the Nitrostat tablet that has opened up his veins "like flower petals uncurling in the sun" (365). The parade is immediately followed by an account of Thelma's death, raving, angry and hallucinating, an American nightmare. A less celebratory communal ritual is staged in her funeral, at which Harry and Thelma's husband, Ron, former basketball teammates, almost come to blows. At the end of the funeral the two, "with a precision as if practiced, execute a criss-cross" (374), games players to the last.

The most skillful player, however, is ultimately revealed to be Pru. When Janice finally tells Harry of her plans, she assures him that there is no way Pru can resist. Janice holds the economic power: she still owns the Springer house. But in revealing her adultery with Harry, Pru plays her trump card, as Janice recognizes: "She didn't seem repentant, just tough, and obviously not wanting me to come live in the house. That's why she told" (427). Pru has defended her breeding grounds in adept fashion, a performer who is both inside and outside the game, able to manipulate the others to her own ends. Nelson is also able to exploit the American commodification of affection. When Nelson learns that his father has made love to his wife, his reaction is telling. He doesn't hit him, or her, or howl, or scream. He sets to work, without delay, to set up a family therapy session: "He says this will need a lot of processing" (427).

Faced with this distinctly unenticing proposition, Harry flees. As Jeff Campbell comments [. . . *ed.*] Nelson's therapy is an extension of the machine world, a creed that is entirely organized around the idea of refining the human product. Nelson does not seem to think or feel, he processes. Fatter, he resembles in equal parts Harry's mother-in-law (395) and a television evangelist (396). As the heir to the Reverend Eccles, his faith is "faith that the process will work" (398), faith in "God as we understand him (sic)" (397). Ironically, his recovery is total. He has transformed his initial libidinal excess into work (a career opportunity as a social worker) and rewritten it in "family" terms, as a mere symptom of his problems with Harry. For Nelson, the addiction is now less important than "getting the relational poison out of your system" (416).

Harry's flight, a completion of the interrupted escape attempt of _Rabbit, Run_, is not, however, a straightforward escape. On the debit side he has escaped responsibility, indulged his libido handsomely, and fled the world of work to that of permanent holiday. On the other hand, the Florida to which he returns is not the same world as that of the opening sequence. On his daily walks he moves away from the mass vacation locale to an older working community that supplies the labor for the hotels and condos. It is important to note here that Updike displays the economic underpinnings, other people's sacrifices, that make the permanent holiday possible and that they are black sacrifices. The black area of town, with its old-fashioned houses, chicken coops, and general stores is reminiscent of Harry's childhood, familiar and vital. Harry's identification with the black community may be naive, but it marks, at least, a clear advance on his earlier racism.

What is it exactly that kills Rabbit? Or who? Play (as the immediate cause)? Overindulgence (hence a heart attack)? Adultery? Flight from the consequences of adultery (and an angry Janice)? Or is her "hardheartedness" more responsible than his? Should responsibility be laid at the door of Pru, fighting for her family? Or Nelson, indulging his desires? Or is Harry's death in part a return to individual responsibility in opposition to the therapeutic, the commodified, the fantasy? Three points are important here. In the first place, if Updike doesn't _quite_ kill Harry at the end, it is perhaps for good reason. In a sense this is not the novel in which Harry dies, but the novel in which he comes back from the dead (a form of living death), albeit briefly, to choose a better death. Second, it is important to emphasize that this death is a choice, and third, that it is a choice which aligns him with a different political and economic position.

Updike multiplies a plethora of suggestions that Harry is ready for death. Watching the basketball game, Harry thinks of Mike Schmidt, "who had the grace to pack it in when he could no longer produce," and Chrissie Evert, who "packed it in too. There comes a time" (481). He makes a last call north, to speak to his grandchildren, but is unable to hang up: "He had to make the child do it first. Chicken in a suicide pact" (490). Thereafter, in the Mead Hall of Valhalla Village, the former cold warrior sets to work to eat-to-die, retiring to dream of a curious reunion with all his dead, including, in some future incarnation, Roy, now fully grown. In choosing to play his final game, Harry also opts out of a commodified and materialist world. In his youth Harry had been an ardent believer in capitalism, as represented by Kroll's department store, despite his awareness of "the panicky gamble of all this merchandising" (454). When Kroll's closes, he realizes that "the world was not solid and benign, it was a shabby set of temporary arrangements rigged up for the time being, all for the sake of money." He comes to the conclusion that the gamble of capitalism, its deals and speculations, is no longer based on "good faith" and that nothing is sacred: "If Kroll's could go, the courthouse could go, the banks could go. When the money stopped, they could close down God himself (sic)" (455). In the event, this turns out not to be so easy. On the drive south, _play_ actually does turn into _pray_, if in somewhat farcical terms. A Supreme Court ruling against organized prayer before football matches has infuriated the South. The mayor of Montgomery leads prayers at the fifty-yard line, in Alabama local ministers in the bleachers join spectators in the Lord's Prayer, and in Pensacola prayers are declaimed through bullhorns to the audience. As a result of his heart attack, Harry comes to feel that he is "in His hand already. Like you're out on the court instead of on the bench swallowing down butterflies and trying to remember the plays" (443). For Harry, the rehearsals are over. "Play" in its indulgent, "bread and circuses" sense no longer stands between him and a firm grasp of political and social reality. His bedtime reading suddenly reveals to him the costs of the American Revolution, in Tuchman's account of atrocities. Up to this point, "He has always thought of the Revolution as a kind of playful toy war, without any of that grim stuff" (492). Harry has always been torn between rebellion and conformity. Now he decides that "he loves freedom but a grassy field is his idea of enough" (479).

The end game (on a grassy court) is clearly emblematic. In the alterative Florida that Harry has discovered, work and play seem to be held in creative balance. The game is played in an "unhurried" and cooperative fashion, "all together making a weave, nobody trying too hard" (480). Harry also advances beyond his earlier, defensive homophobia, unworried by the boys' suspicion of him (they take him for a "cheesecake" who is after "a black boy's dick" [483]). In the final game, Harry plays alone against an opponent who, in symbolic terms, embodies all his former nightmares. The boy is black, with "Indian" (495) high cheekbones, and is wearing a tank top decorated with a snarling tiger. He unites in one person the threats of black America, the Asian tiger economies, and ancestral guilts. Harry notes that he is an extremely skillful and deliberate performer "making good serious economical moves" (495).He is also a dealer. He offers Harry some "Scotty"– a euphemism for crack, as his gesture of cracking a whip implies. (The reference is once more to television: *Star Trek* and its catchphrase, "Beam Me Up Scotty.") Yet although Tiger clearly has the whip hand in the game, he is also described as "gracious" (498) and his play is based on an honor system, calling his own fouls on himself. Harry has plenty of warning of impending death, but courts it as if it were paradise. He feels "as if his tree of veins and arteries is covered with big pink blossoms," while the pain in his back is "spreading, like clumsy wings" (498).As he leaps, to die in play, he goes "way up toward the torn clouds," beaming up in a fashion that is about as transcendent as Harry's own limited consciousness will allow: "He feels something immense persistently fumble at him" (499). As "the social net twitches" and a neighbor calls the emergency services, Tiger, the heir to the younger Rabbit, feels "the impulse to run" (499) and takes off, one step ahead of the paramedics, whose emergency sirens suggest to the bystanders the beginnings of hurricane Hugo, the natural cataclysm that coincides with Harry's death.

The tetralogy ends on an ambivalent note. On the plus side, Harry has (at least in his own experience) swapped commodified gratification for real sex, and anesthetized deathliness for a real death. Janice also experiences a reawakening of naked emotion. When she sees Harry, she is hit by a wave of enormous feeling and realizes that her hardhearted silence had been "a kind of addiction" (503). Janice is nonetheless still ready to maintain her toughness with Nelson ("after a while the mother in you dies just like heart muscle" [501]), who appears to be quite unregenerate. At the close, as Nelson whines by his deathbed, Harry wants to put him out of his misery: *"Nelson,* he wants to say, *you have a sister"* (504). But the message is garbled. The existence of Annabelle remains "an old story, going on and on, like a radio nobody's listening to" (275). Here there is no soap opera deathbed confession and reunion. The story– in its secrecy, its repression– is from another era in content and medium. It is not just a question here of lost content, but of a form of story that can no longer be told to the television-attuned Angstroms. As a result, Nelson's little sister is lost to silence– as Harry falls into the embrace of her proverbial namesake– Little Sister Death.

*Judie Newman, "Rabbit at Rest: The Return of the Work Ethic" *Rabbit Tales: Poetry and Politics in John Updike's Rabbit Novels.* Lawrence R. Broer Ed. Tuscaloosa, Alabama: University of Alabama Press, 1998.

"Rabbit at Rest: The Seed of Death Within"

James A. Schiff*

The subject of *Rabbit at Rest* was inevitable, given that the final image of *Rabbit Is Rich* is of Harry's coffin and that the first three novels of the tetralogy are filled with images and allusions to death and the dead. Updike even published an essay,"Why Rabbit Had to Go," two months before publication of his novel, and he made sure the dust jacket of *Rabbit at Rest* bore the image of a tombstone with the funereal colors of black, gray, and purple.[68] Updike had decided Rabbit's death, all but certain at the novel's conclusion, would not come as a surprise. By revealing his ending in advance and in describing his novel as "a depressed book about a depressed man, written by a depressed man," one would have thought *Rabbit at Rest* had little chance of success.[69]Yet reviews were largely appreciative, even glowing, and the book went on to win the Pulitzer prize, the National Book Critics Circle Award, and the Howells Medal.[70] The accomplishment of this elegiac novel was that Updike was able to make a depressing work vibrant, an age-old subject fresh, a predictable ending poignant.

Beginning on the day Harry senses the seed of death has been planted inside

---

[68] John Updike, "Why Rabbit Had to Go," I, 24-25. Material concerning Updike's role in the making of the dust jacket to *Rabbit at Rest* is located in the collection of Updike papers at the Houghton Library, Harvard University. MS Storage 279.

[69] Ibid, 24.

[70] The Howells Medal, given by the American Academy of Arts and Letters, is awarded every five years to the most distinguished work of American fiction of the preceding five years.

him (December 28, 1988), and concluding on what is perhaps the final day of his life (September 22, 1989), the novel spans nine months, which suggests Updike treats Harry's death as a birth, from its beginnings as a seed to its explosive and violent arrival on a schoolyard basketball court in Florida. The movement of this novel dealing with heart attacks, hospitals, doctors, and cardiovascular information, is toward Harry's death, though there are other adventurers and episodes: a tour of Edison's Florida house; a sailing expedition with his granddaughter, Judy; a one-night liaison with his daughter-in-law, Pru; a stint as Uncle Sam in the Mt. Judge Independence Day parade; an encounter with Mr. Shimada from Toyota; and a final pickup basketball game with a black youth named Tiger. In addition to Harry's adventurers, there are subplots in the novel that treat Nelson's fall into cocaine abuse and economic ruin, and Janice's rise to competence as family matriarch and working woman.

The novel's subject is introduced immediately as Harry, waiting for his family to arrive on an airplane, "has a funny sudden feeling that what he has come to meet. . .is not [his family] but something more ominous and intimately his: his own death, shaped vaguely like an airplane."[71] How fitting that his son, daughter-in-law, and grandchildren should be bringing death to Harry– as if their very presence and growth are displacing him– and bringing it to him in Florida, "death's favorite state" (146). Furthermore, the plane's association with death relates to the recent bombing of Pan Am Flight 103, a disaster very much on Harry's mind, in which the aircraft was ripped open from inside by an exploding bomb, resulting in "bodies tumbling down like wet melon seeds" (7). Curious about what the passengers on that flight experienced, Harry identifies with them: "[H]e too is falling, helplessly falling, toward death" (159). The destroyed aircraft functions as a metaphor for Harry's body. Both have something ticking inside (a heart, a bomb) that is likely to go off: "Every plane had a bomb ticking away in its belly. We can explode any second" (449). Nine months later the seed of Harry's death, now matured, will explode: "His torso is ripped by a terrific pain, elbow to elbow. He bursts from within" (460).

As a result of his opening premonition, Harry is more conscious of his mortality, and following his first heart attack, he becomes increasingly fearful, careful, and tired. In a novel in which death and disaster are everywhere, Harry, who resides at Valhalla Village, Norse hall for slain warriors, can think of little else. His mind is preoccupied with those who have recently died: Max Robinson, Roy Orbison, Jimmie the Mouseketeer, Peggy Fosnacht, Thelma Harrison, the woman at Fiscal Alternatives, Barbara Tuchman, Bartlett Giamatti, and a host of others. In addition, he dreams about death, imagining it as a gigantic beast that awaits him; he continually wonders what death will feel like and ponders how other living entities, even banyan trees, die; he arrives at the point where he cannot think of sex

---

[71] John Updike, *Rabbit at Rest* (New York: Knopf, 1990; New York: Fawcett Columbine, 1996), 1. Subsequent references, noted parenthetically, are to the Fawcett Columbine paperback edition, which is based on the Knopf/Everyman's Library four-volume collection, *Rabbit Angstrom* (1995).

without death; and he takes nitroglycerin pills and undergoes medical procedures to thwart death.

The focal point of Harry's dying is his heart, which, his doctor reveals, is "tired and stiff and full of crud" (150). The word *heart* first appeared in the tetralogy in the epigraph to *Rabbit, Run* in which Pascal refers to "the hardness of the heart," a characteristic Harry possesses. In that same novel Tothero advised Harry: "Do what the heart commands. The heart is our only guide" and "A boy who has had his heart enlarged by an inspiring coach can never become. . .a failure."[72] The sometimes hardhearted Harry, whose heart eventually becomes "too big," follows his coach's advice and moves to the promptings of his heart (148). However, living in this manner has gotten him into trouble, and ultimately there will be a price to pay for his self-indulgence. As Updike states 30 years later, "In [*Rabbit at Rest*]. . . the hardened heart becomes no longer a metaphor, but an actual physical thing."[73] Through his junk food addiction, Harry has clogged, overworked, and abused his heart to the point it is failing, and thus threatening his life.

The cause of his chest pains and shortness of breath, Harry's heart assumes a crucial presence in the novel and is nearly a character in its own right. At one point Harry dreams "he has become his own heart, a huffing puffing pumping man at midcourt" (69) and later imagines the heart as a "companion" that talks to him (428): "At times it seems a tiny creature, a baby, pleading inside him for attention, for rescue, and at others a sinister intruder, a traitor muttering in code, an alien parasite nothing will expel" (430). The metaphors continue with Harry imagining "his heart as an unwilling captive inside his chest, a galley slave or one of those blinded horses that turn a mill wheel" (185).

The fate of Harry's heart preoccupies a chorus of voices (doctors, family members, Harry himself), and the reader, like Harry, anticipates that the poisoned muscle will either explode like the bomb in the belly of Pan Am Flight 103, or stop ticking, as was the fate of Commissioner Giamatti during cardiac arrest: "That little electric twitch: without it we're so much rotting meat" (406). By focusing on the ailing heart, Updike evokes the precariousness of life and shows how death comes to *everyone*, including otherwise middling Americans like Harry. As Oates states, Updike's "courageous theme [is] the blossoming and fruition of the seed of death we all carry inside us."[74]

Harry's heart problems are the result of his efforts to feed his hunger. From the beginning Harry has sought to satisfy his body, primarily through sex and athletics, but now decades later his appetite has more to do with eating: "[H]e's hungry again, for anything salty and easy to chew" (4). Whereas basketball once offered supreme pleasure, Harry now finds simple delight in the sensations of

---

[72] Updike, *Rabbit, Run* 47, 55.

[73] Melvyn Bragg, "Forty Years of Middle America with John Updike (1990)," in *Conversations with John Updike*, 228.

[74] Oates, "So Young!" 1.

certain foods on his teeth and tongue: "[h]e helps himself generously to, among other items, the scallops wrapped in bacon. The mix of textures, of crisp curved bacon and rubbery yielding scallops, in his sensitive mouth feels so delicious his appetite becomes bottomless" (453). As Updike states, "[Harry's] pleasure centers have become pretty much located in his mouth."[75] The problem is that Harry hungers for foods that are killing him.

Harry's eating functions as an extension of the consumerism theme that dominates *Rabbit Is Rich*. In *Rabbit at Rest* Harry continues to be a great American consumer, though the object of his desire is not gold Krugerrands or a new home but food products high in sodium and fat. With great relish, Harry consumes a vast assortment of taboo foods, which the novel catalogs: peanut brittle, doughnuts, peanuts, almonds, hazelnuts, pretzels, Corn Chips, steak, pecan pie, butter-pecan ice cream, cherry Danish, a Big Mac, cookies, macadamia nuts, fried eggs and bacon, hamburger and french fries, hot pastrami, fried catfish, French toast, link sausages, scallops wrapped in bacon, creamed asparagus, potato pancakes, and so on.

Harry's constant hunger for food, which he can never fully satisfy, relates to the addiction theme Updike posits in the novel: Harry is addicted to junk food and salt, Nelson to cocaine, and Americans to consumerism and the pursuit of happiness. As Updike says of *Rabbit at Rest*, "There's the idea floating around in there that America makes us addictive, that there's so much more food here than we can possibly eat that you feel you should be eating your share all the time."[76] America, as Harry's reading of Barbara Tuchman's *First Salute* reveals, "*was formed for happiness, but not for empire*" (77)– an idea echoed in the novel when, following the parade, Harry thinks, "All in all this is the happiest fucking country the world has ever seen" (337). The pursuit of happiness, however, has its costs: Harry is destroying his heart, Nelson's pursuit of "instant happiness" through cocaine ruins the family business, and the American empire is in decline (51).

The presaged fall of the House of Angstrom, which stems from its reckless pursuit of happiness, reflects the larger decline of America. As Frederick Douglass states in the novel's epigraph, "Food to the indolent is poison, not sustenance," which suggests Harry, Nelson, and America are poisoning themselves. Updike is critical of American culture for its laziness and softness ("[a] nation of couch potatoes" [441]); its overdevelopment; and its lack of discipline and order, as reflected in its continual running up of debt. As a result, America is losing its place in the global economy; like Harry, who is also being replaced, it is no longer "the big cheese" (325). Written at perhaps the height of recent American concern about the rise of the Japanese economy, *Rabbit at Rest* utilizes Mr. Shimada's confiscation of Springer Motors as an act representative of the larger picture.

Nowhere is the vulnerability and yet exuberance of America more apparent than in the scene in which Harry plays Uncle Sam in a Fourth of July parade

---

[75] Bragg, "Forty Years of Middle America," 226.

[76] Ibid.

through the streets of Mt. Judge. Inspired by the author's participation in a parade in his hometown,[77] the scene reveals Updike's vision of America. As the embodiment of his nation, Harry is overweight and hindered by a failing heart (is America's heart dying?) for which he needs to pop pills. In addition, he literally is falling apart at the seams. Early in the novel Updike says of America, "Everything falling apart, airplanes, bridges" (6), and this image holds true for Uncle Sam himself whose trousers are "left unbuttoned at the stomach" (328), whose top hat sits precariously, and whose "goatee doesn't stick" so that Harry is forced to make improvised repairs with Scotch tape to keep himself together (332). Though some in the crowd are aware of his unraveling condition, they nevertheless cheer him on, as if America is oblivious to the fact Uncle Sam is coming apart at the seams. Furthermore, the dialogue Updike employs during this scene is potent with meaning. At one point Janice says of Uncle Sam, "He's not dead, is he?" (329). And when strangers approach Uncle Sam to ask for directions, Harry is forced "to keep telling them he doesn't know anything" (330). Though the parade is a success and Harry is energized by participating, Updike posits an ironic underside to the scene, suggesting Americans will continue to applaud while oblivious to the declining stature of their country.

Decline is pervasive in the novel, and Nelson's fall presages America's fall. At 32, Nelson has become a cocaine addict, and to feed his addiction he has embezzled nearly two hundred thousand dollars from Springer Motors. Though he undergoes rehabilitation and feels optimistic about restarting his life, Nelson seems destined for failure. What is intriguing about *Rabbit at Rest* is how the Angstrom men– Harry, Nelson, and Nelson's son, Roy– are depicted as either frail, declining, weak, or whiny. In contrast, the women exhibit strength. Janice, with newly realized confidence and competence, has become more expressive and intelligent, and has begun a new career as a real estate broker. Inspired by her Florida women's group, the film *Working Girl*, and mentors like Mr. Lister and Charlie Stavros, she has acquired a business-woman's efficiency and is ready to pick up the pieces when her husband's health fails and her son falls into addiction. Pru and Judy, too, display a strength and confidence that gives them a superiority over their male counterparts, Nelson and Roy. Pru maintains order and stability within their family despite Nelson's recklessness, and Judy remains calm and helpful during the sailing outing when her grandfather suffers his heart attack. In Updike's America, women increasingly assume control and authority, though one could argue that in Harry's life women, beginning with his mother, have always been in control.

Like the earlier novels of the tetralogy, *Rabbit at Rest* chronicles Harry's continuing relationships with women. As Updike states,

> It would seem that the novels as a whole trace Rabbit's relations with
> the opposite sex, which have two principle aspects, the paternal and the
> erotic. In each novel– this much was a conscious decision– his sexual
> experience is deepened, his lifelong journey into the bodies of women

---

[77] A fictional account of this event, titled "The Parade," appears in *Odd Jobs* (New York: Knopf, 1991), 13-17.

is advanced. Fellatio, buggery– the sexual specifics are important, for
they mark the stages of a kind of somatic pilgrimage. . . .In *Rabbit at
Rest*, he has very little further to go, just a bit of incest and impotence,
while his old bed partners are joining the dead.[78]

Though sex plays a diminished role in *Rabbit at Rest*, the paternal and erotic merge
in Harry's incestuous encounter with Pru, a scene some reviewers found lacking in
credibility. Despite the outrageousness of the episode– as Janice says, "This is the
worst thing you've ever done, ever, ever" (393)– it seems believable. Harry's
behavior here reminds one of the impulsive, sexually desirous, and equally
outrageous Harry of *Rabbit, Run*. In addition, the possibility of something occurring
between Harry and Pru has been hinted at since *Rabbit Is Rich*, and further
suggestions appear early in *Rabbit at Rest* when Pru kisses her father-in-law "flush
on the mouth," and the narrator states, "She likes Harry and he likes her though they
have never found a way around all these others to express it" (10). Harry has long
been attracted to large women like his mother– Ruth, Annabelle, Pru– and in
drawing close to his equally unhappy daughter-in-law, he gets a taste once again of
"Paradise" (314).

Though most of the women from *Rabbit Is Rich*– Thelma, Annabelle, Cindy–
put in appearances in *Rabbit at Rest*, their roles have been greatly reduced,
signaling their physical decline as well as the decline of Harry's sex drive. Thelma,
with whom Harry has had an affair over the last decade, is now dying of lupus, and
her decay, as well as Harry's fear of sex since the advent of his heart attack,
dissolves their relationship. Annabelle, placed rather incredibly in the role of
Harry's nurse at the hospital in Brewer, no longer stirs Harry, who has lost his
energy and curiosity for her and her mother. Finally Cindy, Harry's former fantasy
woman, is now overweight, divorced, and no longer a part of their social scene,
which has also deteriorated since the prior novel. Besides Pru, Janice is the only
woman in the novel with whom Harry has a sexual relationship, and between them
there is a distance, as Harry resents her growing competence. As Updike states,
"He's increasingly found himself a kind of poor boy to her rich girl. And this is
galling, perhaps, and disheartening. His original credential, which was his own
body and athletic prowess, has become more and more tattered– whereas her little
credential, of Daddy having a car lot, has increased in value."[79]

An interesting feature of *Rabbit at Rest* is the increased identification that
occurs between Rabbit and the reader, who have now shared more than a thousand
pages and three decades worth of narrative memory. In this fourth novel Updike
plants more allusions to the earlier Rabbit novels. For instance, he makes several
comic references to the word *redux*, and he updates the reader on such previously
mentioned figures as the Dalai Lama and the Mousketeers. Furthermore, we see

---

[78] John Updike, "A 'Special Message' for the Franklin Library's First Edition
Society Printing of *Rabbit at Rest* (1990)," in *Odd Jobs*, 870.

[79] Charles Trueheart, "Sex, God and John Updike," *Washington Post*, 28
October 1990, F4.

how scenes and situations from earlier in Harry's life recur and offer him second chances. In the sailing episode with Judy, Harry grapples with the possibility of once again losing a girl to drowning– as if his life will repeat, in a kind of Nietzschean "eternal return," its most tragic event. However, on this occasion Harry redeems himself, much as Janice did by reviving Charlie Stavros in *Rabbit Redux*, and he returns safely to shore with Judy alive. Another familiar situation recurs late in the novel when Harry, feeling squeezed by domestic pressure, decides to run. Reacting instinctively, as he did at the beginning of *Rabbit, Run*, Harry gets into his car and heads south toward the sun. In the earlier novel, Harry failed to get past West Virginia, yet given this second chance he succeeds because he now knows the way and "has acquired the expertise and the money" to get there.[80] As Updike states, "There is a pattern in life whereby you do tend to complete motions that you begin," and so closure is given to an aborted passage from the past.[81]

The novel's conclusion brings us full circle, as the man once known for his running makes his final run south. There is a poignance and deliberateness to the novel's final 70 pages, as Updike describes Harry's last journey in great detail. Attention is given to the bad food Rabbit consumes, and his decision to gorge himself suggests his continued refusal to accept the limitations of his body. As Mary O'Connell states, "Rabbit has always understood limitation. . .as a diminishment of the self"; thus, his destructive eating represents an affirmation of the soul.[82] Yet one wonders whether there isn't something suicidal in Harry's actions. In *Rabbit, Run* Harry spoke of there being *"something that wants me to find it" (Run*, 110), and in this novel the passage is repeated, though the *"it"* now appears to refer to death (*Rest*, 122). One senses Harry is ready to die and is, perhaps, even trying to pursue death. Certainly his telephone calls to his grandchildren, packed with advice, suggest he is saying his final goodbyes.

The conclusion leads back to the event and form of play that began the 1,500-page tetralogy: a pickup basketball game. In the closing pages, while Hurricane Hugo threatens the coast, Harry wanders several times into a black neighborhood in Deleon that reminds him of his own middle-class childhood: "[T]his ignored part of Deleon is in some way familiar, he's been there before, before his life got too soft" (442). Drawn to a basketball court of "pale tamped earth" (443), Harry challenges a black youth named Tiger to a pickup game. As in *Beowulf*, the final episode of individual battle demonstrates that the hero's time has passed.

In the closing pages Updike gives Harry a deathbed scene that is neither maudlin nor cliché and strikes the proper human note to conclude his saga. In some ways the conclusion resembles that of Updike's first novel, *The Poorhouse Fair*, in which Hook, wishing to repair a wound by offering "a small word. . .[to] set

---

[80] Updike, Introduction to *Rabbit Angstrom, xx.*

[81] Bragg, "Forty Years of Middle America," 227.

[82] Mary O'Connell, *Updike and the Patriarchal Dilemma, 228.*

things right," cannot quite settle on the final "advice he must impart."[83] In *Rabbit at Rest* Harry, too, wishes to provide a final word of kindness and connection, to say something to his frantic and anxious son "to put the kid out of his misery" (466). He even tries to tell Nelson, "[*Y]ou have a sister*," but the communication is unsuccessful, just as Hook's mind is unable to land upon the right words of advice. Ultimately Rabbit is able to speak, and his final words to his son are ostensibly about dying, "[A]ll I can tell you is, it isn't so bad" (466). The primary difference between the endings of the two novels is that Hook, though not as near to death as Rabbit, remains overconscientious and troubled whereas Rabbit is more accepting and resigned. This difference reflects, perhaps, Updike's personal evolution from youth to late-middle age. The anxiety found in an early novel like *Rabbit, Run*, written by a man in his twenties, is transformed into the acceptance of *Rabbit at Rest*, although the tension is now passed on to Rabbit's son.

Adding to the impact of the conclusion is that Updike does not sanctify or exalt the deathbed scene; instead he allows comedy to seep in, as he has throughout the tetralogy. When Janice realizes that with Harry gone she can now sell the Penn Park house, she prays, "*Dear God, dear God. Do what You think best*" (464). And when Nelson begins his visit by complaining to his father, Harry thinks, "*O.K., what else am I doing wrong?*" (465). Finally, the novel concludes, like the other Rabbit volumes, on an open note, a chord of ambiguity: "[B]ut enough. Maybe. Enough" (466). There remains the possibility, however unlikely, that Harry is not dead, that he may someday return in a future sequel. *Rabbit Resurrected.*

Rabbit at Rest, in many ways represents Updike's farewell: to his mother, who died two weeks after he completed the novel's first draft; to Harry, his most successful and memorable character; and to Pennsylvania and his mother's family farm, which he was forced to sell. That the author's mother was aging and dying while he composed the novel seems to account for its strongly elegiac tone and texture, and certainly his visits to her in the hospital shaped the hospital scenes of *Rabbit at Rest*. Even the naming of Deleon stands as a tribute to his mother, as Ponce de León, the first European to reach Florida, was "the hero of a frequently revised and never-published novel" that his mother had written.[84]

Finally, *Rabbit at Rest* brings us full circle in a way that relates back to Updike's original plan for *Rabbit, Run* and *The Centaur*, which were to be companion novels that would "illustrate the polarity between running and plodding, between the rabbit and the horse, between the life of instinctual gratification and that of dutiful self-sacrifice."[85] Yet as Updike observes in 1995, "Rabbit, in his near-elderly, grandpaternal condition, more and more talked. . . like George Caldwell in *The Centaur*. My two projected novellas had merged: the dodgy rabbit

---

[83] John Updike, *The Poorhouse Fair* (New York: Knopf, c 1959, 1977), 185.

[84] Updike, "Special Message for *Rabbit at Rest*," 871.

[85] John Updike, "A 'Special Message' to purchasers of the Franklin Library limited edition, in 1977, of *Rabbit, Run*," in *Hugging the Shore*, 849-50.

had become the suffering horse; the man of impulse and appetite had aged into humorous stoicism."[86] Perhaps just as important, one realizes that the tetralogy, completed when Updike was 58, continued to be influenced and shaped by the two people who generated such a presence in his early fiction: his mother and father.

*James A. Schiff, "Rabbit at Rest: The Seed of Death Within." *John Updike Revisited.* New York Twayne Publishers, 1998: 56-65.

From *John Updike and the Cold War*

D. Quentin Miller*

Harry and Janice declare a sort of truce with one another at the end of *Rabbit Redux*, but his competitive instinct must find an outlet. In *Rabbit Is Rich* he transfers this instinct away from Janice and throws himself into the business of making money. His competition is more individualized now, pitting him against his golfing friends as opposed to his wife. He has unconsciously replicated the "kitchen debate" of his youth, amassing the comforts and appliances that herald American prosperity. He takes this pursuit to its grotesque extreme when he spreads gold Krugerrands across his bed and makes love to Janice on top of them (Rich 200-203). An over-abundance of money itself in its most garish form– gold coins– appears to have made the struggles of Harry's life worthwhile. British journalist and social commentator Godfrey Hodgson writes of a "consensus mood" in American culture, which becomes the "dominant American ideology" by 1960, the year *Rabbit, Run* was published; the two notable qualities of this consensus mood, he writes, are that Americans became "Confident to the verge of complacency about the perfectibility of American society, anxious to the point of paranoia about the threat of communism." Hodgson sees this ideology emerge from the discovery of the simple fact that "Capitalism, after all, seemed to work,"[21] while communism led to economic woes. He points to the way American economists put a new spin on the ideas of John Maynard Keynes– that capitalism worked best when combined with aggressive governmental spending and competition– after postwar economic success in the 1940s.

Updike affirms the neo-Keynesian viewpoint as late in the Cold War as 1989, writing that the economic conditions of the superpowers during the Cold War did not render them "six of one and a half-dozen of the other. It was more like eleven of one and one of the other. It was Athens and Sparta, light and shadow. Ours was the distinctly better mousetrap" (SC 139). To see Updike's view of the necessity of

---

[86] Updike, Introduction to *Rabbit Angstrom*, xxii.

[21] Godfrey Hodgson, *America during the Cold War*, 74, 75.

global competition strictly in economic terms would be reductive; yet there is something resonant about the way many of Updike's characters approach their lives in general, but more specifically the idea that American capitalism is competing with Soviet communism for more than just global stability in the nuclear age. Updike's generation believed to varying degrees that America was superior to its global counterpart in terms of the lifestyle of its citizens as well as the strength of its military. Hodgson sums up the essential elements of the predominant ideology of Updike's generation as follows: "the optimism, the confidence that more means better, the faith in the harmony of interests between capitalism and social progress, the cankerous sense that all this must be related to the competition with communism."[22] Harry Angstrom's behavior throughout the Rabbit tetralogy reflects this philosophy exactly; his struggle to gain and maintain power– whether on the basketball court, in the bedroom, or as a functioning member of his local community– is motivated by a strong belief in competition as the mans to success and well-being, and his conservative views on communism bear out and largely explain this competitive instinct.

Harry certainly seems more content, less flappable, and less in danger in *Rabbit Is Rich* than in the previous two novels in the tetralogy. His relative wealth and level of social comfort allows him to transfer the global pressure exerted by the Cold War from his relationship to Janice to his place in the community. Gradually, though, this competition is transferred back to his family, but this time it is directed toward Nelson. Just as America has retreated in order to focus on its own problems in the late 1970s, Harry tries to exist as though he can "go it alone," eliminating from his mind any troubling thoughts from outside his insulated little world. Just before the scene in which he makes love to Janice on top of the gold coins, he meditates on Nelson, concluding, "To hell with this scruffy kid. Rabbit has decided to live for himself" (Rich 199). This isolation from his son can only be temporary despite Harry's efforts to run from Nelson or to set up blockades against him. Similarly, awareness that America's ongoing conflict with the Soviet Union is still very much alive creeps into Harry's consciousness at various times. To a young couple wanting to buy a car early in the novel, he backs off temporarily from his determined sales pitch, claiming, "It's still a free country, the Commies haven't gotten any further than Cambodia" (Rich 14). Underlying this seemingly meaningless banter is the fear that it is still possible for America to fall to communism; Harry's use of the word "Commies" intensifies this sense of fear, as it is a word associated with the paranoia of McCarthy-era rhetoric, and the very word he used to intimidate Jill in *Rabbit Redux*. His use of the word "still" also indicates a lingering fear that America must keep up its guard against communist infiltration. The link between Harry's perception of the Carter years and of the 1950s is later made explicit: "Carter is smart as a whip and prays a great deal but his gift seems to be the old Eisenhower one of keeping much from happening, just a little daily seepage" (Rich 117). This idea is both a comfort and a bane to Harry; coupled with the absence of a direct threat to global stability, which characterized

---

[22] Ibid., 81.

the Kennedy years, is the notion that a threat is seeping into the American landscape, definitely and steadily, toward some inevitable end.

Harry's friends in *Rabbit Is Rich* cling to the notion that the world behind the Iron Curtain must continue to be stigmatized; Buddy Inglefinger believes that "in countries like East Germany or China they're pumping these athletes full of steroids, like beef cattle, they're hardly human" (Rich 53). Inglefinger expresses a typical American perception of Soviet athletes during the early 1980s, rendered heavy-handedly in media images and films like the propagandistic *Rocky IV* in which the American boxing hero, literally wrapped in the American flag, defeats his Soviet opponent who has been made inhuman through countless steroid injections. Athletic competition with the Soviet Union was prevented the year before *Rabbit Is Rich* was published when President Carter canceled U. S. participation in the 1980 Moscow Olympics due to Soviet military involvement in Afghanistan. The atmosphere during the late Carter years was tense due to the renewal of such showdowns between the superpowers; one unnamed Carter administration official declared in 1980, "this is the Cold War in the most classic, extreme form."[23] After making his pronouncement about Russian athletes, Inglefinger has no problem transferring old Cold War rhetoric to the new Cold War situation: "Jesus, those Arabs," he says, "Wouldn't it be bliss just to nuke 'em all?" (Rich 159). Buddy later treats Harry and his friends to a banal pun about a Russian ballet dancer who defected to the United States "because Communism wasn't Goodunov" (Rich 168). The presence of Buddy and his old-fashioned xenophobic attitudes in the novel signals a lingering paranoia in Harry's world, as well as a tinge of fear about America's economic slide, which Harry uses as a metaphor for his fear that he will fall from the position of power that he has attained; he muses, "Get out of it in this society and you're as good as dead, an embarrassment. Not Goodunov" (Rich 168). Competition is still the core of Harry's philosophy of success, and even when the Soviet Union and its global allies do not provide an immediate threat to American hegemony, they seem to lurk in the margins of Harry's consciousness, ready to take over if America falters. To Americans at this time the nation's primary weakness was its fragile economy, so Harry fights this battle by getting rich.

As is the case with many of the protagonists of Updike's 1970s novels, Harry in *Rabbit Is Rich* is trapped by nostalgia, and resents this quality in himself when Janice points it out to him: "It stung him, that she thinks he lives in the past" (Rich 229). Immediately after this realization, he "switches on the radio to shut off their conversation," and he hears about "Soviet tanks patrolling the streets of Kabul in the wake of last Sunday's mysterious change of leadership in Afghanistan" (Rich 229). Harry's resistance to being caught in the past is coupled with the sense that the past, at least in terms of the Cold War, has parallels in the present. His ideas about competition and about the Cold War have essentially not changed since the late 1950s; "he pulls for the Rams [to win the Super Bowl] the way he does for the Afghan rebels against the Soviet military machine" (Rich 435). He proclaims, in his support of the long-shot football team and the Afghan rebels, that "he doesn't

---

[23] Bernard A. Weisberger, *Cold War, Cold Peace*, 292.

like overdogs," but in the case of Afghanistan, he would also be uncomfortable if the Russians were to exert power successfully.

It is obvious to the reader, if not to Harry, that the Cold War in 1979 resembles the old Cold War only on the surface. The new enemy of middle-class America, according to Harry's coworker (and Janice's former lover) Charlie Stavros, is Big Oil, an extension of OPEC, which represents the new area of countries with divided loyalties between the United States and the Soviet Union. The narrator notes that a riot over gasoline on television "looks like old films of Vietnam or Budapest but it is Levittown right down the road" (Rich 44). The connection between the suburban gasoline riots and former Cold War battlefields is subtle, yet terrifying for Harry, who still retains his crucial need for space around him– a concept he developed in relation to Vietnam in *Rabbit Redux*– and his need to feel as if he can still compete. Like other Americans, Harry in 1979 feels strongly about America's inability to do anything about the hostages in Iran or about the angry Iranians who could be seen on the nightly news desecrating the American flag. It is evident from Updike's "Notes and Comment" pieces from the late 1950s that mainstream Americans believed the way to counter Soviet achievements was to revel in the triumphs of American culture. Having been raised on that paradigm, Harry fights back by making money. But like the 1950s quiz shows, there is something false about the way Harry achieves his wealth. He is no more satisfied with his job as a car salesman than he was with his job as a Magipeel (sic) salesman in *Rabbit, Run* or as a linotype setter in *Rabbit Redux*. Moreover, he has essentially inherited this job and the money that accompanies it from Janice's father. Finally, he amasses his wealth on gold speculation, the purest gamble and the most fleeting and illusory form of wealth.

Despite the relative bliss of Harry's world in this novel, then, things may not be what they seem. Updike believed that America would pay a price for its blithe dismissal of the quiz show scandals, and he also believed that Harry would have to pay a price for becoming rich on the inflationary fears of others. That price comes not in the form of a devastated marriage but rather in the form of a ruined son.[24] The fourth section of the book begins bluntly with a reaction to the crisis in Iran: "The hostages have been taken," and is followed immediately by, "Nelson has been working at Springer Motors for five weeks" (Rich 292), as though these two events are directly related to one another. There is, of course, no causal relationship between the two, but in Harry's mind, hiring Nelson has been catastrophic, as much of a criss as the taking of political hostages in the new battleground of the Cold War. Harry has spent the majority of the novel avoiding both the global crisis and the deep problems that exist in his family, and the two crises resurface at the same moment. The old Cold War solution of making money works for Harry, but since he has dismissed the perspective of the younger generation in *Rabbit Redux* he has yet to account for the complexities of the new Cold War.

Harry makes a weak, narcissistic effort to care about his son, declaring,

---

[24] See D. Quentin Miller, "Updike's Rabbit Novels and the Tragedy of Parenthood," 195-216.

"You're too much me" (Rich 194). There are many ways in which they are alike, of course, in that Nelson impregnates a woman and tries to run from his responsibilities, but these comparisons are to the young Harry of *Rabbit, Run*. Nelson and Harry may be the same type of man, but they are from different generations. As a young man Harry had a completely different context for the way he thought about the world. His relatively simple version of the way the world works cannot be compared to Nelson, who grew up during the turbulent 1960s and was exposed to profound turmoil when Janice moved out and Jill and Skeeter moved in. Nelson has no idea of the larger ramifications of the hostage crisis, and no insight into its effect on his life or his new career at Springer Motors; he muses, "This Iranian thing is going to scare gas prices even higher but it'll blow over, they won't dare keep them long, the hostages" (Rich 297). Yet something bothers Nelson about the hostage situation, as though he senses the threat of another empire to his existence despite the fact that he was not indoctrinated in the Cold War the way Harry was. Nelson recognizes his own fear, using an image similar to Kenneth's perception of Khrushchev's visit in "Dear Alexandros" ("like swallowing a penny"): "[Nelson] thinks of those hostages in Tehran and its like a pill caught in his throat" (Rich 298). His earlier thought that the hostage crisis will not last long is undermined by this fear, and he reacts accordingly: "Drop a little tactical A-bomb on a minaret as a calling card" (Rich 298). We see evidence here that the Cold War affects Nelson's generation in much the same way that it affected Harry's generation, as represented by Buddy Inglefinger. There is an illusion of national solidarity shared by the two generations demonstrated by Nelson's and Buddy's desire to flex America's nuclear muscle against Iran, a Soviet ally. However, the differences in perspective between the younger and older generations (made evident in the late 1960s) simmer dangerously under the nation's surface. The hostage crisis bogs down into the same type of standoff that occurred with failed negotiations in earlier decades; the news in *Rabbit Is Rich* becomes in Harry's mind "the latest version of nothing happening. Khomeini and Carter both trapped by a pack of kids who need a shave and don't know shit" (Rich 331). Harry tries to blame the standoff (like everything else) on the new generation, and it is clear that he regards this generation as his new enemy, with Nelson as its point man.

Despite some superficial similarities between Nelson and Harry, their differences underscore how dramatically the early Cold War consensus has broken down. Their opposite interpretations of the new Cold War build into a crisis at a rare scene in which the two actually talk to one another. The generational differences between the father and the son have always been a point of contention between them, but in this scene their differences are contextualized specifically in terms of the Cold War. Harry is on the verge of firing his son as a car salesman; he begins the conversation by talking about basketball, the game from his youth that he still holds dear, even though he admits, "it's changed a lot since my day." Nelson's reaction to the conversation is, "Basketball is all goons, if you ask me" (Rich 353). Harry senses that the discussion is off to a poor start and switches to politics; he begins,

> "What do you think about those Russkis in Afghanistan? They sure
> gave themselves a Christmas present."

"It's stupid," Nelson says. "I mean, Carter's getting all upset. It's no worse that what we did in Vietnam, it's not even as bad because at least it's right next door and they've had a puppet government there for years."

"Puppet governments are O. K., huh?"

"Well, *everybody* has 'em. All of South America is our puppet governments."

"I bet that'd be news to the spics."

"At least the Russians, Dad, *do* it when they're going to do it. We *try* to do it and then everything gets all bogged down in politics. We can't do *any*thing anymore."

"Well not with people talking like you we can't," Harry says to his son. "How would you feel about going over and fighting in Afghanistan?" (Rich 353-54)

Nelson, who came of age during Vietnam when the new Cold War began, laughs off Harry's question and says, "Dad, I'm a married man. And way past draft age besides" (Rich 354). Harry is startled by this response, first because he himself "doesn't feel too old to fight" and second because he was prepared to go to Korea when he was in the army during the early Cold War. He reminisces about the "straight-on way of looking at the world" (Rich 353) that characterized his time in the army. The distance between them is evident; Harry belligerently addresses his son as "people like you" as if he is back discussing Vietnam with Charlie Stavros in *Rabbit Redux*. He accuses Nelson of getting married to avoid going to war and Nelson replies, "There won't be any next war, Carter will make a lot of noise but wind up letting them have it, just like he's letting Iran have the hostages. Actually, Billy Fosnacht was saying the only way we'll get the hostages back is if Russia invades Iran. Then they'd give us the hostages and sell us the oil because they need our wheat" (Rich 354). Harry uses this opportunity to voice his negative opinion of Billy Fosnacht, and a confrontation ensues about the fateful night when Jill died in the house fire. As he becomes heated Harry feels "his heart rising to what has become a confrontation" (Rich 354) with his son just as he hopefully felt his heart "lift off" in *Rabbit Redux* as he prepared to fight against Janice. Even though Harry has recently demonstrated his nostalgia for the past, his advice to Nelson is, "You got to let it go, kid. Your mother and me have let it go. . . .The past is the past" (Rich 355). Since Harry returns to the past when it is more appealing than the present, his advice to Nelson is inconsistent and perhaps insincere, just one of many instances when he effectively dismisses his son. Nelson's troubled presence in Harry's life is testimony to the fact that the world is more complex than Harry allows, and the "straight-on way of looking at the world" that characterized his youth is only a temporary defense against the difficulties of the present. As in the previous novel of the tetralogy, Nelson disappears at the end of this one and Harry seems happy enough to be isolated, crowing, "Fuck the Russkis. . . .We'll go it alone, from sea to shining sea" (Rich 436). His will to withdraw despite his competitive instinct emphasizes how poorly he has adapted to changes in the Cold War world. Nelson's disappearance is only temporary; neither personal nor global conflicts have been truly resolved.

Even so, Harry's competitive instinct is perfectly understandable in terms of his Cold War upbringing, which fostered a deeply ingrained belief that America is a better place, in terms of military power and economic health, because of its rivalry with the Soviet Union. Yet since marriages and family relationships deteriorate in Updike's fiction as a direct result of the competitive instincts exhibited by his patriarchal protagonists like Harry, we can conclude that competition for its own sake does not lead to happiness. At some level, the object of the competition becomes less clear. If Americans were trying to demonstrate the superiority of their lifestyle through the promulgation of happy, well-apportioned (sic) homes, then why are those homes the sites of so much despair in Updike's fiction? It is clear from these stories and novels that the competitive global structure was not meant to infiltrate the domestic sphere, but there was no way to stop it. The tension between the global power structure and the mistranslation of this structure into the private worlds of characters is often at the heart of Updike's fiction, especially during the middle period of his writings– the period spanned by the two middle novels in the Rabbit tetralogy. The threat is heightened by the division of public opinion during Vietnam, the subject of my next chapter. Though theoretical competition with the global "other" put pressure on the fragile domestic sphere in Updike's writing, America's divisive response to actual competition in the mysterious jungles of Vietnam threatened to shatter it altogether.

*D. Quentin Miller. *John Updike and the Cold War*. Columbia (Mo): University of Missouri Press, 2001: 63-71.

Rabbit Angstrom

"Why Rabbit Had to Go"

John Updike*

Rabbit at Rest will be the fourth and last of my so-called Rabbit books. Each of them occurs in the ninth year of a decade, and was written, more or less, in the ninth year of the decade.

The first one, *Rabbit, Run*, was written in 1959 with no thought of there being a sequel. It was composed by a youngish man, 27 I believe I was, who had received a Guggenheim grant by promising to write a novel– hence, having accepted the grant, I felt obliged to write the book. I had published one previous, quite short novel, *The Poorhouse Fair*. My sense of myself was of a sort of sprinter. My name, if known, was known by way of contributions to *The New Yorker* magazine. My original concept had been to write two novellas, to be bound into one volume, which would contrast two approaches to the game of life: one would be the rabbit approach, a kind of dodgy approach– spontaneous, unreflective, frightened, hence my character's name, Angstrom– and the second was to be the horse method of coping with life, to get into harness and pull your load until you drop. And this was eventually *The Centaur*. But I began the rabbit book first.

It was subtitled, in my conception of it, "A Movie"; I imagined the opening scene as something that would happen behind credits, and I saw the present tense of the book as corresponding to the present tense in which we experience the cinema. There is no real past in the movies; things happen, one after the other, right there in front of us. The present tense, in the late 50's, was not at all a common device in American fiction. The only instance that I had encountered was in a novel by Joyce Cary, the British writer, called *Mister Johnson*, about an African civil servant. I don't know if it's remembered or forgotten, but it's a wonderful book, one of the best novels about Africa– certainly one of the best books written by a white man about Africa that there is. I have been told since that Damon Runyon wrote in the present tense, but for me Joyce Cary opened the door.

I discovered as I began to write how delicious the present tense is. Instead of writing "she said and he said"it's "he says and she says," and not "he jumped" at some past moment, but "he jumps," right now in front of you. Action takes on a wholly different, flickering quality; thought and feeling and event are brought much closer together.

And so the present tense proved to be a happy one and I wrote on and on in a little room in the corner of East Street and County Road in Ipswich, Mass., a town I'd moved to in an attempt to get away from the charms and distractions of New York City. I was there provisionally, seeing if I could be a freelance writer. I had had a job in New York, I had done my New York thing, I could tell Uptown from Downtown, I had undergone the Manhattan initiation rites that writers should undergo, and was up in New England experimentally, out on a limb as it were. I sat in that little room, the old sewing room, looking out at a very complex telephone pole, and the excitement of writing a novel was so great for me that my feet, in scuffing, wore two bare spots in the floor, which might still be there.

Anyway, I completed the book; it was indeed a full-length book, too full-length to include with the horse novel, which I then made into another separate book. And that of course is the way we accumulate a shelf of books, every idea subdivides and becomes two and then four, and in that manner you can have written 37 books and not have had very many ideas.

Rabbit, Run was published, with mild sales, fair reviews. People asked me about the ending; they found it ambiguous. What really happened? The hero is last seen running. I thought that Rabbit's immersion in the blind act of running was a sufficient ending for the novel; it didn't occur to me we needed to know more about this man.

But the decade passed, a decade that brought me good news and bad, and that brought the country a lot of news. The 60's were an exceedingly newsworthy decade, from John F. Kennedy's assassination on. A lot of things happened, things that were more or less distressing to Americans older than 30.

I had written a book called *Couples*, which had sold enough to make me feel entitled to write a long poem, all about myself, under the false impression that that would be interesting to people. But I made the useful discovery that in fact an author is interesting only as a storyteller, only as the conduit whereby certain imaginary events get onto the page. And so my long poem about myself, called "Midpoint," fell quietly into the void– more quietly than a stone down a well, which at least does make a sort of little plip.

It was then my notion to complete a kind of Pennsylvania tetralogy. I'd written a book that took place in the future, *The Poorhouse Fair*, one that took place in the immediate present, *Rabbit, Run*, one that took place in the remembered past, *The Centaur*, and I wanted to write a historical novel about James Buchanan, Pennsylvania's only President– a fascinating man, at least to me. I did so much research I began to dream about him. One day I woke up and told my wife, "James Buchanan is my best friend."

Well, it was one thing to fall in love with James Buchanan but another to try to write a historical novel. I found that I couldn't bring myself to do all the fakery necessary in writing a historical novel. Never having lived in a log cabin, I found myself inhibited about describing one; never having participated in a Washington 19th-century political parley, I found myself at a loss to imagine exactly what went on. Even things like buggies and spittoons loomed as mysterious. So I found myself balked in the attempt to write the Buchanan novel and I finally made it into a play, putting upon the director and the set designer all these difficult particulars that eluded me.

By now it was high time for me to write a novel. I had made a deal with myself at the beginning of this freelance career I've spoken of: I would give my publishers, to make up for the loses they'd suffered on the intervening books, a novel every other book, with collections of something or other in between. So the rhythm would go, presumably, loss, small gain, loss, small gain. It was novel time, and Buchanan hadn't worked out as a hero.

And there was all this distress around me– Vietnam distress, race riots, marches, agitation of all sorts. Suddenly it seemed to me that Rabbit Angstrom of Pennsylvania, about whose future some people had expressed curiosity, might be the vehicle in which to package some of the American unease that was raging all around us. And so I wrote *Rabbit Redux*. It felt good to be back in the present tense and good to try to locate in this small section of southeastern Pennsylvania echoes and ramifications of the national and international disturbances that were so preoccupying in the late 60's.

Having composed, then, one sequel, and having had the sequel fairly well received, obliged me, it seemed, to write another; one sequel leads to another. A motive of the artistic life, after all, is the completion of sets. That childhood instinct we have to make collections, to tidy up and round out, affects adult enterprises as well.

But in the meantime, I had a whole decade to live, on my own track. People would ask me, "What's Harry doing?" as though he was a real person, but I had no idea what he was doing. For one thing, I lived in Massachusetts and he was living in Pennsylvania. I didn't even know he'd become a car dealer.

When the time came, when 1979 came– each novel, by the way, was written in a different house, as it turned out, at a different address– I was in a different town, I had a different wife, a different sense of myself. I was full of beans, really, looking back on it from my present relatively beanless condition. I was in my mid-40's, just a kid. The town we lived in, I should say, was away from the sea and in size and social atmosphere reminded me of the town in Pennsylvania, Shillington, that I had grown up in. The house was even the same shape– long and narrow, with a deep backyard. From the room I wrote in, I saw rows of yellow school buses. I was at home in America, all right.

I needed a hook, into 1979. I mean, what can you say? Although the first novel had had a few overheard news items in it, it wasn't really in a conscious way about the 50's. It just was a product of the 50's; it was a helplessly 50's kind of book written by a sort of helplessly 50's guy. The 60's were much more self-conscious, much more conscious of themselves as a decade. The 70's seemed somewhat amorphous.

But we happened to be in Pennsylvania, staying with some friends of my wife's, and it was June, and there was some anxiety about our getting away because there were terrible gas lines all over the state. And my host was so hostly, or else so keen on our departure, that he rose very early in the morning and got in my car and went and waited in a gas line to get me gas to get out of there. So the gas crunch became my hook: running out of gas, which is the first phrase in *Rabbit Is Rich*. The general sense of exhaustion, inflation, Jimmy Carter's fainting during one of his trots– all that seemed to add up to a national picture.

The paradox was that although the theme was running out of gas, I was feeling pretty good. And so the book is kind of an upbeat book in spite of itself. It's really a cheerful book, very full, it seems to me insofar as I can be a critic, of itself and its material. I really had to cut it short at the end– it was threatening to go on forever. Tennyson said what he wanted was a novel that would go on forever, but it's not what I want. So I moved briskly to the arrival of Angstrom's granddaughter in his arms; the book is really about his becoming a grandfather, written years before I myself became one. He is rich in a number of ways, and discovers of course that to be rich is just another way of being poor, that your needs expand with your income and the world eventually takes away what it gives.

But it's a big, basically bouncy book that won prizes. Why some books win prizes and others don't is a mystery. In part it was that by this time, I'd been around so long, and was obviously working so hard, that people felt sorry for me and furthermore hoped that if Rabbit and I received a prize we would go away and put an end to this particular episode in American letters. But no, I've felt obliged to produce a fourth!

Again, I groped for the hook. It was quite easy to have a blank mind about the 80's; there was a distinct fuzziness about it. It was Ronald Reagan's decade and very cool, in the McLuhanesque sense, and all I really knew was that my hero would be 10 years older and probably feeling no better than I did, and maybe even a little worse– since he had peaked earlier than I did. I saw him in Florida. I thought a new state might perk up Rabbit readers. The Updikes– a branch of them, my father's brother and sister– went down to Florida in the 1920's when their own father, my grandfather, became ill with tuberculosis, and so Florida has some personal relevancy for me– a warm spot in my heart, you might say. Also, my mother for almost as long as I knew her had been trying to write a novel about the discoverer of Florida, Ponce de León. So I made some trips, in 1988 I think it must have been, to gather background.

I couldn't wait to begin the book; the opening of it occurs late in 1988, after the Presidential election and just after the crash of Pan Am Flight 103 in Lockerbie. In writing, I several times had to stop to let real time catch up with my fictional time. The private events are the main thing, of course, but you don't want some public event, atomic war or a giant earthquake, to cancel the world and make everything anachronistic. A few months after I began, in April of 1989, my mother was hospitalized, and from then on I had to keep making trips to Pennsylvania to check on things. I had a hard time keeping momentum, and noticed in rereading, even on the last set of proofs, some repetitions and inconsistencies.

You might say it's a depressed book about a depressed man, written by a depressed man. Deciding to wind up the series was a kind of death for me. Even though I left Pennsylvania in the early 50's, as long as my parents were alive I had a living link with the state. My father died in 1972 but my mother lived on, and so I had continuing reasons to visit Rabbit's territory, to refresh my sense of it and check up on changes. But as she became older I saw that my link would end someday, and end with it my grip on Rabbit's world. My mother died in October, 10 days after I finished the first draft; her dying became interwoven with my own sense of aging and my hero's even more severe sense of aging.

Yet all those visits, to her in the hospital and out of it– I hadn't had such a strong dose of my native turf since leaving it for college. My fictional city of Brewer is, I guess it's no secret to say, based on Reading, in Berks County. And though I was raised in a suburb of Reading, I had never lived there, and putting Rabbit into Brewer in *Rabbit, Run* was actually an act of fantasy, something like the country of Kush in *The Coup*, and I got the geography all scrambled up, and it's all rather vague and, as it seemed to me at the time, enchanted. In *Rabbit at Rest* it's less vague– the area at last, in my taking leave of it, began to make sense.

Another reason for winding up: I felt that if I was going to make a kind of meganovel out of the series, and bring all the threads to a gathering, four novels was about the limit. We've all heard of tetralogies, but after that there's no word for it. And with sequels, there is an accumulation of loose threads, of characters you invented and used, so that the elements increase geometrically, and beyond four would become very messy. Even so, each Rabbit book has been longer than the preceding, and this is the longest.

The action ends in October; I used Hurricane Hugo to round out the climax, but of course the events that now seem important about 1989– the collapse of Communism in Eastern Europe– occurred quite late in the year. But Rabbit feels them coming– at one point he asks himself, "if there's no Cold War, what's the point of being an American?" His sense of being useless, of being pushed to one side by his wife and son, has this political dimension, then. Like me, he has lived his adult life in the context of the cold war. He was in the Army, ready to go to Korea, hawkish on Vietnam, proud of the moon shot, and in some sense always justified, at the back of his mind, by a concept of freedom, of America, that took sharpness from contrast with Communism. If that contrast is gone, then that's another reason to put him, regretfully, to rest in 1990.

*John Updike, "Why Rabbit Had to Go." *The New York Times Book Review* 8 Aug. 1990: 1, 24-25.

"Introduction," from *Rabbit Angstrom*

John Updike*

The United states, democratic and various though it is, is not an easy country for a fiction-writer to enter: the slot between the fantastic and the drab seems too narrow. An outsiderish literary stance is traditional; such masterpieces as *Moby-Dick* and *Huckleberry Finn* deal with marginal situations and eccentric, rootless characters; many American writers have gone into exile to find subjects of a congenial color and dignity. The puritanism and practicality of the early settlers imposed a certain enigmatic dullness, it may be, upon the nation's affective life and social texture.

The minimization of class distinctions suppressed one of the articulating elements of European fiction, and a close, delighted grasp of the psychology of sexual relations– so important in French and English novels– came slowly amid the New World's austerities. Insofar as a writer can take an external view of his own work, my impression is that the character of Harry 'Rabbit' Angstrom was for me a way in– a ticket to the America all around me. What I saw through Rabbit's eyes was more worth telling than what I saw through my own, though the difference was often slight; his life, less defended and logocentric than my own, went places mine could not. As a phantom of my imagination, he was always, as the contemporary expression has it, *there* for me, willing to generate imagery and motion. He kept alive my native sense of wonder and hazard.

A writer's task is not to describe his work but to call it into being. Of these four related novels, I know principally– and that by the fallible light of recollection– what went into them, what stimuli and ambitions and months of labor. Each was composed at the end of a decade and published at the beginning of the next one; they became a kind of running report on the state of my hero and his nation, and their ideal reader became a fellow-American who had read and remembered the previous novels about Rabbit Angstrom. At some point between the second and third of the series, I began to visualize four novels that might together make a single coherent volume, a mega-novel. Now, thanks to Everyman's Library, this volume exists, titled, as I had long hoped, with the name of the protagonist, an everyman who, like all men, was unique and mortal.

Rabbit, Run was begun, early in 1959, with no thought of a sequel. Indeed, it was not yet clear to me, though I had one short novel to my credit, that I was a novelist at all. At the age of twenty-seven I was a short-story writer by trade, a poet and light-versifier on the side, and an ex-reporter for *The New Yorker*. I had come, two yeas before, to New England to try my luck at freelancing. *Rabbit, Run* at first was modestly conceived as a novella, to form with another, *The Centaur*, a biune study of complementary moral types: the rabbit and the horse, the zigzagging creature of impulse and the plodding beast of stoic duty. *Rabbit* took off; as I sat at a little upright desk in a small corner room of the first house I owned, in Ipswich, Massachusetts, writing in soft pencil, the present-tense sentences accumulated and acquired momentum. It was a seventeenth-century house with a soft pine floor, and my kicking feet, during those excited months of composition, wore two bare spots in the varnish. The handwritten draft was completed, I noted at the end, on 11 September 1959. I typed it up briskly and sent it off to my publisher just as the decade ended and headed, with my family, to the then-remote Caribbean island of Anguilla.

There, after some weeks of tropical isolation, I received a basically heartening letter from my publisher, Alfred A. Knopf himself, indicating acceptance with reservations. The reservations turned out to be (he could tell me this only face to face, so legally touchy was the matter) sexually explicit passages that might land us– this was suggested with only a glint of irony– in jail. Books were still banned in Boston in those days; no less distinguished an author than Edmund Wilson had been successfully prosecuted, in New York State in 1946, for *Memoirs of Hecate County*. My models in sexual realism had been Wilson and D. H. Lawrence and

Erskine Caldwell and James M. Cain and of course James Joyce, whose influence resounds, perhaps all too audibly, in the book's several female soliloquies. Not wishing, upon reflection, to lose the publisher who made the handsomest books in America, and doubting that I could get a more liberal deal elsewhere, I did, while sitting at the elbow of a young lawyer evidently expert in this delicate area, consent to a number of excisions– not always the ones I would have expected. It was, I thought, a tactful and non-fatal operation. The American edition appeared toward the end of 1960 without legal incident; in England, Victor Gollancz asked for still more cuts and declined to publish the Knopf text as it was, but the youthful firm of André Deutsch did. The dirty-word situation was changing rapidly, with the legally vindicated publication of Lawrence's *Lady Chatterley's Lover* and Henry Miller's *Tropic of Cancer*. Censorship went from retreat to rout, and when I asked Penguin Books, late in 1962, if I could make some emendations and restorations for their edition, they permissively consented. For ten pages a day that winter, sitting in a rented house in Antibes, France, I went through *Rabbit, Run*, restoring the cuts and trying to improve the prose throughout. The text was the one that appeared in the Modern Library and eventually in Knopf hardcover; I have made a few further corrections and improvements for this printing. *Rabbit, Run*, in keeping with its jittery, indecisive protagonist, exists in more forms than any other novel of mine.

Yet my intent was simple enough: to show a high-school athletic hero in the wake of his glory days. My father had been a high-school teacher, and one of his extra-curricular duties was to oversee the ticket receipts for our basketball games. Accompanying him, then, at home and away, I saw a great deal of high-school basketball, and a decade later was still well imbued with its heroics, as they are thumpingly, sweatily enacted in the hotly lit intimacy of jam-packed high-school gymnasiums. Our Pennsylvania town of Shillington was littered, furthermore, with the wrecks of former basketball stars, and a thematically kindred short story, `Ace in the Hole', and poem, `Ex-Basketball Player', had preceded Rabbit into print:

> Once Flick played for the high-school team, the Wizards.
> He was good: in fact, the best. In '46
> He bucketed three hundred ninety points,
> A county record still. The ball loved Flick.
> I saw him rack up thirty-eight or forty
> In one home game. His hands were like wild birds.

To this adolescent impression of splendor my adult years had added sensations of domestic interdependence and claustrophobia. Jack Kerouac's *On the Road* came out in 1957 and, without reading it, I resented its apparent instruction to cut loose; *Rabbit, Run* was meant to be a realistic demonstration of what happens when a young American family man goes on the road- the people left behind get hurt. There was no painless dropping out of the Fifties' fraying but still tight social weave. Arriving at so prim a moral was surely not my only intention: the book ends on an ecstatic, open note that was meant to stay open, as testimony to our heart's stubborn amoral quest for something once called grace. The title can be read as a piece of advice. (My echo of a British music show tune from 1939, by Noel Gay and Ralph Butler, was unintentional; just recently I was given the sheet music of `Run, Rabbit, - Run!' and read the lyrics' injunction `Don't give the farmer his fun,

fun, fun./ He'll get by without his rabbit pie.')

The present tense was a happy discovery for me. It has fitfully appeared in English -language fiction– Damon Runyon used it in his tough tall tales, and Dawn Powell in the mid-Thirties has a character observe, 'It was an age of the present tense, the stevedore style.' But I had encountered it only in Joyce Cary's remarkable *Mister Johnson,* fifteen or so years after its publication in 1939. In a later edition of that ground-breaking portrait of a West African entrapped by colonialism, Cary wrote of the present tense that it 'can give to a reader that sudden feeling of insecurity (as if the very ground were made only of a deeper kind of darkness) which comes to a traveller who is bushed in unmapped country, when he feels all at once that not only has he utterly lost his way, but also his own identity.' At one point Rabbit is literally lost, and tears up a map he cannot read; but the present tense, to me as I began to write in it, felt not so much ominous as exhilaratingly speedy and free– free of the grammatical bonds of the traditional past tense and of the subtly dead, muffling hand it lays upon every action. To write 'he says' instead of 'he said' was rebellious and liberating in 1959. In the present tense, thought and act exist on one shimmering plane; the writer and reader move in a purged space, on the travelling edge of the future, without vantage for reflection or regret or a seeking of proportion. It is the way motion pictures occur before us, immersingly; my novella was originally to bear the sub-title 'A Movie', and I envisioned the credits unrolling over the shuffling legs of the boys in the opening scuffle around the backboard, as the reader hurried down the darkened aisle with his box of popcorn.

A non-judgmental immersion was my aesthetic and moral aim, when I was fresh enough in the artistic enterprise to believe that I could, in the Poundian imperative, 'make it new'. *The Centaur's* fifteen-year-old narrator, Peter Caldwell, awakes with a fever after three trying days with his plodding, prancing father, and looks out the window. He is a would-be painter:

> The stone bare wall was a scumble of umber; my father's footsteps
> thumbs of white in white. I knew what this scene was– a patch of
> Pennsylvania in 1947– and yet I did not know, was in my softly fevered
> state mindlessly soaked in a rectangle of colored light. I burned to paint
> it, just like that, in its puzzle of glory; it came upon me that I must go
> to Nature disarmed of perspective and stretch myself like a large
> transparent canvas upon her in the hope that, my submission being
> perfect, the imprint of a beautiful and useful truth would be taken.

The religious faith that a useful truth will be imprinted by a perfect artistic submission underlies these Rabbit novels. The first one, especially, strives to convey the quality of existence itself that hovers beneath the quotidian details, what the scholastic philosophers called the *ens.* Rather than arrive at a verdict and a directive, I sought to present sides of an unresolvable tension intrinsic to being human. Readers who expect novelists to reward and punish and satirized their characters from a superior standpoint will be disappointed.

Unlike such estimable elders as Vonnegut, Vidal, and Mailer, I have little reformist tendency and instinct for social criticism. Perhaps the Lutheran creed of my boyhood imbued me with some of Luther's conservatism; perhaps growing up

Democrat under Franklin Roosevelt inclined me to be unduly patriotic. In any case the rhetoric of social protest and revolt which roiled the Sixties alarmed and, even, disoriented me. The calls for civil rights, racial equality, sexual equality, freer sex, and peace in Vietnam were in themselves commendable and non-threatening; it was the savagery, between 1965 and 1973, of the domestic attack upon the good faith and common sense of our government, especially of that would-be Roosevelt Lyndon B. Johnson, that astonished me. The attack came, much of it, from the intellectual elite and their draft-vulnerable children. Civil disobedience was antithetical to my Fifties education, which had inculcated, on the professional level, an impassioned but cool aestheticism and implied, on the private, salvation through sensibility, which included an ironical detachment from the social issues fashionable in the Thirties. But the radicalizing Thirties had come round again, in psychedelic colors.

I coped by moving, with my family, to England for a year, and reading in the British Museum about James Buchanan. Buchanan (1791-1868) was the only Pennsylvanian ever elected to the White House; the main triumph of his turbulent term (1857-61) was that, though elderly, he survived it, and left it to his successor, Abraham Lincoln, to start the Civil War. A pro-Southern Democrat who yet denied any Constitutional states' right to secede, he embodied for me the drowned-out voice of careful, fussy reasonableness. For over a year, I read American history and tried unsuccessfully to shape this historical figure's dilemmas into a work of fiction. But my attempted pages showed me too earthbound a realist or too tame a visionary for the vigorous fakery of a historical novel.

By the first month of 1970, back in the United States, I gave up the attempt. But then, what to do? I owed my publisher a novel, and had not come up with one. From the start of our relationship, I had thought it a right and mutually profitable rhythm to offer Knopf a novel every other book. In the ten years since *Rabbit, Run* had ended on its ambiguous note, a number of people asked me what happened to him. It came to me that he would have run around the block, returned to Mt. Judge and Janice, faced what music there was, and be now an all-too-settled working man– a Linotyper. For three summers I had worked as a copy boy in a small-city newspaper and had admired the men in green eyeshades as they perched at their square-keyed keyboards and called down a rain of brass matrices to become hot lead slugs, to become columns of type. It was the blue-collar equivalent of my sedentary, word-productive profession. He would be, my thirty-six-year-old Rabbit, one of those middle Americans feeling overwhelmed and put upon by all the revolutions in the air; he would serve as a receptacle for my disquiet and resentments, which would sit more becomingly on him than on me. Rabbit to the rescue, and as before his creator was in a hurry. An examination of the manuscript reveals what I had forgotten, that I typed the first draft– the only novel of the four of which this is true. I began on 7 February 1970, finished that first draft on 11 December, and had it typed up by Palm Sunday 1971– which means that my publisher worked fast to get it out before the end of that year. If the novel achieved nothing else, it revived the word *redux*, which I had encountered in titles by Dryden and Trollope. From the Latin *reducere*, 'to bring back', it is defined by Webster's as 'led back; specif., *Med.*, indicating return to health after disease'. People wanted to pronounce it 'raydoo', as if it were French, but now I often see it in print, as a staple of journalese.

Rabbit became too much a receptacle, perhaps, for every item in the headlines. A number of reviewers invited me to think so. But though I have had several occasions to reread the novel, few excisions suggested themselves to me. As a reader I am carried along the curve that I described in my flap copy: 'Rabbit is abandoned and mocked, his home is invaded, the world of his childhood decays into a mere sublunar void; still he clings to semblances of patriotism and paternity.' The novel is itself a moon shot: Janice's affair launches her husband, as he and his father witness the takeoff of Apollo 11 in the Phoenix bar, into the extraterrestrial world of Jill and Skeeter. The eventual reunion of the married couple in the Safe Haven Motel is managed with the care and gingerly vocabulary of a spacecraft docking. It is the most violent and bizarre of these four novels, but then the Sixties were the most violent and bizarre of these decades. The possibly inordinate emphasis on sexual congress– and enthusiastic mixture of instruction manual and de Sadeian ballet– also partakes of the times.

In *Rabbit, Run,* there is very little direct cultural and political reference, apart from the burst of news items that comes over his car radio during the night of fleeing home. Of these, only the disappearance of the Dalai Lama from Tibet engages the fictional themes. In *Rabbit Redux,* the trip to the moon is the central metaphor. 'Trip' in Sixties parlance meant an inner journey of some strangeness; the little apple-green house in Penn Villas plays host to space invaders– a middle-class runaway and a black rhetorician. The long third chapter– longer still in the first draft– is a Sixties invention, a 'teach-in'. Rabbit tries to learn. Reading aloud the words of Frederick Douglass, he becomes black, and in a fashion seeks solidarity with Skeeter.   African Americans, Old-World readers should be reminded, have an immigrant pedigree almost as long as that of Anglo- Americans; 'the Negro problem' is old in the New World. The United States is more than a tenth black; black music, black sorrow, black jubilation, black English, black style permeate the culture and have contributed much of what makes American music, especially, so globally potent. Yet the society continues racially divided, in the main, and Rabbit's reluctant crossing of the color line represents a tortured form of progress.

The novel was meant to be symmetric with *Rabbit, Run*: this time, Janice leaves home and a young female dies on Harry's watch. Expatiation of the baby's death is the couple's joint quest throughout the series; Harry keeps looking for a daughter, and Janice strives for competence, for a redeemed opinion of herself. Nelson remains the wounded, helplessly indignant witness. He is ever shocked by 'the hardness of heart' that enables his father to live to egocentrically, as if enjoying divine favor. *Rabbit, Run's* epigraph is an uncompleted thought by Pascal: 'The motions of Grace, the hardness of the heart; external circumstances.' In *Rabbit Redux,* external circumstances bear nightmarishly upon my skittish pilgrim; he achieves a measure of recognition that the rage and destructiveness boiling out of the television set belong to him. Many of the lessons of the Sixties became part of the *status quo.* Veterans became doves; bankers put on love beads. Among Harry's virtues, self-centered though he is, are the national curiosity, tolerance, and adaptability. America survives its chronic apocalypses. I did not know, though, when I abandoned to motel sleep the couple with a burnt-out house and a traumatized child, that they would wake to such prosperity.

Rabbit is rich, of course, in 1979, only by the standards of his modest working-class background. It was a lucky casual stroke of mine to give the used-car dealer Fred Springer a Toyota franchise in *Rabbit Redux*, for in ten years' time the Japanese-auto invasion had become one of the earmarks of an inflated and teetering American economy, and the Chief Sales Representative of a Toyota agency was well situated to reap advantage from American decline. As these novels had developed, each needed a clear background of news, a 'hook' uniting the personal and national realms. In late June, visiting in Pennsylvania for a few days, I found the hook in the OPEC-induced gasoline shortage and the panicky lines that cars were forming at the local pumps; our host in the Philadelphia suburbs rose early and got our car tank filled so we could get back to New England. A nuclear near-disaster had occurred at Three-Mile Island in Harrisburg that spring; Carter's approval rating was down to thirty per cent; our man in Nicaragua was being ousted by rebels; our man in Iran was deposed and dying; John Wayne was dead; Sky-Lab was falling; and Rabbit, at forty-six, with a wife who drinks too much and a son dropping out of college, could well believe that he and the U. S. were both running out of gas. Except that he doesn't really believe it; *Rabbit Is Rich*, for all its shadows, is the happiest novel of the four, the most buoyant, with happy endings for everybody in it, even the hapless Buddy Inglefinger. The novel contains a number of scenes distinctly broad in their comedy: amid the inflationary abundance of money, Harry and Janice copulate on a blanket of gold coins and stagger beneath the weight of 888 silver dollars as they lug their speculative loot up the eerily deserted main drag of Brewer. A Shakespearian swap and shuffle of couples takes place in the glimmering Arcadia of a Caribbean Island, and a wedding rings out at the novel's midpoint. 'Life is sweet, that's what they say,' Rabbit reflects in the last pages. Details poured fast and furious out of my by now thoroughly mapped and populated Diamond County. The novel is fat, in keeping with its theme of inflation, and Pru is fat with her impending child, whose growth is the book's secret action, its innermost happiness.

My own circumstances had changed since the writing of *Rabbit Redux*. I was married to another wife, which may help account for Janice's lusty rejuvenation, and living in another town, called Georgetown, twenty minutes inland from Ipswich. Each of the Rabbit novels was written in a different setting— *Redux* belonged to my second house in Ipswich, on the winding, winsomely named Labor-in-Vain Road, and to my rented office downtown, above a restaurant whose noontime aromas of lunch rose through the floor each day to urge my writing to its daily conclusion. Whereas Ipswich had a distinguished Puritan history and some grand seaside scenery, Georgetown was an unassuming population knot on the way to other places. It reminded me of Shillington, and the wooden house that we occupied for six years was, like the brick house I had spent my first thirteen years in, long and narrow, with a big back yard and a front view of a well-trafficked street. The town was littered with details I only needed to stoop over and pick up and drop into Mt. Judge's scenery; my evening jogs through Georgetown could slip almost unaltered into Rabbit's panting peregrinations three hundred miles away. In two respects his fortunes had the advantage of mine: I was not a member of any country club, nor yet a grandfather. Within five years, I would achieve both privileged states, but for the time being they had to be, like the procedures of a Toyota agency, dreamed up. A dreamy mood pervades the book; Rabbit almost has to keep pinching himself to make sure that his bourgeois bliss is real— that he is, if not as utterly a master of householdry and husbandry as the ineffable Webb Murkett, in the same exalted league.

Once in an interview I had rashly predicted the title of this third installment to be *Rural Rabbit*; some of the words Harry and Janice exchange in the Safe Haven Motel leave the plot open for a country move. But in the event he remained a small-city boy, a creature of sidewalks, gritty alleys, roaring highways, and fast-food franchises. One of *Rabbit, Run*'s adventures in my mind had been its location in Brewer, whose model, the city of Reading, had loomed for a Shillington child as an immense, remote, menacing, and glamorous metropolis. Rabbit, like every stimulating alter ago (sic), was many things the author was not: a natural athlete, a blue-eyed Swede, sexually magnetic, taller than six feet, impulsive, and urban. The rural rabbit turns out to be Ruth, from the first novel, whom he flushes from her cover in his continued search for a daughter. Farms I knew first-hand, at least in their sensory details, from the years of rural residence my mother had imposed on her family after 1945. Rabbit spying on Ruth from behind the scratchy hedgerow is both Peter Rabbit peeking from behind the cabbages at the menacing Mr. McGregor and I, the self-exiled son, guiltily spying on my mother as, in plucky and self-reliant widowhood, she continued to occupy her sandstone farmhouse and eighty acres all by herself. She did not, in fairness, keep the shell of a school bus in her yard; rather, the town fleet of yellow school buses was visible from the window of my drafty study in Georgetown.

Though 1979 was running out, I seem to have worked at a leisurely speed: the end of the first draft is dated 19 April 1980, and seven more months went by before my typing of the manuscript was completed on 23 November. Happily, and quite to my surprise, *Rabbit Is Rich* won all three of 1981's major American literary prizes for fiction (as well as a place in the Washington critic Jonathan Yardley's list of the Ten Worst Books of the Year). An invigorating change of mates, a move to a town that made negligible communal demands, a sense of confronting the world in a fresh relation cleared my head, it may be. The Rabbit novels, coming every ten years, were far from all that I wrote; the novel that precedes it, *The Coup*, and the semi-novel that followed it, *Bech Is Back*, in retrospect also seem the replete but airy products of a phase when such powers as I can claim were exuberantly ripe.

Ripeness was the inevitable theme of my fourth and concluding entry in this saga. By 1989 my wife and I had moved to Beverly Farms, a bucolic enclave of old summer homes. Most of our neighbors and new acquaintances were elderly; many spent part of their year in Florida. My children were all adult, and three stepsons nearly so; as it happened, my wife and I each had a widowed mother living in solitude. My mother, well into her eighties, was my principal living link with Rabbit's terrain; countless visits over the years had refreshed my boyhood impressions and reassured me that southeastern Pennsylvania was changing in tune with the rest of the nation. Thirty years before, a reader had asked me if Harry didn't die at the end of *Rabbit, Run*, and it did seem possible that death might come early to him, as it often does to ex-athletes, especially those who are overweight and not usefully employed. All men are mortal; my character was a man. But I, too, was a man, and by no means sure how much of me would be functioning in 1999. The more research I did to flesh out my hero's cardio-vascular problems, the more ominous pains afflicted my own chest. As a child, just beginning to relate my birth year to the actuarial realities, I had wondered if I would live to the year 2000. I still wondered. I wanted Harry to go out with all the style a healthy author could give him, and had a vision of a four-book set, a squared-off tetralogy, a boxed life. I began *Rabbit at Rest* early in 1989, on 12 January, as if anxious to get started, and finished the first draft on the last day of September, and the typed draft on 20 January 1990. Like *Rabbit, Run*, it was published in a zero year.

And like *Rabbit, Run*, it is in three parts. The hero of both novels flees south from domestic predicaments. In March of 1959 'his goal is the white sun of the south like a great big pillow in the sky'. He fails to get there and, lost and exasperated on the dark roads of West Virginia, turns back; but his fifty-six-year-old self knows the way. Harry has acquired the expertise and the money and he gets there, and lays his tired head upon that great big pillow. No distinctly American development, no moon shot or gas crunch, offered itself as a dominant metaphor, at this end of Reagan's decade; instead, the mid-air explosion of Pan Am Flight 103 over Lockerbie, which occurred before Christmas of 1988, haunts Rabbit acrophobically. And he senses the coming collapse of the Soviet Union and its empire, whose opposition to the free world has shadowed and shaped his entire adult life. Freedom has had its hazards for him, and capitalist enterprise its surfeit, but he was ever the loyal citizen. God he can doubt, but not America. He is the New World's new man, armored against eventualities in little but his selfhood.

The novel's two locales have an exceptional geographical density. For the Florida city of Deleon, I did several days of legwork in the vicinity of Fort Myers. To give substance to Harry's final, solitary drive south, I drove the route myself, beginning at my mother's farm and scribbling sights, rivers, and radio emissions in a notebook on the seat beside me, just as, more than three decades previous, I turned on my New England radio on the very night, the last night of winter, 1959, and made note of what came. Accident rules these novels more than most, in their attempt to take a useful imprint of the world that secretes in newspapers clues to its puzzle of glory. The fictional name Deleon, along with the murals Rabbit notices in the hospital lobby, constitutes homage to my mother, whose cherished project it had long been to write and publish a novel about the Spanish governor of Puerto Rico and discoverer of Florida, Juan Ponce de León. She enriched, too, the city of Brewer, for a grim interplay developed between my novel, in the year of its writing, and her physical decline. Her several hospitalizations generated medical details that I shamelessly fed into Rabbit's ordeal; my frequent filial visits exposed me more intensely to Reading and its environs than at any time since the Fifties, and so Rabbit's home turf, especially as evoked at the beginning of Chapter II, acquired substance and the poignance of something slipping away. I became, as I have written elsewhere,'conscious of how powerfully, inexhaustibly rich real places are, compared with the paper cities we make of them in fiction. Even after a tetralogy, almost everything is still left to say. As I walked and drove the familiar roads and streets, I saw them as if for the first time with more than a child's eyes and felt myself beginning, at last, to understand the place. But by then it was time to say goodbye.'

My mother died two weeks after I had competed the first draft of *Rabbit at Rest*. If she pervades its landscape and overall mortal mood, my father, who died in 1972, figures strongly also. Rabbit, in his near-elderly, grandpaternal condition, more and more talked, I could not but notice, like George Caldwell in *The Centaur*. My two projected novellas had merged: the dodgy rabbit had become the suffering horse; the man of impulse and appetite had aged into humorous stoicism. In trying to picture a grandfather (my own enactment of that role had just barely begun) I fell back upon memories of my father, whose patient bemusement and air of infinite toleration had enchanted my own children. A number of readers told me how much more lovable Harry had become. My intention was never to make him– or any character– lovable. He was imagined, at a time when I was much taken with Kierkegaard, as a creature of fear and trembling; but perhaps my college exposure to Dostoevsky was more central. Rabbit is, like the Underground Man, *incorrigible*; from first to last he bridles at good advice, taking direction only from his personal, also incorrigible God.

His adventure on the Sunfish with Judy rehearses once more the primal trauma of *Rabbit, Run*, this time successfully, with the baby saved by a self-sacrificing parent. Ripeness brings to fruition many of the tendencies of Rabbit's earthly transit. His relations with the opposite sex appear to have two main aspects, the paternal and erotic; they come to a momentarily triumphant climax in his contact with his daughter-in-law. His lifelong involvement with Ronnie Harrison– that repugnant locker-room exhibitionist whose very name seems a broken mirroring of Rabbit's– reaches its terminus in a tied golf match. Harry's shy but determined advance into the bodies of women slowly brings him to a kind of forgiveness of the flesh. Whatever his parental sins, their wages are generously paid him by his son in an act of corporate destruction. Harry's wary fascination with his black fellow-Americans leads him to explore the black section of Deleon, in its stagnation comfortingly similar to the Depression world of his childhood. So many themes convene in *Rabbit at Rest* that the hero could be said to sink under the burden of the accumulated past, and to find relief in that 'wide tan emptiness under the sun', the recreation fields next to the abandoned Florida high school.

A problem for the author of sequels is how much of the previous books to carry along. The nuclear family– Harry, Janice, Nelson– and Ronnie Harrison figure in all four installments of *Rabbit Angstrom*. The older generation, potently present in the first two novels, has dwindled to the spunky figure of Bessie Springer in *Rabbit Is Rich*; I was charmed to find her so spirited and voluble as she manipulated the purse strings of her little dynasty. Characters dominant in one novel fall away in the next. Ruth vanishes from *Rabbit Redux* but returns in the next decade. I have restored to *Redux* an omitted brief reappearance by Jack Eccles, who almost became the co-protagonist of Rabbit's first outing, and whose own 'outing' seemed to deserve a place in the full report. Skeeter, who takes over

Redux, dwindles to a news item and a troubling memory; what later novel could hold him? Perhaps he returns in the form of Tiger. That the neo-Babbitt of the third volume contains the witness to the apocalyptic events of the second would strain plausibility did not so many peaceable citizens contain lethal soldiers, so many criminals contain choirboys, so many monogamous women contain promiscuous young things. An adult human being consists of sedimentary layers. We shed more skins than we can count, and are born each day to a merciful forgetfulness. We forget most of our past but embody all of it.

For this fresh printing, apt to be the last I shall oversee, I have tried to smooth away such inconsistencies as have come to my attention. Various automotive glitches-- a front engine assigned to a rear-engine make of car, a convertible model that never existed in all of Detroit's manufacture— have been repaired. The flora and fauna of commercial products and popular culture posted many small spelling problems that should be now resolved. Birthdays: real people have them, but fictional characters usually do without, unless an extended chronicle insists. To my best knowledge Harold C. (a mystery initial) Angstrom was born in February 1933, and Janice Springer sometime in 1936. They were married in March of 1956, and their son Nelson was born the following October, seven months later– on the 22nd, by my calculations. *Rabbit, Run* takes place from 20 March 1959 to 24 June of that year; *Rabbit Redux* from 16 July 1969 to late October; *Rabbit Is Rich* from 23 June 1979 to 20 January 1980; and *Rabbit at Rest* from 28 December 1988 to 22 September 1989. Spring, fall, summer, winter: a life as well as a year has its seasons.

*John Updike, "Introduction." *Rabbit Angstrom*. New York Knopf/Everyman, 1999. ix-xxiv.

"Rabbit Reread"

David Heddendorf*

For the first time since 1950, Americans are leaving a decade behind without the company of Harry "Rabbit" Angstrom, John Updike's fictional Toyota dealer and former high-school basketball star. Not only is Rabbit dead, he's been ceremonially interred in *Rabbit Angstrom* (1995), the one-volume Everyman's Library edition of the four novels that bear his name. In the forty years since the publication of *Rabbit, Run*, a literary phenomenon that began life as a scandal has achieved a kind of revered, grand-old-man status—still delighting and surprising, certainly selling, but no longer capable of shocking. By 1990 there was something inevitable and almost taken for granted about the Rabbit books, as though Updike owed the world another installment as surely as the world owed Updike another round of awards. The arrival of the next in the series was one of those comforting recurrences like spring or a visit from a favorite uncle. Now, with no further novels to anticipate, we can finally look back and see Harry whole, from the young man crashing a back-alley pickup game to the sad retiree literally playing his heart out on a dusty Florida playground.

To which Rabbit, though, do we look back? Do we reread the originals or the collected, corrected *Rabbit Angstrom*? It's like trying to decide between the 1881 version and the New York Edition of *The Portrait of a Lady*. But where Henry James's late manner superseded his earlier style, charting a new course of indirectness and qualification, Updike's career, while remarkably varied, follows a more continuous line. His aim with the new edition seems restorative rather than revisionary, the alterations limited mostly to repairing "automotive glitches" (as he calls his mistakes with cars) and correcting other minor errors.

What astonishes, on rereading the novels in their original versions, is how much Updike got right the first time. To return again and again over decades to a detailed chronicle, picking up where one left off and bringing a unified work to completion, must feel like doing a lifelong crossword puzzle in indelible ink. Yet not only do Harry, his wife Janice, and son Nelson endure, looking and sounding like the same complex characters; Updike's language as well—the ever-youthful hero of the tetralogy—reverberates through the novels with widely scattered refrains and sly internal references.

Sometimes a word or phrase from a major scene is repeated from book to book, as with Rabbit's surprised "Hey" from his first night with Ruth in *Rabbit, Run*. Elsewhere a line rings such a faint bell that only a hunch and some backward paging can locate the source. In *Rabbit at Rest*, for example, Harry contemplates the perfect golf swing, the way the ball makes "a tiny tunnel into the absolute." "That would be *it*," the rapturous paragraph concludes—oddly, yet with something familiar about the phrase. Sure enough, in *Rabbit, Run* Harry hits a gorgeous tee shot, admires the ball's protracted flight, and exclaims, "That's *it*!" to the minister Jack Eccles, who has been asking Rabbit what mysterious presence he seeks.

Later in *Rabbit, Run*, after the birth of the doomed baby, one of the novel's showier sentences occurs: "Sunshine, the old clown, rims the room." It reappears verbatim in *Rabbit Redux*, again placed prominently at the beginning of a section. (In the new *Rabbit Angstrom* the echo is clipped to "Sunshine, the old clown"—as in the golf epiphany only grazing the ear, stirring memory like a symphony theme.)

Since the novels are narrated, with occasional exceptions, from Rabbit's expansive point of view, these verbal echoes occur as Harry remembers words of warning, command, joy, and love. He hears his mother whispering "Hassy," Ruth in bed saying "Work," and a gruff gas-station attendant telling him, his first time on the road, "The only way to get somewhere, you know, is to figure out where you're going before you go there." These catchwords and aphorisms lodge in Harry's teeming mind, to surface unpredictably as the decades pass. The wholeness Rabbit feels in his life derives, like the novelistic wholeness wrought by Updike's brimming language, from a lengthy accretion of verbal textures.

When *Rabbit, Run* first appeared, the explicit sex obliged Updike to consult a lawyer. The threat of legal repercussions had abated by the time of *Rabbit Redux*, but Updike still wonders if that novel didn't contain a "possibly inordinate emphasis on sexual congress." The third and fourth installments continued to abound in inventive couplings as Updike explored the variations of desire with a candor still relatively new to mainstream literature. Who can forget, after all, that Harry's final sexual partner is his daughter-in-law?

Updike has explained that his objective with Rabbit was "[a] non-judgmental immersion." The phrase, from the *Rabbit Angstrom* introduction, nicely captures what it feels like to witness Harry's inner life—a moist drama that if rendered by a literal-minded director would promptly win an NC-17 rating. And just as Rabbit's fantasies go uncensored by a public self, his conduct receives an unblinking account from Updike the neutral, meticulous recorder. Since there's no telling where a magnetic ex-jock's appetites will lead, the author, who merely describes events in objective detail, can claim he's a realist, not a pornographer.

But of course Updike's genius really lies in an entirely different sphere, a third category that combines art and blunt description under uneasy labels like "poetic realism." To read the Rabbit novels from a decade's distance is to encounter neither a prurient imagination—Updike as lecher—nor a dispassionate report—Updike as lens—but an elaborately structured vision of life that encompasses the sleazy and the sublime. In *Rabbit is Rich*, home from vacation and the swap night with Thelma Harrison, Harry decides to confront his old lover Ruth about a girl he believes is their daughter. He loses his nerve at the last minute and almost flees: "But as with dying there is a moment that must be pushed through, a slice of time more transparent than plate glass; it is in front of him and he takes the step, drawing heart from that loving void Thelma had confided to him." What Harry is psyching himself up with here is an episode of anal sex, depicted graphically twenty pages earlier. His recalling it puts the act in a new light: Does he love Thelma? Is he merely sentimentalizing their nascent affair? Is he groping absurdly for anything to bolster his obsessive interrogation of Ruth? Thus have sexual mechanics joined the vocabulary of the revealing gesture. (So much for knuckle-cracking and fiddling with ashtrays.)

Despite this now common permissiveness in fiction, Harry's one-night stand with his son's wife, Pru, might strain readers' patience. "This is the worst thing you've ever done, ever, ever," cries Janice when she learns of it—and that's saying something. Presumably we're meant to keep caring for Harry as he begins his final descent toward Florida and the grave; but his behavior, in swerving toward the outrageous and extreme, tests not credulity so much as understanding, sympathy, tolerance.

As a structural device, Rabbit's tryst with Pru—in the works since *Rabbit Is Rich*—functions perfectly to trigger his symmetrical second flight, the road trip aborted in *Rabbit, Run*. There is a kind of amoral inner logic to the deed, with Harry just out of the hospital after angioplasty, watching Janice's real-estate career take off, and Pru back from driving her no-good husband to a drug clinic. Both feel as good as dead, their lives skidding onto some narrow berm where they can at least comfort each other for a night. Immersed in these characters' converging fates, we can sense how provisional the rules must seem, for Pru as well as for Harry. This night confirms the longstanding affinities between them, affinities that have already called into question the contingent bonds of family.

But the strongest justification for the scene, if it needs one, might be the penumbra cast by Harry's increasingly otherworldly imagination. On returning to Pennsylvania the spring following his heart attack, he drives around Brewer visiting sites from his past. He stumbles on a block of recently planted pear trees, their blossoms forming "a white tunnel." While the pedestrians around him bustle on with their lives, Harry stops his car and gets out to admire "the beauty suspended above them, enclosing them, already shedding a confetti of petals: they are in Heaven." Then Harry drives home, and earthly life resumes. The full extent of Nelson's drug use and embezzling comes out; Harry undergoes his heart operation; and on a rainy night in his mother-in-law's old house, Pru comes to him: "Her tall pale wide-hipped nakedness in the dimmed room is lovely much as those pear trees in blossom along that block in Brewer last month were lovely, all his it had seemed, a piece of paradise blundered upon, incredible."

Maybe this only shows what can run through a man's mind while he's having sex with his daughter-in-law. One could argue that Harry's thoughts here will naturally be self-serving, throwing a blanket of religiosity over his worst betrayal. But we've been with Harry too long, seen too much of his divided nature, to reduce his meandering associations to this. Something happened to him on that petal-strewn street, and he relives the extraordinary experience while he is with Pru. Could it be that, with the heightened spiritual perception of the dying, he glimpses a divine presence in the very occasion of sin?

If the theological term jars, it shouldn't. This scene takes us back, like so much else in *Rabbit at Rest*, to the mysterious world of *Rabbit, Run*. One of the earliest facts we're told about Rabbit and Janice is that they, first impressions notwithstanding, are Christians, and the story that follows seems designed to elaborate this statement, exploring senses in which it could conceivably be true. After leaving Janice and making his way back to Brewer, Harry wakes up with Ruth, makes love with her again, says a prayer and starts pestering her about God. Recent movies have inured us to characters who chatter about the cosmos while having sex or blowing people away, but in *Rabbit, Run* Harry sounds like a man with genuine experience, for whom God really is just down the next fairway. Even the minister who adopts him as a personal cause seems to envy Rabbit's matter-of-fact faith. "Well I don't know all this about theology," Harry confesses to Jack Eccles. "I *do* feel, I guess, that somewhere behind all this . . . there's something that wants me to find it."

In *Rabbit, Run* more than in the later novels, Harry is the central problem, the baffling source of all the action. He leaves Janice before we quite know who he is, tells Ruth he loves her when she's little more to him than a prostitute, returns to Janice for the baby's birth, and runs again. Where the later novels bulge with events and people to whom Rabbit must respond, *Rabbit, Run* dwells probingly on Harry himself, introducing others mainly so they can try to figure him out. "Oh, my Rabbit," Ruth laughs, charmed yet mystified. "You just wander, don't you?" Jack Eccles, sent by Janice's parents to bring Harry home, winds up on the golf course soliciting his views about God.

Updike has said he intended his hero to show the cruelty of unrestrained, Kerouac-inspired romanticism, a temperament that characterizes one side of Rabbit. "All I know is what feels right," says this selfish, impulsive Harry to Ruth. But because his feelings are torn between the flesh and the spirit, he can also embody what his earthly creator calls "our heart's stubborn amoral quest for something once called grace." The novels issue periodic bulletins on this quest of Rabbit's, monitoring his spiritual state as, in his fashion, he nurses a wavering, unfocused faith. On the night his child is born he stands in the hospital parking lot, praying to the moon. Flying to the tropics with adultery on his mind, he is filled with religious awe: "God, having shrunk in Harry's middle years to the size of a raisin lost under the car seat, is suddenly great again, everywhere like a radiant wind." There is nothing phony or hypocritical about these transports of Harry's. They simply come over him, out of the blue as it were, moving him with the same irresistible force as lust. All he knows is what feels right.

The relatively empty, God-haunted universe of *Rabbit, Run* gives way to the worldly incursions of the later novels: the Apollo 11 landing of *Rabbit Redux*, the gas shortage of *Rabbit Is Rich*, the Pan Am bombing of *Rabbit at Rest*. AIDS and cocaine add their destructive plot engines, while hurricanes and Super Bowl crowds roar offstage. Harry, who began as a cryptic central presence, diminishes to a ten-year time capsule. We learn what's on TV, what songs are on the radio, how Mike Schmidt and the Phillies are doing. Harry starts to react with his familiar surly growl—rereading *Rabbit, Run*, one is startled by the boyish voice—as celebrities, headlines, and commercial jingles compete for his sensitive notice. A marked change comes over the novels. Details that once appeared as background, fixing us in time and space, become prominent in their own right. We still get the news and hype through Harry's point of view, with his opinions as our escort through the cultural landscape, but both the landmarks and the minutiae claim considerable space on their own.

Rabbit participates in his inundation—rushing to catch the nightly news, annoyed when family duties delay him. The Toyotas he selects for his personal use must have high-quality radios among their features. Yet even as Harry invites the media tide, he resents and fears a dark undercurrent he can't help hearing. Vacationing in the Poconos in *Rabbit Is Rich*, he remembers boyhood summer drives to the Jersey Shore: "Town after town numbingly demonstrated to him that his life was a paltry thing, roughly duplicated by the millions in settings where houses and porches and trees mocking those in Mt. Judge fed the illusions of other little boys that their souls were central and dramatic and invisibly cherished." The older Rabbit gets, the more his soul feels squeezed by multitudinous America. Duplication, it turns out, was just getting warmed up. With his copy of *Consumer Reports* promising a world of choices, he watches his surroundings collapse into wearying sameness, a boulevard of malls and fast-food chains. His daily joys, robbed of singularity, seem transient as the songs that clog the memories of millions like himself.

Harry can't endure immersion in the crowd—he used to be the crowd's high-scoring favorite. As an older man he relinquishes local fame, reduced to a benevolent Uncle Sam in a Fourth of July parade, but he still demands some minimal notice, as if proving to himself he exists. He needs the reassurance of "earning his paycheck, filling his slot in the big picture, doing his bit, getting a little recognition. That's all we want from each other, recognition."

After four lengthy volumes we readers, at least, do recognize Harry. We're acquainted with his uncircumcised penis, his tendency to sneeze, his queasiness about eating animals. We've been told the address of every place he's lived. We know the eyebrow cowlick he's handed down to his son, Nelson, and granddaughter, Judy. These enumerated particulars begin to seem insistent, as if claiming more than the conventional roundedness of fictional characterization. "Here stands (walks, talks, copulates) an individual," say these traits, "despite the best efforts of mass society." But Harry requires the ultimate recognition, the one he believes in as the ground of all others. To his friend and fellow heart patient Charlie Stavros, who asks what *else* Harry is but a machine for pumping blood, Harry replies silently, defiantly, "A God-made one-of-a-kind with an immortal soul breathed in." In a uniform, flattening America of disposable identities, Rabbit calls on a resource that exceeds his traits: his dogged faithfulness in being himself.

As Updike observes in the *Rabbit Angstrom* introduction, the first of the novels contains the fewest topical references. After the strange and faraway *Rabbit, Run, Rabbit at Rest* can feel almost pushily familiar, accosting us with our own obsessive murmurings and daydreams. But the sense of being overrun by brand names and current events might be partly a trick of historical perspective. Compared to Deion Sanders and Toyota slogans, the pop culture of thirty and forty years ago will sound faintly, if at all. The voices buzzing around us might amount to little more than static, but *Cheers* and *Night Court* remain, after a little over a decade, *our* static. Reading the novels in succession, gradually nearing our own time, we see Harry's world grow larger and more distinct book by book, like an object approaching from beyond the horizon.

But what of Harry himself? To recognize him by his quirks isn't necessarily to know him, and his noisy, garish world, much of it with us still, threatens to obstruct our view of the man. In forty more years, the gleam of the contemporary having rubbed off at last, Harry might emerge in a clearer light, if at a greater distance. Perhaps he'll join on the remote heights of literature such flawed idealists as Ahab, Hester Prynne, and Huckleberry Finn—ambiguous yet unmistakable, repugnant yet beloved. Already Harry seems destined for such an afterlife, with his contradictions, his moral failures redeemed by moral outrage, his American distrust of collective identity. To know and understand these tendencies in Harry–loving him one moment, fearing him the next–is to recognize ourselves in his disappointed faith, his alert and articulate pain.

*David Heddendorf, "Rabbit Reread." *Southern Review* Sum. 2000: 641-47.

"Rabbit Remembered"

"Noticers in Chief: John Updike and Rabbit"

D[aniel] T. Max

Rabbit is dead. If there was any doubt about that at the end of the last book in John Updike's remarkable series of novels about Harry "Rabbit" Angstrom– *Rabbit, Run, Rabbit Redux, Rabbit Is Rich* and *Rabbit at Rest*--it is laid to rest in the first moments of Updike's new novella, "Rabbit Remembered."

There was a chance Updike hadn't killed him off ten years ago in *Rabbit at Rest*, when Rabbit lay in a hospital room after a heart attack. His final words were "Enough. Maybe. Enough." There was torture in that "maybe" between the two "enoughs" on the last page. Updike says he received plenty of letters over the years asking what he planned to do and even a few plot suggestions. "They would send me schemes to bring him back," he remembers. "One guy had what I thought was a rather clever notion to give him a heart transplant from a young black man which would bring the Negro theme, the minority theme, the diversity theme..." Was he tempted to use it? "Ugh," he says, "it seems like something that would happen in someone else's novel." In general, he was not tempted. "To revive [Rabbit] would be a little like bringing back Sherlock Holmes from Reichenbach Falls and if he was brought back he would be brought back as a cardiac invalid in his late fifties. Who wants to read about that?" he says. No plot was the right plot. Rabbit was dead and had to stay dead.

Those who surrounded him in life, however, live on to talk about him. They are a querulous group trying to make sense of a difficult man and the warren of dysfunctional relationships he left behind: his son, Nelson; his wife, Janice; now remarried to his high-school enemy Ronnie; along with various people who knew him less well– Thelma, Doris, Billy. Janice, remembering her unhappy years with Harry, tries to resist the tug back into the past, while Nelson, still focused on a father who was more competitive than loving, can't. "Another reason I like you," he tells Ronnie at one point, "is that you and I are about the last people left on earth my father still bugs." Thus Rabbit is remembered by those who knew him– and not too fondly. But for us, a new Rabbit story is an unanticipated piece of good luck. It's a chance to be back within the memories and the reflections of those books. It gives us again Updike's excellent observations on our culture and vivid descriptions of people and place in his smooth prose. Like returning to an old dream, it awakens feelings we used to have about ourselves. There is the sense of triumph: Time has passed but we are still here, changed, but here.

Harry "Rabbit" Angstrom was not one of the most attractive men, but he was memorable. He was many things: an average mid-century middle-aged American male with multiple flaws--chauvinism, racism, misogyny. He loved kitchen gadgets, respected power and feared water. Some of his sins rose to biblical levels. He was responsible for the death of a daughter and slept with his daughter-in-law. "If you have the guts to be yourself," he said once, "other people'll pay the price." But he was also a dreamer, a seeker, an embodiment of the idea that in the midst of all the messy commerce of America some magic could be found. Forty years ago, a character in *Rabbit, Run* called the then-twenty-six year old "a son of the morning" and that description stayed true into the evening of his life. He believed he was on some sort of quest.

"Rabbit Remembered" resolves a particular mystery that haunted Rabbit: Did he father a daughter when he lived with a woman named Ruth during one of his many flights from Janice four decades ago? Was there a daughter to replace the one who had died? Rabbit believed so. He looked for her quite hard in later years. But it might have been just an obsession. He was full of such egotistical illusions. The first chapter of "Rabbit Remembered" reveals that there is a daughter. Annabelle Byer is now thirty-nine years old, and her descending on Janice, Nelson and Ronnie stirs up the feelings of the people Rabbit left behind. Updike lets this play out over 180 pages. It's a busy story, as messy as forty years of life would be expected to make it. If you are just meeting Rabbit, be warned: This novella may at first be more baffling than elevating, like being in a family counseling session without any notes. Who are Nelson and Ronnie and why are they so pissy with each other? Why doesn't Janice want to see Annabelle? Who was Billy Fosnacht? "The beautiful thing about history," Harry once commented, "is it puts you right to sleep." Updike says he considered that readers new to Rabbit's history might not get what was going on. "It was on my mind," he says, "how much you should try to fill in the reader coming upon this cold, and I think I decided to just let the reader swim. I wanted the story to be a letter to people who have been with me previously."

Even those who have been following Rabbit since the end of the Eisenhower era may be surprised by what they don't remember. The Rabbit books came out on the turns of decades: *Rabbit, Run* in 1960, *Rabbit Redux* in 1971, *Rabbit Is Rich* in 1981 and *Rabbit at Rest* in 1990. The action of each book takes place in the last year of the decade and lays out the ambitions and anxieties of that moment. The books are brilliant time capsules. But ten years between books is a long time. An attentive reader might remember Nelson and Janice's names, but who were Doris and Billy, Ronnie and Thelma? What really stays all these years is intense, depressive, narcissistic Rabbit, Rabbit on his quixotic quest. Now he's gone.

"Rabbit Remembered"— which Updike calls a "redemptive postscript"---is over quickly. This is perhaps the price that has to be paid if you want to put forty years of history into a novella, but why did Updike want to keep the new one so short? Why this act of self-limitation? The novella isn't even published on its own but folded into a collection called *Licks of Love*. Updike is the author of fifty-one books. At sixty-eight he does not seem to be winding down. In fact, the reverse is true. He is writing harder, throwing his imagination further afield, taking more risks. In the past three years, he has written *Toward the End of Time*, a novel set in New England in 2020 and *Gertrude and Claudius*, a prequel to *Hamlet*, as well as many of the stories in *Licks of Love*, plus a lot of criticism. No one could say he is shy about using up the paper. One wants- -feels entitled to– another Rabbit tome, a long book instead of a short one, something to fill in and push the story forward, a meal instead of a snack.

Updike's response is that "there was something sacred about the four books about Harry." "When I finished *Rabbit at Rest* I wasn't sure I wouldn't be at rest myself by the time ten years went by," he says.

> But the ten years did go by, and there I was. I was nagged by the fact that I'd left the problematical daughter up in the air, a loose end that should have been tied up. I thought the novella was the least obtrusive way to– well, I thought that there was only a novella in it. And without Rabbit these. . .he, uh, haunts the novella, but as I wrote it I was very aware of his absence. Indeed, it's a book about the absence of a presence in a way. Does that answer your question? I wanted to kind of sneak it in, I guess, is the short answer.

This is a typical Updike utterance. There is a Lutheran— almost Calvinist-morbidity, the sense that writing is a practical craft rather than divine inspiration ("a loose end that had to be tied up"), and the syntax that moves between the literary and the ordinary, the fun with words. Last, there is the laugh he gives as he conveys his hope that we are not disappointed. It's not hard to imagine his reddish face, the Roman nose, the smile as he says these things. He both tells you more than you expect and less. He's forthcoming about his own sense of mortality but disingenuous about how we see him. Doesn't he realize that hundreds of thousands of readers were waiting to see if Rabbit would somehow, mysteriously, survive?

In recounting Rabbit's story, Updike both holds the mirror up to himself and holds the mirror up to us. This is a trick that comes out of the relationship between Updike and Rabbit, as well as out of the way by which Rabbit serves as our eyes and ears.

Who is Rabbit to Updike? When interviewers ask him, he demurs. When Updike talks about Rabbit, he still refers to him in the present tense, though he's been dead for ten years. Rabbit is both an ego projection of Updike and a nightmare, his ideal self and the self he barely avoided being. When we first met Rabbit it was 1959. The book was *Rabbit, Run*. He was a twenty-six-year-old living in the town of Brewer, a grimy midsized Pennsylvania city that resembled Updike's native Reading. He was roughly Updike's age, and they shared the dour Lutheran-almost-Calvinist flavor of the town. Rabbit was gifted but already fading. He'd been a high-school basketball star. Now he was a MagiPeel demonstrator. His nickname came from "the breadth of his white face, the pallor of his blue irises, and a nervous flutter under his brief nose. . ." There were other reasons. On the court he was quick like a bunny. He was also horny as a rabbit. And when he was in a tight spot, he would run.

Updike has described himself as a shy, inward-gazing adolescent, the only child in a shabby genteel household. He liked to draw and to write. His father was a teacher and his mother a frustrated creative writer. He remembers feeling different from the other kids in his high school in the middle of Pennsylvania coal country, the Rabbits of the world. "I sat in the grandstand and watched them," he says, "I felt almost like an alien." Through the Rabbit books, the author realized that the Rabbits of the world felt like aliens too.

Rabbit, Run takes place toward the end of the heyday of American sublimation. Nothing could be named but everything could be implied, by no means the worst conditions under which to write. Trying to decide between his pregnant young wife Janice and Ruth, whom he has also made pregnant, Rabbit remembers what it feels like to shoot baskets: "There was you and sometimes the ball and then the hole, the high perfect hole with its pretty skirt of net. It was you, just you and that fringed ring, and sometimes it came down right to your lips it seemed and sometimes it stayed away." Another time Rabbit is playing golf with a minister and hits a great drive and has an intimation of God. Unhappiness is infused with a domesticity that America would soon lose. The minister asks him what is bugging him. "In what way do you think you're exceptional?" he asks. And Rabbit says: "You don't think there's any answer to that but there is. I once did something right. I played first-rate basketball. I really did. And after you're first-rate at something, no matter what, it kind of takes the kick out of being second-rate."

Updike was on an opposite trajectory. He had gone to Harvard, graduated summa cum laude and now lived in the small Massachusetts coastal town of Ipswich. The novels came steadily– first *The Poorhouse Fair* in 1959, then *Rabbit, Run*, a year later, which was a protest against the norms of Eisenhower America, then *Couples* in 1968, which made him notorious and rich. He was the youngest person ever elected to the American Academy of Arts & Letters. At age thirty-six, *Time* put him on its cover with the banner "The Adulterous Nation." Updike was overnight the bard of suburban sex. He was rising and Rabbit sinking. You might think the books would weaken, that Updike would lose interest as he lost his connection to Rabbit's world, but one of the surprising things about the series is the way Updike and Rabbit stayed in sync. They were both questers in *Rabbit, Run*. In *Rabbit Redux*, Updike's novel of the Sixties, they were both stupefied watchers. *Rabbit Redux* is turned on, tuned in, and full of sex and violence. The euphemisms are gone and the four-letter words are out. "All our bad checks are being cashed," one character grimly says. Vietnam was on the nightly news. There was crime on Brewer's streets, and on Reading's. Men were about to land on the moon. Rabbit's personal life was in free fall. Janice moved out on him, leaving Nelson, now twelve, behind with his thirty-six-year (sic) old father. Most unsettling was the arrival (not entirely plausible) into Rabbit's empty home of Skeeter, a wiry, skinny, black man, who did drugs and read to Rabbit from *The Life of Frederick Douglass*. Skeeter believed he was the next messiah, that all the craziness was there to prepare for him. To Harry's homegrown fantasy of destiny was counterpoised Skeeter's own wilder version.

Rabbit Redux is a raw book. You get the feeling that even from the relative quiet of Ipswich, the Sixties nearly overwhelmed its author. He was, as he remains, an incrementalist, an observer of the subtle changes in American consciousness. Seismic changes intimidate him. The speed with which he absorbs cultural change is closer to John Cheever's than Philip Roth's. This turned out to be Rabbit's case as well. He is a rebel when America is conservative and a seeker when others are content. But when everyone is on a quest, he loses heart. His status as an iconoclast has been compromised.

Soon after *Redux* the society calmed down and began to lick its wounds. This was a break for Updike. *Rabbit Is Rich* takes place from Christmas 1979 to spring 1980. It was the era of Skylab, stagflation and America "disgraced and barren, mourning her hostages" in Iran. Ironically, tough times for America were good times for Rabbit. Updike by now was a star, America's author, the explainer-in-chief of our social habits and mores. But Rabbit too had gotten lucky. His father-in-law had hired him to sell cars on his Toyota lot at the moment when gas got expensive. He and Janice drank and hung out and golfed at the new-money country club. They moved out of Janice's mother's into a two-story stone house complete with a downstairs bathroom, like Rabbit had always dreamed of. Rabbit had gotten fat.

He was also stultified. Excessive money has never been good for artists or mystics. In those days, Rabbit could name the profits of different Toyota models. He read *Consumer Reports* and carried its odd bits of knowledge wherever he went. But his sense of purpose was beginning to fade. He no longer cared about basketball. He lost for the first time, he tells a friend, the "old inkling. . .that there was something that wanted him to find it, that he was here on earth on a kind of assignment." Inflation was in double digits. "Poor pop," he thought. "He didn't live to see money get unreal." As unreal as he had become: "Another shadowy presence jars his heart: A man in blue suit trousers and rumpled white shirt with cuffs folded back and a loosened necktie, looking overweight and dangerous, is watching him. Jesus. It is himself, his own full-length reflection."

One finished *Rabbit Is Rich* with the sense that Updike was going to quit. Rabbit had lost what made him sexy. Updike had followed him from his anxious working-class roots to affluence, and spiritually from the world of John Cheever to the bourgeois complacency of John O'Hara. Rabbit hadn't found God, but he'd found a substitute many of us find adequate: the American dream. What was there left to look for? But assuming that was the last we'd hear from Rabbit meant underrating both him and Updike and how much old age (that Calvinist morbidity) would scare both of them.

In 1990, Updike came back with *Rabbit at Rest,* a long, spectacular and excruciating novel in the maximalist vein. It may be his finest. The book goes from the last days of 1988 to late 1989. Rabbit was fifty-five. He had retired, because Janice had turned the Toyota lot over– against his wishes– to Nelson, freeing Rabbit to again become a seeker, a creator without the tools to create. Who made the stars? Why is sex so interesting? Overwhelmed by leisure, Rabbit moved constantly. He and Janice divided their time between the area around Fort Myers, Florida, and a newly revitalized Brewer. When, at the warm waters of the Gulf, Rabbit takes off his Nikes, Updike writes, "the sand bites his bare feet with an unexpected chill– the tide of night still cold beneath the sunny top layer of grains. The tops of his feet show wormy blue veins, and his shins are all chalky and crackled, as if he is standing up to his knees in old age. A tremor of fright comes alive in his legs. The sea, the sun are so big: cosmic wheels he could be ground between. He is playing with fire." Family was just another reminder that death was coming. Rabbit was the head of the pride displaced by the younger lions. Here is Rabbit waiting for Nelson, Pru, now Nelson's wife, and their two children to arrive for a visit: "He sees them. Just this side of the zebra crossing, coming this way, struggling with suitcases. He first sees Nelson, carrying Roy on his shoulders like a two-headed monster, and then Pru's head of red hair puffed out like the Sphinx, and Janice's white tennis dress. Harry, up to his chest in car roofs, waves his arms back and forth like a man on a desert island." Fear made Rabbit a world-class recorder of the world around him. No longer protected by his physical grace, he was exposed to the full anxiety of his nihilism. He was looking everywhere for an answer– to the Jewish residents dominating his condo, to the wisdom of the blacks in the inner city, to a book of American history he picked up. His body was beginning to complain about all those years of junk food (Rabbit was an inveterate nibbler). Doctors had put him on Nitrostat pills. Time was running out.

In an instinctive act of connection and revenge on Janice and Nelson, he slept with Nelson's wife Pru. This was the act no one could forgive. When he subsequently fled to Florida, for the first time, no one went after him. He had become redundant. He wandered lonely and lost through out-of-season Florida, "still trying to keep up with America, as it changes styles and costumes and vocabulary, as it dances ahead ever young, ever younger." He returned to basketball, his first love, his only genuine experience, and had a massive heart attack playing a pick-up game with a teen-ager near his condo. He fell where he first was given life– on the basketball court.

Throughout the books, there was a suggestion that Harry might really have been called for something, that this wasn't all just emptiness. The rabbit is also a symbol of Christian resurrection. But we never really find out. All we know– we who aren't in God's mind, who are just observers of Rabbit's intense quest through these sixteen hundred pages, his hunt for the white whale of life's meaning– is that when Rabbit hit the ground, it seemed to be over. Updike wrote: "Seen from above, his limbs splayed and bent, Harry is as alone on the court as the sun in the sky, in its arena of clouds." It wasn't much of an ending in terms of hope, redemption or caring. Dead is dead.

"My idea of happy and other people's idea of happy isn't necessarily the same," Updike points out when reminded how brutal the end of *Rabbit at Rest* is. He agrees that what he calls his and Rabbit's "vague but authentic religious impulses" came to nothing. The Rabbit series is among other things a shaggy-dog story. He adds, "There *is* something depressing about being a human being, you're able to think, you're able to foresee your own death, you're able to observe quasars on the edge of the universe." Yet you do all this, Updike observes, locked in a body perpetually going downhill. Rabbit felt this inconsistency and fled from it. Updike's own response has been steady productivity. "My way of looking for the peace beyond understanding," he says, "...is to do something creative, to make something out of nothing. That's still exciting to me." For many years he has written three hundred to four hundred words a day six days a week. He stops when he has gotten to his goal. If he finishes early, he gives himself a treat. Like Rabbit, he likes to play golf. But where Rabbit had only wanting, Updike has discipline. He has lashed himself to the mast of literature.

Thirty-two works of fiction, six books of poetry, seven books of criticism, a memoir and five children's books have come from Updike's pen– and more recently his computer. When he isn't writing, he is thinking about writing or critiquing other writers or writing about art. He is unique in the scope of his literary life. Updike reviews books for *The New Yorker* and art exhibitions for *The New York Review of Books*. If a reporter calls him for a comment on a current event, he picks up his phone and talks to them. This is highly unusual. We live in an era in which writers have either walled themselves up in universities (Toni Morrison, Saul Bellow) or limited what we are allowed to know about them to their fiction (Don DeLillo, Philip Roth). They are trying to reclaim their former status as cultural shamans. That's not Updike. He's out there in his chinos and polo shirt. You always know what he is thinking. And he knows what we are thinking.

This engagement helps fuel the creativity that keeps Updike from falling into the nihilism that ultimately got Rabbit. His life is not– as he describes Rabbit's– "the saga of a man who didn't have quite enough to live for after adolescence." It is the reverse. It also explains what gives the Rabbit books their unique punch. Every writer reveals himself through his characters. But chronicling how we live in the world is much rarer. Unlike their Victorian predecessors, contemporary novelists are not teachers. They try to depict life as they sense it to be and not as consensus opinion regards it. One wouldn't, for example, trust Saul Bellow on 1930s Chicago or J.D. Salinger on postwar New York. Their vision is too personal, too internal. They make a world, for all that it is drawn from reality, that is primarily accountable to their artistic vision. But Updike's special genius, not just in the Rabbit books but in many of his thirty-one works of fiction, is that he has the disposition to fulfill the roles of novelist and social historian. This is useful right now. Our insides have become too broad, too varied, too agitated for nonfiction. Daily newspapers publish five sections of news each morning without a breath of life lived in them. Updike's novels give us a view of our times as rich, human and entertaining as they really were. He can create a wholly satisfying fictional universe and tell us about our own, taking us on an inner and outer journey at once.

Being different from other literary writers has had its advantages for him. It's allowed him to create average Americans, like Harry Angstrom, whom other novelists cannot conceive of. The great gift of the books– the way in which they extend literature– is the way in which they plausibly put thoughts generated by a brilliant, educated man into the mouth of an uneducated but intuitively intelligent one. They are populist remedies for our deficient education system. They flatter us with our potential. They tell the reader: Keep thinking! There's glory in it! This democratic message has made Updike lot (sic) of money over the years. His books have been enormous sellers. At times he's been the closest thing America has to a people's novelist. He's been on the cover of *Time* twice. He's won two Pulitzer Prizes, two National Book Critics Circle Awards and a National Book Award.

But being different– more human, more like the rest of us– has also cost him. Critics speculate that his casting his net so wide has dissipated his talents. *The New York Times* critic Michiko Kakutani, in giving *Toward the End of Time* a negative review, was typical in wondering whether the problem was Updike's self-imposed "pressure of publishing at least one new book a year? . . .Is it simply that many prolific authors, regardless of their talent, produce their share of lemons?"

Another rap is that everything he writes is pretty good but nothing great. He has never given us a *Herzog* or *Beloved*. Bellow and Morrison have won the Nobel Prize, but he has not. He lacks the highest kind of seriousness. This is a difficult charge to respond to, just as it is a difficult charge to sustain. It gets into the question of why we read. Which book is more likely to be read in fifty years, *Beloved* or *Rabbit at Rest*? One suspects that at that point *Beloved* will feel arch and self-important, like the poetry of Henry Wadsworth Longfellow does today– America dressing up for a visit from the in-laws. The Rabbit series will feel honest and cleanly observed, the equivalent of Herman Melville's fiction. We will grow into Rabbit. Updike's own response to the criticism has been to become more who he is. He once said: "There's a yes-but quality about my writing that evades entirely pleasing anybody. It seems that critics get increasingly querulous and impatient for madder music and stronger wine, when what we need is a greater respect for reality, its secret, its music."

Because he assumes such music exists, Updike has made his life quiet enough to hear it. He has long had the dullest life of any major American writer. For all his fondness for writing about sex, there is little to scandalize– or even to entertain. Updike married his first wife while they were still in college. They had three (sic) children. The marriage lasted twenty years. After a separation, it ended in divorce– to be followed by Updike's remarriage to a therapist. John and Martha Updike have been together twenty-three years. With his first wife, he lived in the coastal town of Ipswich in Massachusetts (the model for Tarbox in *Couples*) and now he lives in the town of Beverly Farms, about forty miles south. "I'm a domestic creature," he has said.

Domesticity was not Rabbit's gift, but Updike sees other points of contact. "We share certainly a watchful eye, and a watchful eye for a pretty leg," he says, "for a well-turned ankle as they used to say, though most men can claim that. He and I are also gut patriots in a way that is not always fashionable." But whereas Updike is at peace, Rabbit, Updike points out, "never quite comes to terms" with the fact that "to be in any social situation is to give up some of the freedom that American males are obsessed with." He is Updike acting out, desublimated, freed from his desk to make trouble in the world. Updike doesn't think Rabbit would respond to him if they met. There's not enough angst in the writer. "Rabbit would be distant and friendly," he says, "but I wouldn't seem very real to him. He'd recognize that I wasn't the real thing but a rabbit manqué, a would-be rabbit. Whereas he's the real article."

The difference between real and fake Rabbits is also at the center of "Rabbit Remembered." The story, which begins with Annabelle's knocking on Janice's door, comes to focus on Rabbit's son, Nelson, now a counselor for troubled adults. For Nelson, the great trauma of his life remains his loving, competitive father. He is beginning to get some perspective. He and Annabelle talk about Rabbit's golf game:

> Nelson: "He just got up on the tee and expected to be terrific."
> Annabelle: "And was he?"
> Nelson: "Not very actually . . . But in his mind he had all this potential."

"You need sometimes the space a dead father gives you," says Updike, whose own father died in 1972, when he was forty. Nelson also takes on Rabbit's burden of wanting, his obsession with sex, his worrying about the state of the world, his running away when he's angry, and some of his gift for noticing. Rabbit took notice over the years of the fate of a particular restaurant in downtown Brewer. Johnny Frye's Chophouse became Cafe Barcelona and then the Crepe House in the 1970s and then Salad Binge in the 1980s. Now Nelson sees it has changed once again. It is Casa di Pasta. He records plane crashes and natural disasters, as his father did. When Nelson's friend Billy asks him if he's afraid of death, he responds the way Rabbit would:

> "It's like a nap. Only you don't wake up and have to find your shoes. He
> is being hard-hearted; there is agony here, even if Billy is a comical old
> friend. Not only are his lips fat, his nose has gotten fat; it sits there in
> the middle of his face, like something added, its flesh faintly off-color.

Fans might hope that the forty-two-year-old Nelson will be the new Rabbit, a way to continue the series, but Updike says no. "I don't know if I'll be alive in nine years, and if I am I can't believe that there'll be. . .anything left to say. Maybe [he's good for] a short story." Updike wants to move on. Maybe he's still in mourning over the death of his forty-year alter ego, a relationship that lasted longer than either of his marriages. You don't get over that in a mere decade. There will always be a part of him that misses Rabbit– or that part of himself that died with him. Maybe too he is glad to be relieved of the burden of being our official noticer. "I'm not sure I have very many thoughts about the '90s," Updike says. That's hard to believe, but the motive for the answer is easy enough to understand. Enough. Maybe. Enough.

There's so much that is left behind when a person dies. Updike is not the only one who misses Rabbit. What would Rabbit have thought of the hapless Phillies? The loss of a Russian submarine? The drop in the crime rate? *Survivor*? (The guy who won in the summer was reminiscent of Ronnie.) What about the nuclear face-off between India and Pakistan over Kashmir? Rabbit was fascinated with how exposed America was to unforeseen dangers. Would he have noticed that George W. Bush has learned to avoid smirking by tightening and pulling down his face muscles when he speaks? Or the way that Americans have snuck out of their compacts and into SUVs– our relentless need to conquer nature reasserting itself? "Most of American life is driving somewhere and then driving back wondering why the hell you went," Rabbit says in *Rabbit at Rest*. Nelson makes similar observations to this in "Rabbit Remembered," but there was something in Rabbit's make-up that made him perfect for them. His narcissism made him look at the world with only one question: What does this mean for me? That's exactly what a writer does too.

Updike says "there's a little Rabbit in all of us," a good explanation for the success of the series. There's also a little Updike. Things frequently show up that seem perfect for the Rabbit books. Last week on the New Jersey Turnpike, a road Rabbit surely must have driven in his multiple attempts to get away, there was the following advertisement for the Toyota Avalon. "You did something to deserve this?" The perfect epitaph, perhaps, for Rabbit, Nelson, Updike and all the rest of us.

*Max., D[aniel] T. "Noticers in Chief: John Updike and Rabbit." *Book* Nov.-Dec. 2000: 32-36, 38-39.

"Still Wild About Harry"

A. O. Scott*

Each of John Updike's four Rabbit novels concludes with a one-word sentence, a condensed, almost ideogrammatic summation of the moral state of the hero, his nation and, perhaps, his creator. The first book, *'Rabbit, Run,'* published in 1960, left Harry Angstrom, the former high school basketball star, in flight and in flux: it ends with the breathless, subjectless verb "Runs." A decade later, *'Rabbit Redux* faded out with an anxious question – " O.K.?" -- as though both author and character were seeking reassurance after the marital and social upheavals of the 60's. By the end of the 70's, with the Reagan presidency on the horizon and his father-in-law's Toyota dealership thriving, Harry Angstrom could settle, with satisfied amazement, into the comfort and complacency of worldly success: the last word in *Rabbit Is Rich'* is "His." Finally, 10 years ago, as his maker pushed poor Rabbit, too young at 56, toward his final rest, the two men let go of each other with a sigh of resignation, regret and perhaps a measure of relief: "Enough."

But of course it wasn't. Not even the grave, or the 1,516 cloth-bound pages of the Everyman's Library edition of *Rabbit Angstrom: The Four Novels*, could exhaust Rabbit's life force. Updike, who has found in Rabbit an indispensable, if unlikely, vehicle for his truest insights into the mysteries of manhood, the promise of American life and the operations of divine grace, could no more pass up the opportunity for a further Rabbit report than Rabbit himself could forgo a bowl of macadamia nuts. Another decade has come and gone and here, miraculously and just in time, is the latest (one hesitates to declare it the final) installment in the saga, a 182-page novella called "Rabbit Remembered," appended to a collection of a dozen recent short stories.

Updike once noted that Rabbit was "many things his author was not: a natural athlete, a blue-eyed Swede, sexually magnetic, taller than six feet, impulsive and urban." He was also a child of the working class -- a typesetter before he was a car dealer -- who remained rooted in his hometown even when he and Janice took to wintering in Florida. The other stories in *Licks of Love* seem, in contrast, like self-portraits, some rendered with minimal embellishment. These stories, most of which appeared in *The New Yorker*, share a theme of retrospect and a bittersweet tone of forgiveness. Not all the memories are sexual -- two particularly touching stories, "My Father on the Verge of Disgrace" and "The Cats," are about parents and children -- but most of them chase after the vapors of vanished erotic contact. The narrators and third-person protagonists of these stories seem to have their carnal histories perpetually at their fingertips and to remember the intimate smells and shapes of women they knew many years ago, and sometimes barely at all.

A few stories may not win over readers who have previously been turned off by Updike's occasional bursts of satyriasis. The title of *Licks of Love*, about a banjo player on a State Department tour of the Soviet Union in the mid-60's, is a naughty play on words. A "lick" is a musician's term that also refers to, well, just what you might expect. More often, though, Updike uses eros as a window onto the past, and the value of *Licks of Love*, apart from the pleasure of catching up with Rabbit's friends and relations, is the wry, measured sense of perspective it brings to Updike's earlier work. The best story, in this regard, may be the one that seems at first glance the slightest-- a brief, quizzical inquiry into changing approaches to child-rearing and marriage called "How Was It, Really?," in which the narrator, a father of four grown children, now settled into grand parenthood, can't quite formulate an answer to his question. He should go back and reread *Too Far to Go*.

In the years since *Rabbit at Rest*, Updike, whose unstraining industry seems calculated to put every other American novelist (except maybe Joyce Carol Oates) to shame, has been a restless traveler, forsaking the familiar habitats of coastal New England and southeastern Pennsylvania for the humid exoticism of *Brazil*, the multigenerational historical pomp of *In the Beauty of the Lilies*, the dystopian science fiction of *Toward the End of Time* and the Shakespearean mischief of *Gertrude and Claudius*. (This is not to mention the two story collections, the children's picture book, the volumes of poetry, criticism and golf writing or the unclassifiable *Memories of the Ford Administration*. This kind of productivity pre-empts the potential critic with a smiling, implicit rebuke: So how did *you* spend these past 10 years?) Just as "Rabbit at Rest" brought Updike back to the hard ground of realism after the quasi-allegorical flights of his mid-80's Hawthorne phase, so "Rabbit Remembered"-- narrated, like the other Angstrom books, in the present tense-- returns his attention to the Heraclitean flow of current events, both intimate and public.

Ever since *Rabbit Redux* juxtaposed the calamity of Harry and Janice's marriage with the Apollo moon landing, the news of the day has served each novel as intermittent background noise, intruding on the consciousness of characters and readers alike with the buzz of fact and the resonance of metaphor. The final reel of "Rabbit Remembered" unspools in the frenetic sham apocalypse of Y2K-- how far away it already seems-- and along the way there are references to, among other things, the Elián González affair, the Columbine shootings and the death of John F. Kennedy Jr. There are also barrages of pop-culture shorthand, like a movie marquee advertising "BLUE EYES BLAIR WITCH SIXTH SENSE CROWN AFFAIR," and a dinner-table mention (how could Updike resist it?) of *The Vagina Monologues*.

Sometimes, these refractions of recent history seem overly willed, like black-and-white newsreel footage inserted into a Hollywood costume drama. At one point, Janice, Harry's widow, now married to his nemesis, the boorish Ronnie Harrison, contemplates a smudged drinking glass and thinks: "Fingerprints on fingerprints. Now they use DNA-- not that O. J. didn't go free anyway. That long-legged prosecutor outsmarted herself, and that black lawyer was slick." This sounds less like a representation of thought than a piece of convenient ventriloquism, a lepidopterist's pin piercing a middle-aged woman's consciousness in order to fix her in the velvet-lined display case of her time. Still, the question of how, bombarded with information and cocooned within the tedium and safety of daily life, we actually experience distant happenings may pose an insoluble puzzle for an American novelist. Updike's occasional clumsiness is at least evidence of an honest effort too few writers bother to make. And he is also remarkably attentive to alterations in the finer grain of social life-- the ever-shifting culinary fads, the impact of technology, from e-mail to the S.U.V. – and the rapid, nearly untraceable fluctuations of taste, real estate values and religious practice. His observations eddy and swirl into the main stream of his narrative, swelling it with life.

Recent history has also given Updike, as it gave Philip Roth in *The Human Stain*, a windfall in the form of the Clinton-Lewinsky imbroglio. The president's impeachment, still raw in the autumn of 1999, provides "Rabbit Remembered" with a brilliant central set piece, a contentious Thanksgiving dinner that brings together, somewhat against their wills, Rabbit's scattered and scarred survivors. Janice and Ronnie-- whose late wife, Thelma, was one of Rabbit's lovers, and who also had a fling with Ruth Leonard, Rabbit's first mistress-- are living in Janice's parents' old house at 89 Joseph Street in Brewer, where the whole cycle began. Janice and Harry's son, Nelson, recovered from his cocaine addiction and separated from his wife, Pru (another of Rabbit's conquests), is living with them. Joining Ronnie, Janice, Nelson and Ronnie's unpleasant children for the holiday meal is Annabelle Byer, Rabbit and Ruth's daughter, who briefly surfaced in *Rabbit at Rest* and whose appearance on Janice's doorstep sets the brief, packed plot of "Rabbit Remembered" in motion.

Nelson seethes, Janice slips into her usual tipsy detachment and Ronnie insults Annabelle. The dinner is a tableau of dysfunction, a perverse tribute to the wreckage Rabbit left in his wake. "He was narcissistically impaired," Nelson explains, flaunting the diagnostic language of his new career as a social worker before moving on to a brutally reductive summary of the first four Rabbit novels: "I mean, he *did* things, too. He ran away from Mom to shack up with your mother. He got involved with a megalomaniacal black guy and a masochistic runaway white girl and got our house burned down. He had a crush on this nitwit young wife of a friend of my parents when they were in a country-club phase. Then he had a long secret affair with his oldest friend's wife."

But if Rabbit was an unapologetic sinner -- specializing in lust and gluttony, with strong side interests in vanity and sloth -- he was also, in Updike's perverse, persuasive version of Protestant theology, a saint. His earthly appetites, however destructive to himself and others, were signs of election, his carnal enthusiasm an ecstatic embrace of creation. Nelson, without irony, thinks back on his father as "the spectacular man" and intuits his spectral presence everywhere around him -- in his dreams, in Annabelle's face, in his own crippled and compromised capacity for joy. The subtext of the Thanksgiving argument, in which he and Annabelle unite to defend the president against the disgust and derision of the others, is clear enough. They are speaking up for a reckless, charming man who takes mulligans on the golf course and gobbles unhealthy food -- a man not unlike their father. "Yes, it was too bad about -- about his needing a little affection," Annabelle admits, "but maybe he was entitled to some." Janice, deep in Sauternes, thinks "of how much like Harry Nelson was, defending presidents. . . . Why do they do it, care so about those distant men? They identify. They think the country is as fragile as they are."

Harry's patriotism-- reflexive and sometimes complacent-- was, like Updike's, the expression of an embattled, stubborn optimism. "God he can doubt," Updike wrote in the introduction to the Everyman's edition, "but not America. He is the New World's new man, armored against eventualities in little but his selfhood." Such Emersonian confidence contains a paradoxical element of political conservatism, but this book, and the Rabbit cycle taken as a whole, transcends any obvious political label. Forty years ago, when he quit New York for the bourgeois towns of Massachusetts, Updike symbolically threw in his artistic lot with the provincial American middle class. Ten years later, when he declined to join the literary fifth column of the New Left, he renewed the bet, accepting what looked like very long odds. At the end of the 20th century, it seems his gamble has paid off: the car dealers and sales executives and suburban professionals in whose midst he has flourished have turned out to be history's true revolutionary class.

Near the end of "Rabbit Remembered," Nelson and Annabelle, along with Pru and Nelson's old buddy Bobby (sic) Fosnacht, drive to a New Year's Eve showing of *American Beauty*. Pru finds it "overdone and unconvincing," and of course she's right, but it's also a lurid rehash of a half-dozen John Updike novels. In the abstract, Lester Burnham's predicament looks a lot like Rabbit Angstrom's-- the lust, the restlessness, the atmosphere of casual adultery and sexual hypocrisy. But*American Beauty* tries to turn Updike's realism into Gothic, and to impose a ready-made tragic vision on a story that turns out to have been a comedy all along. "The very motion of our life is towards happiness," Nelson tells Annabelle at the end, quoting the Dalai Lama (whose flight from Tibet was part of the historical backdrop of "Rabbit, Run"). It may take an incarnate deity to articulate such a notion, but only an artist can prove it. "Rabbit Remembered" ends, as the laws of classical comedy stipulate, with the prospect of a marriage -- and also, true to form, with a sentence consisting of a single word. The word is "Gladly."

*A. O. Scott. "Still Wild About Harry,"*New York Times Book Review*. 19 Nov. 2000: 11-12.

Appendix

The "Rabbit" Angstrom Timetable

Jack De Bellis*

As he reviewed his four novels for *Rabbit Angstrom*, Updike wrote, "by my calculations, *Rabbit, Run* takes place from 20 March 1959 to 24 June of that year; *Rabbit Redux* from 16 July 1969 to late October; *Rabbit Is Rich* from 23 June 1979 to 20 January 1980; *Rabbit at Rest* from 28 December 1988 to 22 September 1989.Spring, fall, summer, winter: a life as well as a year has its seasons" [xxiv].My intention is to guide the reader's attention to the passage of time Updike has so carefully constructed. The dating of events in this chronology is derived from *Rabbit Angstrom*, and the novella "Rabbit Remembered." Since Updike was creating the felt apprehension of reality in his fiction and not a dated log, the dates listed are sometimes followed by "?" to indicate my informed guess.

The purpose of this timetable is thus: 1) to provide an accurate record of the succession of events that form the days of the life of Harry Angstrom; 2) to reveal how careful Updike was in integrating those events to a chronicle of events in American culture; and 3) to suggest how some dates contain metaphorical or symbolical meaning. The important days of a life are not necessarily those the rolling calendar advertizes as the most significant– Christmas, birthdays. And the date everyone on earth awaited, the turning of the millennium, is encountered in confusion and painful purgation.

While the timetable may at times provide some sense of the plot of the 'Rabbit' saga, that is only incidental to these other purposes. Though Updike is often highly specific in his dating (in the case of e-mail, down to the tenth of a second), often dates need to be construed by a named or suggested event (a Mike Schmidt home run, the moon landing)or the approximate time implied by meal times, bedtimes etc. I have noted where the obvious or conjectural dating may be found in Updike's definitive *Rabbit Angstrom* (*RA*), and in "Rabbit Remembered" in *Licks of Love* (*LL*). I have occasionally indicated where dating conflicts in the texts arise. The valuable chronology of *Rabbit at Rest* in Dilvo Ristoff's *John Updike's Rabbit at Rest: Appropriate History* is more event-centered than mine, and we disagree on some dates. But in my timetable I have sought to include only events which can be attached to a specific or implied time. For page citations, I have listed only the first or most important page.

"Time has turned the spectacular man to powder in just ten years"(*LL*, 255) Updike's narrator observes in "Rabbit Remembered," and the minutes, hours, days and seconds included in the texts show how time does in fact turn people into "powder" with its inexorable ticking, yet Updike's people often produce an explosive "powder" in the events that round their lives. But as the narrator of *Rabbit at Rest* remarks, time is not an enemy but the element in which we exist. So this timetable operates both as a melancholy march through moments of Harry "Rabbit" Angstrom's life and an appreciation, respect, and even reverence, for the temporal dimension that is at one and the same time our most fragile and our most durable element.

As a social realist, Updike places the action in each Rabbit novel in so specific a moment in time he seems to have created a timetable for *Rabbit Angstrom*. More detailed in some novels than in others but constantly propelled by the present tense Updike found so liberating, the timetable provides the reader both a moment-by-moment participation in Rabbit's life and a subtle sense, as he reads, of the passage of his own time as well. This constant presence of minutes, hours and days in the saga also produces an awareness of the presence of symbolic meaning time too. Harry deserts his family in *Rabbit, Run* on Friday, March, 20, 1959, the first day of spring. An apparent rebirth, the season leads to an abrupt finish to his freedom and the death of one of Rabbit's babies and threatened abortion of another.

Rabbit Redux confirms that what should have been a rebirth in spring for Rabbit had delivered him to life-in-death: the womb had become a tomb. *Rabbit Redux* opens on the day of the Apollo 11 moon launch, July 16, 1969, a false "lifting," since the space age has no perceptible impact on Harry or his personal world. Astronauts may land on the moon, but Janice Angstrom's flight from her husband brings a "moonchild" in Jill and an alien Skeeter into Harry's sterile world. Near Columbus Day he, like Columbus, finds a better direction by going the wrong way. Around Halloween Rabbit dreams of Jill's ghost, buries the ghost of his baby who died a decade before and reconciles with Janice, who had nearly caused her lover's death. Updike had used the liturgical calendar to some extent in *Rabbit, Run* when Rabbit slept with Ruth on Palm Sunday. In *Rabbit Redux* the sacred calendar is counterbalanced mordantly by Hallowe'en, the eve of the Feast of All Saints.

The calendar becomes distinctly secular in *Rabbit Is Rich*, ending with the secular "holy day"of Super Bowl Sunday. The action starts in a kind of purgatorial summer in which Teresa "Pru" Lubelle, carrying Nelson's child, arrives on a date she embodies, Labor Day Eve; they marry on September 22, the first day of fall (foreshadowing the day on which Rabbit will die ten years hence). She "falls" (with Nelson's help) and breaks her arm the day before the anniversary of the cessation of hostilities ending World War I, November 10. Meanwhile, on Webb Murkett's advice Rabbit gambles on the rise of the price of gold and silver: time turns into money. Rabbit becomes a parody of Santa Claus, straining to carry sacks of silver to the bank during the Christmas season. On New Year's Day, the Angstroms buy a new home, which, in time, is converted again into money in *Rabbit at Rest*. On

Super Bowl Sunday, January 20, 1980, Rabbit apparently gains an advantage over death when Pru presents his granddaughter Judy to him, but the symbolic victory over death is overwhelmed by Harry's realization that, Judy is a clock who carries his doom, a "nail in his coffin."

Rabbit at Rest begins with a thoroughly secularized Christmas, as Nelson's family visits Rabbit and Janice in Florida. Judy, Nelson and Pru parody the three Wise Men with symbolic gifts that conspire to kill Rabbit, though their pernicious effects take nine months to be effective, as though Rabbit had experienced a gestation of death. Judy provides a prank that creates Rabbit's near-fatal heart attack. Nelson has embezzled from Springer Motors to support his cocaine addiction, forcing Rabbit out of retirement. Though spring finds him symbolically reborn among the Brewer Bradford pear trees, Pru's gift of her body and subsequent confession of their sexual evening forces Rabbit to flee to Florida and to his death. In the ironic garden of Florida he dies at summer's height.

"Rabbit Remembered" begins in the fall of the year and moves inexorably through the decade toward the year 2000, a fearful date which in the past was filled with religious terror, but now is fraught only with predictions of terrorism and computer disaster. Yet the birth of a new thousand years brings Nelson to maturity as he enables his half-sister Annabelle to restore her faith in men, it provides him with the strength to leave his mother and re-establish his life with his estranged wife. Fall gives way to winter without discontent because Harry Angstrom, who entered the saga on the first day of spring, is reborn through the rebirth of his son and daughter.

The Time before *Rabbit, Run*

1904
July 20: Mary Renninger Angstrom is born ("I'm sixty-five" *RA*, 346).

1905
Earl W. Angstrom is born (*LL*, 271).

1920s
Frank Byer is born ("in his forties" in 1961 when Annabelle was about one year old *LL*, 185).
Mt. Judge High School built(*RA*, 1380).

1924
Mary Angstrom tells her boyfriend to shoot her if she lives to be thirty (RA346).

1927
Webb Murkett is born ("He enlisted in '45 when he was eighteen" *RA*, 369).
St. John's Episcopal Church is built (*RA*, 206).

1929

Fred and Bessie Springer buy a breakfront (*RA*, 905).

1930s

The house Harry and Janice buy was built in this decade (*RA*, 1031), like the block where they lived when first married (*RA*, 1346).

1932

Fritz Kruppenbach arrives in Mt. Judge ("I've been here twenty-seven years" *RA*, 146).

1933

Harry "Rabbit" Angstrom (hereafter, Rabbit) is born the same year Brewer High school is built *(RA*, 651, 1275) in February *(RA, 51)*. Ruth Leonard is born ("both of them twenty-six" *RA*, 1314).

1934

Thelma Harrison is born ("she was only fifty-five" in 1989 *RA*, 1387.)

1935

Earl and Mary Angstrom buy a brick house at 303 Jackson Road for $4,200 *(RA, 18*, 654).

1936

Janice Springer Angstrom is born ("age forty-three" RA, 655, "fifty-two" *RA*, 1126). Her birthday is probably before the end of July, since she is fifty-two in Dec. 1988, and fifty-three (2 years younger than Thelma) at the funeral (*RA*, 1387).
Charlie Stavros "is Janice's age" (*RA*, 1266).

1939

Miriam "Mim" Angstrom born ("Born when he [Rabbit] was six" *RA*, 430).
Rabbit tells Reverend Jack Eccles that he "must have been six or seven" when he was saved from being "a Fosnacht" by his grandfather (*RA*, 108).

1940

Rabbit's mother's father, grandfather Renninger, dies *(RA*, 108).

1942

Rabbit Angstrom's "big time" was buying peanuts in Brewer on Saturday (*RA*, 1274).

1944

The Springers buy a home on 89 Joseph Street ("The Springers moved to this house when Janice was eight" *RA*, 1338).

Rabbit caddies at the Chestnut Grove Golf Course where he and Eccles later golf (*RA*, 110). He flattens cans and buys War Stamps (*RA*, 120).

Mrs. Smith's son is killed in the war (*RA*, 120).

1945

Rabbit sees his father's sad buttocks (he was twelve or thirteen" *RA*, 813), and on a Sunday walk with his mother fears his sister will fall in the quarry (*RA*, 139, 210). He starts practicing basketball at home (*RA*, 140).

April 12, Thursday: Rabbit learns of President Franklin Roosevelt's death (*RA*, 436).

Webb Murkett joins the navy ("He enlisted in `45 when he was eighteen" *RA*, 980).

Rabbit recalls V-E Day (*RA*, 216).

1946

Fred Springer buys his car lot ("after the war" *RA*, 1438).

1947

Rabbit experiences his first sexual desire (for Lotty Bingaman) as a freshman at Mt. Judge Senior High ("Rabbit was fourteen in soc sci class" *RA*, 898).

Ruth Leonard desperately tries to lose weight (*RA*, 166).

1949

April: Cindy Murkett is born ("I'll be thirty this April" *RA*, 887).

Manager of "The Blasts" has been a client of Fred Springer since 1949 *(RA*, 330).

1949-51
Rabbit attends Mt. Judge Senior High school.

1950
Rabbit scores 23 points in his first varsity game and sets a record with 817 points in a season (*RA*, 7, 24, 1250). He has his first sexual experience with Mary Ann after the Senior Prom at the Ben Franklin hotel (*RA*, 1219). They continue their intimacy the next year in his father's new blue Plymouth (*RA*, 170, 793, 1447).

1951
Rabbit breaks his own "B" League scoring record for points in a basketball game ("not broken until four years later, that is, four years ago" *RA*, 7). His team wins the league championship two of his three years at Mt. Judge (*RA*, 1226). He graduates from Mt. Judge High. Ruth Leonard graduates from West Brewer High. (*RA*, 49). Jill Pendleton is born (*RA*, 376).

1952-54
Rabbit serves in the army at Fort Larson, Lubbock, Texas, near El Paso (*RA*, 347, 689), and has his appendix out in case he was sent to Korea, but he is grateful that he never was (*RA*, 375, 1105). He sleeps with a prostitute after his mother writes that Mary Ann has married (*RA*, 171, 1468). He buys a '39 Nash for $125 (*RA*, 21).

1953
Back from the army, Rabbit refuses to work as a typesetter with his father (*RA*, 140).

1954
June: Janice Springer graduates from Mt. Judge High ("she was two years out of high school" *RA*, 11).
August: Janice loses her virginity (*LL*, 202).

1955
Summer. While working at Kroll's Department Store opening packing crates and moving furniture (*RA*, 277), Rabbit meets Janice who is selling candy and nuts. She was "turning twenty" (*LL*, 203). They become intimate in his father's DeSoto and later, when work ends at 5:30, use Linda Hammacher's Eighth Street apartment to make love (*RA*, 13, 339, 1468).
September: Teresa "Pru" Lubell is born. ("I'm thirty-three" she says in May, 1989, *RA*, 1362).

1956
February: Janice tells Rabbit "in early February" she is pregnant (*RA*, 216).
March : Janice and Rabbit marry ("their marriage is seven months older than their child" *RA*, 294).
October 22: Nelson Frederick Angstrom is born ("tomorrow is his birthday"

RA, 593).
  Rev. Jack and Lucy Eccles have a daughter, Joyce (*RA*, 101).
  Jill Pendleton's favorite brother is born (*RA*, 396).

1957
  June Billy Fosnacht is born *(RA, 280)*.
  Mr. Springer gives Janice a mink stole on her twenty-first birthday. Rabbit
buys a 1955 Ford from Springer Motors for $1,000 (*RA*, 21).
  Jack and Lucy Eccles arrive in Mt. Judge.

1958
  Mim goes to Las Vegas *("*at nineteen Mim. . .went west" *RA,* 1305).
  Rev. Jack and Lucy Eccles have a second daughter (*RA*, 101).

1959
  Charlie Stavros starts at Springer Motors *("*he has been with Springer Motors
twice as long as Rabbit" RA, 626-7).
  February 21?: Rabbit begins demonstrating the MagiPeel peeler. (By March
20 "he's had the job for four weeks *RA*, 10).

The Time of *Rabbit, Run*

1959
  March 20, Friday: ("winter's last day" *RA*, 7, 22). After work, Rabbit shoots
some baskets with neighborhood kids and then runs home. He watches *The Mickey
Mouse Club* with Janice, and walks to his in-laws' home to retrieve their Ford
Falcon. He then drives to his parents' home to get his son, Nelson, but when he sees
Nelson being fed, Rabbit decides to drive south. Rabbit asks directions at a gas
station at 7:30 (*RA*, 24), at 8:04 passes Lancaster (*RA*, 27), at 9:20 he stops at a
diner (*RA*, 30) and stops for coffee in West Virginia before midnight (*RA*, 30).At
"two o'clock in the morning," Fred and Bessie Springer phone their minister, Rev.
Jack Eccles (*RA*, 89).
  March 21, Saturday: Near dawn Rabbit returns to Brewer (*RA*, 35). Just
after six o'clock Rabbit awakens (*RA*, 43) in the attic room of his former coach,
Marty Tothero at the Sunshine Athletic Association. They go to dinner with Ruth
Leonard and Margaret Kosko.
  March 22, Palm Sunday: "Palm Sunday is always blue" (*RA*, 87). Rabbit
moves in with Ruth, so he returns to his home for clothes and encounters Rev.
Eccles who arranges a golf date for Tuesday. Rabbit hikes to the top of Mt. Judge
with Ruth in "the sloping sunlight" (*RA*, 99).
  March 23, Monday: Rev. Eccles visits Janice and her high school friend
Peggy Gring Fosnacht to tell them Rabbit is still "in the county" (*RA*, 108). Ruth
and Rabbit have seen four films; *Bell, Book and Candle* prompts him to purchase
bongo drums (*RA*, 99).

March 24, Tuesday: Rabbit golfs with Eccles at the Chestnut Hill Golf Course and it becomes a regular Tuesday meeting (*RA*, 128). He is offered a job gardening for Mrs. Horace Smith (*RA*, 99).

April-May: Rabbit works ("for these two months" *RA*, 117) as a gardener for 83-year-old Mrs. Smith. About this time Janice takes Nelson to look at the apartment on Summer Street where Rabbit and Ruth live(*RA*, 768).

May 20 Wednesday:? "Memorial Day's next Saturday" Rabbit tells Mrs. Smith (*RA*, 120).

May 30, Saturday, Memorial Day: (*RA*, 122).Ruth fears she is pregnant while she and Rabbit swim in the Brewer pool (*RA*, 123).

Early June? Eccles visits the Springers for the second time in three weeks (*RA*, 130) and he sees Earl and Mary Angstrom in order to reconcile Rabbit and Janice. Near dinner time Eccles also talks to the Angstrom's Lutheran minister, Fritz Kruppenbach, who accuses him of diluting his spiritual office by becoming a social worker.

June 6, Saturday: At Club Castanet, Rabbit and Ruth drink with Rabbit's former teammate Ronnie Harrison. Rabbit infers that Ronnie had been one of Ruth's clients. Later he coerces Ruth into fellating him as she had Ronnie. After Janice goes into labor, Mrs. Springer calls Eccles at 8 P.M., and after two hours of calls Eccles locates Rabbit at 11P.M. at Ruth's apartment (*RA, 161*). A few minutes later Rabbit tells Ruth they are finished and goes to the hospital.

June 7, Sunday: After a six-hour labor Rebecca June Angstrom is born at 2A.M. (*RA*, 171). Rabbit sleeps at Eccles' s home until 12:20 P.M. (*RA, 177*). He visits Tothero who has suffered two strokes, and from 1 to 3 P.M. watches television quiz shows with Janice, then meets his baby (*RA*, 182-88).

June 8-15: During this week Rabbit and Nelson watch softball games, go to the playground, visit his parents and his in-laws. He stops gardening for Mrs. Smith. "The days go all right" (*RA*, 197).

June 12, Friday: Janice and Becky come home. "For the first few days" all is well (*RA*, 200).

June 15, Monday: Rabbit begins selling cars at Springer Motors ("off at his new job since Monday" *RA*, 201).

June 21, Sunday: ("The day is one of the longest of the year" *RA*, 210). Janice has been out of the hospital "nine days" (*RA*, 201), so Rabbit goes to church alone at 10:45 and is bored by Eccles' s "Forty Days in the Wilderness" sermon, walks Lucy home and rejects what he considers a pass. Becky cries all day and Rabbit's attempt at intimacy alienates Janice, so he takes a bus to Ruth's apartment and, when she doesn't return, sleeps in a hotel (*RA, 231*).

June 22, Monday: "The first day of summer" (*RA, 231*). Becky's cries awaken Janice at 4 A.M. (*RA*, 214). She watches "the sun come up" (*RA*, 244), then watches television and drinks whiskey. Her father calls "after eleven" (*RA*, 222) to see why Rabbit has not come to work; she says he has gone to Allentown to sell a car. At lunchtime her mother calls and when she plans to help Janice, Janice hurries to clean the apartment and accidentally drowns her baby while washing it. Meantime, Rabbit wanders around Brewer all day after again failing to find Ruth and in the afternoon calls Eccles and learns of Becky's death (*RA*, 231-232). He returns to the Springers' home where Mrs. Springer makes a supper; then spends the night in his own home (*RA*, 233-38).

June 23 Tuesday: In the morning Rabbit returns to the Springers and stays with Janice all day. In the afternoon Tothero arrives to say he had warned him tragedy would follow his leaving Janice (*RA*, 240). Eccles comes "later in the afternoon" (*RA*, 241). Visitors pay respects at the Springer home where Rabbit spends the night. Mrs. Springer calls his mother (*RA*, 247).

June 24 Wednesday: After breakfast Rabbit and Janice return to their apartment to dress for the funeral with the "sun nearing the height of noon" (*RA*, 245). Janice changes dresses as it "becomes one o'clock" (*RA*, 245). After Nelson's lunch Janice naps. Rabbit is too upset to eat as "time to the funeral slowly passes" (*RA*, 247). A little after 2:25 (*RA*, 247) the Springers dress then "the minutes ebb in the silver-faced clock" as they await the undertaker's car (*RA*, 248). They gather at the funeral parlor where Eccles reads the service. They go to the cemetery, "beautiful at four o'clock" (*RA*, 251), where Eccles reads again, the baby is buried. Rabbit, feeling accusation in the faces of the mourners, runs. At 5:40 he phones Eccles, but Lucy hangs up on him (*RA*, 259). He returns to Ruth, learns that Eccles had called her "about a half-hour ago" (*RA*, 260), and that she is pregnant. Unable to decide to return to his family or divorce Janice and marry Ruth, he runs into the gathering darkness (*RA*, 264).

The Time between *Rabbit, Run* and *Rabbit Redux*

1959

Sometime in 1959 Rabbit begins working at Verity Press; by 1969 he has worked there "a decade" (*RA*, 269) rising at 7:15 A.M. to go to work with his father (*RA*, 647).

1960

January 8?: Annabelle "Annie," daughter of Ruth Leonard and Rabbit, is born in Pottstown (*LL*, 182, 191, 357).

Christmas?: Ruth Byer deceives Rabbit into thinking her son, Scott, was born at this time (*RA*, 1024).

1961

Spring?: Ruth meets Frank Byer while working at a restaurant "over toward Stogey's Quarry" (*LL*, 184).

November: Annabelle's step-brother Scott born "the next year" (*LL*, 185).

1963

November 22, Friday: News of President John F. Kennedy's assassination comes to Rabbit at Verity Press (*RA*, 436).

1966?

Mrs. Mary Angstrom has had Parkinson's disease "for years" (*RA*, 270).

1966

Rabbit and Janice moved to 26 Vista Crescent, Penn Villas "three years ago" (*RA*, 270).

June 6: Ruth's last child, Morris, is born (*RA*, 1023).

Jill Pendleton is given a Porsche for her sixteenth birthday (*RA*, 383).

1967

Fall: Rabbit meets Ruth at Kroll's and she tells him "You've had your day in the cabbage patch."(*RA*, 323).

Pru muses that "maybe two years ago" Nelson began to steal from Springer Motors to support his cocaine habit (*RA*, 1362).

1968

December: Rabbit attends a Christmas party at Verity Press and is unfaithful to Janice.

1969

Janice's affair with Charlie Stavros has been going on "for months" (*RA*, 322).

"Early this summer" Rabbit meets and hates the doctor attending his mother (*RA*, 483).

July 10, Thursday: Janice's parents go to their vacation home in the Poconos.

The Time of *Rabbit Redux*

1969:

July 16, Wednesday: The day of the Apollo 11 blast-off for the moon, Rabbit and his father drink at the Phoenix bar when work at Verity Press is done at 4:15 P.M. (*RA*, 272, 441). He returns home, to 26 Vista Crescent in Penn Villas, phones Janice who says she will work until "ten or eleven" (*RA*, 274) doing bookkeeping for her father at Springer Motors, makes TV dinners for Nelson and himself, watches the news at 6 P.M. (*RA*, 285) and at 9 P.M. *The Carol Burnett Show* with a skit about the Lone Ranger (*RA*, 285). Janice arrives at 10:55 P.M. with Rabbit nearly asleep (*RA*, 289).

July 17, Thursday: Rabbit's father tells him during the 10:30 A.M. coffee break that the Springers are in the Poconos, revealing that Janice had lied (*RA*, 292). Rabbit and Janice dine at "The Taverna," on Quince Street, arriving at 6:20 P.M.; Charlie Stavros, a salesman at Springer Motors, joins them (*RA*, 298) and Rabbit argues with him about the Vietnam war until after 6:50 P.M. (*RA*, 302), making the Angstroms late for the 7:30 P.M. start of *2001: A Space Odyssey* (*RA*, 295). Janice joins them after twenty minutes of coffee and stolen kisses with her lover (*RA*, 310). After they return home and Rabbit falls asleep, Janice masturbates thinking of Charlie (*RA*, 315).

July 18, Friday: "Next day, Friday" (*RA*, 316) after work Rabbit's father tells him his mother thinks Janice is having an affair. She returns home "after six" (*RA*, 318) and confesses her adultery when Rabbit beats her, but they then make love from twilight until "after two" (*RA*, 326-327).

July 19, Saturday: After breakfast Rabbit decides to let Janice live with Stavros, and she accepts the gambit. At 12:30 P.M. (*RA*, 331) Fred Springer takes Rabbit and Nelson to see the Brewer "Blasts" play baseball. On returning at about 4 P.M. Rabbit finds a farewell note from Janice.

July 20, Sunday: During 8 A.M. breakfast Rabbit watches news of race riots, Senator Edward Kennedy's car accident, and the preparation for lunar landing. At "around nine" (*RA*, 340) Nelson comes to breakfast and Rabbit returns to bed and sleeps until 10:55 A.M.. After lunch he and Nelson wait twenty minutes for a bus to Brewer, then shop for Mary Angstrom's birthday present (*RA*, 342). They arrive at her home at 4:20 P.M. (*RA*, 345) and have dinner with his father and mother who, though suffering from Parkinson's disease, has made her own birthday cake. As "dusk thickens" they watch the Eagle land on the moon, and though Rabbit suggests at 9 P.M. that they go home (*RA*, 351), they stay to watch Armstrong step on the moon at 10:56 P.M. (*RA*,352).

At about this time Jill Pendleton arrives at Jimbo's Lounge (*RA*, 377).

July 26?: Rabbit phones Janice at work to see if she is working (*RA*, 355).

August 2, Saturday: "One Saturday in August" (*RA*, 353) Buchanan, a "Negro" co-worker at Verity, during morning coffee break, invites Rabbit to Jimbo's Friendly Lounge "around nine or ten" (*RA*, 354). Rabbit allows Nelson to stay overnight with Billy Fosnacht and watch the film *The Longest Day* on television (*RA*, 393). He kisses Peggy before leaving. At Jimbo's, Rabbit enjoys the piano playing of Beatrice "Babe" Green, meets Hubert "Skeeter" Farnsworth, a black Vietnam vet, and Jill Pendleton. Jill goes home with Rabbit at 12:10 A.M. (*RA*, 387).

August 3, Sunday: Nelson discovers Jill at 9:45 A.M.. They all go with Ollie and Billy Fosnacht to the New Jersey Shore at 10:30 A.M. (*RA*, 395).

August 4, Monday: Rabbit insists Jill leave their home.

mid-August: During a "succession of nights" (*RA*, 401) Rabbit and Jill talk a good deal about religion. During the "crystalline week before school begins" Jill teaches Nelson to drive her Porsche (*RA*, 405).

August 25, Monday: Jill has been living with Rabbit for three weeks (*RA*, 409). At 11 A.M. Rabbit and his father discuss his mother's response to L-Dopa for her Parkinson's disease and he conveys Janice's warnings about Jill. After work Rabbit beats Jill when he discovers that Jill and Nelson had been panhandling. Jill relates her history in talking blues while strumming the guitar bought panhandling; they are reconciled.

August 28, Thursday: "one day after work" (*RA*, 417) in the Phoenix bar Rabbit and Stavros discuss the possibility of Janice returning to Rabbit. Rabbit watches a film being made (perhaps *Rabbit, Run*?) (*RA*, 424).

August 29, Friday: "Labor Day is coming on" (*RA*, 425) when Janice announces she will buy Nelson's school clothes the next day, and Rabbit adds "he's going to be thirteen next month" (in reality, in the fall) (*RA*, 425)."The other night" (*RA*, 430) Jimbo's is raided early in the morning, and Babe, Skeeter and eight others are taken into custody, but Skeeter escapes (*RA*, 454, 445).

August 30, Saturday: In the morning Jill goes to Valley Forge so Rabbit visits his parents, Mrs. Angstrom attacking Janice and relating nightmares prompted by L-Dopa; Rabbit leaves at 3:30 P.M. during a Phillies baseball game. He meets Jack Eccles on the bus, and walks home in the 4 P.M. "September brightness" (*RA*, 440).After making love to Jill he watches the news with its estimates of Labor Day fatalities at 6 P.M. as Nelson returns from shopping with Janice (*RA*, 443).

September 2, Tuesday: "One day in September" (*RA*, 444) Rabbit encounters Skeeter hiding in his home and beats him for having sex with Jill. Nelson and Billy Fosnacht, home from school, observe the fight (*RA*, 450). Those arrested at Jimbo's are sentenced (*RA*, 454).

September 8, Wednesday: Rabbit and his father at the Phoenix discuss Janice's reaction to Skeeter while they watch television images of the lying-in-state of Senator Everett Dirsken who died the previous day (*RA*, 471-72) . After dinner he listens to Skeeter's description of slave history and his reading of *The Autobiography of Frederick Douglass*. At 8 P.M. they watch the satiric television show *Laugh-In* in which Sammy Davis, Jr. and Arte Johnson, dressed alike, seem "one man looking into a crazy mirror" (*RA*, 481).

September 12: Friday: Rabbit visits Peggy near the time Billy Fosnacht will return from school (*RA*, 458) and asks Peggy not to spread the word that Skeeter lives with him. Rabbit returns home to find Jill, Nelson and Skeeter watching news of the arrival of Robert Williams in Detroit (*RA*, 461). After supper they have their first "educational" evening in which Rabbit is told the history of America from the viewpoint of the dispossessed blacks (*RA*, 466-69) . [Note: In this novel Updike has the events of September 8 follow those of September 12, and I have noted this anomaly by indicating the pagination in *RA* which errs by placing Williams's arrival before Dirksen's lying-in-state. *Ed.*]

"Nights with Skeeter blend together" as Skeeter explains how a Negro feels, expresses his hatred of privileged persons (*RA*, 483), and demonstrates white oppression of black women by forcing a kiss on Jill (*RA*, 484). Skeeter instructs Rabbit about class hatred and describes the exploitation of black women.

October 1, Wednesday: Peggy Fosnacht invites Rabbit to dinner October 11 ("Saturday" (*RA*, 486); he accepts. "This fall" Nelson discovers junior high school soccer (*RA*, 488).

(The Following dates are conjectural since "one of these afternoons" is all that is indicated until October 11 [*RA*, 497]).

October 2, Thursday: Skeeter relates his Vietnam experiences after dinner.

October 3, Friday: Rabbit thinks he loves Jill.

(October 4, Saturday?): Skeeter and Jill watch quiz shows all day, and Nelson fights with a boy who objects to Skeeter living in his home.

October 5, Sunday: Skeeter relives his Vietnam experiences.

October 6, Monday: Rabbit has a beer with his father and learns L-Dopa has helped his mother.

October 7, Tuesday: Skeeter offers a cosmic theory of the relation of God and Vietnam to Black Holes and colonialism. (*RA*, 494-95).

October 8, Wednesday: After dinner Skeeter provides his "Beatitudes" (*RA*, 496). They all cruise the area in Jill's Porsche, but it "seizes up" an hour before sunset *(RA,*497-503).

October 9, Thursday: At 6 P.M. they all watch Students for a Democratic Society riots on TV, and after the 11 P.M. news discuss the relation of technology to Vietnam. Rabbit reads from *The Life and Times of Frederick Douglass*, prompting Skeeter to masturbate.

October 10, Friday: Rabbit phones Peggy during his lunch hour and confirms their date for "tomorrow" (*RA*, 514). After work, Rabbit is accosted by Mahlon Showalter and Eddie Brumbach who threaten him if he doesn't evict Skeeter and stop having visible sex with Jill. At home, Nelson insists Rabbit get rid of Skeeter because Skeeter has apparently hooked Jill on heroin. After the 6 P.M. news Skeeter explains how "you may recognize My coming." (*RA*, 523). Later Skeeter enacts the rape of black women by assigning Rabbit and Jill roles as slaves, while Skeeter plays the role of a white slave-owner who forces Jill to fellate him. When Rabbit turns on the lamp to see them better, they are seen by "a face" at the window.

October 11, Saturday: Janice and Charlie drive to the Poconos to see the fall colors and Nelson plans to visit her tomorrow. Rabbit puts off seeing his mother, hunts for Skeeter's drugs, watches some of game one of the World Series, washes the windows, and tends the lawn. At 5 P.M. Skeeter and Jill return from selling the Porsche for $600, and about 6 P.M. Rabbit takes Nelson for an overnight with Billy Fosnacht in anticipation of an "early birthday party" the next day on Ollie Fosnacht's boat. Peggy Fosnacht makes dinner for Rabbit, and after watching the 11 P.M. news they make love. When he takes his leave she protests "it's only midnight" (*RA*, 539) so he stays until 1:20A.M. when Skeeter phones (*RA*, 540), urging Rabbit to return home. Rabbit drives home in Peggy's car. He finds his home on fire, Jill dead.

October 12, Sunday: Rabbit inspects the ruin around 6 A.M. and finds Skeeter hiding in his car (*RA*, 555). Rabbit drives him out of town. In the first of "a dreadful three days" Rabbit spends the day driving back and forth with things from the burned house to his parents' home in Mt. Judge, driving through the Columbus Day parade (*RA*, 566).

October 13, Monday: When Verity Press converts to off-set printing, Rabbit is fired as a linotyper (*RA*, 563), effective October 17. At noon Jill's parents and her husband confront Rabbit (*RA*, 567). Billy Fosnacht photographs the burned house (*RA*, 571); Nelson keeps the Polaroids in his scrapbook. Mim calls from New York, having flown from Las Vegas the day before (*RA*, 569).

October 14, Tuesday: Rabbit sleeps late and has to be roused for work.

October 15, Wednesday: Mim visits her family, after spending two days in New York (*RA*, 573). "Moratorium Day" provides one day of peaceful demonstrations against the Vietnam war. Janice has phoned several times, threatening to sue him for the burning of the house.

October 16, Thursday: After work Rabbit finds Mim amusing Nelson with imitations of the Disney automatons of presidents. She tells Rabbit she is seeing

Stavros.

October 17, Friday: Rabbit's last day at work (*RA, 585*). Mim tells him she slept with Stavros, then takes the family out to dinner.

October 18, Saturday: In the morning Mim takes Nelson to the Fosnachts and sleeps with Stavros a second time.

October 19, Sunday: The family takes Mrs. Angstrom to dinner, then to visit the quarry; she dislikes her dinner, but she does like *Funny Girl* which they see at 6:30 P.M. (*RA, 58 8*).

October 20, Monday: Rabbit awakens at 7 A.M., his first day out of work in ten years (*RA, 588*). At 11 A.M. Mim leaves to sleep with Stavros for the last time (*RA, 589*). Returning at 2 P.M., Mim explains while playing basketball with Rabbit that she wanted to drive Stavros away from Janice (*RA, 593*). She gives Nelson a mini-bike for his birthday "tomorrow" (*RA, 593*), though in fact he was born on October 22.

Undated, but several nights later: Rabbit imagines Jill comes to his bed (*RA, 596*) . About 2 A.M. Janice helps Stavros overcome a heart attack (*RA, 601*) and comforts him until 6 A.M..

Late October "two nights later": "Be November pretty soon" (*RA, 616*). At noon Janice phones (*RA, 606*) Rabbit to arrange a meeting at 2 P.M.; they decide to sell their burned home. At 2:30 P.M. they check into the *Safe Haven Motel*, watch *The Dating Game* on television and sleep.

The Time Between *Rabbit Redux* and *Rabbit Is Rich*

1969

Rabbit, Janice and Nelson move into the Springer home, 89 Joseph Street. (*RA, 654*). Rabbit and Nelson watch *Lost in Space* on television (*RA, 785*).

1970

Rabbit starts work at Springer Motors as Associate Sales Representative.
May 4: Kent State Shootings (*RA, 907*).
Rabbit recalls seeing Nelson's penis (*RA, 813*).
Unspecified. Nelson practices on Jill's guitar and collects rock and roll music (*RA, 1290*).

1971

Rabbit resumes golfing (*RA, 601*).   Janice quizzes Nelson about his masturbation (*RA, 1183*).
Annabelle's step-father teaches her to ride a tractor, work the farm (*LL, 183*).

1972

Rabbit conjectures Cindy and Webb Murkett might have begun their relationship on this date, when she was 22 years old (*RA, 887*).
Mrs. Mary R. Angstrom dies (*LL, 271*) .

1973

Nelson may have stolen condoms from Rabbit (*RA*, 813).

Janice has a tubal ligation after she and Rabbit stop using condoms (*RA*, 666, 887).

By the time Nelson graduates from high school Fred Springer has had his first stroke (*RA*, 659).

1974

Rabbit first sees the Springer Motors books (*RA*, 825).

Fred Springer gives his wife, Bessie Koerner Springer, a Chrysler Newport (*RA*, 655).

Nelson visits Kent State University (*RA*, 654-55).

Cindy Murkett has her first child (*RA*, 672).

During the year, Frank Byer abuses his step-daughter Annabelle (*LL*, 281).

1975

"One summer day" Fred Springer dies of a heart attack "(*RA*, 624) "brought on by Watergate" (*RA*, 1331).

Rabbit assumes control of Springer Motors.

1976

March: Rabbit gives Janice a gold necklace for their twentieth wedding anniversary(*RA*, 704).

August: Frank Byer, Ruth Leonard's husband, dies of cancer (*RA*, 1024).

September: Nelson enrolls at Kent State.

Earl W. Angstrom dies (*LL*, 271).

Cindy Murkett has her second child (*RA*, 672).

1977

Jamie Nunemacher takes Annabelle to the senior prom (*LL*, 290).

1978?

Annabelle works as a nurse's aide in Sunnyside nursing home (*LL*, 183).

Rabbit reads an article about Professor Julian Jaynes's theory of the origin of consciousness in the breakdown of the bi-cameral mind (*RA*, 1040).

1979

April: Rabbit learns of Skeeter's death. (*RA*, 647). He cites the April *Consumer Reports* to sell Toyotas (*RA*, 624). Nelson impregnates Teresa "Pru" Lubell: "She missed her first period in May" Janice reports (*RA*, 789).

June 19: Thursday: A terrible thunderstorm strikes Brewer (*RA*, 695).

June 20, Friday: Rabbit sells a 1974 Barracuda. At night a big hail storm floods Eisenhower and Seventh(*RA*, 626). The Philadelphia Phillies lose a ball game 7-0 (*RA*, 640). Nelson and Melanie spend the night in a field in western Ohio (*RA*, 688).

Billy Fosnacht enters Tufts University dental school (*RA*, 709, 911).

The Time of *Rabbit Is Rich*

1979

June 21, Saturday: (" This longest Saturday in June and the first of calendar summer" *RA*, 626). Rabbit awakens at 6:30 A.M., rises at 7 A.M. (*RA*, 667). In the afternoon, he tries to sell a Toyota to Annabelle Byer and Jamie Nunemacher (*RA*, 632-43). Leaving work at 6 P.M., Rabbit drives to where he thinks Ruth Leonard Byer lives and hears a tale about a goose "murder" on his car radio (*RA*, 652). At 6:32 P.M. (*RA*, 656) he arrives home and learns that Nelson will return from Kent State University with a friend. After a night of television and Gallo Chablis, which intoxicates Janice by 10 P.M. (*RA*, 666), the Angstroms make love near midnight (*RA*, 667), the best for Rabbit in months (*RA*, 670).

June 22, Sunday: "The next day" Rabbit and Bill Inglefinger lose a golf match to Ronnie Harrison and Webb Murkett at the Flying Eagle Tee and Racquet Club. While drinking with them, discussing the Phillies, and trying to tell his "goose" joke, Rabbit ogles Cindy Murkett. When "the pool side is in shadow" Rabbit learns that Nelson has arrived with a friend, Melanie (*RA*, 683). Around 8 P.M. Nelson goes out for pizza while Mrs. Springer watches *All in the Family* and Rabbit reads the July *Consumer Reports* (*RA*, 693-4). After dinner Rabbit falls asleep when Janice shows no interest in sex.

July 7? Monday: Melanie has been living with the Angstroms "two weeks" and works as a waitress at the "the Crêpe House." She serves lunch to Rabbit and Charlie, who is attracted to her (*RA*, 700).

"One night" during **"these July nights"** Janice agrees to have Charlie to dinner, Rabbit arranging to have him meet Melanie (*RA*, 703).

July 20, Sunday: Former president Richard Nixon gives a moon-landing anniversary party, which upsets Charlie Stavros (*RA*, 713).

July 26, Saturday?: Charlie dines at the Angstroms' and meets Melanie. Nelson returns after 8 P.M., having gone off with Billy Fosnacht at 6 P.M. *(RA*, 709). He damages Rabbit's car.

July 30 Wednesday?: "Toward the end of July" Rabbit discovers Ruth Byer's farm but runs before they can meet (*RA*, 722).

"One night" Melanie dates Charlie (*RA*, 724). While it rains, Rabbit discusses selling cars with Nelson who then leaves angry.

Next day, August, first week:. Rabbit quizzes Charlie about his date with Melanie (*RA*, 735) and considers Charlie's idea of having Nelson join Springer Motors while the Angstroms vacation in the Poconos (*RA*, 738). About this time Janice learns of Pru's pregnancy (RA, 787).

"A month and more" since Melanie and Nelson arrived, Nelson vilifies his father to her, she tells him she's conflicted about dating Charlie, and they have intercourse while smoking pot (*RA*, 738).

August 7-26: Rabbit, Janice and Mrs. Angstrom vacation in the Springers' Poconos cottage "three weeks of August" (*RA*, 744) where he jogs, plays three-handed pinochle with Janice and Mrs. Springer, and plays tennis. Meanwhile Nelson buys convertibles, after 10 P. M goes to the "Laid-Back," and sleeps with

Melanie while complaining about his father (*RA,* 739-60).

August 18, Saturday: Charlie takes Melanie to the Amish areas near Lancaster (*RA,* 763).

August 24, Friday: Nelson and Melanie watch *Charlie's Angels* and discuss Nelson's lack of responsibility to Pru and his parents who will be "back Sunday" (*RA,* 760).

August 26, Sunday: The Angstroms arrive "on a sparkling Sunday noon late in August" (*RA,* 760). Charlie takes Melanie to Valley Forge. Nelson shows Rabbit the convertibles he has purchased, but he smashes them together when Rabbit criticizes his poor business judgment (*RA,* 773-74).

August 27-September 10: Charlie takes a two-week vacation (*RA,* 775).

August 29, Wednesday: "By Wednesday" Rabbit sells the TR-6 for $5,500, thus vindicating Nelson (*RA,* 775). Melanie leaves (*RA,* 775), presumably to join Charlie in Florida.

September 2, Sunday, Labor Day Eve: "The Sunday before Labor Day" Rabbit plays in a "Four Ball" tournament until 5:45 P.M. (*RA,* 783) and Webb Murkett suggests he buy gold. Janice tells him to come home to meet Teresa "Pru" Lubell, Nelson's fiancée. Rabbit guesses she is pregnant and "with this guess a backwards roll of light illumines the months past" (*RA,* 787).

September 5, Wednesday?: "A few nights later" (*RA,* 794) Reverend Archie "Soupy" Campbell discusses the wedding of Nelson and Pru.

September 6, Thursday:"the next day" driving to the lot in the rain, Rabbit fails to convince Nelson not to marry Pru (*RA,* 804).

September 12, Wednesday: Rabbit notices a new store, "Fiscal Alternatives" (*RA,* 811).

September 13, Thursday: Rabbit buys thirty Krugerrands at "Fiscal Alternatives" at Webb Murkett's suggestion *(RA,* 811). Nelson and Pru have their third counseling session with "Soupy," returning at 9:30 P.M. *(RA,* 813) . While the others watch *M*A*S*H,* Rabbit showers Janice with the Krugerrands and makes love to her (*RA,* 816-19).

September 17, Monday: Charlie returns to Springer Motors (*RA,* 819) and describes his affair with Melanie.

September 21 Friday: Rabbit jogs "each night" (*RA,* 827). Nelson damages Rabbit's Corona while running a stop sign, after he, Pru and Melanie get "drunk as skunks" (*RA,* 831, 837) in a pre-wedding celebration.

September 22, Saturday: "This holiday they have made just for themselves from a mundane Saturday, this last day of summer." Nelson and Pru marry at 4 P.M., on the last day of summer (*RA,* 843); a 4:30 reception follows (*RA,* 844).

September 23, Sunday-October 5: Nelson and Pru honeymoon at the Springers' cottage in the Poconos (*RA,* 856) and are "due back from the Poconos Friday." (*RA,* 866) . Mim flies home (*RA,* 855).

"One Evening" Bessie and Janice tell Rabbit they have agreed to give Charlie a six-month leave with half pay and hire Nelson. Rabbit strenuously objects (*RA,* 856). Bessie reminds him who is boss and goes off to watch *Charlie's Angels* (*RA,* 863).

September 29, Saturday: Jamie Nunemacher buys a Corolla from Charlie Stavros (*RA*, 868).

September 30, Sunday: While Rabbit plays golf, Mrs. Springer tells Charlie that Nelson has replaced him. Rabbit is impressed by new photos of Jupiter (*RA*, 867).

October 1, Monday: ("October first falls on a Monday" (*RA*, 864) as Rabbit and Charlie stare through a window at rain and discuss Charlie's termination. Rabbit learns of Jamie Nunemacher's purchase of the Corolla but can't be there to see him (and Annabelle) when he picks it up tomorrow because he has "Rotary" "tomorrow" (that is, Tuesday, but normally Rotary meets on Thursday *RA*, 868).

October 2, Tuesday: At Rotary, Rabbit hears a former track star Eddie Pastorelli tell a joke and propose civic improvements. At 4:30 P. M. Rabbit goes to Ruth's farm a second time (*RA*, 870).

October 6, Saturday: Charlie works his last day at Springer Motors (*RA*, 883).After golf, the Murketts host the Harrisons, Angstroms, and Fosnachts (*RA*, 880). Rabbit explores the Murkett bedroom and bathroom discovering nude photos of Cindy. The Fosnachts become embarrassing; after they leave, the other couples plan to vacation in the Caribbean. The Angstroms drive home at 1 A.M. (*RA*, 901).

October 7, Sunday: Nelson and Pru return from their Poconos honeymoon (*RA*, 900). Peggy Fosnacht attends an anti-nuclear meeting at a Universalist church (*RA*, 890).

October 8, Monday: Nelson has been working at Springer Motors for five weeks (*RA*, 905).

November 10, Saturday: "Here it is the middle of November" (*RA*, 909) as Nelson meets Annabelle Byer at the "Laid-Back." She has just started working in Brewer at the Sunnyside nursing home (*RA*, 916). Nelson and Pru leave about 11:30 P. M. as news of the Iranian hostages appears on the television (*RA*, 925).Pru falls with his connivance down a stairwell and breaks her left arm (*RA*, 927). Meanwhile, the Angstroms enjoy striptease at "The Gold Cherry" with their friends. Nelson takes Pru to the hospital and stays from 1 A.M. until he falls asleep at 3:30 A.M. He calls home to Mt. Judge at 1:15 A.M., but his grandmother is asleep (*RA*, 928).

November 11, Sunday: Pru calls "Soupy" Campbell at 7 A.M. because she fears she is starting labor. Rabbit first learns of Pru's accident when Nelson awakens him at 9 A.M. (*RA*, 928).At 9:30 A.M. Campbell visits Pru at St. Joseph's hospital, then meets Mrs. Springer at the 10 A.M. service; he sees her later at a fund-raiser for a new church organ (*RA*, 929). Rabbit had driven her there by 9:55 A.M. (*RA*, 938).

November 17?: At 11:30 A.M. on the eve of Pru's return from her seven-day stay in the hospital (*RA*, 940), Harry and Janice discuss their new house while having sex (*RA*, 941-45).

December: "The Christmas lights are up" (*RA*, 946), and Pru guesses that Nelson had betrayed her with Melanie as they drive to the "Laid-Back" where he scratches Mrs. Springer's Chrysler (*RA*, 951).

December 14, Friday?: After noon Rabbit and Janice convert their

Krugerrands to scrap silver bought "three months ago" (*RA*, 951).

December, the Christmas season: Nelson is outraged that his parents intend to buy a new house. At about this time Pru removes her cast (*RA*, 931).

"The week between the holidays": Rabbit and Nelson discuss Jill while working together, and how the Ruskies "gave themselves a Christmas present" with their war in Afghanistan (*RA*, 964). Janice and Rabbit select a new house (*RA*, 968).

December 25, Tuesday: Janice gives Rabbit a sheepskin overcoat and suede hat (*RA*, 1015).

December 31, Monday, New Year's Eve: Buddy Ingelfinger gives a party, which the Angstroms leave at 3 A.M. (*RA*, 968); Nelson and Bessie Springer watch Guy Lombardo's brother on TV. Charlie Stavros's mother takes a turn for the worse during the month (*RA*, 1012).

1980

January 1, Tuesday, New Year's Day: While Pru and Nelson watch the Cotton Bowl parade, Rabbit and Janice tell Bessie that they intend to leave her home, "announcing the break on a significant day, the first day of a new decade" (*RA*, 968).

January 7, Monday: Rabbit and Janice sell their silver at a profit (*RA*, 975).

January 8, Tuesday: The Angstroms "pass papers" on the house (*RA*, 975). It will be mortgaged until Rabbit is sixty-six (*RA*, 1041).

January 10, Thursday: The Angstroms fly to a Caribbean island after an 11 A.M. (*RA*, 973) drink in the lounge, arriving at 2 P.M. (*RA*, 977). Thelma Harrison burns badly at the beach. They watch crab races at night. Meanwhile Peggy Fosnacht has a mastectomy.

January 11, Friday: Thelma stays in the cabin. At night they observe Limbo dancing (*RA*, 979). In Brewer, Nelson goes alone to the "Laid-Back."

January 12, Saturday: After the men play golf, they all lie in the sun till 4 P.M.. Thelma buys a big hat and wrapper for sun protection. They all dance to a steel band till 4 A.M. (*RA*, 979-80). In Brewer, Nelson and Pru argue about his going to a party at Slim's, so Nelson drives to Ohio in Rabbit's Corona, as Pru learns Sunday morning (*RA*, 1006-1007).

January 13, Sunday night: At the Casino, Rabbit loses $300 but Ronnie has an exciting winning streak in craps, only to lose it all. They return about 2 A.M. (*RA*, 984). The women hatch a plot.

January 14, Monday: Rabbit swims alone before breakfast (*RA*, 985) then plays golf poorly. After lunch he rents a Sunfish, and Cindy saves Rabbit when he swamps their boat (*RA*, 986-9). After the bar-b-q buffet dinner (*RA*, 989), the couples swap spouses, Rabbit getting Thelma, Webb Janice, and Ronnie Cindy (*RA*, 993). They make love until dawn (*RA*, 1004).

January 15, Tuesday: Harrison and Murkett awaken Rabbit and the men play disgruntled golf. At 1P.M., Janice tells him Bessie Springer phoned the news that Nelson has deserted his family and driven to Ohio with Rabbit's Corona (*RA*, 1005). Nelson goes to Melanie (*RA*, 1030). They fly to San Juan, Puerto Rico at 3P.M.

and stay overnight. Pru delivers her baby, Judith (*RA*, 1010). Meanwhile, Bessie rehires Charlie Stavros (*RA*, 1012) and he sells a Corvette (*RA*, 1014).

January 16, Wednesday: After a poor night's sleep, the Angstroms fly to Atlanta, then Philadelphia where Bessie drives them to Brewer. They visit Pru and Judith in the hospital (*RA*, 1013). Charlie sells a snowmobile (*RA*, 1014).

January 17, Thursday: Rabbit discusses Nelson's behavior with Charlie at the lot, then drives a Celica Supra at 11:17 A. M. (*RA*, 1016) to visit Ruth who refuses to declare Annabelle his daughter (*RA*, 1020). He meets Janice at 1P.M. at Schaechner's Furniture Store where they buy a Sony TV so Rabbit can watch the Super Bowl Game (*RA*, 1030). The Murketts and Harrisons return from the island (*RA*, 1032).

January 18, Friday: Because Harrison works until 10 P.M., he can't help Rabbit move the next day (*RA*, 1030). The Sony TV is delivered (*RA*, 1032).

January 19, Saturday: In two hours Webb and Buddy help Rabbit move into his new house at 14½ Franklin Drive (*RA*, 1030). At 1:30 he receives a letter with a clipping of the goose story containing new details; since Thelma may have sent it, Janice decides she is still attached to Rabbit (*RA*, 1033). Nelson writes asking for tuition money; he plans to return to Kent State on the 28th (*RA*, 1035). The Angstroms have a party with the Murketts, Harrisons, and Buddy Inglefinger and Valerie (*RA*, 1036).

January 20, Super Bowl Sunday: Rabbit tours the house and burns 70's *Playboy* and *Penthouse* magazines (*RA*, 1037). Janice returns after 2 P.M., and "all afternoon" they clean house(*RA*, 1039). Janice shops, returns at 6 P. M. and awakens Rabbit from his nap (*RA*, 1043). He watches the Super Bowl game between the Steelers and the Rams about 8 P.M. Early in the fourth quarter, Janice and Pru arrive and after a Pittsburgh touchdown, Pru places Judith ("Judy") Rebecca Angstrom in grandfather Rabbit's arms (*RA*, 1042).

The Time Between *Rabbit Is Rich* and *Rabbit at Rest*

1980
    January: Rabbit and Thelma begin a ten-year affair. Annabelle Byer begins training as a nurse (*RA*, 920).

1980 or 1981: Peggy Fosnacht dies of breast cancer (*RA*, 1217). Her husband Ollie moves to New Orleans (*RA*, 1235).
    Rabbit and Janice visited Mim in Las Vegas "seven or eight years ago" (*RA*, 1306).

1980s
    Webb Murkett divorces Cindy and marries a woman in her twenties; they move to Galilee. Cindy works in a boutique in Oriole, Pennsylania (*RA*, 1235).
    Buddy Inglefinger marries Valerie (*RA*, 1112).
    Marcia of "Fiscal Alternatives" commits suicide (*RA*, 1245).

1981

March: The twenty-fifth wedding anniversary of Rabbit and Janice Angstrom (*RA*, 1282).

1982

June 22: Bessie Koerner Springer dies of diabetes (*RA*, 1052), "the day after Princess Di gave birth to little Prince William" (*RA*, 1222).

1984

October: Harold Roy Angstrom, son of Nelson and Pru Angstrom, is born (*RA*, 1500); Pru, who had given up cocaine when pregnant, never resumes using it (*RA*, 1184).

Mr. Shimada comes from Torrance, California (*RA*, 1405).

The Angstroms begin spending six months in their condominium in Deleon, Florida, six in Brewer (*RA*, 1055, 1087). In their "first year or two in Florida" they buy a telescope (*RA*, 1157).

Ruth Leonard Byer begins a fifteen-year career with an investments advisory firm in Brewer (*LL*, 192).

1986

Annabelle Byer begins work as a practical nurse at St Joseph's hospital (*LL*, 182).

1986-87? Ronnie Harrison's son, Ron Jr., goes to Lehigh University in Bethlehem, Pennsylvania for two years (*RA*, 1224).

1987

December: Charlie has open-heart surgery (*RA*, 1264).

Jimmie, the Big Mouseketeer, dies (*RA*, 1149). Nelson becomes a big cocaine user "maybe two years ago" (*RA*, 1362).

Ron Harrison decides to withdraw from the Flying Eagle Country Club (*RA*, 1226).

After Christmas?: Nelson and Pru Angstrom and their children Roy and Judy visit Rabbit and Janice at the condo in Deleon, Florida. They visit the Circus Museum in Sarasota (*RA*, 1092).

1988

Lyle suffers at least a year with AIDS (*RA*, 1243).

Annabelle Byer trades in her Corolla (*RA*, 1301).

April?: Pru enters Narc-Anon in Brewer (*RA*, 1278).

November: the Angstroms leave for Florida (*RA*, 1230).

"Before Christmas" Angus "Slim" Barfield dies of AIDS (*RA*, 1249).

December 22: Pan Am jet 103 is blown up, killing 259, near Lockerbie, Scotland (*RA*, 1055).

December 25: Janice gives Rabbit *The Final Salute*, by Barbara Tuchman (*RA*, 1436). Deion Sanders punches an auxiliary cop; he will be sued September

5, 1989 (*RA*, 1477).
   "Yesterday" A fourteen-inch hole in a plane forces landing in West Virginia.

The Time of *Rabbit at Rest*

1988
   December 27, Tuesday: "This Tuesday after Christmas in the last year of Ronald Reagan's reign" (*RA*, 1053) Rabbit and Janice pick up Nelson, his wife and children at Southwest Regional Airport in the afternoon, then drive to Valhalla Village by 4 P.M. (*RA*, 1077). They will visit for five days (*RA*, 1079). While awaiting dinner, the children swim in the pool and Rabbit and Nelson discuss the car business.
   December 28, Wednesday: "Today is Wednesday" (*RA*, 1090) and the Angstroms breakfast with the *Today* show (*RA*, 1094). Rabbit watches a "Lassie" movie, and then at 9:40 A. M. golfs with Bernie Drechsel vs. Ed Silberstein and Joe Gold "right through lunch"(*RA*, 1098) until 2:45 P. M. (*RA*, 1109).Rabbit naps with Judy then plays games with her while Janice goes to a women's group meeting. They dine at the Mead Hall, in Building B (*RA*, 1121). Rabbit becomes interested in a film on television, *The Return of Martin Guerre,* and drifts to sleep reading *The First Salute* and hearing the women and late-arriving Nelson laughing (*RA*, 1125-1128). Janice goes to sleep at 1 A.M. (*RA*, 1128).
   December 29, Thursday: At 9:30A.M. the Angstroms (without Nelson) tour the Edison Winter Home (*RA*, 1133). At noon they eat at McDonald's, then visit Jungle Gardens, where Rabbit accidentally eats parrot food (*RA*, 1142). At 2:45 they see the movie *Working Girl* (*RA*, 1145). After forty minutes in traffic, they return to Valhalla Village about 6 P.M., in time for the local evening news. Pru makes a healthful dinner, and, after channel surfing, Rabbit reads *The First Salute*; Janice reads the magazine *Elle.*
   December 30, Friday: A little after 10A.M., Rabbit takes Judy sailing but their Sunfish capsizes and Rabbit's effort to rescue Judy, who appears to be drowning, prompts his heart attack as the sun "has moved past noon" (*RA*, 1173). The paramedics arrive seven minutes later (*RA*, 1196). When Nelson awakens at 11A.M. (*RA*, 1178), Janice quizzes him about his drug use and Nelson makes promises he doesn't keep. A 12:25 P. M. phone call tells her Rabbit is in intensive care (*RA*, 1189). His doctor tells him he has "athlete's heart" and is told to choose heart bypass surgery or angioplasty (*RA*, 1198).
   December 31, Saturday: About 2 P.M. "twenty-six hours later" (*RA*, 1197) Janice talks to Rabbit on the phone and two hours later visits him in the hospital with Nelson, Pru and the children (*RA*, 1193). They speak to him separately while he monitors the Eagles vs. Bears football game. Roy pulls the oxygen tubes from his nose (*RA*, 1213-28). At night Janice takes Nelson and his family to the airport, then visits Rabbit again, then leaves to attend an origami lecture (*RA*, 1193).
   (From December, 1988 to April, 1989 Nelson and Lyle reported sales of a Toyota a month to the deceased Angus "Slim" Barfield (*RA*, 1375).

1989

January: Rabbit has a catheterization to reveal the damage done by his heart attack (*RA*, 1229). Elvira Ollenbach starts at Springer Motors after three years with Datsun (*RA*, 1240).

March: The weather is miserable in Florida (*RA*, 1225).

April 11?, Tuesday: Rabbit likes to be back "around April tenth" (*RA*, 1214) in Brewer. Rabbit and Janice return from Florida, since, on April 18, they have been "up here a week" (*RA*, 1249). He takes a tour of the town and is affected by the pear trees because in April Brewer brims "with innocent energy" (*RA*, 1217).

April 18, Tuesday: "Exactly two years ago" Mike Schmidt hit his five hundredth homer for the Phillies (*RA*, 1249). Rabbit has been "up here a week" (*RA*, 1230). At noon he visits Thelma Harrison (*RA*, 1225) for a half hour, and they end their affair. At Springer Motors he just misses Nelson who left for lunch at 1 P.M. (*RA*, 1239), so he confronts Lyle. Janice takes real estate courses at the Penn State extension, and after dinner she watches *Jeopardy* and Rabbit watches the Mets-Phils game (*RA*, 1251). In bed Rabbit tells Janice he suspects embezzlement at Springer Motors and she refuses to help until she talks to Nelson alone (*RA*, 1254).

April 19, Wednesday?: Nelson's cocaine creditors call and threaten the Angstroms.

April 20, Thursday: The Philadelphia Phillies's Mike Schmidt breaks former Phillie Richie Ashburn's hit record (*RA*, 1261).

April 21, Friday: Rabbit lunches with Charlie Stavros at Salad Binge, and Charlie advises him to have the bypass. He also agrees to find out if Janice intends to confront Nelson about drugs (*RA*, 1269). Rabbit is awakened at 2:10A.M. by Pru whom Nelson has beaten (*RA*, 1270) and in twenty minutes they arrive at her side and talk till past 3A.M. about Nelson's drug problem, wife-beating and embezzlement. They return at 3:50A.M. (*RA*, 1294).

Mid-May: (*RA*, 1330).

May, Friday: Rabbit has angioplasty at St. Joseph's hospital (*RA*, 1295). He guesses that his nurse is his and Ruth's daughter. He stays in the hospital "for five nights" (*RA*, 1303).

May, Saturday: Janice visits, says she had lunch with Charlie, and on his advice she called an accountant and visited the former accountant, Mildred Kroust. Then she confronts Lyle (*RA*, 1304).

May, Sunday: Dr. Breit visits Rabbit and encourages heart bypass in a few months (*RA*, 1309). Rabbit has a visit from a young girl dressed in black (*RA*, 1312). An hour later his sister Mim calls.

May, Monday: In the evening Annabelle asks if he wants to see her mother, and he rejects the offer. Janice has a real estate class (*RA*, 1303).

May, Tuesday: Rabbit watches television programs about nature and history. At 6 P.M. Janice (*RA*, 1318) reveals how Nelson embezzled from Springer Motors, and how she demanded he go into drug rehab for ninety days (*RA*, 1323). Rabbit watches *Antarctica* until the Harrisons arrive at 7:30 P.M. since Thelma is seeing her own doctor at the same hospital. Janice meets Charlie at a Vietnamese restaurant for dinner, then hurries home for the last ten minutes of *thirtysomething* at about 10:50 P. M. . She can't sleep because it rains for an hour (*RA*, 1331).

May, Wednesday: After quarreling with him, Janice sees Nelson off to therapy at 9A.M. (*RA*, 1330). Then she picks up Rabbit when Pru returns late from Philadelphia with the car after 1 P.M. While Janice studies for her quiz, Rabbit takes a walk past his old Mt. Judge home, then sleeps until the children return from school (*RA*, 1349). He dines on Pru's healthful dinner with Janice and the children, then watches news and the *Cosby Show* with Pru and Judy. Janice goes to her quiz as it begins to rain, promising to return at 10:30 or 11 P. M. (*RA*, 1355). At about 9 P.M. Pru goes to Rabbit's room and they have sex (*RA*, 1364). Janice returns "less than an hour later" (*RA*, 1373).

late May, early June: Rabbit and Janice have visited Nelson twice in his Philadelphia rehab (*RA*, 1365). Mike Schmidt says he is only in a hitting slump, but then retires (*RA*, 1369).

June 17, Saturday: Rabbit can't resist pizza from the Pizza Hut across the road (*RA*, 1365).

June18, Father's Day, Sunday: Rabbit fails to do a good cookout (*RA*, 1366).

June19, Monday: "The day after Father's Day" (*RA*, 1365) Rabbit again heads Springer Motors.

June 24, Saturday: the week after Father's Day; the weeds take over.

late June ("A week before the 4th of July") Janice and Rabbit fuss with his Uncle Sam costume (*RA*, 1378).

July 4 Tuesday: For Judy's sake Rabbit marches in the parade as Uncle Sam (*RA*, 1378).

July: Dying, Thelma Harrison tells her minister that God is responsible only for people's experience, not "for anything at the microscopic level" (*RA*, 1389). In her last week in the hospital she tells him she deserves her ailment (*RA*, 1388).

July 19, Wednesday: Thelma dies of kidney failure (*RA*, 1387) "the same week" a plane crashes in Sioux City, Iowa. At her funeral Ronnie reveals he knew of her affair with Rabbit.

August: Rabbit reflects on playing Uncle Sam "last month" (*RA*, 1395). At 11A.M. Mr. Natsume Shimada explains Toyota's position to Rabbit (*RA*, 1395), and Rabbit promises to make restitution by the "end of August," three weeks away (*RA*, 1404). Janice, who anticipates her real estate license in October, suggests they sell the Florida condo (*RA*, 1410).

Next Day: Nelson, back from rehab, has dinner with his parents about 6 P.M. in Mt. Judge (*RA*, 1414).Rabbit disputes Nelson's plan to make Springer Motors into a half-way house with the Toyota bill due "in two weeks" (*RA*, 1417).

Next day: Nelson returns to Springer Motors (*RA*, 1419).

August 30, Wednesday: "Middle weeks": Rabbit golfs with Ronnie Harrison (they tie), and they quarrel over Thelma (*RA*, 1421). Rabbit rejects Nelson's idea to sell jet skis (*RA*, 1427). Rabbit tells Elvira that he affirms "the Pete Rose settlement" made August 24 (*RA*, 1430).

"Thursday before Labor Day Weekend": August 31: (*RA*, 1432).Janice suggests selling their house and moving in with Nelson's family in her mother's place to get her started selling real estate. Rabbit hates this as much as he hates having not beaten Harrison "yesterday" at golf (*RA*, 1436). Janice goes to Nelson's to discuss the plan and Rabbit watches the news, with the "invasion of Poland fifty years ago tomorrow" (*RA*, 1441). At 9:20 P. M. he is awakened by Janice's phone call. Pru has told her she slept with Rabbit. He runs from the house and drives to Florida at 10:07 P. M. (*RA*, 1446). By 11 P. M. he's in Amish country (*RA*, 1448) and listens to news and music till midnight when he checks into a Best Western motel north of Baltimore (*RA*, 1450).

September 1, Friday: After breakfast Rabbit calls Pru to find out why she betrayed him. He spends the afternoon driving to Fayetteville, North Carolina.

September 2, Saturday: Rabbit drives though South Carolina and talks to a trucker who expects to be in Boston "twenty-four hours from now" (*RA*, 1462). He stops for the night at a Ramada Inn near Brunswick, Georgia, and the ten o'clock news repeats the story of baseball commissioner Bart Giamatti's fatal heart attack at age fifty-one (*RA*, 1464).

September 3, Sunday: Rabbit travels across Florida to Deleon. The sun is high and the heat "wrathful" (*RA*, 1470). "Tomorrow is Labor Day" (*RA*, 1473).

"One day": Rabbit is in his condo and tries golfing again (*RA*, 1474). He feels "bogged down into nothingness" "those four days before the phone got connected on Thursday" (*RA*, 1476).

September 5, Tuesday: Lightning kills a young football player "the day after Labor Day" (*RA*, 1477).

September 7, Thursday Though the phone has been installed, Janice doesn't call or answer his calls which scares Rabbit (*RA*, 1476).

September 10, Sunday: Rabbit watches Boris Becker defeat Ivan Lendl for the U. S. Open Tennis championship (*RA*, 1477).

September 11, Monday: He makes an appointment with Dr. Morris "day after next" (*RA*, 1480).

September 13, Wednesday: Sees Dr. Morris and is told to return in "four weeks" (*RA*, 1483).

"Late-summer" (*RA*, 14 85). He walks for his health twice a day and cuts out bad food (*RA*, 1484).

September 17, Sunday: "I've been down two weeks" (*RA*, 1487), Rabbit says to Nelson who calls to say Rabbit needs to sign the papers in order to sell the Penn Park house. Debbye Turner, the first black woman, is chosen Miss America (*RA*, 1492).

September 18, Monday: "On. . . Monday" at 4 P.M. Rabbit watches a basketball game (*RA*, 1493) as Hurricane Hugo arrives in Puerto Rico (*RA*, 1494).

September 19, Tuesday: Rabbit looks for signs of the hurricane's arrival and wonders if Mrs. Zabritski wants him to escort her to dinner tomorrow night (*RA*, 1495).

September 20, Wednesday: Rabbit finds the hurricane heading for Florida (*RA*, 1495). It rains from 12-3 P.M. and afterward he walks to the basketball courts; this time he joins the boys in a game of "Horse." After the news and a TV dinner, he calls home and learns Janice has sold a house. He wishes Roy a Happy Birthday. He has a second unnutritious dinner at 7:30 in the Mead Hall (*RA*, 1503).

September 21, Thursday:. At 10A.M. he returns to the basketball court, where a player named Tiger plays him a game of "one-on-one." Rabbit wins, but his last shot brings on a heart attack (*RA*, 1511). At night the police bring news of the tragedy to Janice and she and Nelson's family fly to Florida (*RA*, 1512).

September 22, Friday: At about 9A.M. Dr. Olman tells Janice that Rabbit's heart cannot be repaired(*RA*, 1513). Rabbit wants to tell her "I won." Then he tells Nelson (or thinks he tells him) that he has a sister and pronounces, perhaps about dying, "It isn't so bad" and dies. It is Nelson's tenth wedding anniversary.

The Time between *Rabbit at Rest* and "Rabbit Remembered"

1989

September?: Rabbit is cremated and Janice, Nelson, Pru and the children drive back to Brewer (*LL*, 269).

September? "The next night": Janice and Pru sleep in one room and Nelson in another because he and Pru are still estranged over her sleeping with Rabbit (*LL*, 270).

September? "In the morning": they have to drive back to the Comfort Inn for Rabbit's forgotten ashes (*LL*, 270).

September?: Mim attends Rabbit's funeral (*LL*, 269), her last return to Brewer.

1991

Janice marries Ronnie Harrison (*LL*, 213).

Nelson earns his counselor's certificate at Hubert F. Johnson Community College (*LL*, 218).

1995

Annabelle Byer works in home care "these last five" years (*LL*, 182).

1996?: Charlie Stavros has died "two or was it three years ago" of infection following cardiac surgery, age sixty? (*LL*, 195, 275).

1998

August: Pru has moved back to Akron, Ohio with Roy and Judy "a year and a half ago" and works for a lawyer (*LL*, 273, 312).

1999

May 3: President Bill Clinton visits Oklahoma City after a tornado strikes the city (*LL*, 262).

July: "Two months ago" Ruth Leonard Byer died (*LL*, 179).

August: Janice Harrison spends two weeks in the Poconos with her grandchildren, Judy and Roy (*LL*, 120). Her husband Ronnie plays golf all summer at the Flying Eagle (*LL*, 212).

The Time of "Rabbit Remembered"

1999
   September **"early fall"** (*LL*, 180): Annabelle, now an L. P. N. (*LL*, 182), visits Janice Angstrom, now Janice Harrison (*LL*, 179) with the news that she is Rabbit and Ruth's child. At noon Janice shows a house to prospective buyers, lunches in Brewer, drives to West Brewer to play bridge with friends, then drives home by 5:20 P.M. (*LL*, 208).
   September 16th, the following Thursday (*LL*, 223): During the morning, while rain and wind from hurricane Floyd arrive, Nelson works at the Fresh Start Adult Day Treatment Center, counseling schizoid Michael DiLorenzo and his parents until the center closes at noon. At 12:30 Nelson then lunches with Annabelle at the Greenery (*LL*, 223).
   "That night or the next": Ronnie agrees to invite Annabelle to Thanksgiving dinner. Annabelle lunches with Nelson (*LL*, 261).
   October 22, Friday, 8:04 P.M.: Roy Angstrom, Nelson's son, e-mails a birthday wish to Nelson, age forty-three (*LL*, 262). Nelson plans to see Roy, Pru and Judy at Christmas (*LL*, 268).
   October 24, Sunday: 9:31P.M.: Nelson e-mails his son Roy and tells him of Annabelle (*LL*, 267).
   October?: Nelson phones Mim Angstrom (*LL*, 272) and is disappointed that she isn't more responsive to his news about Annabelle.
   early November "One night": Nelson dreams that he sees Rabbit chipping golf balls (*LL*, 275).
   mid-November "Next morning": Nelson leads a Relationships group and recounts the event at lunch with Annabelle at The Greenery (*LL*, 276). Annabelle leaves for her dentist at 2 P.M. (*LL*, 280).
   November 25, Thursday, Thanksgiving: Annabelle joins the Harrisons and others for Thanksgiving dinner and is insulted by Ronnie (*LL*, 300). Nelson defends her, then leaves home with Annabelle in the rain (*LL*, 303).
   November 28, Sunday: Nelson comes by for his things while Ronnie is at church (*LL*, 304), and Janice apologizes for Ronnie.
   November 29, Monday: At Janice's urging, Ronnie apologizes to Nelson, and Nelson makes Ronnie realize he had really attacked Rabbit, not Annabelle (*LL*, 302).
   December 10, Friday: 5:11 P.M.: Nelson e-mails Roy to tell him he is now living in an apartment (*LL*, 309).
   December 11, Saturday: Pru phones Nelson to ask why he left Janice's home (*LL*, 304).
   December?: **March**: Nelson is asked to Christmas dinner and he refuses (*LL*, 319).

December? : Nelson and Annabelle have lunch (*LL*, 319).

December: 24, Friday, Christmas Eve: Christmas feels "least phony" at the Center for Nelson (*LL*, 327).

December: Christmas: Nelson gives Janice a computer program about bridge which he needs to return since she can't learn it, but Ronnie's gift to him of a book by the Dalai Lama seems to contain an aura of Rabbit (*LL*, 329). He leaves before midday, called back to the Center because of the suicide of Michael Di Lorenzo. Nelson dines alone (*LL*, 334). Pru spends Christmas with her mother and siblings, then comes to Brewer later with Roy and Judy. Annabelle visits Las Vegas with a friend (*LL*, 320).

December 27, Monday: Pru arrives with Roy but Judy stays in Akron (*LL*, 335).

December 28, Tuesday: Nelson stays in Janice's home with Pru and Roy but doesn't sleep with his wife(*LL*, 335). Ron Jr. takes Roy to a basketball game (*LL*, 336).

December 29: Wednesday On the phone, Annabelle tells Nelson she discovered a good deal about her father Rabbit from aunt Mim in Las Vegas and that she got her seats to *Cirque du Soleil* and other shows. Nelson invites her to double date on New Year's Eve (*LL*, 336).

December 30: A one hundred-nineteen-year-old Allentown, Pennsylvania, woman dies (*LL*, 342).

December 31, Friday, New Year's Eve: Roy plays pinochle and watches David Letterman with Janice and Ronnie (*LL*, 354). At 6:30 P. M. Annabelle and Billy Fosnacht pick up Pru and Nelson at Janice's home, then go to dinner at 7 P.M. at the Lookout in the Pinnacle Hotel, then see the film *American Beauty* and at 11:20 P. M. they drive in the millennium traffic congestion, get lost and "close to midnight" are still "nowhere" (*LL*, 349) until the Sunflower Beer clock "says it's midnight" (*LL*, 351). The clock is wrong and a minute later they see the fireworks in the center of Brewer, as Nelson and Pru begin to reconcile and Annabelle and Billy become familiar.

2000

January 8, Saturday: Roy e-mails thanks to Janice and Ronnie for spending New Year's Eve with him. He explains that Nelson will live with his family in Akron (*LL*, 354).

Some Days Later: Nelson talks to Annabelle on the phone and he wishes her happy birthday. She asks him to give her away if she should marry Billy Fosnacht.

*This Appendix was prepared especially for this book.

Primary and Selected Bibliography

PRIMARY SOURCES

I. Novels

The Poorhouse Fair. New York: Knopf, 1959.
Rabbit, Run. New York: Knopf, 1960.
The Centaur. New York: Knopf, 1963.
Of the Farm. New York: Knopf, 1965.
Couples. New York: Knopf, 1968.
Rabbit Redux. New York: Knopf, 1970.
A Month of Sundays. New York: Knopf, 1975.
Marry Me: A Romance. New York: Knopf, 1976.
The Coup. New York: Knopf, 1978.
Rabbit Is Rich. New York: Knopf, 1981.
The Witches of Eastwick. New York: Knopf, 1984.
Roger's Version. New York: Knopf, 1986.
S. New York: Knopf, 1988.
Rabbit at Rest. New York: Knopf, 1990.
Memories of The Ford Administration. New York: Knopf, 1992.
Brazil. New York: Knopf, 1994.
Rabbit Angstrom: A Tetralogy. No. 214 in Everyman's Library. New York: Knopf, 1995.
In the Beauty of the Lilies. New York: Knopf, 1996.
Toward the End of Time. New York: Knopf, 1997.
Gertrude and Claudius. New York: Knopf, 2000.
Seek My Face. New York: Knopf, 2002.
Villages. New York: Knopf, 2004.

II. Short Fiction Collections

The Same Door. New York: Knopf, 1959.
Pigeon Feathers. New York: Knopf, 1962.
Olinger Stories. New York: Vintage, 1964.
The Music School. New York: Knopf, 1966.
Bech: A Book. New York: Knopf, 1970.
Museums and Women and Other Stories. New York: Knopf, 1972.
Problems and Other Stories. New York: Knopf, 1979.
Too Far To Go: The Maples Stories. New York: Fawcett, 1979.
Bech Is Back. New York: Knopf: 1982.
Trust Me, New York: Knopf, 1987.
The Afterlife. New York: Knopf, 1994.
Bech at Bay. New York: Knopf, 1998.
Licks of Love: Stories and a Novella, "Rabbit Remembered." New York: Knopf, 2000.
The Complete Henry Bech. New York: Knopf/Everyman, 2001.
The Early Stories. New York: Knopf, 2003.

III. Uncollected Short Fiction
"Personal Archeology." *The New Yorker* 29 May 2000: 124-127.
"Free." *The New Yorker* 8 Jan. 2001: 74-77.
"The Guardians." *The New Yorker* 26 March. 2001: 82-85.
"The Laughter of the Gods." *The New Yorker* 11 Feb. 2002: 76-81.
"Spanish Prelude to a Second Marriage." *Harper's* Nov. 2002: 71-75.
"Varieties of Religious Experience." *Atlantic* Nov. 2002: 93-96, 98-100, 102-04.
"Sin: Early Impressions." *The New Yorker* 9 Dec. 2002: 110-117.
"The Walk with Elizanne." *The New Yorker* 7 July 2003: 66-71.
"Pluie, Pluie, Allez-Vous-En." *The Paris Review* Fall 2003: 315-17.
"Delicate Wives." *The New Yorker* 2 Feb. 2004: 76-9.

IV. Poetry
The Carpentered Hen. New York: Harper's, 1958.
Telephone Poles. New York: Knopf, 1963.
Verse. New York: Fawcett, 1965.
Midpoint. New York: Knopf, 1965.
Tossing and Turning. New York: Knopf, 1977.
Facing Nature. New York: Knopf, 1985.
Collected Poems, 1953-1993. New York: Knopf, 1993.
Americana and Other Poems.. New York: Knopf, 2002.
Not Cancelled Yet. Boise, Idaho: Limberlost Press, 2004.

V. Uncollected Poetry
"Compliment." *Poetry* 164(Aug. 1994): 259.
"New York." *The New Republic* 211(22-29 Aug. 1994): 44.
"Upon Winning One's Flight in the Senior Four-Ball." *The New Yorker* 69 (7 Aug. 1995): 50.
"Elderly Sex." In *It Could Be Verse*. Ed., John Timpane. Albany, CA: Boaz, 1995. 63-4.
"The Witnesses." *Ontario Review* 46 (Spg./Sum. 1997): 73.
"Big Bard." *The American Scholar* 70(Autumn 2001): 40.
"Evening Concert, Sainte-Chapelle." *The New Yorker* 30 June 2003: 45.
"TV." *Atlantic* Sept. 2003: 104.
"Mars as Bright as Venus." *The New York Times Book Review* 28 Sept. 2003: 24.
"Duet on Mars." *The New Yorker* 1 Mar. 2004: 35.

VI. Literary Essays and Criticism
Assorted Prose. New York: Knopf, 1965.
Picked-Up Pieces. New York: Knopf, 1975.
Hugging The Shore. New York: Knopf, 1981.
Odd Jobs: Essays and Criticism. New York: Knopf, 1991.
More Matter. New York: Knopf, 1998.

VII. Memoir
Self-Consciousness. New York: Knopf, 1989.

VIII. Other Collections
Just Looking. New York: Knopf, 1989.
Concerts at Castle Hill. Northridge, California: Lord John Press, 1993.
Golf Dreams. New York: Knopf, 2000.

IX. Children's Books
The Magic Flute. New York: Knopf, 1962.
The Ring. New York: Knopf, 1964.
A Child's Calendar. New York: Knopf, 1965; rev. Holiday House, 1969.
Bottom's Dream: New York: Knopf, 1969.
A Helpful Alphabet of Friendly Objects. New York: Knopf, 1995.

SECONDARY WORKS

I. Books

A. Bibliography:
Bozeman, Pat. *John Updike: An Exhibition*. M. D. Anderson Library: University Park, Tex.: 1985.
De Bellis, Jack. *John Updike, 1967-1993: A Bibliography of Primary and Secondary Sources*. Foreword by John Updike. Westport, Conn: Greenwood Publishing Group, 1994.
De Bellis, Jack and Michael Broomfield. *John Updike: A Bibliography of Primary and Secondary Sources for Collectors, Critics and General Readers*. New Castle, Del.: Oak Knoll Press. Forthcoming.
Falsey, Elizabeth A. *The Art of Adding and the Art of Taking Away: Selections from John Updike's Manuscripts, an Exhibition at the Houghton Library*. Cambridge: Harvard College Library, 1987.
Greiner, Donald J. and Elizabeth A. Falsey. "John Updike." *First Printings of American Authors: Contributions Toward Descriptive Checklists*. Volume V. Ed. Philip B. Eppard. Detroit: Gale, 1987. 329-43.
Taylor, C. Clarke. *John Updike: A Bibliography*. Kent, Ohio: Kent State University Press, 1968.

B. Interviews
Plath, James. *Conversations with John Updike*. Jackson, Mississippi: University Press Mississippi, 1994.

C. Resources
De Bellis, Jack. *The John Updike Encyclopedia*. Westport, Conn: Greenwood Publishing Group, 2000.
Markle, Joyce, Anthony Olivas and Herb Yellin, et al, eds. *The John Updike Newsletter*. n. p. 1975-1981.

II: Books: Individual Studies

Baker, Nicholson. *U and I*. New York: Random House, 1991.

Boswell, Marshall. *John Updike's Rabbit Tetralogy: Mastered Irony in Motion*. Columbia, Missouri: University of Missouri Press, 2001.

Campbell, Jeff H. *Updike's Novels: Thorns Spell a Word*. Wichita Falls: Midwestern State University Press, 1987.

Detweiler, Robert. *John Updike*. New York: Twayne, 1972. Revised, 1984.

Greiner, Donald J. *John Updike's Novels*. Athens: Ohio University Press, 1984.

Greiner, Donald J. *The Other John Updike: Poems/ Short Stories/ Prose/ Play*. Athens: Ohio University Press, 1981.

Hamilton, Alice and Kenneth. *The Elements of John Updike*. Grand Rapids, Mich.: Eerdmans, 1970.

Hunt, George. *John Updike and the Three Great Secret Things: Sex, Religion, and Art*. Grand Rapids: Eerdmans, 1980.

Luscher, Robert M. *John Updike: A Study of the Short Fiction*. Boston: Hall, 1992.

Markle, Joyce B. *Fighters and Lovers: Theme in the Novels of John Updike*. New York: New York University Press, 1973.

Miller, D. Quentin. *John Updike and the Cold War: Drawing the Iron Curtain*. Columbia, Missouri: University of Missouri Press, 2001.

Newman, Judie. *John Updike*. New York: St. Martin's Press, 1988.

O'Connell, Mary. *Updike and the Patriarchal Dilemma: Masculinity in the Rabbit Novels*. Carbondale: University of So Illinois., 1996.

Pritchard, William. *John Updike*. South Royalton, Vermont: Steerforth Press, 2000.

Ristoff, Dilvo. *John Updike's* Rabbit at Rest: *Appropriating History*. New York: Lang, 1998.

_____. *Updike's America: The Presence of Contemporary American History in John Updike's Rabbit Trilogy*. New York: Lang, 1988.

Samuels, Charles T. *John Updike*. U of Minnesota Pamphlets on American Writers, No. 79. Minnesota: University of Minnesota Press, 1969.

Schiff, James A. *Updike's Version: Rewriting The Scarlet Letter*. Columbia: University of Missouri, 1992.

_____. *John Updike Revisited*. Boston: Twayne, 1998.

Searles, George J. *The Fiction of Philip Roth and John Updike*. Carbondale: Southern Illinois University Press, 1985.

Tallent, Elizabeth. *Married Men and Magic Tricks: John Updike's Erotic Heroes*. Berkeley: Creative Arts, 1982.

Taylor, Larry E. *Pastoral and Anti-Pastoral Patterns in John Updike's Fiction*. Carbondale: Southern Illinois University Press, 1971.

Uphaus, Suzanne Henning. *John Updike*. New York: Ungar, 1980.

Vargo, Edward P. *Rainstorms and Fire*. Port Washington, New York: Kennikat Press, 1973.

Vaughan, Philip H. *John Updike's Images of America*. Reseda: Mojave, 1981.

IV. Collections of Essays

Broer, Lawrence R., Ed. *Rabbit Tales: Poetry and Politics in John Updike's Rabbit Novels*. Tuscaloosa, Alabama: University of Alabama Press, 1998.

Harold Bloom, Ed. *Modern Critical Views: John Updike*. New York: Chelsea House, 1987.

Macnaughton, William R. *Critical Essays on John Updike*. Boston: Hall, 1982.

Perkins, Wendy, ed. "A & P." New York: Harcourt Brace College Publishers, 1998.

Stafford, William T., ed. *Modern Fiction Studies* (John Updike Number) 20 (Spring 1974).

Thorburn, David and Howard Eiland, Ed. *John Updike: A Collection of Critical Essays*. Englewood Cliffs: Prentice, 1979.

Trachtenberg, Stanley. Ed. *New Essays on* Rabbit, Run. New York: Cambridge University Press, 1993.

Yerkes, James. Ed. *John Updike and Religion*. Grand Rapids, Michigan: Eerdmans, 1999.

V. Articles or Essays in Books

Allen, Mary. "John Updike's Love of 'Dull Bovine Beauty.'" *The Necessary Blankness: Women in Major American Fiction of the Nineteen Sixties*. Urbana: University of Illinois Press, 1976. 97-132.

Crews, Frederick. "Mr. Updike's Planet." *The New York Review of Books* 33 (4 Dec. 1986): 7-10, 12, 14.

Detweiler, Robert. "John Updike and the Indictment of Culture-Protestantism." *Four Spiritual Crises in Mid-Century American Fiction*. Gainesville: University of Florida Press, 1963. 14-24.

Galloway, David D. "The Absurd Man as Saint: The Novels of John Updike." *The Absurd Hero in American Fiction*. Austin: University of Texas Press, 2nd rev. ed.. 1981. 17-80.

Greiner, Donald J. *Adultery in the American Novel: Updike, James, and Hawthorne*. Columbia: The University of South Carolina Press, 1985. 3-71, 97-131.

_____. "John Updike." *Dictionary of Literary Biography Yearbook: 1980*. Detroit, Mich.: Gale, 1981. 107-16.

_____. adv. ed. "John Updike." *Dictionary of Literary Biography: Ed. Mary Bruccolli. Documentary Series: An Illustrated Chronicle*. Volume 3. Detroit, Mich.: Gale, 1983. 251-320.

_____. "John Updike" in *American Novelists Since World War II*, ed. James R. Giles and Wanda H. Giles. Volume 143. 250-276. Dictionary of Literary Biography, Third Series. Detroit, Mich.: Gale, 1994.

_____. "John Updike." *Broadening Views, 1968-88: Concise Dictionary of American Literature Biography*. Detroit, Mich.: Gale, 1989. 276-297.

Karl, Frederick R. *American Fictions 1940-1980*. New York: Harper, 1983. 35-36, 169-172, 251-52, 259-61, 347-55.

Richard Lyons, "A High E. Q." *The Minnesota Review* Spring., 1961: 385-9.

Neary, John M. *Something and Nothingness: The Fiction of John Updike and John Fowles*. Carbondale, Ill.: Southern Illinois University Press, 1991. (Chapters 3, 5, and 6 concern Updike.)

Olster, Stacy ."Rabbit Rerun: Updike's Replay of Popular Culture in *Rabbit at Rest*." *Modern Fiction Studies* Spr. 1991: 45-59.

Wills, Gary. "Long-Distance Runner." *The New York Review of Books* 25 Oct. 1990: 11-14.

Wood, Ralph C. *The Comedy of Redemption: Christian Faith and Comic Vision in Four American Novelists*. South Bend, Indiana: University of Notre Dame Press, 1988. 178-206.

Wright, Stuart. "John Updike's Contributions to *Chatterbox*." *Bulletin of Bibliography* 42 (Dec. 1985): 171-78.

Index

ABOUT THE EDITOR

JACK DE BELLIS is Professor Emeritus of English at Lehigh University.